Praise for *Key Marketing Metrics*

Measurement is critical to the health of any business, and Key Marketing Met
*highlights key tools and techniques across many measurement landscapes – ~~from~~
the consumer, to the sales force, to the ever-changing media environment. It's a
'must-read' for any business leader who wants to optimize the way they measure
business activities and results in order to grow their business.*

KIMBERLEY B. DEDEKER, VICE PRESIDENT,
GLOBAL CONSUMER & MARKET KNOWLEDGE, PROCTER & GAMBLE

Why read Key Marketing Metrics? *Because better metrics lead to better decisions,
which lead to better outcomes. This book does a superb job of helping marketers,
and all executives, understand which metrics to use and how to use them.*

ERV SHAMES, FORMER CEO, KRAFT FOODS

Why was this book not written earlier? Key Marketing Metrics *presents an excellent
compendium of the metrics you really need to know, along with a structural
framework that ties them together and helps you steer your business successfully.*

DR HANS-WILLI SCHROIFF, VICE PRESIDENT,
MARKET RESEARCH/BUSINESS INTELLIGENCE, HENKEL

*Marketing is being challenged, as never before, to be accountable. This book, by
describing metric options and their risks, will help address this challenge.*

DAVID AAKER, AUTHOR OF BRAND PORTFOLIO STRATEGY

*Measurement is central to our business discipline. What gets measured matters,
and having the right measures is key.* Key Marketing Metrics *provides an insightful
compilation of what to measure and how to measure it for today's marketing-savvy
executives.*

GLENN RENWICK, CEO OF THE PROGRESSIVE CORPORATION
(PROGRESSIVE DIRECTSM AND DRIVE® INSURANCE FROM PROGRESSIVE)

*Marketing, as a function, is under increasing pressure to develop business-oriented
metrics to justify marketing mix investments.* Key Marketing Metrics *offers clear
advice on how to develop common marketing metrics that are relevant and
accessible to both marketing and non-marketing decision makers.*

ANIL MENON, VICE PRESIDENT, MARKETING,
SYSTEMS & TECHNOLOGY GROUP, IBM

Key marketing metrics

₩ Wharton School Publishing

In the face of accelerating turbulence and change, business leaders and policy makers need new ways of thinking to sustain performance and growth.

Wharton School Publishing offers a trusted source for stimulating ideas from thought leaders who provide new mental models to address changes in strategy, management, and finance. We seek out authors from diverse disciplines with a profound understanding of change and its implications. We offer books and tools that help executives respond to the challenge of change.

Every book and management tool we publish meets quality standards set by The Wharton School of the University of Pennsylvania. Each title is reviewed by the Wharton School Publishing Editorial Board before being given Wharton's seal of approval. This ensures that Wharton publications are timely, relevant, important, conceptually sound or empirically based, and implementable.

To fit our readers' learning preferences, Wharton publications are available in multiple formats, including books, audio, and electronic.

To find out more about our books and management tools, visit us at whartonsp.com and Wharton's executive education site, exced.Wharton.upenn.edu

UNIVERSITY *of* PENNSYLVANIA

PAUL W. FARRIS
NEIL T. BENDLE
PHILLIP E. PFEIFER
DAVID J. REIBSTEIN

Key marketing metrics

The 50+ metrics every manager needs to know

Ideas.Action.Impact.
Wharton School Publishing

An imprint of **Pearson Education**

Harlow, England • London • New York • Boston • San Francisco • Toronto
Sydney • Tokyo • Singapore • Hong Kong • Seoul • Taipei • New Delhi
Cape Town • Madrid • Mexico City • Amsterdam • Munich • Paris • Milan

PEARSON EDUCATION LIMITED

Edinburgh Gate
Harlow CM20 2JE
Tel: +44 (0)1279 623623
Fax: +44 (0)1279 431059
Website: www.pearsoned.co.uk

Original edition, entitled MARKETING METRICS: 50+ METRICS EVERY EXECUTIVE SHOULD MASTER, 1st edition, by FARRIS, PAUL W.; BENDLE, NEIL T.; PFEIFER, PHILLIP E.; REIBSTEIN, DAVID J., published by Pearson Education, Inc., publishing as Wharton School Publishing, Copyright © 2006.

First edition published by PEARSON EDUCATION LTD, Copyright © 2009.

This edition is manufactured in the UK and is authorised for sale only in the UK, EUROPE, MIDDLE EAST AND AFRICA.

The rights of Paul W. Farris, Neil T. Bendle, Phillip E. Pfeifer and David J. Reibstein to be identified as authors of this work have been asserted by them in accordance with the Copyright, Designs and Patents Act 1988.

ISBN: 978-0-273-72203-8

British Library Cataloguing-in-Publication Data
A catalogue record for this book is available from the British Library

11
16

Typeset in Swiss Light 9.25 pt/12 pt by 3
Printed by Ashford Colour Press Ltd., Gosport

*We dedicate this book to our students, colleagues
and consulting clients who convinced us that
a book like this would fill a real need.*

Contents

Acknowledgements x
About the authors xi
Foreword xii

1 | Introduction 1

2 | Share of hearts, minds and markets 9

3 | Margins and profits 43

4 | Product and portfolio management 89

5 | Customer profitability 129

6 | Sales force and channel management 155

7 | Pricing strategy 195

8 | Promotion 239

9 | Advertising media and Web metrics 263

10 | Marketing and finance 305

11 | The marketing metrics X-ray 325

Conclusion 337
Endnotes 338
Select bibliography 342
Index 344

Acknowledgements

We hope this book will be a step, however modest, toward clarifying the language, construction and meaning of many of our important marketing metrics. If we have succeeded in making such a step, we owe thanks to a number of people.

Jerry Wind reviewed our initial concept and encouraged us to set our sights higher. Rob Northrop, Simon Bendle and Vince Choe read early drafts and gave valuable feedback on the most important chapters. Eric Larson, Jordan Mitchell, Tom Disantis and Francisco Simon helped develop material for important sections and provided their research skills. Gerry Allan and Alan Rimm-Kauffman allowed us to cite liberally from their materials on customers and Internet marketing.

Marc Goldstein combined business savvy with deft editing touches that improved the readability of almost every chapter. Paula Sinnott, Tim Moore, Kayla Dugger and their colleagues also made significant improvements in moving from a raw manuscript to the book in your hands.

Erv Shames, Erjen van Nierop, Peter Hedlund, Fred Telegdy, Judy Jordan, Lee Pielemier and Richard Johnson have collaborated on our "Allocator" management simulation and "Management by the Numbers" online tutorials. That work helped us set the stage for this volume. Finally, we thank Kate, Emily, Donna and Karen, who graciously tolerated the time sacrificed from home and social lives for the writing of this book.

About the authors

Paul W. Farris is Landmark Communications Professor and Professor of Marketing at the Darden Graduate Business School, University of Virginia, where he has taught since 1980. Professor Farris's research has produced award-winning articles on retail power and the measurement of advertising effects. He has published more than 50 articles in journals such as the *Harvard Business Review*, *Journal of Marketing*, *Journal of Advertising Research* and *Marketing Science*. He is currently developing improved techniques for integrating marketing and financial metrics and is co-author of several books, including *The Profit Impact of Marketing Strategy Project: Retrospect and Prospects*. Farris's consulting clients range from Procter & Gamble to Apple and IBM. He has served on boards of manufacturers, retailers and e-commerce companies. Currently, he is a director of Sto, Inc., and GSI Group.

Neil T. Bendle is a Ph.D. student in marketing at the Carlson School of Management, University of Minnesota. He holds an MBA from Darden, and has nearly a decade's experience in marketing management, consulting, business systems improvement and financial management. He was responsible for measuring the success of marketing campaigns for the Labour Party.

Phillip E. Pfeifer, Alumni Research Professor of Business Administration at the Darden Graduate Business School, currently specialises in interactive marketing. He has published a popular MBA textbook and over 25 refereed articles in journals such as the *Journal of Interactive Marketing*, *Journal of Database Marketing*, *Decision Sciences* and the *Journal of Forecasting*. Pfeifer was recognised in 2004 as the Darden School's faculty leader in external case sales. His teaching has won student awards and has been recognised in *Business Week*'s Guide to the Best Business Schools. His recent clients include Circuit City, Procter & Gamble and CarMax.

David J. Reibstein is Managing Director of CMO Partners and William Stewart Woodside Professor of Marketing at the Wharton School. Regarded as one of the world's leading authorities on marketing, he served as Executive Director of the Marketing Sciences Institute, and co-founded Wharton's CMO Summit, which brings together leading CMOs to address their most pressing challenges. Reibstein designed and teaches the Wharton Executive Education course on marketing metrics. He has an extensive track record consulting with leading businesses, including GE, AT&T Wireless, Shell Oil, HP, Novartis, Johnson & Johnson, Merck and Major League Baseball. He has served as Vice Dean and Director of Wharton's Graduate Division, as visiting professor at Stanford and INSEAD, and as faculty member at Harvard. He serves on the Board of Directors of Shopzilla, And1 and several other organizations.

Foreword

Despite its importance, marketing is one of the least understood, least measurable functions at many companies. With sales force costs, it accounts for 10 per cent or more of operating budgets at a wide range of public firms. Its effectiveness is fundamental to stock market valuations, which often rest upon aggressive assumptions for customer acquisition and organic growth. Nevertheless, many corporate boards lack the understanding to evaluate marketing strategies and expenditures. Most directors – and a rising percentage of Fortune 500 CEOs – lack deep experience in this field.

Marketing executives, for their part, often fail to develop the quantitative, analytical skills needed to manage productivity. Right-brain thinkers may devise creative campaigns to drive sales but show little interest in the wider financial impact of their work. Frequently, they resist being held accountable even for top-line performance, asserting that factors beyond their control – including competition – make it difficult to monitor the results of their programmes.

In this context, marketing decisions are often made without the information, expertise and measurable feedback needed. As Procter & Gamble's Chief Marketing Officer has said, "Marketing is a $450 billion industry, and we are making decisions with less data and discipline than we apply to $100,000 decisions in other aspects of our business." This is a troubling state of affairs. But it can change.

In a recent article in *The Wall Street Journal*, I called on marketing managers to take concrete steps to correct it. I urged them to gather and analyse basic market data, measure the core factors that drive their business models, analyse the profitability of individual customer accounts and optimise resource allocation among increasingly fragmented media. These are analytical, data-intensive, left-brain practices. Going forward, I believe they'll be crucial to the success of marketing executives and their employers. As I concluded in the *Journal*:

> *Today's boards want chief marketing officers who can speak the language of productivity and return on investment and are willing to be held accountable. In recent years, manufacturing, procurement and logistics have all tightened their belts in the cause of improved productivity. As a result, marketing expenditures account for a larger percentage of many corporate cost structures than ever before. Today's boards don't need chief marketing officers who have creative flair but no financial discipline. They need ambidextrous marketers who offer both.*

In *Key Marketing Metrics*, Farris, Bendle, Pfeifer and Reibstein have given us a valuable means toward this end. In a single volume, and with impressive clarity, they have outlined the sources, strengths and weaknesses of a broad array of marketing metrics. They have explained how to harness those data for insight. Most importantly, they have explained how to act on this insight – how to apply it not only in planning campaigns, but also in measuring their impact, correcting their courses and optimising their results. In essence, *Key Marketing Metrics* is a key reference for managers who aim to become skilled in both right- and left-brain marketing. I highly recommend it for all ambidextrous marketers.

JOHN A. QUELCH, LINCOLN FILENE PROFESSOR OF
BUSINESS ADMINISTRATION AND SENIOR ASSOCIATE DEAN FOR
INTERNATIONAL DEVELOPMENT, HARVARD BUSINESS SCHOOL.

Introduction

In recent years, data-based marketing has swept through the business world. In its wake, measurable performance and accountability have become the keys to marketing success. However, few managers appreciate the range of metrics by which they can evaluate marketing strategies and dynamics. Fewer still understand the pros, cons and nuances of each.

In this environment, we have come to recognise that marketers, general managers and business students need a comprehensive, practical reference on the metrics used to judge marketing programmes and quantify their results. In this book, we seek to provide that reference. We wish our readers great success with it.

What is a metric?

A metric is a measuring system that quantifies a trend, dynamic or characteristic. In virtually all disciplines, practitioners use metrics to explain phenomena, diagnose causes, share findings and project the results of future events. Throughout the worlds of science, business and government, metrics encourage rigour and objectivity. They make it possible to compare observations across regions and time periods. They facilitate understanding and collaboration.

Why do you need metrics?

> When you can measure what you are speaking about, and express it in numbers, you know something about it; but when you cannot measure it, when you cannot express it in numbers, your knowledge is of a meager and unsatisfactory kind: it may be the beginning of knowledge, but you have scarcely, in your thoughts, advanced to the stage of science.
>
> WILLIAM THOMSON, LORD KELVIN, POPULAR LECTURES AND ADDRESSES (1891–94)[1]

Lord Kelvin, a British physicist and the manager of the laying of the first successful transatlantic cable, was one of history's great advocates for quantitative investigation. In his day, however, mathematical rigour had not yet spread widely beyond the worlds of science, engineering and finance. Much has changed since then.

Today, numerical fluency is a crucial skill for every business leader. Managers must quantify market opportunities and competitive threats. They must justify the financial risks and benefits of their decisions. They must evaluate plans, explain variances, judge performance and identify leverage points for improvement – all in numeric terms. These responsibilities require a strong command of measurements and of the systems and formulas that generate them. In short, they require metrics.

Managers must select, calculate and explain key business metrics. They must understand how each is constructed and how to use it in decision-making. Witness the following, more recent quotes from management experts:

> ... every metric, whether it is used explicitly to influence behavior, to evaluate future strategies, or simply to take stock, will affect actions and decisions.[2]

> If you can't measure it, you can't manage it.[3]

Marketing metrics: opportunities, performance and accountability

Marketers are by no means immune to the drive toward quantitative planning and evaluation. Marketing may once have been regarded as more an art than a science. Executives may once have cheerfully admitted that they knew they wasted half the money they spent on advertising, but they didn't know which half. Those days, however, are gone.

Today, marketers must understand their addressable markets quantitatively. They must measure new opportunities and the investment needed to realise them. Marketers must quantify the value of products, customers and distribution channels – all under various pricing and promotional scenarios. Increasingly, marketers are held accountable for the financial ramifications of their decisions. Observers have noted this trend in graphic terms:

> For years, corporate marketers have walked into budget meetings like neighborhood junkies. They couldn't always justify how well they spent past handouts or what difference it all made. They just wanted more money – for flashy TV ads, for big-ticket events, for, you know, getting out the message and building up the brand. But those heady days of blind budget increases are fast being replaced with a new mantra: measurement and accountability.[4]

Choosing the right numbers

The numeric imperative represents a challenge, however. In business and economics, many metrics are complex and difficult to master. Some are highly specialised and best suited to specific analyses. Many require data that may be approximate, incomplete or unavailable.

Under these circumstances, no single metric is likely to be perfect. For this reason, we recommend that marketers use a portfolio or "dashboard" of metrics. By doing so, they can view market dynamics from various perspectives and arrive at "triangulated" strategies and solutions. Additionally, with multiple metrics, marketers can use each as a check on the others. In this way, they can maximise the accuracy of their knowledge.[5] They can also estimate or project one data point on the basis of others. Of course, to use multiple metrics effectively, marketers must appreciate the relations between them and the limitations inherent in each.

When this understanding is achieved, however, metrics can help a firm maintain a productive focus on customers and markets. They can help managers identify the strengths and weaknesses in both strategies and execution. Mathematically defined and widely disseminated, metrics can become part of a precise, operational language within a firm.

Data availability and globalisation of metrics

A further challenge in metrics stems from wide variations in the availability of data between industries and geographies. Recognising these variations, we have tried to suggest alternative sources and procedures for estimating some of the metrics in this book.

Fortunately, although both the range and type of marketing metrics may vary between countries,[6] these differences are shrinking rapidly. Ambler et al.,[7] for example, report that performance metrics have become a common language among marketers, and that they are now used to rally teams and benchmark efforts internationally.

Mastering metrics

Being able to "crunch the numbers" is vital to success in marketing. Knowing which numbers to crunch, however, is a skill that develops over time. Toward that end, managers must practise the use of metrics and learn from their mistakes. By working through the examples in this book, we hope our readers will gain both confidence and a firm understanding of the fundamentals of data-based marketing. With time and experience, we trust that you will also develop an intuition about metrics, and learn to dig deeper when calculations appear suspect or puzzling.

Ultimately, with regard to metrics, we believe many of our readers will require not only familiarity but also fluency. That is, managers should be able to perform relevant calculations on the hoof – under pressure, in board meetings and during strategic deliberations and negotiations. Although not all readers will require that level of fluency, we believe it will be increasingly expected of candidates for senior management positions, especially those with significant financial responsibility. We anticipate that a mastery of data-based marketing will become a means for many of our readers to differentiate and position themselves for career advancement in an ever more challenging environment.

Organisation of the text

This book is organised into chapters that correspond to the various roles played by marketing metrics in enterprise management. Individual chapters are dedicated to metrics used in promotional strategy, advertising and distribution, for example. Each chapter is composed of sections devoted to specific concepts and calculations.

Inevitably, we must present these metrics in a sequence that will appear somewhat arbitrary. In organising this text, however, we have sought to strike a balance between two goals: (1) to establish core concepts first and build gradually toward increasing sophistication, and (2) to group related metrics in clusters, helping our readers recognise patterns of mutual reinforcement and interdependence. In Figure 1.1, we offer a graphical presentation of this structure, demonstrating the interlocking nature of all marketing metrics – indeed of all marketing programmes – as well as the central role of the customer.

The central issues addressed by the metrics in this book are as follows:

- *Chapter 2 – Share of hearts, minds and markets:* Customer perceptions, market share and competitive analysis.
- *Chapter 3 – Margins and profits:* Revenues, cost structures and profitability.
- *Chapter 4 – Product and portfolio management:* The metrics behind product strategy, including measures of trial, growth, cannibalisation and brand equity.
- *Chapter 5 – Customer profitability:* The value of individual customers and relationships.
- *Chapter 6 – Sales force and channel management:* Sales force organisation, performance and compensation. Distribution coverage and logistics.
- *Chapter 7 – Pricing strategy:* Price sensitivity and optimisation, with an eye toward setting prices to maximise profits.
- *Chapter 8 – Promotion:* Temporary price promotions, coupons, rebates and trade allowances.
- *Chapter 9 – Advertising media and Web metrics:* The central measures of advertising coverage and effectiveness, including reach, frequency, rating points and impressions. Models for consumer response to advertising. Specialised metrics for Web-based campaigns.
- *Chapter 10 – Marketing and finance:* Financial evaluation of marketing programmes.
- *Chapter 11 – The marketing metrics X-ray:* The use of metrics as leading indicators of opportunities, challenges and financial performance.

Figure 1.1 Marketing metrics: marketing at the core of the organisation

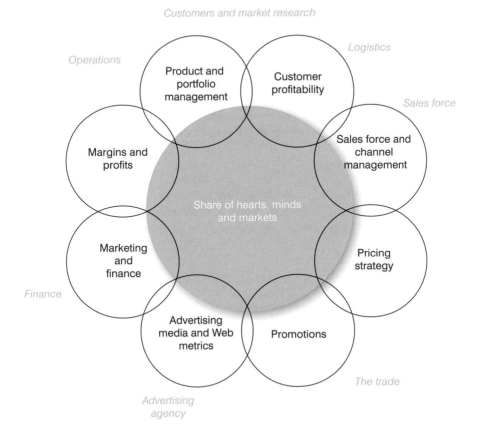

Components of each chapter

As shown in Table 1.1, the chapters are composed of multiple sections, each dedicated to specific marketing concepts or metrics. Within each section, we open with definitions, formulas and a brief description of the metrics covered. Next, in a passage titled **Construction**, we explore the issues surrounding these metrics, including their formulation, application, interpretation and strategic ramifications. We provide examples to illustrate calculations, reinforce concepts and help readers verify their understanding of key formulas. That done, in a passage titled **Data Sources, Complications and Cautions**, we probe the limitations of the metrics under consideration, and potential pitfalls in their use. Toward that end, we also examine the assumptions underlying these metrics. Finally, we close each section with a brief survey of **Related Metrics and Concepts**.

In organising the text in this way, our goal is straightforward: most of the metrics in this book have broad implications and multiple layers of interpretation. Doctoral theses could be devoted to many of them, and have been written about some. In this book, however, we want to offer an accessible, practical reference. If the devil is in the details, we want to identify, locate and warn readers against him, but not to elaborate his entire demonology. Consequently, we discuss each metric in stages, working progressively toward increasing levels of sophistication. We invite our readers to sample this information as they see fit, exploring each metric to the depth that they find most useful and rewarding.

With an eye toward accessibility, we have also avoided advanced mathematical notation. Most of the calculations in this book can be performed by hand, on the back of the proverbial envelope. More complex or intensive computations may require a spreadsheet. Nothing further should be needed.

Reference materials

Throughout this text, we have highlighted formulas and definitions for easy reference. We have also included outlines of key terms at the beginning of each chapter and section. Within each formula, we have followed this notation to define all inputs and outputs.

£ (monetary terms) **A monetary value. We have used the pound sign for brevity, but any other currency, including the euro, dollar, yen, dinar or yuan, would be equally appropriate.**

% (percentage) **Used as the equivalent of fractions or decimals. For readability, we have intentionally omitted the step of multiplying decimals by 100 to obtain percentages.**

N (number) **Used for such measures as unit sales or number of competitors.**

R (rating) **Expressed on a scale that translates qualitative judgements or preferences into numeric ratings. Example: a survey in which customers are asked to assign a rating of "1" to items that they find least satisfactory and "5" to those that are most satisfactory. Ratings have no intrinsic meaning without reference to their scale and context.**

I (index) **A comparative figure, often linked to or expressive of a market average. Example: the consumer price index. Indexes are often interpreted as a percentage.**

£ – pound   % – percentage   N – number   R – rating   I – index

References and suggested further reading

Abela, A., B.H. Clark and T. Ambler. (2004). "Marketing Performance Measurement, Performance, and Learning", working paper, 1 September.

Ambler, T. and C. Styles. (1995). "Brand Equity: Toward Measures That Matter", working paper no. 95-902, London Business School, Centre for Marketing.

Barwise, P. and J.U. Farley. (2003). "Which Marketing Metrics Are Used and Where?", Marketing Science Institute (03-111), working paper.

Clark, B.H., A.V. Abela and T. Ambler. (2004). "Return on Measurement: Relating Marketing Metrics Practices to Strategic Performance", working paper, 12 January.

Hauser, J. and G. Katz. (1998). "Metrics: You Are What You Measure", *European Management Journal*, 16(5), 517–528.

Kaplan, R.S. and D.P. Norton. (1996). *The Balanced Scorecard: Translating Strategy into Action*, Boston, MA: Harvard Business School Press.

Table 1.1 Major metrics list

Chapter	Metric	Chapter	Metric
2	Share of hearts, minds and markets		Customer satisfaction
			Willingness to search
	Market share	3	Margins and profits
	Unit share		Unit margin
	Relative market share		Margin (%)
	Brand development index		Channel margins
	Category development index		Average price per unit
	Market share		Price per statistical unit
	Market penetration		Variable and fixed costs
	Brand penetration		Marketing spending
	Penetration share		Contribution per unit
	Share of requirements		Contribution margin (%)
	Heavy usage index		Break-even sales
	Hierarchy of effects		Target volume
	Awareness		Target revenues
	Top of mind	4	Product and portfolio management
	Ad awareness		
	Knowledge		Trial
	Beliefs		Repeat volume
	Intentions		Penetration
	Purchase habits		Volume projections
	Loyalty		Growth – percentage
	Likeability		Growth – CAGR
	Willingness to recommend		Cannibalisation rate

Table 1.1 *Continued*

Chapter	Metric	Chapter	Metric
	Fair share draw rate		Residual elasticity
	Brand equity metrics	8	*Promotion*
	Conjoint utilities and consumer preferences		Baseline sales
			Incremental sales/promotion lift
	Segment utilities		Redemption rates
	Conjoint utilities and volume projections		Costs for coupons and rebates
			Percentage sales with coupon
5	*Customer profitability*		Per cent sales on deal
	Customers		Per cent time on deal
	Recency		Average deal depth
	Retention rate		Pass-through
	Customer profit		Price waterfall
	Customer lifetime value	9	*Advertising media and Web metrics*
	Prospect lifetime value		
	Average acquisition cost		Impressions
	Average retention cost		Gross rating points (GRPs)
6	*Sales force and channel management*		Cost per thousand impressions (CPM)
	Workload		Net reach
	Sales potential forecast		Average frequency
	Sales total		Frequency response
	Sales force effectiveness		Effective reach
	Compensation		Effective frequency
	Break-even number of employees		Share of voice
			Pageviews
	Sales funnel, sales pipeline		Clickthrough rate
	Numeric distribution %		Cost per click
	All commodity volume (ACV)		Cost per order
	Product category volume (PCV)		Cost per customer acquired
	Total distribution %		Visits
	Facings		Visitors
	Out of stock %		Abandonment rate
	Inventories	10	*Marketing and finance*
	Mark-downs		Net profit
	Direct product profitability (DPP)		Return on sales – (ROS)
	Gross margin return on inventory investment (GMROII)		Return on investment – (ROI)
			Economic profit – (EVA)
7	*Pricing strategy*		Payback
	Price premium		Net present value (NPV)
	Reservation price		Internal rate of return (IRR)
	Per cent good value		Return on marketing investment – (ROMI); revenue
	Price elasticity of demand		
	Optimal price		

Share of hearts, minds and markets

2

Metrics covered in this chapter:

- Market share

- Relative market share

- Market concentration

- Brand development index (BDI)

- Category development index (CDI)

- Penetration

- Share of requirements

- Heavy usage index

- Awareness, attitudes and usage (AAU)

- Customer satisfaction

- Willingness to recommend

- Willingness to search

Introduction

As Wal-Mart aggressively rolls out more stores, it continues to capture an increasing share of wallet. Three out of five consumers shopped for gifts at Wal-Mart this past holiday season. U.S. households now buy, on average, 22% of their groceries at Wal-Mart. A quarter of all shoppers indicate that they are spending more of their clothing budget at Wal-Mart now compared with a year ago. These ShopperScape findings lend credence to Retail Forward's premise that Wal-Mart will continue to push the boundaries of what consumers will allow it to be.[1]

At first glance, market share appears to involve a relatively simple calculation: "us/(us + them)". But this raises a host of questions. Who, for example, are "they"? That is, how broadly do we define our competitive universe? Which units are used? Where in the value chain do we capture our information? What time frame will maximise our signal-to-noise ratio? In a metric as important as market share, and in one as closely monitored for changes and trends, the answers to such questions are crucial. In this chapter, we will address them and also introduce key components of market share, including penetration share, heavy usage index and share of requirements.

Probing the dynamics behind market share, we'll explore measures of awareness, attitude and usage – major factors in the decision-making process by which customers select one brand over another. We'll discuss customer satisfaction with products and dealers, the quantification of which is growing in importance among marketing professionals. Finally, we'll consider metrics measuring the depth of consumer preference and satisfaction, including customers' willingness to search if a brand is unavailable and their disposition to recommend that brand to others. Increasingly, marketers rely on these as leading indicators of future changes in share.

Metric	Construction	Considerations	Purpose
Revenue market share	Sales revenue as a percentage of market sales revenue.	Scope of market definition. Channel level analysed. Before/after discounts. Time period covered.	Measure of competitiveness.
Unit market share	Unit sales as a percentage of market unit sales.	Scope of market definition. Channel level analysed. Time period covered.	Measure of competitiveness.
Relative market share	Brand market share divided by largest competitor's market share.	Can use either unit or revenue shares.	Assesses comparative market strength.
Brand development index	Brand sales in a specified segment, compared with sales of that brand in the market as a whole.	Can use either unit or revenue sales.	Regional or segment differences in brand purchases and consumption.

Metric	Construction	Considerations	Purpose
Category development index	Category sales in a specified segment, compared with sales of that category in the market as a whole.	Can use either unit or revenue sales.	Regional or segment differences in category purchases and consumption.
Decomposition of market share	Penetration Share * Share of Requirements * Heavy Usage Index.	Can be based on unit or revenue shares. Time period covered.	Calculation of market share. Competitive analysis. Historical trends analysis. Formulation of marketing objectives.
Market penetration	Purchasers of a product category as a percentage of total population	Based on population. Therefore, unit/revenue consideration not relevant.	Measures category acceptance by a defined population. Useful in tracking acceptance of new product categories.
Brand penetration	Purchasers of a brand as a percentage of total population.	Based on population. Therefore, unit/revenue consideration not relevant.	Measures brand acceptance by a defined population.
Penetration share	Brand penetration as a percentage of market penetration.	A component of the market share formula.	Comparative acceptance of brand within category.
Share of requirements	Brand purchases as a percentage of total category purchases by buyers of that brand.	Can use either unit or revenue shares. May rise even as sales decline, leaving only most loyal customers.	Level of commitment to a brand by its existing customers.

Metric	Construction	Considerations	Purpose
Heavy usage index	Category purchases by customers of a brand, compared with purchases in that category by average customes in the category.	Can use either unit or revenue sales.	Measures relative usage of a category by customers for a specific brand.
Hierarchy of effects	Awareness; attitudes, beliefs; importance; intentions to try; buy; trial, repeat.	Strict sequence is often violated and can be reversed.	Set marketing and advertising objectives. Understand progress in stages of customer decision process.
Awareness	Percentage of total population that is aware of a brand.	Is this prompted or unprompted awareness?	Consideration of who has heard of the brand.
Top of mind	First brand to consider.	May be subject to most recent advertising or experience.	Saliency of brand.
Ad awareness	Percentage of total population that is aware of a brand's advertising.	May vary by schedule, reach and frequency of advertising.	One measure of advertising effects. May indicate "stopping power" of ads.
Knowledge	Percentage of population with knowledge of product, recollection of its advertising.	Not a formal metric. Is this prompted or unprompted knowledge?	Extent of familiarity with product beyond name recognition.
Beliefs	Customers'/ consumers' view of product, generally captured via survey responses, often through ratings on a scale.	Customers/ consumers may hold beliefs with varying degrees of conviction.	Perception of brand by attribute.

Metric	Construction	Considerations	Purpose
Purchase intentions	Probability of intention to purchase.	To estimate probability of purchase, aggregate and analyse ratings of stated intentions (for example, top two boxes).	Measures pre-shopping disposition to purchase.
Purchase habits	Frequency of purchase. Quantity typically purchased.	May vary widely among shopping trips.	Helps identify heavy users.
Loyalty	Measures include share of requirements, willingness to pay premium, willingness to search.	"Loyalty" itself is not a formal metric, but specific metrics measure aspects of this dynamic. New product entries may alter loyalty levels.	Indication of base future revenue stream.
Likeability	Generally measured via ratings across a number of scales.	Often believed to correlate with persuasion.	Shows overall preference prior to shopping.
Willingness to recommend	Generally measured via ratings across a 1–5 scale.	Non-linear in impact.	Shows strength of loyalty, potential impact on others.
Customer satisfaction	Generally measured on a 1–5 scale, in which customers declare their satisfaction with brand in general or specific attributes.	Subject to response bias. Captures views of current customers, not lost customers. Satisfaction is a function of expectations.	Indicates likelihood of repurchase. Reports of dissatisfaction show aspects that require improvement to enhance loyalty.
Willingness to search	Percentage of customers willing to delay purchases, change stores or reduce quantities to avoid switching brands.	Hard to capture.	Indicates importance of distribution coverage.

Market share

Market share is the percentage of a market (defined in terms of either units or revenue) accounted for by a specific entity.

$$\text{Unit market share (\%)} = \frac{\text{Unit sales (N)}}{\text{Total market unit sales (N)}}$$

$$\text{Revenue market share (\%)} = \frac{\text{Sales revenue (£)}}{\text{Total market revenue (£)}}$$

Marketers need to be able to translate sales targets into market share because this will demonstrate whether forecasts are to be attained by growing with the market or by capturing share from competitors. The latter will almost always be more difficult to achieve. Market share is closely monitored for signs of change in the competitive landscape, and it frequently drives strategic or tactical action.

Purpose: key indicator of market competitiveness

Market share is an indicator of how well a firm is doing against its competitors. This metric, supplemented by changes in sales revenue, helps managers evaluate both primary and selective demand in their market. That is, it enables them to judge not only total market growth or decline but also trends in customers' selections among competitors. Generally, sales growth resulting from primary demand (total market growth) is less costly and more profitable than that achieved by capturing share from competitors. Conversely, losses in market share can signal serious long-term problems that require strategic adjustments. Firms with market shares below a certain level may not be viable. Similarly, within a firm's product line, market share trends for individual products are considered early indicators of future opportunities or problems.

Construction

Market share: The percentage of a market accounted for by a specific entity.

Unit market share: The units sold by a particular company as a percentage of total market sales, measured in the same units.

$$\text{Unit market share (\%)} = \frac{\text{Unit sales (N)}}{\text{Total market unit sales (N)}}$$

This formula, of course, can be rearranged to derive either unit sales or total market unit sales from the other two variables, as illustrated in the following:

$$\text{Unit sales (N)} = \text{Unit market share (\%)} * \text{Total market unit sales (N)}$$

$$\text{Total market unit sales (N)} = \frac{\text{Unit sales (N)}}{\text{Unit market share (\%)}}$$

> **Revenue market share:** **Revenue market share differs from unit market share in that it reflects the prices at which goods are sold. In fact, a relatively simple way to calculate relative price is to divide revenue market share by unit market share (see "Price premium" on pages 198–203).**

$$\text{Revenue market share (\%)} = \frac{\text{Sales revenue (£)}}{\text{Total market sales revenue (£)}}$$

As with the unit market share, this equation for revenue market share can be rearranged to calculate either sales revenue or total market sales revenue from the other two variables.

Data sources, complications and cautions

Market definition is never a trivial exercise

If a firm defines its market too broadly, it may dilute its focus. If it does so too narrowly, it will miss opportunities and allow threats to emerge unseen. To avoid these pitfalls, as a first step in calculating market share, managers are advised to define the served market in terms of unit sales or revenues for a specific list of competitors, products, sales channels, geographic areas, customers and time periods. They might posit, for example, that "Among grocery stores, we are the revenue market share leader in sales of frozen Italian food entrées in the UK".

Data parameters must be carefully defined

Although market share is probably the single most important marketing metric, there is no generally acknowledged best method for calculating it. This is unfortunate, as different methods may yield not only different computations of market share at a given moment, but also widely divergent trends over time. The reasons for these disparities include variations in the lenses through which share is viewed (units versus money), where in the channel the measurements are taken (shipments from manufacturers versus consumer purchases), market definition (scope of the competitive universe) and measurement error. In the situation analysis that underlies strategic decisions, managers must be able to understand and explain these variations.

Competitive dynamics in the car industry, and at General Motors in the US in particular, illustrate the complexities involved in quantifying market share:

With market share sliding in the first two months of the year, from 27.2% to 24.9% – the lowest level since a two-month strike shut the company down in 1998 – GM as a whole expects a net loss of $846 million the first quarter.[2]

Reviewing this statement, drawn from *Business Week* in 2005, a marketing manager might immediately pose a number of questions:

- Do these figures represent unit (car) or revenue (dollar) market shares?
- Does this trend hold for both unit and revenue market shares at GM?
- Was revenue market share calculated before or after rebates and discounts?
- Do the underlying sales data reflect factory shipments, which relate directly to the manufacturer's current income statement, or sales to consumers, which are buffered by dealer inventories?
- Does the decline in market share translate to an equivalent percentage decrease in sales, or has the total market size changed?

Managers must determine whether a stated market share is based on shipment data, channel shipments, retail sales, customer surveys or some other source. On occasion, share figures may represent combinations of data (a firm's actual shipments, for example, set against survey estimates of competitors' sales). If necessary, managers must also adjust for differences in channels.

The time period measured will affect the signal-to-noise ratio

In analysing short-term market dynamics, such as the effects of a promotion or a recent price change, managers may find it useful to measure market share over a brief period of time. Short-term data, however, generally carry a low signal-to-noise ratio. By contrast, data covering a longer time span will be more stable but may obscure important, recent changes in the market. Applied more broadly, this principle also holds in aggregating geographic areas, channel types or customers. When choosing markets and time periods for analysis, managers must optimise for the type of signal that is most important.

Potential bias in reported shares

One way to find data for market sizing is through surveys of customer usage (see "Awareness, attitudes and usage (AAU)" on pages 32–36). In interpreting these data, however, managers must bear in mind that shares based on reported (versus recorded) sales tend to be biased toward well-known brands.

Related metrics and concepts

> Served market: **That portion of the total market for which the firm competes. This may exclude geographic regions or product types. In the airline industry, for example, as of mid 2005, Ryanair did not fly to the US. Consequently, the US would not be considered part of its served market.**

Relative market share and market concentration

Relative market share indexes a firm's or a brand's market share against that of its leading competitor.

$$\text{Relative market share (I) (\%)} = \frac{\text{Brand's market share (£,N)}}{\text{Largest competitor's market share (£,N)}}$$

Market concentration, a related metric, measures the degree to which a comparatively small number of firms accounts for a large proportion of the market.

These metrics are useful in comparing a firm's or a brand's relative position across different markets and in evaluating the type and degree of competition in those markets.

Purpose: to assess a firm's or a brand's success and its position in the market

A firm with a market share of 25% would be a powerful leader in many markets but a distant "number two" in others. Relative market share offers a way to benchmark a firm's or a brand's share against that of its largest competitor, enabling managers to compare relative market positions across different product markets. Relative market share gains some of its significance from studies – albeit controversial ones – suggesting that major players in a market tend to be more profitable than their competitors. This metric was further popularised by the Boston Consulting Group in its famous matrix of relative share and market growth (see Figure 2.1).

Figure 2.1 The BCG matrix

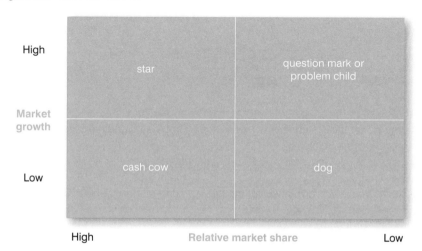

In the BCG matrix, one axis represents relative market share – a surrogate for competitive strength. The other represents market growth – a surrogate for potential. Along each dimension, products are classified as high or low, placing them in one of four quadrants. In the traditional interpretation of this matrix, products with high relative market shares in growing markets are deemed stars, suggesting that they should be supported with vigorous investment. The cash for that investment may be generated by cash cows – products with high relative shares in low-growth markets. Problem child products may have potential for future growth but hold weak competitive positions. Finally, dogs have neither strong competitive position nor growth potential.

Construction

$$\text{Relative market share (I)} = \frac{\text{Brand's market share (£,N)}}{\text{Largest competitor's market share (£,N)}}$$

Relative market share can also be calculated by dividing brand sales (£,N) by largest competitor's sales (£,N) because the common factor of total market sales (or revenue) cancels out.

Example The market for small urban cars consists of five players (see Table 2.1).

Table 2.1 Market for small urban cars

	Units sold (thousands)	Revenue (thousands)
Zipper	25	€375,000
Twister	10.0	€200,000
A-One	7.5	€187,500
Bowlz	5	€125,000
Chien	2.5	€50,000
Market total	50.0	€937,500

In the market for small urban cars, managers at A-One want to know their firm's market share relative to its largest competitor. They can calculate this on the basis of revenues or unit sales.

In unit terms, A-One sells 7,500 cars per year. Zipper, the market leader, sells 25,000. A-One's relative market share in unit terms is thus 7,500/25,000 or 0.30. We arrive at the same number if we first calculate A-One's share (7,500/50,000 = 0.15) and Zipper's share (25,000/50,000 = 0.50) and then divide A-One's share by Zipper's share (0.15/0.50 = 0.30).

In revenue terms, A-One generates €187.5 million in car sales each year. Zipper, the market leader, generates €375 million. A-One's relative market share in revenue terms is thus €187.5m/€375m, or 0.5. Due to its comparatively high average price per car, A-One's relative market share is greater in revenue than in unit terms.

Related metrics and concepts

> Market concentration: **The degree to which a relatively small number of firms accounts for a large proportion of the market. This is also known as the concentration ratio. It is usually calculated for the largest three or four firms in a market.**
>
> Three (four) firm concentration ratio: **The total (sum) of the market shares held by the leading three (four) competitors in a market.**

Example In the small urban car market, the three firm concentration ratio is comprised of the market shares of the top three competitors – Zipper, Twister and A-One (see Table 2.2).

Table 2.2 Market share: small urban cars

	Units sold (thousands)	Unit share	Revenue (thousands)	Revenue share
Zipper	25	50%	€375,000	40.0%
Twister	10.0	20%	€200,000	21.3%
A-One	7.5	15%	€187,500	20.0%
Bowlz	5	10%	€125,000	13.3%
Chien	2.5	5%	€50,000	5.3%
Market total	50.0	100%	€937,500	100%

In unit terms, the three firm concentration ratio is 50% + 20% + 15% = 85%. In revenue terms, it is 40% + 21.3% + 20% = 81.3%.

> Herfindahl Index: **A market concentration metric derived by adding the squares of the individual market shares of all the players in a market. As a sum of squares, this index tends to rise in markets dominated by large players.**

Example The Herfindahl Index dramatically highlights market concentration in the small urban car market (see Table 2.3).

Table 2.3 Calculation of the Herfindahl Index for small urban cars

	Units sold (thousands)	Unit share	Herfindahl Index	Revenue (thousands)	Revenue share	Herfindahl Index
Zipper	25	50%	0.25	€375,000	40%	0.16
Twister	10.0	20%	0.04	€200,000	21%	0.0455
A-One	7.5	15%	0.0225	€187,500	20%	0.04
Bowlz	5	10%	0.01	€125,000	13%	0.0178
Chien	2.5	5%	0.0025	€50,000	5%	0.0028
Market total	50.0	100%	0.325	€937,500	100%	0.2661

On a unit basis, the Herfindahl Index is equal to the square of the unit market share of Zipper (50% ^ 2 = 0.25), plus that of Twister (20% ^ 2 = 0.04), plus those of A-One, Bowlz and Chien = 0.325.

On a revenue basis, the Herfindahl Index comprises the square of the revenue market share of Zipper (40% ^ 2 = 0.16), plus those of all its competitors = 0.2661.

As demonstrated by the Herfindahl Index, the market for small urban cars is slightly more concentrated in unit terms than in revenue terms. The reason for this is straightforward: higher-priced cars in this market sell fewer units.

Note: For a given number of competitors, the Herfindahl Index would be lowest if shares were equally distributed. In a five-firm industry, for example, equally distributed shares would yield a Herfindahl Index of 5 * (20% ^ 2) = 0.2.

Data sources, complications and cautions

As ever, appropriate market definition and the use of comparable figures are vital prerequisites to developing meaningful results.

Related metrics and concepts

Market share rank: **The ordinal position of a brand in its market, when competitors are arranged by size, with 1 being the largest.**

Share of category: **This metric is derived in the same manner as market share, but is used to denote a share of market within a certain retailer or class of retailers (for example, mass merchandisers).**

Brand development index and category development index

The brand development index (BDI) quantifies how well a brand is performing within a specific group of customers, compared with its average performance among all consumers.

$$\text{Brand development index (I)} = \frac{[\text{Brand sales to group (N)}/\text{Households (N) in the group}]}{[\text{Total brand sales (N)}/\text{Total households (N)}]}$$

The category development index (CDI) measures the sales performance of a category of goods or services within a specific group, compared with its average performance among all consumers.

$$\text{Category development index (I)} = \frac{[\text{Category sales to group (N)}/\text{Households in group (N)}]}{[\text{Total category sales (N)}/\text{Total households (N)}]}$$

The brand and category development indexes are useful for understanding specific customer segments relative to the market as a whole. Although defined here with respect to households, these indexes could also be calculated for customers, accounts, businesses or other entities.

Purpose: to understand the relative performance of a brand or category within specified customer groups

The brand and category development indexes help identify strong and weak segments (usually, demographic or geographic) for particular brands or categories of goods and services. For example, by monitoring the CDI (category development index), marketers might determine that the Scots buy twice as many folk music CDs per capita as Britons in general, while consumers living in the southeast buy less than the national average. This would be useful information for targeting the launch campaign for a new folk performer. Conversely, if managers found that a particular product had a low brand development index in a segment that carried a high CDI for its category, they might ask why that brand suffered relatively poor performance in such a promising segment.

Construction

Brand Development Index – BDI (I): **An index of how well a brand performs within a given market group, relative to its performance in the market as a whole.**

$$\text{Brand development index} - \text{BDI (I)} = \frac{[\text{Brand sales to group (N)/} \\ \text{Households in group (N)}]}{\text{Total brand sales (N)/} \\ \text{Total households (N)}]}$$

The BDI (brand development index) is a measure of brand sales per person or per household within a specified demographic group or geography, compared with its average sales per person or household in the market as a whole. To illustrate its use: one might hypothesise that sales per capita of Ben & Jerry's brand ice cream would be greater in the brand's home state, Vermont, than in the rest of the US. By calculating Ben & Jerry's BDI for Vermont, marketers could test this hypothesis quantitatively.

Example Oaties is a minor brand of breakfast cereal. Among households without children, its sales run to one packet per week per 100 households. In the general population, Oaties' sales run to one packet per week per 80 households. This translates to 1/100 of a packet per household in the childless segment, versus 1/80 of a packet in the general populace.

$$\text{BDI} = \frac{(\text{Brand sales/Household})}{(\text{Total brand sales/Household})}$$

$$= \frac{1/100}{1/80} = 0.8$$

Oaties performs slightly less well in the childless segment than in the market as a whole.

> **Category development index (CDI): An index of how well a category performs within a given market segment, relative to its performance in the market as a whole.**

$$\text{Category development index (I)} = \frac{[\text{Category sales to group (N)/} \\ \text{Households in group (N)}]}{[\text{Total category sales (N)/} \\ \text{Total households (N)}]}$$

Similar in concept to the BDI, the category development index demonstrates where a category shows strength or weakness relative to its overall performance. By way of example, Boston in the US enjoys high per-capita consumption of ice cream. Bavaria and Ireland both show higher per-capita consumption of beer than Iran.

Data sources and complications

In calculating BDI or CDI, a precise definition of the segment under study is vital. Segments are often bounded geographically, but they can be defined in any way for which data can be obtained.

Related metrics and concepts

The concept of the category development index has also been applied to retail organisations. In this application, it measures the extent to which a retailer emphasises one category versus others.

$$\text{Category development index (I)} = \frac{\text{Retailer's share of category sales (\%)}}{\text{Retailer's total share of market (\%)}}$$

This use of the term is similar to the category performance ratio (see "Numeric, ACV and PCV distribution, facings/share of shelf" on pages 176–183).

Penetration

> Penetration is a measure of brand or category popularity. It is defined as the number of people who buy a specific brand or a category of goods at least once in a given period, divided by the size of the relevant market population.
>
> $$\text{Market penetration (\%)} = \frac{\text{Customers who have purchased a product in the category (N)}}{\text{Total population (N)}}$$
>
> $$\text{Brand penetration (\%)} = \frac{\text{Customers who have purchased the brand (N)}}{\text{Total population (N)}}$$
>
> $$\text{Penetration share (\%)} = \frac{\text{Brand penetration (\%)}}{\text{Market penetration (\%)}}$$
>
> $$\text{Penetration share (\%)} = \frac{\text{Customers who have purchased the brand (N)}}{\text{Customers who have purchased a product in the category (N)}}$$
>
> Often, managers must decide whether to seek sales growth by acquiring existing category users from their competitors or by expanding the total population of category users, attracting new customers to the market. Penetration metrics help indicate which of these strategies would be most appropriate and help managers to monitor their success. These equations might also be calculated for usage instead of purchase.

> Penetration: **The proportion of people in the target who bought (at least once in the period) a specific brand or a category of goods.**

$$\text{Market penetration (\%)} = \frac{\text{Customers who have purchased a product in the category (N)}}{\text{Total population (N)}}$$

$$\text{Brand penetration (\%)} = \frac{\text{Customers who have purchased the brand (N)}}{\text{Total population (N)}}$$

Two key measures of a product's "popularity" are penetration rate and penetration share. The penetration rate (also called penetration, brand penetration or market penetration as appropriate) is the percentage of the relevant population that has purchased a given brand or category at least once in the time period under study.

Example Over a period of a month, in a market of 10,000 households, 500 households purchased Big Bomb brand flea powder.

$$\text{Brand penetration, Big Bomb} = \frac{\text{Big Bomb customers}}{\text{Total population}}$$

$$= \frac{500}{10,000} = 5\%$$

A brand's penetration share, in contrast to penetration rate, is determined by comparing that brand's customer population to the number of customers *for its category* in the relevant market as a whole. Here again, to be considered a customer, one must have purchased the brand or category at least once during the period.

$$\text{Penetration share (\%)} = \frac{\text{Brand penetration (\%)}}{\text{Market penetration (\%)}}$$

Example Returning to the flea powder market, during the month in which 500 households purchased Big Bomb, 2,000 households bought at least one product of any brand in this category. This enables us to calculate Big Bomb's penetration share.

$$\text{Penetration share, Big Bomb} = \frac{\text{Big Bomb customers}}{\text{Category customers}}$$

$$= \frac{500}{2,000} = 25\%$$

> Relationship of penetration share to market share: **Market share can be calculated as the product of three components: penetration share, share of requirements and heavy usage index.**
>
> $$\text{Market share (\%)} = \text{Penetration share (\%)} * \text{Share of requirements (\%)} * \text{Heavy usage index (I)}$$
>
> Share of requirements: **The percentage of customers' needs in a category that are served by a given brand or product (see "Share of requirements" on pages 26–30).**
>
> Heavy usage index: **A measure of how heavily the people who use a specific product use the entire category of such products (see 'Heavy usage index' on pages 30–31).**

In light of these relationships, managers can use this decomposition of market share to reveal penetration share, given the other inputs.

$$\text{Penetration share (\%)} = \frac{\text{Market share (\%)}}{[\text{Heavy usage index (I)} * \text{Share of requirements (\%)}]}$$

Example Eat Wheats brand cereal has a market share in Urbanopolis of 6%. The heavy usage index for Eat Wheats cereal is 0.75 in Urbanopolis. Its share of requirements is 40%. From these data, we can calculate the penetration share for Eat Wheats brand cereal in Urbanopolis:

$$\text{Penetration share} = \frac{\text{Market share}}{(\text{Heavy usage index} * \text{Share of requirements})}$$

$$= \frac{6\%}{(0.75 * 40\%)} = \frac{6\%}{0.30} = 20\%$$

Data sources, complications and cautions

The time period over which a firm measures penetration can have a significant impact on the penetration rate. For example, even among the most popular detergent brands, many are not purchased weekly. As the time period used to define penetration becomes shorter, managers can expect penetration rates to decline. By contrast, penetration share may be less subject to this dynamic because it represents a comparison between brands, among which the effects of shorter periods may fall approximately evenly.

Total number of active customers: The customers (accounts) who purchased at least once in a given time period. When assessed at a brand level, this is equivalent to brand penetration. This term is often used in shorthand form – total number of customers – though this would not be appropriate when a distinction must be made for ex-customers. This is discussed in more detail in "Customers, recency and retention" on pages 132–137 (customers of a specified recency).

Acceptors: Customers who are disposed to accept a given product and its benefits: the opposite of rejecters.

Ever-tried: The percentage of a population that has tried a given brand at any time. (See "Trial, repeat, penetration and volume projections" on pages 92–105 for more on trial.)

Share of requirements

Share of requirements, also known as share of wallet, is calculated solely among buyers of a specific brand. Within this group, it represents the percentage of purchases within the relevant category, accounted for by the brand in question.

$$\text{Unit share of requirements (\%)} = \frac{\text{Brand purchases (N)}}{\text{Total category purchases by brand buyers (N)}}$$

$$\text{Revenue share of requirements (\%)} = \frac{\text{Brand purchases (£)}}{\text{Total category purchases by brand buyers (£)}}$$

Many marketers view share of requirements as a key measure of loyalty. This metric can guide a firm's decisions on whether to allocate resources toward efforts to expand a category, to take customers from competitors or to increase share of requirements among its established customers. Share of requirements is, in essence, the market share for a brand within a market narrowly defined as the people who have already purchased that brand.

Purpose: to understand the source of market share in terms of breadth and depth of consumer franchise, as well as the extent of relative category usage (heavy users/larger customers versus light users/smaller customers)

Share of requirements is increasingly used to describe customer loyalty in behavioural terms (as opposed to attitudes).

Construction

> Share of requirements: **A given brand's share of purchases in its category, measured solely among customers who have already purchased that brand. Also known as share of wallet.**

When calculating share of requirements, marketers may consider either money or units. They must ensure, however, that their heavy usage index is consistent with this choice.

$$\text{Unit share of requirements (\%)} = \frac{\text{Brand purchases (N)}}{\text{Total category purchases by brand buyers (N)}}$$

$$\text{Revenue share of requirements (\%)} = \frac{\text{Brand purchases (£)}}{\text{Total category purchases by brand buyers (£)}}$$

The best way to think about share of requirements is as the average market share enjoyed by a product among the customers who buy it.

Example In a given month, the unit purchases of AloeHa brand sunscreen ran to 1,000,000 bottles. Among the households that bought AloeHa, total purchases of sunscreen came to 2,000,000 bottles.

$$\text{Share of requirements} = \frac{\text{AloeHa purchases}}{\text{Category purchases by AloeHa customers}}$$

$$= \frac{1,000,000}{2,000,000} = 50\%$$

Share of requirements is also useful in analysing overall market share. As previously noted, it is part of an important formulation of market share.

$$\text{Market share} = \text{Penetration share} * \text{Share of requirements} * \text{Heavy usage index}$$

Share of requirements can thus be calculated indirectly by decomposing market share.

$$\text{Share of requirements (\%)} = \frac{\text{Market share (\%)}}{[\text{Penetration share (\%)} * \text{Heavy usage index (I)}]}$$

Example Eat Wheats brand cereal has a market share in Urbanopolis of 8%. The heavy usage index for Eat Wheats in Urbanopolis is 1. The brand's penetration share in Urbanopolis is 20%. On this basis, we can calculate Eat Wheats' share of requirements in Urbanopolis:

$$\text{Share of requirements} = \frac{\text{Market share}}{(\text{Heavy usage index} * \text{Penetration share})}$$

$$= \frac{8\%}{(1 * 20\%)} = \frac{8\%}{20\%} = 40\%$$

Note that in this example, market share and heavy usage index must both be defined in the same terms (units or revenue). Depending on the definition of these two metrics, the calculated share of requirements will be either unit share of requirements (%) or revenue share of requirements (%).

Data sources, complications and cautions

Double jeopardy

Some marketers strive for a "niche" positioning that yields high market share through a combination of low penetration and high share of requirements. That is, they seek relatively few customers but very loyal ones. Before embarking on this strategy, however, a phenomenon known as "double jeopardy" should be considered. Generally, the evidence suggests that it's difficult to achieve a high share of requirements without also attaining a high penetration share. One reason is that products with high market share generally have high availability, whereas those with low market share may not. Therefore, it can be difficult for customers to maintain loyalty to brands with low market share.

Related metrics and concepts

> Sole usage: **The fraction of a brand's customers who use only the brand in question.**

> Sole usage percentage: **The proportion of a brand's customers who use only that brand's products and do not buy from competitors. Sole users may be die-hard, loyal customers. Alternatively, they may not have access to other options, perhaps because they live in remote areas. Where sole use is 100%, the share of wallet is 100%.**

$$\text{Sole usage (\%)} = \frac{\text{Customers who buy only the brand in question (N)}}{\text{Total brand customers (N)}}$$

Number of brands purchased

During a given period, some customers may buy only a single brand within a category, whereas others buy two or more. In evaluating loyalty to a given brand, marketers can consider the average number of brands purchased by consumers of that brand versus the average number purchased by all customers in that category.

Example Among 10 customers for cat food, 7 bought the Arda brand, 5 bought Bella and 3 bought Constanza. Thus, the 10 customers made a total of 15 brand purchases (7 + 5 + 3), yielding an average of 1.5 brands per customer.

Seeking to evaluate customer loyalty, a Bella brand manager notes that of his firm's 5 customers, 3 bought only Bella, whereas 2 bought both Arda and Bella. None of Bella's customers bought Constanza. Thus, the 5 Bella customers made 7 brand purchases (1 + 1 + 1 + 2 + 2), yielding an average of 1.4 (that is, 7/5) brands per Bella customer. Compared to the average category purchaser, who buys 1.5 brands, Bella buyers are slightly more loyal.

> Repeat rate: **The percentage of brand customers in a given period who are also brand customers in the subsequent period.**
>
> Repurchase rate: **The percentage of customers for a brand who repurchase that brand on their next purchase occasion.**

Confusion abounds in this area. In these definitions, we have tried to distinguish a metric based on calendar time (repeat rate) from one based on "customer time" (repurchase rate). In Chapter 5, "Customer profitability", we will describe a related metric, retention, which is used in contractual situations in which the first non-renewal (non-purchase) signals the end of a customer relationship. Although we suggest that the term "retention" be applied only in contractual situations, you will often see repeat rates and repurchase rates referred to as "retention rates". Due to a lack of consensus on the use of these terms, marketers are advised not to rely on the names of these metrics as perfect indicators of how they are calculated.

The importance of repeat rate depends on the time period covered. Looking at one week's worth of purchases is unlikely to be very illuminating. In a given category, most consumers only buy one brand in a week. By contrast, over a period of years, consumers may buy several brands that they do not prefer, on occasions when they can't find the brand to which they seek to be loyal. Consequently, the right period to consider depends on the product under study and the frequency with which it is bought. Marketers are advised to take care to choose a meaningful period.

Heavy usage index

The heavy usage index is a measure of the relative intensity of consumption. It indicates how heavily the customers for a given brand use the product category to which that brand belongs, compared with the average customer for that category.

$$\text{Heavy usage index (I)} = \frac{\text{Average total purchases in category by brand customers (N,£)}}{\text{Average total purchases in category by all customers for that category (N,£)}}$$

or

$$\text{Heavy usage index (I)} = \frac{\text{Market share (\%)}}{[\text{Penetration share (\%) * Share of requirements (\%)}]}$$

The heavy usage index, also called the weight index, yields insight into the source of volume and the nature of a brand's customer base.

Purpose: to define and measure whether a firm's consumers are "heavy users"

The heavy usage index answers the question, "How heavily do our customers use the category of our product?" When a brand's heavy usage index is greater than 1.0, this signifies that its customers use the category to which it belongs more heavily than the average customer for that category.

Construction

Heavy usage index: **The ratio that compares the average consumption of products in a category by customers of a given brand with the average consumption of products in that category by all customers for the category.**

The heavy usage index can be calculated on the basis of unit or monetary inputs. For a given brand, if the heavy usage index is greater than 1.0, that brand's customers consume an above-average quantity or value of products in the category.

$$\text{Heavy usage index (I)} = \frac{\text{Average total purchases in category by brand customers (N,£)}}{\text{Average total purchases in category by all customers for that category (N,£)}}$$

Example Over a period of one year, the average shampoo purchases by households using Shower Fun brand shampoo totalled six 15-oz bottles. During the same period, average shampoo consumption by households using any brand of shampoo was four 15-oz bottles.

The heavy usage index for households buying Shower Fun is therefore 6/4, or 1.5. Customers of Shower Fun brand shampoo are disproportionately heavy users. They buy 50% more shampoo than the average shampoo consumer. Of course, because Shower Fun buyers are part of the overall market average, when compared with non-users of Shower Fun, their relative usage is even higher.

As previously noted, market share can be calculated as the product of three components: penetration share, share of requirements, and heavy usage index (see "Penetration" on pages 23–26). Consequently, we can calculate a brand's heavy usage index if we know its market share, penetration share and share of requirements, as follows:

$$\text{Heavy usage index (I)} = \frac{\text{Market share (\%)}}{[\text{Penetration share (\%) * Share of requirements (\%)}]}$$

This equation works for market shares defined in either unit or financial terms. As noted earlier, the heavy usage index can measure either unit or financial usage. Comparing a brand's unit heavy usage index to its financial heavy usage index, marketers can determine whether category purchases by that brand's customers run above or below the average category price.

Data sources, complications and cautions

The heavy usage index does not indicate how heavily customers use a specific brand, only how heavily they use the category. A brand can have a high heavy usage index, for example, meaning that its customers are heavy category users, even if those customers use the brand in question to meet only a small share of their needs.

Related metrics and concepts

See also the discussion of brand development index (BDI) and category development index (CDI) on pages 21–23.

Awareness, attitudes and usage (AAU): metrics of the hierarchy of effects

> Studies of awareness, attitudes and usage (AAU) enable marketers to quantify levels and trends in customer knowledge, perceptions, beliefs, intentions and behaviours. In some companies, the results of these studies are called "tracking" data because they are used to track long-term changes in customer awareness, attitudes and behaviours.
>
> AAU studies are most useful when their results are set against a clear comparator. This benchmark may comprise the data from prior periods, different markets or competitors.

Purpose: to track trends in customer attitudes and behaviours

Awareness, attitudes and usage (AAU) metrics relate closely to what has been called the hierarchy of effects, an assumption that customers progress through sequential stages from lack of awareness, through initial purchase of a product, to brand loyalty (see Figure 2.2). AAU metrics are generally designed to track these stages of knowledge, beliefs and behaviours. AAU studies also may track "who" uses a brand or product – in which customers are defined by category usage (heavy/light), geography, demographics, psychographics, media usage and whether they purchase other products.

Figure 2.2 Awareness, attitudes and usage: hierarchy of effects

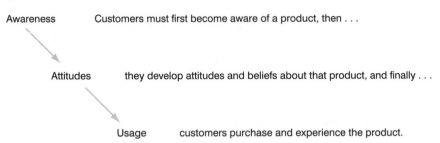

Awareness   Customers must first become aware of a product, then . . .

Attitudes   they develop attitudes and beliefs about that product, and finally . . .

Usage   customers purchase and experience the product.

Information about attitudes and beliefs offers insight into the question of why specific users do, or do not, favour certain brands. Typically, marketers conduct surveys of large samples of households or business customers to gather these data.

Construction

Awareness, attitudes and usage studies feature a range of questions that aim to shed light on customers' relationships with a product or brand (see Table 2.4). For example, who are the acceptors and rejecters of the product? How do customers respond to a replay of advertising content?

Marketers use answers to these questions to construct a number of metrics. Among these, certain "summary metrics" are considered important indicators of performance. In many studies, for example, customers' "willingness to recommend" and "intention to purchase" a brand are assigned high priority. Underlying these data, various diagnostic metrics help marketers understand *why* consumers may be willing – or unwilling – to recommend or purchase that brand. Consumers may not have been aware of the brand, for example. Alternatively, they may have been aware of it but did not subscribe to one of its key benefit claims.

Table 2.4 Awareness, attitudes and usage: typical questions

Type	Measures	Typical questions
Awareness	Awareness and knowledge	Have you heard of Brand X? What brand comes to mind when you think "luxury car"?
Attitudes	Beliefs and intentions	Is Brand X for me? On a scale of 1 to 5, is Brand X for young people? What are the strengths and weaknesses of each brand?
Usage	Purchase habits and loyalty	Did you use Brand X this week? What brand did you last buy?

Awareness and knowledge

Marketers evaluate various levels of awareness, depending on whether the consumer in a given study is prompted by a product's category, brand, advertising or usage situation.

> Awareness: **The percentage of potential customers or consumers who recognise – or name – a given brand. Marketers may research brand recognition on an "aided" or "prompted" level, posing such questions as, "Have you heard of Mercedes?" Alternatively, they may measure "unaided" or "unprompted" awareness, posing such questions as, "Which makes of cars come to mind?"**
>
> Top of mind: **The first brand that comes to mind when a customer is asked an unprompted question about a category. The percentage of customers for whom a given brand is top of mind can be measured.**

▶

Ad awareness: The percentage of target consumers or accounts who demonstrate awareness (aided or unaided) of a brand's advertising. This metric can be campaign- or media-specific, or it can cover all advertising.

Brand/product knowledge: The percentage of surveyed customers who demonstrate specific knowledge or beliefs about a brand or product.

Attitudes

Measures of attitude concern consumer response to a brand or product. Attitude is a combination of what consumers believe and how strongly they feel about it. Although a detailed exploration of attitudinal research is beyond the scope of this book, the following summarises certain key metrics in this field.

Attitudes/liking/image: A rating assigned by consumers (often on a scale of 1–5 or 1–7) when survey respondents are asked their level of agreement with such propositions as, "This is a brand for people like me", or "This is a brand for young people." A metric based on such survey data can also be called relevance to customer.

Perceived value for money: A rating assigned by consumers (often on a scale of 1–5 or 1–7) when survey respondents are asked their level of agreement with such propositions as, "This brand usually represents good value for money."

Perceived quality/esteem: A consumer rating (often on a scale of 1–5 or 1–7) of a given brand's product when compared with others in its category or market.

Relative perceived quality: A consumer rating (often from 1–5 or 1–7) of brand product compared to others in the category/market.

Intentions: A measure of customers' stated willingness to behave in a certain way. Information on this subject is gathered through such survey questions as, "Would you be willing to switch brands if your favourite was not available?"

Intention to purchase: A specific measure or rating of consumers' stated purchase intentions. Information on this subject is gathered through survey respondents' reactions to such propositions as, "It is very likely that I will purchase this product."

Usage

Measures of usage concern such market dynamics as purchase frequency and units per purchase. They highlight not only what was purchased, but also when and where it was purchased. In studying usage, marketers also seek to determine how many people have tried a brand. Of those, they further seek to determine how many have "rejected" the brand, and how many have "adopted" it into their regular portfolio of brands.

> Usage: **A measure of customers' self-reported behaviour.**

In measuring usage, marketers pose such questions as the following: What brand of toothpaste did you last purchase? How many times in the past year have you purchased toothpaste? How many tubes of toothpaste do you currently have in your home? Do you have any Crest toothpaste in your home at the current time?

In the aggregate, AAU metrics concern a vast range of information that can be tailored to specific companies and markets. They provide managers with insight into customers' overall relationships with a given brand or product.

Data sources, complications and cautions

Sources of AAU data include:

- Warranty cards and registrations, often using prizes and random drawings to encourage participation.
- Regularly administered surveys, conducted by organisations that interview consumers via telephone, mail, Web or other technologies, such as hand-held barcode scanners.

Even with the best methodologies, however, variations observed in tracking data from one period to the next are not always reliable. Managers must rely on their experience to distinguish seasonality effects and "noise" (random movement) from "signal" (actual trends and patterns). Certain techniques in data collection and review can also help managers make this distinction.

1 **Adjust for periodic changes** in how questions are framed or administered. Surveys can be conducted via mail or telephone, for example, among paid or unpaid respondents. Different data-gathering techniques may require adjustment in the norms used to evaluate a "good" or "bad" response. If sudden changes appear in the data from one period to the next, marketers are advised to determine whether methodological shifts might play a role in this result.

2 Try to **separate customer from non-customer responses**; they may be very different. Causal links among awareness, attitudes and usage are rarely clear-cut. Though the hierarchy of effects is often viewed as a one-way street, on which awareness leads to attitudes, which in turn determine usage, the true causal flow might also be reversed. When people own a brand, for example, they may be predisposed to like it.

3 **Triangulate customer survey data** with sales revenue, shipments or other data related to business performance. Consumer attitudes, distributor and retail sales, and company shipments may move in different directions. Analysing these patterns can be a challenge but can reveal much about category dynamics. For example, toy shipments to retailers often occur well in advance of the advertising that drives consumer awareness and purchase

intentions. These, in turn, must be established before retail sales. Adding further complexity, in the toy industry, the purchaser of a product might not be its ultimate consumer. In evaluating AAU data, marketers must understand not only the drivers of demand but also the logistics of purchase.

4 **Separate leading from lagging indicators** whenever possible. In the car industry, for example, individuals who have just purchased a new car show a heightened sensitivity to advertisements for its make and model. Conventional wisdom suggests that they're looking for confirmation that they made a good choice in a risky decision. By helping consumers justify their purchase at this time, car manufacturers can strengthen long-term satisfaction and willingness to recommend.

Related metrics and concepts

Likeability: **Because AAU considerations are so important to marketers, and because there is no single "right" way to approach them, specialised and proprietary systems have been developed. Of these, one of the best known is the Q scores rating of "likeability". A Q score is derived from a general survey of selected households, in which a large panel of consumers share their feelings about brands, celebrities and television shows.**[3]

Q scores rely upon responses reported by consumers. Consequently, although the system used is sophisticated, it is dependent on consumers understanding and being willing to reveal their preferences.

Segmentation by geography, or geo-clustering: **Marketers can achieve insight into consumer attitudes by separating their data into smaller, more homogeneous groups of customers. One well-known example of this is Prizm. Prizm assigns US households to clusters based on ZIP code,**[4] **with the goal of creating small groups of similar households. The typical characteristics of each Prizm cluster are known, and these are used to assign a name to each group. "Golden Ponds" consumers, for example, comprise elderly singles and couples leading modest lifestyles in small towns. Rather than monitoring AAU statistics for the population as a whole, firms often find it useful to track these data by cluster.**

Customer satisfaction and willingness to recommend

Customer satisfaction is generally based on survey data and expressed as a rating. For example, see Figure 2.3.

Figure 2.3 Ratings

Very dissatisfied	Somewhat dissatisfied	Neither satisfied nor dissatisfied	Somewhat satisfied	Very satisfied
1	2	3	4	5

Within organisations, customer satisfaction ratings can have powerful effects. They focus employees on the importance of fulfilling customers' expectations. Furthermore, when these ratings dip, they warn of problems that can affect sales and profitability.

A second important metric related to satisfaction is willingness to recommend. When a customer is satisfied with a product, he or she might recommend it to friends, relatives and colleagues. This can be a powerful marketing advantage.

Purpose: customer satisfaction provides a leading indicator of consumer purchase intentions and loyalty

Customer satisfaction data are among the most frequently collected indicators of market perceptions. Their principal use is twofold:

1 Within organisations, the collection, analysis and dissemination of these data send a message about the importance of tending to customers and ensuring that they have a positive experience with the company's goods and services.

2 Although sales or market share can indicate how well a firm is performing *currently*, satisfaction is perhaps the best indicator of how likely it is that the firm's customers will make further purchases *in the future*. Much research has focused on the relationship between customer satisfaction and retention. Studies indicate that the ramifications of satisfaction are most strongly realised at the extremes. On the scale in Figure 2.3, individuals who rate their satisfaction level as "5" are likely to become return customers and might even evangelise for the firm. Individuals who rate their satisfaction level as "1", by contrast, are unlikely to return. Further, they can hurt the firm by making negative comments about it to prospective customers. Willingness to recommend is a key metric relating to customer satisfaction.

Construction

> Customer satisfaction: **The number of customers, or percentage of total customers, whose reported experience with a firm, its products or its services (ratings) exceeds specified satisfaction goals.**
>
> Willingness to recommend: **The percentage of surveyed customers who indicate that they would recommend a brand to friends.**

These metrics quantify an important dynamic. When a brand has loyal customers, it gains positive word-of-mouth marketing, which is both free and highly effective.

Customer satisfaction is measured at the individual level, but it is almost always reported at an aggregate level. It can be, and often is, measured along various dimensions. A hotel, for example, might ask customers to rate their experience with its reception and check-in service, with the room, with the amenities in the room, with the restaurants, and so on. Additionally, in a holistic sense, the hotel might ask about overall satisfaction "with your stay".

Customer satisfaction is generally measured on a five-point scale (see Figure 2.4).

Satisfaction levels are usually reported as either "top box" or, more likely, "top two boxes". Marketers convert these expressions into single numbers that show the percentage of respondents who checked either a "4" or a "5". (This term is the same as that commonly used in projections of trial volumes; see "Trial, repeat, penetration and volume projections" on pages 92–105.)

Figure 2.4 A typical five-point scale

Very dissatisfied	Somewhat dissatisfied	Neither satisfied nor dissatisfied	Somewhat satisfied	Very Satisfied
1	2	3	4	5

Example The general manager of a hotel in Paris institutes a new system of customer satisfaction monitoring (see Figure 2.5). She leaves satisfaction surveys at checkout. As an incentive to respond, all respondents are entered into a draw for a pair of free airline tickets.

Figure 2.5 Hotel customer survey response

	Very dissatisfied	Somewhat dissatisfied	Neither satisfied nor dissatisfied	Somewhat satisfied	Very satisfied
Score	1	2	3	4	5
Responses (200 usable)	3	7	40	100	50
%	2%	4%	20%	50%	25%

The manager collects 220 responses, of which 20 are unclear or otherwise unusable. Among the remaining 200, 3 people rate their overall experience at the hotel as very unsatisfactory, 7 deem it somewhat unsatisfactory, and 40 respond that they are neither satisfied nor dissatisfied. Of the remainder, 50 customers say they are very satisfied, while the rest are somewhat satisfied.

The top box, comprising customers who rate their experience a "5", includes 50 people or, as a percentage, 50/200 = 25%. The top two boxes comprise customers who are "somewhat" or "very" satisfied, rating their experience a "4" or "5". In this example, the "somewhat satisfied" population must be calculated as the total usable response pool, less customers accounted for elsewhere, that is, 200 − 3 − 7 − 40 − 50 = 100. The sum of the top two boxes is thus 50 + 100 = 150 customers, or 75% of the total.

Customer satisfaction data can also be collected on a 10-point scale. Regardless of the scale used, the objective is to measure customers' perceived satisfaction with their experience of a firm's offerings. Marketers then aggregate these data into a percentage of top-box responses.

In researching satisfaction, firms generally ask customers whether their product or service has met or exceeded expectations. Thus, expectations are a key factor behind satisfaction. When customers have high expectations and the reality falls short, they will be disappointed and will likely rate their experience as less than satisfying. For this reason, a luxury resort, for example, might receive a lower satisfaction rating than a budget motel – even though its facilities and service would be deemed superior in "absolute" terms.

Data sources, complications and cautions

Surveys constitute the most frequently used means of collecting satisfaction data. As a result, a key risk of distortion in measures of satisfaction can be summarised in a single question: Who responds to surveys?

"Response bias" is endemic in satisfaction data. Disappointed or angry customers often welcome a means to vent their opinions. Contented customers often do not. Consequently, although many customers might be happy with a product and feel no need to complete a survey, the few who had a bad experience might be disproportionately represented among respondents. Most hotels, for example, place response cards in their rooms, asking guests, "How was your stay?" Only a small percentage of guests ever bother to complete those cards. Not surprisingly, those who do respond probably had a bad experience. For this reason, marketers can find it difficult to judge the true level of customer satisfaction. By reviewing survey data over time, however, they may discover important trends or changes. If complaints suddenly rise, for example, that may constitute early warning of a decline in quality or service. (See number of complaints overleaf.)

Sample selection may distort satisfaction ratings in other ways as well. Because only *customers* are surveyed for customer satisfaction, a firm's ratings may rise artificially as deeply dissatisfied customers take their business elsewhere. Also, some populations may be more frank than others, or more prone to complain. These normative differences can affect perceived satisfaction levels. In analysing satisfaction data, a firm might interpret rating differences as a sign that one market is receiving better service than another, when the true difference lies only in the standards that customers apply. To correct for this issue, marketers are advised to review satisfaction measures over time *within the same market*.

A final caution: because many firms define customer satisfaction as "meeting or exceeding expectations", this metric may fall simply because expectations have risen. Thus, in interpreting ratings data, managers may come to believe that the quality of their offering has declined when that is not the case. Of course, the reverse is also true. A firm might boost satisfaction by lowering expectations. In so doing, however, it might suffer a decline in sales as its product or service comes to appear unattractive.

Related metrics and concepts

Trade satisfaction: **Founded upon the same principles as consumer satisfaction, trade satisfaction measures the attitudes of trade customers.**

Number of complaints: **The number of complaints lodged by customers in a given time period.**

Willingness to search

Although many metrics explore brand loyalty, one has been called the "acid test". That is,

Willingness to search (%) = Percentage of customers willing to delay purchases, change stores, or reduce purchase quantities to avoid switching brands

This metric can tell a company much about the attitudes of its customers and whether its position in the market is likely to be defensible against sustained pressure from a competitor.

Brand or company loyalty is a key marketing asset. Marketers evaluate aspects of it through a number of metrics, including repurchase rate, share of requirements, willingness to pay a price premium, and other AAU measures. Perhaps the most fundamental test of loyalty, however, can be captured in a simple question: When faced with a situation in which a brand is not available, will its customers search further or substitute the best available option?

When a brand enjoys loyalty at this level, its provider can generate powerful leverage in trade negotiations. Often, such loyalty will also give providers time to respond to a competitive threat. Customers will stay with them while they address the threat.

Loyalty is grounded in a number of factors, including:

- Satisfied and influential customers who are willing to recommend the brand.
- Hidden values or emotional benefits, which are effectively communicated.
- A strong image for the product, the user or the usage experience.

Purchase-based loyalty metrics are also affected by whether a product is broadly and conveniently available for purchase, and whether customers enjoy other options in its category.

Construction

> Willingness to search: **The likelihood that customers will not settle for a second-choice product if their first choice is not available. Also called "accept no substitutes".**

Willingness to search represents the percentage of customers who are willing to leave a store without a product if their favourite brand is unavailable. Those willing to substitute constitute the balance of the population.

Data sources, complications and cautions

Loyalty has multiple dimensions. Consumers who are loyal to a brand in the sense of rarely switching may or may not be willing to pay a price premium for that brand or recommend it to their friends. Behavioural loyalty may also be difficult to distinguish from inertia or habit. When asked about loyalty, consumers often don't know what they will do in new circumstances. They may not have accurate recall about past behaviour, especially in regard to items with which they feel relatively low involvement.

Furthermore, different products generate different levels of loyalty. Few customers will be as loyal to a brand of matches, for example, as to a brand of baby formula. Consequently, marketers should exercise caution in comparing loyalty rates across products. Rather, they should look for category-specific norms.

Degrees of loyalty also differ between demographic groups. Older consumers have been shown to demonstrate the highest loyalty rates.

Even with these complexities, however, customer loyalty remains one of the most important metrics to monitor. Marketers should understand the worth of their brands in the eyes of the customer – and of the retailer.

Margins and profits

3

Metrics covered in this chapter:

- Margins

- Selling prices and channel margins

- Average price per unit and price per statistical unit

- Variable costs and fixed costs

- Marketing spending – total, fixed and variable

- Break-even analysis and contribution analysis

- Target volume

Introduction

Peter Drucker has written that the purpose of a business is to create a customer. As marketers, we agree. But we also recognise that a business can't survive unless it makes a margin as well as a customer. At one level, margins are simply the difference between a product's price and its cost. This calculation becomes more complicated, however, when multiple variations of a product are sold at multiple prices, through multiple channels, incurring different costs along the way. For example, a recent *Business Week* article noted that less "than two-thirds of GM's sales are retail. The rest go to rental-car agencies or to company employees and their families – sales that provide lower gross margins."[1] Although it is still the case that a business can't survive unless it earns a positive margin, it can be a challenge to determine precisely what margin the firm actually does earn.

In the first section of this chapter, we'll explain the basic computation of unit and percentage margins, and we'll introduce the practice of calculating margins as a percentage of selling price.

Next, we'll show how to "chain" this calculation through two or more levels in a distribution channel and how to calculate end-user purchase price on the basis of a marketer's selling price. We'll explain how to combine sales through different channels to calculate average margins and how to compare the economics of different distribution channels.

In the third section, we'll discuss the use of "statistical" and standard units in tracking price changes over time.

We'll then turn our attention to measuring product costs, with particular emphasis on the distinction between fixed and variable costs. The margin between a product's unit price and its variable cost per unit represents a key calculation. It tells us how much the sale of each unit of that product will contribute to covering a firm's fixed costs. "Contribution margin" on sales is one of the most useful marketing concepts. It requires, however, that we separate fixed costs from variable costs, and that is often a challenge. Frequently, marketers must take "as a given" which of their firm's operating and production costs are fixed and which are variable. They are likely, however, to be responsible for making these fixed versus variable distinctions for marketing costs. That is the subject of the fifth section of this chapter.

In the sixth section, we'll discuss the use of fixed- and variable-cost estimates in calculating the break-even levels of sales and contribution. Finally, we'll extend our calculation of break-even points, showing how to identify sales and profit targets that are mutually consistent.

Metric	Construction	Considerations	Purpose
Unit margin	Unit price less the unit cost.	What are the standard units in the industry? May not reflect contribution margin if some fixed costs are allocated.	Determine value of incremental sales. Guide pricing and promotion.
Margin (%)	Unit margin as a percentage of unit price.	May not reflect contribution margin if some fixed costs are allocated.	Compare margins across different products/sizes/ forms of product. Determine value of incremental sales. Guide pricing and promotion decisions.

Metric	Construction	Considerations	Purpose
Channel margins	Channel profits as percentage of channel selling price.	Distinguish margin on sales (usual) from mark-up on cost (also encountered).	Evaluate channel value added in context of selling price. Calculate effect of price changes at one level of channel on prices and margins at other levels in the same channel (supply chain).
Average price per unit	Can be calculated as total revenue divided by total unit sales.	Some units may have greater relevance from producers' perspective than consumers' (e.g. ounces of shampoo vs. bottles). Changes may not be result of pricing decisions.	Understand how average prices are affected by shifts in pricing and product mix.
Price per statistical unit	SKU prices weighted by relevant percentage of each SKU in a statistical unit.	Percentage SKU mix should correspond over medium term to actual mix of sales.	Isolate effect of price changes from mix changes by standardising the SKU mix of a standard unit.
Variable and fixed costs	Divide costs into two categories: those that vary with volume (variable) and those that do not (fixed).	Variable costs may include production, marketing and selling expenses. Some variable costs depend on units sold; others depend on revenue.	Understand how costs are affected by changes in sales volume.
Marketing spending	Analyse costs that comprise marketing spending.	Can be divided into fixed and variable marketing costs.	Understand how marketing spending changes with sales.

Metric	Construction	Considerations	Purpose
Contribution per unit	Unit price less unit variable cost.	Ensure that marketing variable costs have not already been deducted from price.	Understand profit impact of changes in volume. Calculate break-even level of sales.
Contribution margin (%)	Contribution per unit divided by unit price.	Ensure that variable costs are consistently based on units or revenue, as appropriate.	Same as above, but applies to financial sales.
Break-even sales level	For unit break-even, divide fixed costs by contribution per unit. For revenue break-even, divide fixed costs by contribution margin (%).	Variable and fixed cost estimates may be valid only over certain ranges of sales and production.	Rough indicator of project attractiveness and ability to earn profit.
Target volume	Adjust break-even calculation to include profit target.	Variable marketing costs must be reflected in contribution margins. Sales increases often require increased investment or working capital.	Ensure that unit sales objectives will enable firm to achieve financial hurdle rates for profit, ROS or ROI.
Target revenues	Convert target volume to target revenues by using average prices per unit. Alternatively, combine cost and target data with knowledge of contribution margins.	Same as above.	Same as above, applied to revenue objectives.

Margins

Margin (on sales) is the difference between selling price and cost. This difference is typically expressed either as a percentage of selling price or on a per-unit basis.

$$\text{Unit margin (£)} = \text{Selling price per unit (£)} - \text{Cost per unit (£)}$$

$$\text{Margin (\%)} = \frac{\text{Unit margin (£)}}{\text{Selling price per unit (£)}}$$

Managers need to know margins for almost all marketing decisions. Margins represent a key factor in pricing, return on marketing spending, earnings forecasts and analyses of customer profitability.

Purpose: to determine the value of incremental sales, and to guide pricing and promotion decisions

Margin on sales represents a key factor behind many of the most fundamental business considerations, including budgets and forecasts. All managers should, and generally do, know their approximate business margins. Managers differ widely, however, in the assumptions they use in calculating margins and in the ways they analyse and communicate these important figures.

Percentage margins and unit margins

A fundamental variation in the way people talk about margins lies in the difference between percentage margins and unit margins on sales. The difference is easy to reconcile, and managers should be able to switch back and forth between the two.

What is a unit?

Every business has its own notion of a "unit", ranging from a ton of margarine, to 64 ounces of cola, to a bucket of plaster. Many industries work with multiple units and calculate margin accordingly. The cigarette industry, for example, sells "sticks", "packs", "cartons" and 12M "cases" (which hold 1,200 individual cigarettes). Banks calculate margin on the basis of accounts, customers, loans, transactions, households and branch offices. Marketers must be prepared to shift between such varying perspectives with little effort because decisions can be grounded in any of these perspectives.

Construction

$$\text{Unit margin (£)} = \text{Selling price per unit (£)} - \text{Cost per unit (£)}$$

$$\text{Margin (\%)} = \frac{\text{Unit margin (£)}}{\text{Selling price per unit (£)}}$$

Percentage margins can also be calculated using total sales revenue and total costs.

$$\text{Margin (\%)} = \frac{[\text{Total sales revenue (£)} - \text{Total cost (£)}]}{\text{Total sales revenue (£)}}$$

When working with either percentage or unit margins, marketers can perform a simple check by verifying that the individual parts sum to the total.

To verify a unit margin (£): Selling price per unit = Unit margin + Unit cost

To verify a margin (%): Cost as % of sales = 100% − Margin %

Example A company in the US markets sailcloth by the linear yard. Its cost basis and selling price for standard cloth are as follows:

Unit selling price = $24 per linear yard

Unit cost = $18 per linear yard

To calculate unit margin, we subtract the cost from the selling price:

Unit margin = $24 per yard − $18 per yard

= $6 per yard

To calculate the percentage margin, we divide the unit margin by the selling price:

$$\text{Margin (\%)} = \frac{(\$24 - \$18) \text{ per yard}}{\$24 \text{ per yard}}$$

$$= \frac{\$6}{\$24} = 25\%$$

Let's verify that our calculations are correct:

Unit selling price = Unit margin + Unit cost

$24 per yard = $6 per yard + $18 per yard   **correct**

A similar check can be made on our calculations of percentage margin:

100% − Margin on sales (%) = Cost as % of selling price

$$100\% - 25\% = \frac{\$18}{\$24}$$

75% = 75%   **correct**

When considering multiple products with different revenues and costs, we can calculate overall margin (%) on either of two bases:

- total revenue and total costs for all products, or
- the money-weighted average of the percentage margins of the different products.

Example The sailcloth company produces a new line of deluxe cloth, which sells for $64 per linear yard and costs $32 per yard to produce. The margin on this item is 50%.

$$\text{Unit margin (\$)} = \$64 \text{ per yard} - \$32 \text{ per yard}$$
$$= \$32 \text{ per yard}$$
$$\text{Margin (\%)} = \frac{(\$64 - \$32)}{\$64}$$
$$= \frac{\$32}{\$64}$$
$$= 50\%$$

Because the company now sells two different products, its average margin can only be calculated when we know the volume of each type of goods sold. It would not be accurate to take a simple average of the 25% margin on standard cloth and the 50% margin on deluxe cloth, unless the company sells the same dollar volume of both products.

If, one day, the company sells 20 yards of standard cloth and 2 yards of deluxe cloth, we can calculate its margins for that day as follows (see also Table 3.1):

$$\text{Total sales} = 20 \text{ yards at } \$24, \text{ and } 2 \text{ yards at } \$64$$
$$= \$608$$

$$\text{Total costs} = 20 \text{ yards at } \$18, \text{ and } 2 \text{ yards at } \$32$$
$$= \$424$$
$$\text{Margin (\$)} = \$184$$
$$\text{Margin (\%)} = \frac{\text{Margin (\$184)}}{\text{Total sales (\$608)}}$$
$$= 30\%$$

Because dollar sales differ between the two products, the company margin of 30% is not a simple average of the margins of those products.

Table 3.1 Sales, costs and margins

	Standard	Deluxe	Total
Sales in yards	20	2	22
Selling price per yard	$24.00	$64.00	
Total sales $	$480.00	$128.00	$608.00
Cost per yard	$18.00	$32.00	
Total costs $	$360.00	$64.00	$424.00
Total Dollar margin ($)	$120.00	$64.00	$184.00
Unit margin	$6.00	$32.00	$8.36
Margin (%)	25%	50%	30%

Data sources, complications and cautions

After you determine which units to use, you need two inputs to determine margins: *unit costs* and *unit selling prices*.

Selling prices can be defined before or after various "charges" are taken

Rebates, customer discounts, brokers' fees and commissions can be reported to management either as costs or as deductions from the selling price. Furthermore, external reporting can vary from management reporting because accounting standards might dictate a treatment that differs from internal practices. Reported margins can vary widely, depending on the calculation technique used. This can result in deep organisational confusion on as fundamental a question as what the price of a product actually is.

Please see pages 257–261 on price waterfalls for cautions on deducting certain discounts and allowances in calculating "net prices". Often there is considerable latitude on whether certain items are subtracted from list price to calculate a net price or are added to costs. One example is the retail practice of providing gift certificates to customers who purchase certain amounts of goods. It is not easy to account for these in a way that avoids confusion among prices, marketing costs and margins. In this context, two points are relevant: (1) certain items can be treated either as deductions from prices or as increments to cost, but not both; (2) the treatment of such an item will not affect the unit margin, but will affect the percentage margin.

Margin as a percentage of costs

Some industries, particularly retail, calculate margin as a percentage of costs, not of selling prices. Using this technique in the previous example, the percentage margin on a yard of standard sailcloth would be reckoned as the $6.00 unit margin divided by the $18.00 unit cost, or 33%. This can lead to confusion. Marketers must become familiar with the practices in their industry and stand ready to shift between them as needed.

Mark-up or margin?

Although some people use the terms "margin" and "mark-up" interchangeably, this is not appropriate. The term "mark-up" commonly refers to the practice of adding a percentage to costs in order to calculate selling prices.

To get a better idea of the relationship between margin and mark-up, let's calculate a few. For example, a 50% mark-up on a variable cost of £10 would be £5, yielding a retail price of £15. By contrast, the margin on an item that sells at a retail price of £15 and that carries a variable cost of £10 would be £5/£15, or 33.3%. Table 3.2 shows some common margin/mark-up relationships.

Table 3.2 Relationship between margins and mark-ups

Price	Cost	Margin	Mark-up
£10	£9.00	10%	11%
£10	£7.50	25%	33%
£10	£6.67	33.3%	50%
£10	£5.00	50%	100%
£10	£4.00	60%	150%
£10	£3.33	66.7%	200%
£10	£2.50	75%	300%

One of the peculiarities that can occur in retail is that prices are "marked up" as a percentage of a store's purchase price (its variable cost for an item) but "marked down" during sales events as a percentage of retail price. Most customers understand that a 50% "sale" means that retail prices have been marked down by 50%.

Example An apparel retailer buys T-shirts for £5 and sells them at a 50% mark-up. As noted previously, a 50% mark-up on a variable cost of £5 yields a retail price of £7.50. Unfortunately, the goods don't sell, and the store owner wants to sell them at cost to clear shelf space. He carelessly asks a sales assistant to mark the goods down by 50%. This 50% mark-down, however, reduces the retail price to £3.25. Thus, a 50% mark-up followed by a 50% mark-down results in a loss of £1.25 on each unit sold.

It is easy to see how confusion can occur. We generally prefer to use the term "margin" to refer to margin on sales. We recommend, however, that all managers clarify with their colleagues what is meant by this important term.

Example A mobile-phone network provider sells a handset for $100. The handset costs $50 to manufacture and includes a $20 mail-in rebate (cashback sum). The provider's internal reports add this rebate to the cost of goods sold. Its margin calculations therefore run as follows:

$$\text{Unit margin (\$)} = \text{Selling price} - \text{Cost of goods sold and rebate}$$

$$= \$100 - (\$50 + \$20) = \$30$$

$$\text{Margin (\%)} = \frac{\$30}{\$100} = 30\%$$

Accounting standards mandate, however, that external reports deduct rebates from sales revenue (see Table 3.3). Under this construction, the company's margin calculations run differently and yield a different percentage margin:

$$\text{Unit margin (\$)} = \text{Selling price, net of rebate} - \text{Cost of goods sold}$$

$$= (\$100 - \$20) - \$50 = \$30$$

$$\text{Margin (\%)} = \frac{\$30}{(\$100 - \$20)}$$

$$= \frac{\$30}{\$80} = 37.5\%$$

Table 3.3 Internal and external reporting may vary

	Internal reporting	External reporting
Money received from customer	$100	$100
Rebates	—	$20
Sales	$100	$80
Manufacturing cost	$50	$50
Rebate	$20	—
Cost of goods sold	$70	$50
Unit margin (£)	$30	$30
Margin (%)	30.0%	37.5%

In this example, managers add the rebate to cost of goods sold for the sake of internal reports. In contrast, accounting regulations require that the rebate be deducted from sales for the purpose of external reports. This means that the percentage margin varies between the internal and external reports. This can cause considerable angst within the company when quoting a percentage margin.

As a general principle, we recommend that internal margins follow formats mandated for external reporting in order to limit confusion.

Various costs may or may not be included
The inclusion or exclusion of costs generally depends on the intended purpose of the relevant margin calculations. We'll return to this issue several times. At one extreme, if all costs are included, then margin and net profit will be equivalent. On the other hand, a marketer may choose to work with "contribution margin" (deducting only variable costs), "operating margin" or "margin before marketing". By using certain metrics, marketers can distinguish fixed costs from variable costs and can isolate particular costs of an operation or of a department from the overall business.

Related metrics and concepts

> **Gross margin:** This is the difference between revenue and cost before accounting for certain other costs. Generally, it is calculated as the selling price of an item, less the cost of goods sold (production or acquisition costs, essentially). Gross margin can be expressed as a percentage or in total financial terms. If the latter, it can be reported on a per-unit basis or on a per-period basis for a company.

Prices and channel margins

> **Channel margins can be expressed on a per-unit basis or as a percentage of selling price. In "chaining" the margins of sequential distribution channels, the selling price of one channel member becomes the "cost" of the channel member for which it serves as a supplier.**
>
> Supplier selling price (£) = Customer selling price (£) − Customer margin (£)

$$\text{Customer selling price (£)} = \frac{\text{Supplier selling price (£)}}{[1 - \text{Customer margin (\%)}]}$$

When there are several levels in a distribution chain – including a manufacturer, distributor and retailer, for example – one must not simply add all channel margins as reported in order to calculate "total" channel margin. Instead, use the selling prices at the beginning and end of the distribution chain (that is, at the levels of the manufacturer and the retailer) to calculate total channel margin. Marketers should be able to work forward from their own selling price to the consumer's purchase price and should understand channel margins at each step.

Purpose: to calculate selling prices at each level in the distribution channel

Marketing often involves selling through a series of "value-added" resellers. Sometimes, a product changes form through this progression. At other times, its price is simply "marked up" along its journey through the distribution channel (see Figure 3.1).

Figure 3.1 Example of a distribution channel

Remember: Selling price = Cost + Margin

In some industries, such as imported beer, there may be as many as four or five channel members that sequentially apply their own margins before a product reaches the consumer. In such cases, it is particularly important to understand channel margins and pricing practices in order to evaluate the effects of price changes.

Construction

First, decide whether you want to work "backward", from customer selling prices to supplier selling prices, or "forward". We provide two equations to use in working backward, one for economic margins and the other for percentage margins:

Supplier selling price (£) = Customer selling price (£) − Customer margin (£)

Supplier selling price (£) = Customer selling price (£)
* [1 − Customer margin (%)]

Example Aaron owns a small furniture store. He buys BookCo brand bookcases from a local distributor for £100 per unit. Aaron is considering buying directly from BookCo, and he wants to calculate what he would pay if he received the same price that BookCo charges his distributor. Aaron knows that the distributor's percentage margin is 30%.

The manufacturer supplies the distributor. That is, in this link of the chain, the manufacturer is the supplier, and the distributor is the customer. Thus, because we know the customer's percentage margin, in order to calculate the manufacturer's price to Aaron's distributor, we can use the second of the two previous equations.

Supplier selling price (£) = Customer selling price (£)
* [1 − Customer margin (%)]

= £100 * 70% = £70

Aaron's distributor buys each bookcase for £70 and sells it for £100, earning a margin of £30 (30%).

Although the previous example may be the most intuitive version of this formula, by rearranging the equation, we can also work forward in the chain, from supplier prices to customer selling prices. In a forward-looking construction, we can solve for the customer selling price, that is, the price charged to the next level of the chain, moving toward the end consumer.[2]

$$\text{Customer selling price (£)} = \frac{\text{Supplier selling price (£)}}{[1 - \text{Customer margin (\%)}]}$$

$$\text{Customer selling price (£)} = \text{Supplier selling price (£)} + \text{Customer margin (£)}$$

Example Clyde's Concrete in the US sells 100 cubic yards of concrete for $300 to a road construction contractor. The contractor wants to include this in her bill of materials, to be charged to a local government (see Figure 3.2). Further, she wants to earn a 25% margin. What is the contractor's selling price for the concrete?

Figure 3.2 Customer relationships

This question focuses on the link between Clyde's Concrete (supplier) and the contractor (customer). We know the supplier's selling price is $300 and the customer's intended margin is 25%. With this information, we can use the first of the two previous equations.

$$\text{Customer selling price} = \frac{\text{Supplier selling price}}{(1 - \text{Customer margin \%})}$$

$$= \frac{\$300}{(1 - 25\%)}$$

$$= \frac{\$300}{75\%} = \$400$$

To verify our calculations, we can determine the contractor's percentage margin, based on a selling price of $400 and a cost of $300.

$$\text{Customer margin} = \frac{(\text{Customer selling price} - \text{Supplier selling price})}{\text{Customer selling price}}$$

$$= \frac{(\$400 - \$300)}{\$400}$$

$$= \frac{\$100}{\$400} = 25\%$$

Equipped with these equations and with knowledge of all the margins in a chain of distribution, we can work all the way back to the selling price of the first channel member in the chain.

First channel member's selling price (£) = Last channel member's selling price (£) ∗ [1 − Last channel margin (%)] ∗ [1 − Next-to-last channel margin (%)] ∗ [1 − Next-to-next-to-last channel margin (%)] . . . and so on

Example The following margins are received at various steps along the chain of distribution for a jar of pasta sauce that sells for a retail price of £2.50 (see Table 3.4).

What does it cost the manufacturer to produce a jar of pasta sauce? The retail selling price (£2.50), multiplied by 1 less the retailer margin, will yield the wholesaler selling price. The wholesaler selling price can also be viewed as the cost to the retailer. The *cost* to the wholesaler (distributor selling price) can be found by multiplying the wholesaler selling price by 1 less the wholesaler margin, and so forth. Alternatively, one might follow the next procedure, using a channel member's percentage margin to calculate its economic margin, and then subtracting that figure from the channel member's selling price to obtain its cost (see Table 3.5).

Thus, a jar of pasta that sells for £2.50 at retail actually costs the manufacturer 25 pence to make.

Table 3.4 Example: pasta sauce distribution margins

Distribution stage	Margin
Manufacturer	50%
Distributor	50%
Wholesaler	33%
Retailer	40%

Table 3.5 Cost (purchase price) of retailer

Stage	Margin %	£
Cost to consumer		£2.50
Retailer margin	40%	£1.00
Cost to retailer		£1.50
Wholesaler margin	33%	£0.50
Cost to wholesaler		£1.00
Distributor margin	50%	£0.50
Cost to distributor		£0.50
Manufacturer margin	50%	£0.25
Manufacturer's cost		£0.25

The margins taken at multiple levels of a distribution process can have a dramatic effect on the price paid by consumers. To work backward in analysing these, many people find it easier to convert mark-ups to margins. Working forward does not require this conversion.

Example To show that margins and mark-ups are two sides of the same coin, let's demonstrate that we can obtain the same sequence of prices by using the mark-up method here. Let's look at how the pasta sauce is marked up to arrive at a final consumer price of £2.50.

As noted previously, the manufacturer's cost is £0.25. The manufacturer's percentage mark-up is 100%. Thus, we can calculate its financial mark-up as £0.25 ∗ 100% = £0.25. Adding the manufacturer's mark-up to its cost, we arrive at its selling price: £0.25 (cost) + £0.25 (mark-up) = £0.50. The manufacturer sells the sauce for £0.50 to a distributor. The distributor applies a mark-up of 100%, taking the price to £1.00, and sells the sauce to a wholesaler. The wholesaler applies a mark-up of 50% and sells the sauce to a retailer for £1.50. Finally, the retailer applies a mark-up of 66.7% and sells the pasta sauce to a consumer for £2.50. In Table 3.6, we track these mark-ups to show the pasta sauce's journey from a manufacturer's cost of £0.25 to a retail price (consumer's cost) of £2.50.

Table 3.6 Mark-ups along the distribution channel

Stage	Mark-up %	£	Margin
Manufacturer's cost		£0.25	
Manufacturer mark-up	100%	£0.25	50%
Cost to distributor		£0.50	
Distributor mark-up	100%	£0.50	50%
Cost to wholesaler		£1.00	
Wholesaler mark-up	50%	£0.50	33.3%
Cost to retailer		£1.50	
Retailer mark-up	67%	£1.00	40%
Cost to consumer		£2.50	

Data sources, complications and cautions

The information needed to calculate channel margins is the same as for basic margins. Complications arise, however, because of the layers involved. In this structure, the selling price for one layer in the chain becomes the cost to the next layer. This is clearly visible in consumer goods industries, where there are often multiple levels of distribution between the manufacturer and the consumer, and each channel member requires its own margin.

Cost and selling price depend on location within the chain. One must always ask, "Whose cost is this?" and "Who sells at this price?" The process of "chaining" a sequence of margins is not difficult. One need only clarify who sells to whom. In tracking this, it can help first to draw a horizontal line, labelling all the channel members along the chain, with the manufacturer at the far left and the retailer on the right. For example, if a beer exporter in Germany sells to an importer in the US, and that importer sells to a distributor in Virginia, who sells the beer to a retailer, then four distinct selling prices and three channel margins will intervene between the exporter and retail store customer. In this scenario, the exporter is the first supplier. The importer is the first customer. To avoid confusion, we recommend mapping out the channel and calculating margins, purchase prices and selling prices at each level.

Throughout this section, we've assumed that all margins are "gross margins", calculated as selling price minus cost of goods sold. Of course, channel members will incur other costs in the process of "adding value". If a wholesaler pays his salespeople a commission on sales, for example, that would be a cost of doing business.

But it would not be a part of the cost of goods sold, and so it is not factored into gross margin.

Related metrics and concepts

Hybrid (mixed) channel margins

> **Hybrid channel:** **The use of multiple distribution systems to reach the same market. A company might approach consumers through stores, the Web and telemarketing, for example. Margins often differ among such channels. Hybrid channels may also be known as mixed channels.**

Increasingly, businesses "go to market" in more than one way. An insurance company, for example, might sell policies through independent agents, freephone telephone lines and the Web. Multiple channels often generate different channel margins and cause a supplier to incur different support costs. As business migrates from one channel to another, marketers must adjust pricing and support in economically sensible ways. To make appropriate decisions, they must recognise the more profitable channels in their mix and develop programmes and strategies to fit these.

When selling through multiple channels with different margins, it is important to perform analyses on the basis of *weighted* average channel margins, as opposed to a simple average. Using a simple average can lead to confusion and poor decision-making.

As an example of the variations that can occur, let's suppose that a company sells 10 units of its product through six channels. It sells 5 units through one channel at a 20% margin, and 1 unit through each of the other five channels at a 50% margin. Calculating its average margin on a weighted basis, we arrive at the following figure:

$$\text{Percentage margin (\%)} = \frac{[(5 * 20\%) + (5 * 50\%)]}{10} = 35\%$$

By contrast, if we calculate the average margin among this firm's six channels on a simple basis, we arrive at a very different figure:

$$\text{Percentage margin (\%)} = \frac{[(1 * 20\%) + (5 * 50\%)]}{6} = 45\%$$

This difference in margin could significantly blur management decision-making.

Average margin

When assessing margins in financial terms, use percentage of unit sales.

Average margin (£) = [Percentage of unit sales through channel 1 (%) * Margin earned in channel 1 ($)] + [Percentage of unit sales through channel 2 (%) * Margin earned in channel 2 ($)] + Continued to last channel

When assessing margin in percentage terms, use percentage of financial sales.

Average margin (%) = [Percentage of financial sales through channel 1 (%) * Margin earned in channel 1 (%)] + [Percentage of financial sales through channel 2 (%) * Margin earned in channel 2 (%)] + Continued to last channel

Example Gael's Glass sells through three channels: phone, online and store. These channels generate the following margins: 50%, 40% and 30%, respectively. When Gael's wife asks what his average margin is, he initially calculates a simple margin and says it's 40%. Gael's wife investigates further, however, and learns that her husband answered too quickly. Gael's company sells a total of 10 units. It sells 1 unit by phone at a 50% margin, 4 units online at a 40% margin, and 5 units in the store at a 30% margin. To determine the company's average margin among these channels, the margin in each must be weighted by its relative sales volume. On this basis, Gael's wife calculates the weighted average margin as follows:

Average channel margin = (Percentage of unit sales by phone * Phone channel margin) + (Percentage of unit sales online * Online channel margin) + (Percentage of unit sales through store * Store channel margin)

= (1/10 * 50%) + (4/10 * 40%) + (5/10 * 30%)

= 5% + 16% + 15%

Average channel margin = 36%

Example Sadetta Ltd has two channels – online and retail – which generate the following results:

One customer orders online, paying £10 for 1 unit of goods that costs the company £5. This generates a 50% margin for Sadetta. A second customer shops at the store, buying 2 units of product for £12 each. Each costs £9. Thus, Sadetta earns a 25% margin on these sales. Summarising:

Online margin (1) = 50%. Selling price (1) = £10. Supplier selling price (1) = £5.

Store margin (2) = 25%. Selling price (2) = £12. Supplier selling price (2) = £9.

In this scenario, the relative weightings are easy to establish. In unit terms, Sadetta sells a total of 3 units: 1 unit (33.3%) online, and 2 (66.6%) in the store. In financial terms, Sadetta generates a total of £34 in sales: £10 (29.4%) online, and £24 (70.6%) in the store.

Thus, Sadetta's average unit margin (£) can be calculated as follows: the online channel generates a £5.00 margin, while the store generates a £3.00 margin. The relative weightings are online 33.3% and store 66.6%.

Average unit margin (£) = [Percentage unit sales online (%) * Unit margin online (£)]
+ [Percentage unit sales in store (%) * Unit margin in store (£)]

= 33.3% * £5.00 + 66.6% * £3.00

= £1.67 + £2.00

= £3.67

Sadetta's average margin (%) can be calculated as follows: the online channel generates a 50% margin, while the store generates a 25% margin. The relative weightings are online 29.4% and store 70.6%.

Average margin (%) = [Percentage financial sales online (%) * Margin online (%)]
+ [Percentage financial sales in store (%) * Margin in store (%)]

= 29.4% * 50% + 70.6% * 25%

= 14.70% + 17.65%

= 32.35%

Average margins can also be calculated directly from company totals. Sadetta Ltd generated a total gross margin of £11 by selling 3 units of product. Its average unit margin was thus £11/3, or £3.67. Similarly, we can derive Sadetta's average percentage margin by dividing its total margin by its total revenue. This yields a result that matches our weighted previous calculations: £11/£34 = 32.35%.

The same weighting process is needed to calculate average selling prices.

Average selling price ($) = [Percentage unit sales through channel 1 (%)
* Selling price in channel 1 ($)] + [Percentage unit sales through channel 2 (%) * Selling price in channel 2 ($)] + Continued to [Percentage unit sales through the last channel (%)
* Last channel's selling price ($)]

Example Continuing the previous example, we can see how Sadetta Ltd calculates its average selling price.

Sadetta's online customer pays £10 per item. Its store customer pays £12 per item. Weighting each channel by unit sales, we can derive Sadetta's average selling price as follows:

Average selling price (£) = [Percentage unit sales online (%) * Selling price online (£)] + [Percentage unit sales in store (%) * Selling price in store (£)]

$$= 33.3\% * £10 + 66.6\% * £12$$

$$= £3.33 + £8$$

$$= £11.33$$

The calculation of average supplier selling price is conceptually similar.

Average supplier selling price (£) = [Percentage unit sales through channel 1 (%) * Supplier selling price in channel 1 (£)] + [Percentage unit sales through channel 2 (%) * Supplier selling price in channel 2 (£)] + Continued to [Percentage unit sales through the last channel (%) * Last channel supplier's selling price (£)]

Example Now, let's consider how Sadetta Ltd calculates its average supplier selling price.

Sadetta's online merchandise cost the company £5 per unit. Its in-store merchandise cost £9 per unit. Thus:

Average supplier selling price (£) = [Percentage unit sales online (%) * Supplier selling price online (£)] + [Percentage unit sales through store (%) * Supplier selling price in store (£)]

$$= 33.3\% * £5 + 66.6\% * £9$$

$$= £1.66 + £6 = £7.66$$

With all these pieces of the puzzle, we now have much greater insight into Sadetta's business (see Table 3.7).

▶

Table 3.7 Sadetta's channel measures

	Online	In store	Average/total
Selling price (SP)	£10.00	£12.00	
Supplier selling price (SSP)	£5.00	£9.00	
Unit margin (£)	£5.00	£3.00	
Margin (%)	50%	25%	
Units sold	1	2	3
% Unit sales	33.3%	66.7%	
Financial sales	£10.00	£24.00	£34.00
% financial sales	29.4%	70.6%	
Total margin	£5.00	£6.00	£11.00
Average unit margin (£)			£3.67
Average margin (%)			32.4%
Average selling price			£11.33
Average supplier selling price			£7.67

Average price per unit and price per statistical unit

Average prices represent, quite simply, total sales revenue divided by total units sold. Many products, however, are sold in multiple variants, such as bottle sizes. In these cases, managers face a challenge: they must determine "comparable" units.

Average prices can be calculated by weighting different unit selling prices by the percentage of unit sales (mix) for each product variant. If we use a standard, rather than an actual mix of sizes and product varieties, the result is price per statistical unit. Statistical units are also known as equivalent units.

$$\text{Average price per unit (£)} = \frac{\text{Revenue (£)}}{\text{Units sold (N)}}$$

or

$$= [\text{Price of SKU 1 (£)} \times \text{SKU 1 percentage of sales (\%)}]$$
$$+ [\text{Price of SKU 2 (£)} \times \text{SKU 2 percentage of sales (\%)}]$$

$$\text{Price per statistical unit (£)} = \text{Total price of a bundle of SKUs comprising a statistical unit (£)}$$

$$\text{Unit price per statistical unit (£)} = \frac{\text{Price per statistical unit (£)}}{\text{Total units in the bundle of SKUs comprising that statistical unit (N)}}$$

Average price per unit and prices per statistical unit are needed by marketers who sell the same product in different packages, sizes, forms or configurations at a variety of different prices. As in analyses of different channels, these product and price variations must be reflected accurately in overall average prices. If they are not, marketers may lose sight of what is happening to prices and why. If the price of each product variant remained unchanged, for example, but there was a shift in the mix of volume sold, then the average price per unit would change, but the price per statistical unit would not. Both of these metrics have value in identifying market movements.

Purpose: to calculate meaningful average selling prices within a product line that includes items of different sizes

Many brands or product lines include multiple models, versions, flavours, colours, sizes, or – more generally – stock-keeping units (SKUs). Brita water filters, for example, are sold in a number of SKUs. They are sold in single-filter packs, double-filter packs, and special banded packs that may be restricted to club stores. They are sold on a stand-alone basis and in combination with jugs. These various packages and product forms may be known as SKUs, models, items and so on.

Stock-keeping unit (SKU): A term used by retailers to identify individual items that are carried or "stocked" within an assortment. This is the most detailed level at which the inventory and sales of individual products are recorded.

Marketers often want to know both their own average prices and those of retailers. By reckoning in terms of SKUs, they can calculate an average price per unit at any level in the distribution chain. Two of the most useful of these averages are as follows:

1 A unit price average that includes all sales of all SKUs, expressed as an average price per defined unit. In the water filter industry, for example, these might include such figures as $2.23/filter, $0.03/filtered ounce, and so on.

2 A price per statistical unit that consists of a fixed bundle (number) of individual SKUs. This bundle is often constructed so as to reflect the actual mix of sales of the various SKUs.

The average price per unit will change when there is a shift in the percentage of sales represented by SKUs with different unit prices. It will also change when the prices of the individual SKUs are modified. This contrasts with price per statistical unit, which, by definition, has a fixed proportion of each SKU. Consequently, a price per statistical unit will change only when there is a change in the price of one or more of the SKUs included in it.

The information gleaned from a price per statistical unit can be helpful in considering price movements within a market. Price per statistical unit, in combination with unit price averages, provides insight into the degree to which the average prices in a market are changing as a result of shifts in "mix" – proportions of sales generated by differently priced SKUs – versus price changes for individual items. Alterations in mix – such as a relative increase in the sale of larger versus smaller ice cream tubs at retail grocers, for example – will affect average unit price, but not price per statistical unit. Pricing changes in the SKUs that make up a statistical unit, however, will be reflected by a change in the price of that statistical unit.

Construction

As with other marketing averages, average price per unit can be calculated either from company totals or from the prices and shares of individual SKUs.

$$\text{Average price per unit (£)} = \frac{\text{Revenue (£)}}{\text{Unit sales (N)}}$$

or

$$= [\text{Unit price of SKU 1 (\$)} * \text{SKU 1 percentage of sales (\%)}] + [\text{Unit price of SKU 2 (\$)} * \text{SKU 2 percentage of sales (\%)}] + \text{and so forth}$$

The average price per unit depends on both unit prices and unit sales of individual SKUs. The average price per unit can be driven upward by a rise in unit prices, or by an increase in the unit shares of higher-priced SKUs, or by a combination of the two.

An "average" price metric that is not sensitive to changes in SKU shares is the price per statistical unit.

Price per statistical unit

Procter & Gamble and other companies face a challenge in monitoring prices for a wide variety of product sizes, package types and product formulations. There are as many as 25 to 30 different SKUs for some brands, and each SKU has its own price. In these situations, how do marketers determine a brand's overall price level in order to compare it to competitive offerings or to track whether prices are rising or falling? One solution is the "statistical unit", also known as the "statistical case" or – in volumetric or weight measures – the statistical litre or statistical ton. A statistical case of 288 ounces of liquid detergent, for example, might be defined as comprising:

Four 4-oz bottles = 16 oz

Twelve 12-oz bottles = 144 oz

Two 32-oz bottles = 64 oz

One 64-oz bottle = 64 oz

Note that the contents of this statistical case were carefully chosen so that it contains the same number of ounces as a standard case of 24 12-ounce bottles. In this way, the statistical case is comparable in size to a standard case. The advantage of a statistical case is that its contents can approximate the mix of SKUs the company actually sells.

Whereas a statistical case of liquid detergent will be filled with whole bottles, in other instances a statistical unit might contain fractions of certain packaging sizes in order for its total contents to match a required volumetric or weight total.

Statistical units are composed of fixed proportions of different SKUs. These fixed proportions ensure that changes in the prices of the statistical unit reflect only changes in the *prices* of the SKUs that comprise it.

The price of a statistical unit can be expressed either as a total price for the bundle of SKUs comprising it, or in terms of that total price divided by the total volume of its contents. The former might be called the "price per statistical unit"; the latter, the "unit price per statistical unit".

Example Carl's Coffee Creamer (CCC) is sold in three sizes: a one-litre economy size, a half-litre "fridge-friendly" package and a 0.05 litre single serving. Carl defines a 12 litre statistical case of CCC as:

Two units of the economy size = 2 litres (2 * 1.0 litre)

19 units of the fridge-friendly package = 9.5 litres (19 * 0.5 litre)

Ten single servings = 0.5 litre (10 * 0.05)

Prices for each size and the calculation of total price for the statistical unit are shown in the following table:

SKU names	Size	Price of item	Number in statistical case	Litres in statistical case	Total price
Economy	1 litre	$8.00	2	2.0	$16.00
Fridge-friendly	0.5 litre	$6.00	19	9.5	$114.00
Single serving	0.05 litre	$1.00	10	0.5	$10.00
TOTAL				12	$140.00

Thus, the total price of the 12 litre statistical case of CCC is $140. The per-litre price within the statistical case is $11.67 ($140/12).

If the proportions of the SKUs in the statistical case exactly match the actual proportions sold, then the per-litre price of the statistical case will match the average per-litre price of the actual litres sold.

Example Carl sells 10,000 one-litre economy packs of CCC, 80,000 fridge-friendly half litres and 40,000 single servings. What was his average price per litre?

$$\text{Average price per unit (\$)} = \frac{\text{Revenue (\$)}}{\text{Unit sales (N)}}$$

$$= \frac{(\$8 * 10k + \$6 * 80k + \$1 * 40k)}{(1 * 10k + 0.5 * 80k + 0.05 * 40k)}$$

$$= \frac{\$600k}{52k} = \$11.54$$

Note that Carl's average price per litre, at $11.54, is less than the per-litre price in his statistical case. The reason is straightforward: whereas fridge-friendly packs outnumber economy packs by almost ten to one in the statistical case, the actual sales ratio of these SKUs was only eight to one. Similarly, whereas the ratio of single-serving items to economy items in the statistical case is five to one, their actual sales ratio was only four to one. Carl's company sold a smaller percentage of the higher (per litre) priced items than was represented in its statistical case. Consequently, its actual average price per litre was less than the per-litre price within its statistical unit.

Example In the following table, we illustrate the calculation of the average price per unit as the weighted average of the unit prices and unit shares of the three SKUs of Carl's Coffee Creamer. Unit prices and unit (per-litre) shares are provided.

SKU name	Size	Price	SKUs sold	Units sold (litres)	Unit price (per litre)	Unit share
Economy	1 litre	$8	10k	10k	$8	19.23%
Fridge-friendly	0.5 litre	$6	80k	40k	$12	76.92%
Single serving	0.05 litre	$1	40k	2k	$20	3.85%
TOTAL			130k	52k		100%

On this basis, the average price per unit ($) = ($8 * 0.1923) + ($12 * 0.7692) + ($20 * 0.0385) = $11.54.

Data sources, complications and cautions

With complex and changing product lines, and with different selling prices charged by different retailers, marketers need to understand a number of methodologies for calculating average prices. Merely determining how many units of a product are sold, and at what price, throughout the market is a major challenge. As a standard method of tracking prices, marketers use statistical units, which are based on constant proportions of sales of different SKUs in a product line.

Typically, the proportions of SKUs in a statistical unit correspond – at least approximately – to historical market sales. Sales patterns can change, however. In consequence, these proportions need to be monitored carefully in evolving markets and changing product lines.

Calculating a meaningful average price is complicated by the need to differentiate between changes in sales mix and changes in the prices of statistical units. In some industries, it is difficult to construct appropriate units for analysing price and sales data. In the chemical industry, for example, a herbicide might be sold in a variety of different sizes, applicators and concentration levels. When we factor in the complexity of different prices and different assortments offered by competing retail outlets, calculating and tracking average prices becomes a non-trivial exercise.

Similar challenges arise in estimating inflation. Economists calculate inflation by using a basket of goods. Their estimates might vary considerably, depending on the goods included. It is also difficult to capture quality improvements in inflation figures. Is a 2005 car, for example, truly comparable to a car built 30 years earlier?

In evaluating price increases, marketers are advised to bear in mind that a consumer who shops for large quantities at discount stores may view such increases very differently from a pensioner who buys small quantities at local stores. Establishing a "standard" basket for such different consumers requires astute judgement. In seeking to summarise the aggregate of such price increases throughout an economy, economists may view inflation as, in effect, a statistical unit price measure for that economy.

Variable costs and fixed costs

Variable costs can be aggregated into a "total" or expressed on a "per-unit" basis. Fixed costs, by definition, do not change with the number of units sold or produced. Variable costs are assumed to be relatively constant on a per-unit basis. Total variable costs increase directly and predictably with unit sales volume. Fixed costs, on the other hand, do not change as a direct result of short-term unit sales increases or decreases.

Total costs (£) = Fixed costs (£) + Total variable costs (£)

Total variable costs (£) = Unit volume (N) * Variable cost per unit (£)

Marketers need to have an idea of how costs divide between variable and fixed. This distinction is crucial in forecasting the earnings generated by various changes in unit sales and thus the financial impact of proposed marketing campaigns. It is also fundamental to an understanding of price and volume trade-offs.

Purpose: to understand how costs change with volume

At first glance, this appears to be an easy subject to master. If a marketing campaign will generate 10,000 units of additional sales, we need only know how much it will cost to supply that additional volume.

The problem, of course, is that no one really knows how changes in quantity will affect a firm's total costs – in part because the workings of a firm can be so complex. Companies simply can't afford to employ armies of accountants to answer every possible expense question precisely. Instead, we often use a simple model of cost behaviour that is good enough for most purposes.

Construction

The standard linear equation, $Y = mX + b$, helps explain the relationship between total costs and unit volume. In this application, Y will represent a company's total cost, m will be its variable cost per unit, X will represent the quantity of products sold (or produced), and b will represent the fixed cost (see Figure 3.3).

Total cost (£) = Variable cost per unit (£) * Quantity (N) + Fixed cost (£)

Figure 3.3 Fixed and variable costs

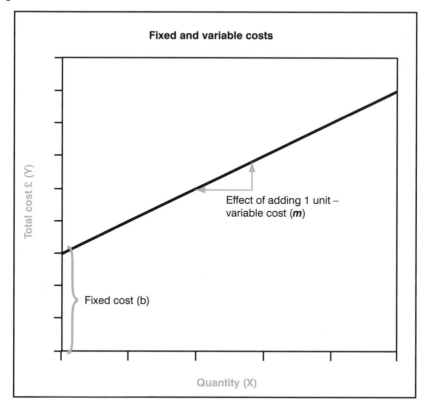

On this basis, to determine a company's total cost for any given quantity of products, we need only multiply its variable cost per unit by that quantity and add its
fixed cost.

To communicate fully the implications of fixed costs and variable costs, it may
help to separate this graph into two parts (see Figure 3.4).

By definition, fixed costs remain the same, regardless of volume. Consequently,
they are represented by a horizontal line across the graph in Figure 3.4. Fixed costs
do not increase vertically – that is, they do not add to the total cost – as quantity
rises.

The result of multiplying variable cost per unit by quantity is often called the total
variable cost. Variable costs differ from fixed costs in that, when there is no production, their total is zero. Their total increases in a steadily rising line, however, as
quantity increases.

We can represent this model of cost behaviour in a simple equation.

$$\text{Total cost (£)} = \text{Total variable cost (£)} + \text{Fixed cost (£)}$$

Figure 3.4 Total cost consists of fixed and variable costs

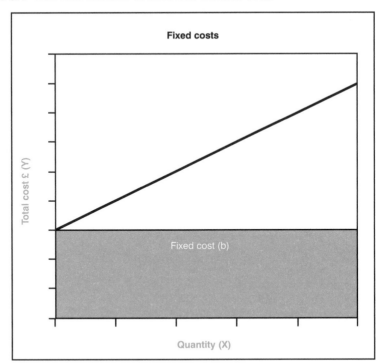

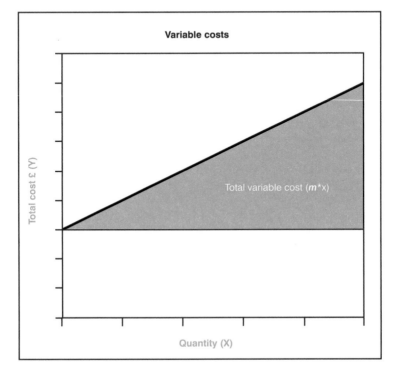

To use this model, of course, we must place each of a firm's costs into one or the other of these two categories. If an expense does not change with volume (rent, for example), then it is part of fixed costs and will remain the same, regardless of how many units the firm produces or sells. If a cost *does* change with volume (sales commissions, for example), then it is a variable cost.

$$\text{Total variable costs (£)} = \text{Unit volume (N)} * \text{Variable cost per unit (£)}$$

Total cost per unit
It is also possible to express the total cost for a given quantity on a per-unit basis. The result might be called total cost per unit, unit total cost, average cost, full cost, or even fully loaded cost. For our simple linear cost model, the total cost per unit can be calculated in either of two ways. The most obvious would be to divide the total cost by the number of units.

$$\text{Total cost per unit (£)} = \frac{\text{Total cost (£)}}{\text{Quantity (N)}}$$

This can be plotted graphically, and it tells an interesting tale (see Figure 3.5). As the quantity rises, the total cost per unit (average cost per unit) declines. The shape

Figure 3.5 Total cost per unit falls with volume (typical assumptions)

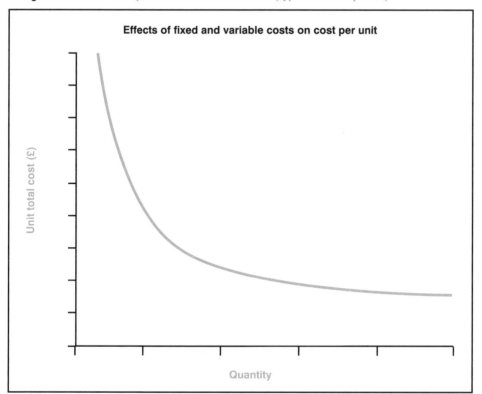

Effects of fixed and variable costs on cost per unit

Unit total cost (£)

Quantity

of this curve will vary among firms with different cost structures, but wherever there are both fixed and variable costs, the total cost per unit will decline as fixed costs are spread across an increasing quantity of units.

The apportionment of fixed costs across units produced leads us to another common formula for the total cost per unit.

Total cost per unit (£) = Variable cost per unit (£) + [Fixed cost (£)/Quantity (N)]

As the quantity increases – that is, as fixed costs are spread over an increasing number of units – the total cost per unit declines in a non-linear way.[3]

Example As a company's unit sales increase, its fixed costs hold steady at £500. The variable cost per unit remains constant at £10 per unit. Total variable costs increase with each unit sold. The total cost per unit (also known as average total cost) decreases as incremental units are sold and as fixed costs are spread across this rising quantity. Eventually, as more and more units are produced and sold, the company's total cost per unit approaches its variable cost per unit (see Table 3.8).

Table 3.8 Fixed and variable costs at increasing volume levels

Units sold	1	10	100	1,000
Fixed costs	£500	£500	£500	£500
Variable costs	£10	£100	£1,000	£10,000
Total costs	£510	£600	£1,500	£10,500
Total cost per unit	£510.00	£60.00	£15.00	£10.50
Variable cost per unit	£10	£10	£10	£10

In summary, the simplest model of cost behaviour is to assume total costs increase linearly with quantity supplied. Total costs are composed of fixed and variable costs. Total cost per unit decreases in a non-linear way with rising quantity supplied.

Data sources, complications and cautions

Total cost is typically assumed to be a linear function of quantity supplied. That is, the graph of total cost versus quantity will be a straight line. Because some costs are fixed, total cost starts at a level above zero, even when no units are produced. This is because fixed costs include such expenses as factory rent and salaries for full-time employees, which must be paid regardless of whether any goods are produced and sold. Total variable costs, by contrast, rise and fall with quantity. Within our model, however, variable cost *per unit* is assumed to hold constant – at £10 per unit for example – regardless of whether one unit or 1,000 units are produced. This is a useful model. In using it, however, marketers must recognise that it fails to account for certain complexities.

The linear cost model does not fit every situation

Quantity discounts, expectations of future process improvements, and capacity limitations, for example, introduce dynamics that will limit the usefulness of the fundamental linear cost equation: Total cost = Fixed cost + Variable cost per unit * Quantity. Even the notion that quantity determines the total cost can be questioned. Although firms pay for *inputs*, such as raw materials and labour, marketers want to know the cost of the firm's *outputs*, that is, finished goods sold. This distinction is clear in theory. In practice, however, it can be difficult to uncover the precise relationship between a quantity of outputs and the total cost of the wide array of inputs that go into it.

The classification of costs as fixed or variable depends on context

Even though the linear model may not work in all situations, it does provide a reasonable approximation for cost behaviour in many contexts. Some marketers have trouble, however, with the fact that certain costs can be considered fixed in some contexts and variable in others. In general, for shorter time frames and modest changes in quantity, many costs are fixed. For longer time frames and larger changes in quantity, most costs are variable. Let's consider rent, for example. Small changes in quantity do not require a change in workspace or business location. In such cases, rent should be regarded as a fixed cost. A major change in quantity, however, would require more or less workspace. Rent, therefore, would become variable over that range of quantity.

Don't confuse total cost per unit with variable cost per unit

In our linear cost equation, the variable cost per unit is the amount by which total costs increase if the firm increases its quantity by one unit. This number should not be confused with the total cost per unit, calculated as: Variable cost per unit + (Fixed cost/Quantity). If a firm has fixed costs, then its total cost per unit will always be greater than the variable cost per unit. Total cost per unit represents the firm's average cost per unit at the current quantity – and *only* at the current quantity. Do not make the mistake of thinking of total cost per unit as a figure that applies to changing quantities. Total cost per unit only applies at the volume at which it was calculated.

A related misunderstanding may arise at times from the fact that total cost per unit generally decreases with rising quantity. Some marketers use this fact to argue for aggressively increasing quantity in order to "bring our costs down" and improve profitability. Total cost, by contrast with total cost *per unit*, almost always increases with quantity. Only with certain quantity discounts or rebates that "kick in" when target volumes are reached can total cost decrease as volume increases.

Marketing spending: total, fixed and variable

To predict how selling costs change with sales, a firm must distinguish between fixed selling costs and variable selling costs.

Total selling (marketing) costs (£) = Total fixed selling costs (£)
+ Total variable selling costs (£)

Total variable selling costs (£) = Revenue (£) * Variable selling cost (%)

Recognising the difference between fixed and variable selling costs can help firms account for the relative risks associated with alternative sales strategies. In general, strategies that incur variable selling costs are less risky because variable selling costs will remain lower in the event that sales fail to meet expectations.

Purpose: to forecast marketing spending and assess budgeting risk

Marketing spending: **Total expenditure on marketing activities. This typically includes advertising and non-price promotion. It sometimes includes sales force spending and may also include price promotions.**

Marketing costs are often a major part of a firm's overall discretionary expenditures. As such, they are important determinants of short-term profits. Of course, marketing and selling budgets can also be viewed as investments in acquiring and maintaining customers. From either perspective, however, it is useful to distinguish between fixed marketing costs and variable marketing costs. That is, managers must recognise which marketing costs will hold steady, and which will change with sales. Generally, this classification will require a "line-item by line-item" review of the entire marketing budget.

In previous sections, we have viewed total variable costs as expenses that vary with unit sales volume. With respect to selling costs, we'll need a slightly different conception. Rather than varying with unit sales, total variable selling costs are more likely to vary directly with the monetary value of the units sold – that is, with revenue. Thus, it is more likely that variable selling costs will be expressed as a percentage of revenue, rather than a certain monetary amount per unit.

The classification of selling costs as fixed or variable will depend on an organisation's structure and on the specific decisions of management. A number of items, however, typically fall into one category or the other – with the proviso that their status as fixed or variable can be time-specific. In the long run, all costs eventually become variable.

Over typical planning periods of a quarter or a year, fixed marketing costs might include:

- Sales force salaries and support.
- Major advertising campaigns, including production costs.
- Marketing staff.
- Sales promotion material, such as point-of-purchase sales aids, coupon production and distribution costs.
- Cooperative advertising allowances based on prior-period sales.

Variable marketing costs might include:

- Sales commissions paid to sales force, brokers or manufacturer representatives.
- Sales bonuses contingent on reaching sales goals.
- Off-invoice and performance allowances to trade, which are tied to current volume.
- Early payment terms (if included in sales promotion budgets).
- Coupon face-value payments and rebates, including processing fees.
- Bill-backs for local campaigns (a bill-back requires customers to submit proof of performance to receive payment or credit whereas an off-invoice is simply deducted from invoice totals). These are conducted by retailers but reimbursed by national brand and cooperative advertising allowances, based on current period sales.

Marketers often don't consider their budgets in fixed and variable terms, but they can derive at least two benefits by doing so.

First, if marketing spending is in fact variable, then budgeting in this way is more accurate. Some marketers budget a *fixed* amount and then face an end-of-period discrepancy or "variance" if sales miss their declared targets. By contrast, a flexible budget – that is, one that takes account of its genuinely variable components – will reflect actual results, regardless of where sales end up.

Second, the short-term risks associated with fixed marketing costs are greater than those associated with variable marketing costs. If marketers expect revenues to be sensitive to factors outside their control – such as competitive actions or production shortages – they can reduce risk by including more variable and less fixed spending in their budgets.

A classic decision that hinges on fixed marketing costs versus variable marketing costs is the choice between engaging third-party contract sales representatives versus an in-house sales force. Hiring a salaried – or predominantly salaried – sales force entails more risk than the alternative because salaries must be paid even if the firm fails to achieve its revenue targets. By contrast, when a firm uses third-party brokers to sell its goods on commission, its selling costs decline when sales targets are not met.

Construction

$$\text{Total selling (marketing) costs (£)} = \text{Total fixed selling costs (£)}$$
$$+ \text{Total variable selling costs (£)}$$

$$\text{Total variable selling costs (£)} = \text{Revenue (£)} * \text{Variable selling cost (\%)}$$

Commissioned sales costs

Sales commissions represent one example of selling costs that vary in proportion to revenue. Consequently, any sales commissions should be included in variable selling costs.

Example Henry's Ketchup spends £5 million a year to maintain a sales force that calls on grocery chains and wholesalers. A broker offers to perform the same selling tasks for a 5% commission.

At £50 million in revenue,

$$\text{Total variable selling cost} = \text{£50 million} * 5\% = \text{£2.5 million}$$

At £100 million in revenue,

$$\text{Total variable selling cost} = \text{£100 million} * 5\% = \text{£5 million}$$

At £200 million in revenue,

$$\text{Total variable selling cost} = \text{£200 million} * 5\% = \text{£10 million}$$

If revenues run at less than £100 million, the broker will cost less than the in-house sales force. At £100 million in revenue, the broker will cost the same as the sales force. At revenue levels greater than £100 million, the broker will cost more.

Of course, the transition from a salaried sales staff to a broker may itself cause a change in revenues. Calculating the revenue level at which selling costs are equal is only a starting point for analysis. But it is an important first step in understanding the trade-offs.

There are many types of variable selling costs. For example, selling costs could be based upon a complicated formula, specified in a firm's contracts with its brokers and dealers. Selling costs might include incentives to local dealers, which are tied to the achievement of specific sales targets. They might include promises to reimburse retailers for spending on cooperative advertising. By contrast, payments to a website for a fixed number of impressions or click-throughs, in a contract that calls for specific financial compensation, would more likely be classified as fixed costs. On the other hand, payments for conversions (sales) would be classified as variable marketing costs.

Example A small manufacturer of a regional food delicacy must select a budget for a television advertising campaign that it plans to launch. Under one plan, it might pay to create a commercial and air it in a certain number of time slots. Its spending level would thus be fixed. It would be selected ahead of time and would not vary with the results of the campaign.

Under an alternative plan, the company could produce the advertisement – still a fixed cost – but ask retailers to air it in their local markets and pay the required media fees to television stations as part of a cooperative advertising arrangement. In return for paying the media fees, local stores would receive a discount (a bill-back) on every unit of the company's product that they sell.

Under the latter plan, the product discount would be a variable cost, as its total amount would depend on the number of units sold. By undertaking such a cooperative advertising campaign, the manufacturer would make its marketing budget a mix of fixed and variable costs. Is such cooperative advertising a good idea? To decide this, the company must determine its expected sales under both arrangements, as well as the consequent economics and its tolerance for risk.

Data sources, complications and cautions

Fixed costs are often easier to measure than variable costs. Typically, fixed costs might be assembled from payroll records, lease documents or financial records. For variable costs, it is necessary to measure the rate at which they increase as a function of activity level. Although variable selling costs often represent a predefined percentage of revenue, they may alternatively vary with the number of *units* sold (as in a £1-per-case discount). An additional complication arises if some variable selling costs apply to only a portion of total sales. This can happen, for example, when some dealers qualify for cash discounts or full-truckload rates and some do not.

In a further complication, some expenses may appear to be fixed when they are actually stepped. That is, they are fixed to a point, but they trigger further expenditures beyond that point. For example, a firm may contract with an advertising agency for up to three campaigns per year. If it decides to buy more than three campaigns, it would incur an incremental cost. Typically, stepped costs can be treated as fixed – provided that the boundaries of analysis are well understood.

Stepped payments can be difficult to model. Rebates for customers whose purchases exceed a certain level, or bonuses for salespeople who exceed quota, can be challenging functions to describe. Creativity is important in designing marketing discounts. But this creativity can be difficult to reflect in a framework of fixed and variable costs.

In developing their marketing budgets, firms must decide which costs to write off as an expense in the current period and which to amortise over several periods. The latter course is appropriate for expenditures that are correctly viewed as investments. One example of such an investment would be a special allowance for financing receivables from new distributors. Rather than adding such an allowance to the current period's budget, it would be better viewed as a marketing item that increases the firm's investment in working capital. By contrast, advertising that is projected to generate long-term impact may be loosely called an investment, but it would be better treated as a marketing expense. Although there may be a valid theoretical case for amortising advertising, that discussion is beyond the scope of this book.

Related metrics and concepts

Levels of marketing spending are often used to compare companies and to demonstrate how heavily they "invest" in this area. For this purpose, marketing spending is generally viewed as a percentage of sales.

> **Marketing as a percentage of sales: The level of marketing spending as a fraction of sales. This figure provides an indication of how heavily a company is marketing. The appropriate level for this figure varies among products, strategies and markets.**

$$\text{Marketing as a percentage of sales (\%)} = \frac{\text{Marketing spending (£)}}{\text{Revenue (£)}}$$

Variants on this metric are used to examine components of marketing in comparison with sales. Examples include trade promotion as a percentage of sales, or sales force as a percentage of sales. One particularly common example is:

> **Advertising as a percentage of sales: Advertising expenditures as a fraction of sales. Generally, this is a subset of marketing as a percentage of sales.**

Before using such metrics, marketers are advised to determine whether certain marketing costs have already been subtracted in the calculation of sales revenue. Trade allowances, for example, are often deducted from "gross sales" to calculate "net sales".

Slotting allowances

These are a particular form of selling costs encountered when new items are introduced to retailers or distributors. Essentially, they represent a charge made by retailers for making a "slot" available for a new item in their stores and warehouses. This charge may take the form of a one-time cash payment, free goods or a special discount. The exact terms of the slotting allowance will determine whether it constitutes a fixed or a variable selling cost, or a mix of the two.

Break-even analysis and contribution analysis

The break-even level represents the sales amount – in either unit or revenue terms – that is required to cover total costs (both fixed and variable). Profit at break-even is zero. Break-even is only possible if a firm's prices are higher than its variable costs per unit. If so, then each unit of product sold will generate some "contribution" toward covering fixed costs. The difference between price per unit and variable cost per unit is defined as contribution per unit.

$$\text{Contribution per unit (£)} = \text{Selling price per unit (£)} - \text{Variable cost per unit (£)}[4]$$

$$\text{Contribution margin (\%)} = \frac{\text{Contribution per unit (£)}}{\text{Selling price per unit (£)}}$$

$$\text{Break-even volume (N)} = \frac{\text{Fixed costs (£)}}{\text{Contribution per unit (£)}}$$

$$\text{Break-even revenue (£)} = \text{Break-even volume (units) (N)} \times \text{Price per unit (£)}$$

or

$$= \frac{\text{Fixed costs (£)}}{\text{Contribution margin (\%)}}$$

Break-even analysis is the Swiss Army knife of marketing economics. It is useful in a variety of situations and is often used to evaluate the likely profitability of marketing actions that affect fixed costs, prices or variable costs per unit. Break-even is often derived in a "back-of-the-envelope" calculation that determines whether a more detailed analysis is warranted.

Purpose: to provide a rough indicator of the earnings impact of a marketing activity

The break-even point for any business activity is defined as the level of sales at which neither a profit nor a loss is made on that activity – that is, where total revenues = total costs. Provided that a company sells its goods at a price per unit that is greater than its variable cost per unit, the sale of each unit will make a "contribution" toward covering some portion of fixed costs. That contribution can be calculated as the difference between price per unit (revenue) and variable cost per unit. On this basis, break-even constitutes the minimum level of sales at which total contribution fully covers fixed costs.

Construction

To determine the break-even point for a business programme, one must first calculate the fixed costs of engaging in that programme. For this purpose, managers do not need to estimate projected volumes. Fixed costs are constant, regardless of activity level. Managers do, however, need to calculate the difference between revenue per unit and variable costs per unit. This difference represents contribution per unit (£). Contribution rates can also be expressed as a percentage of selling price.

Example Apprentice Mousetraps wants to know how many units of its "Magic Mouse Trapper" it must sell to break even. The product sells for €20. It costs €5 per unit to make. The company's fixed costs are €30,000. Break-even will be reached when total contribution equals fixed costs.

$$\text{Break-even volume} = \frac{\text{Fixed costs}}{\text{Contribution per unit}}$$

$$\text{Contribution per unit} = \text{Sale price per unit} - \text{Variable cost per unit}$$

$$= €20 - €5 = €15$$

$$\text{Break-even volume} = \frac{€30,000}{€15} = 2,000 \text{ mousetraps}$$

This dynamic can be summarised in a graph that shows fixed costs, variable costs, total costs and total revenue (see Figure 3.6). Below the break-even point, total costs exceed total revenue, creating a loss. Above the break-even point, a company generates profits.

> Break-even: **Break-even occurs when the total contribution equals the fixed costs. Profits and losses at this point equal zero.**

One of the key building blocks of break-even analysis is the concept of contribution. Contribution represents the portion of sales revenue that is not consumed by variable costs and so contributes to the coverage of fixed costs.

$$\text{Contribution per unit (£)} = \text{Selling price per unit (£)} - \text{Variable cost per unit (£)}$$

Contribution can also be expressed in percentage terms, quantifying the fraction of the sales price that contributes toward covering fixed costs. This percentage is often called the contribution margin.

$$\text{Contribution margin (\%)} = \frac{\text{Contribution per unit (£)}}{\text{Selling price per unit (£)}}$$

Figure 3.6 At break-even, total costs = total revenues

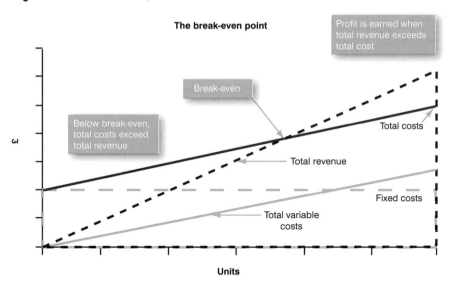

Formulas for total contribution include the following:

$$\text{Total contribution (£)} = \text{Units sold (N)} * \text{Contribution per unit (£)}$$

$$\text{Total contribution (£)} = \text{Total revenues (£)} - \text{Total variable costs (£)}$$

As previously noted,

$$\text{Total variable costs} = \text{Variable costs per unit} * \text{Units sold}$$

$$\text{Total revenues} = \text{Selling price per unit} * \text{Units sold}$$

> **Break-even volume:** **The number of units that must be sold to cover fixed costs.**

$$\text{Break-even volume (N)} = \frac{\text{Fixed costs (£)}}{\text{Contribution per unit (£)}}$$

Break-even will occur when an enterprise sells enough units to cover its fixed costs. If the fixed costs are £10 and the contribution per unit is £2, then a firm must sell 5 units to break even.

> **Break-even revenue:** **The level of financial sales required to break even.**

$$\text{Break-even revenue (£)} = \text{Break-even volume (units) (N)} * \text{Price per unit (£)}$$

This formula is the simple conversion of volume in units to the revenues generated by that volume.

Example Apprentice Mousetraps wants to know how many euros' worth of its "Deluxe Mighty Mouse Trapper" it must sell to break even. The product sells for €40 per unit. It costs €10 per unit to make. The company's fixed costs are €30,000.

With fixed costs of €30,000, and a contribution per unit of €30, Apprentice must sell €30,000/€30 = 1,000 deluxe mousetraps to break even. At €40 per trap, this corresponds to revenues of 1,000 * €40 = €40,000.

$$\text{Break-even revenue (€)} = \text{Break-even volume (N)} * \text{Price per unit (€)}$$

$$= 1,000 * €40 = €40,000$$

Break-even in financial terms can also be calculated by dividing fixed costs by the fraction of the selling price that represents contribution.

$$\text{Break-even revenue} = \frac{\text{Fixed costs}}{[(\text{Selling price} - \text{Variable costs})/\text{Selling price}]}$$

$$= \frac{€30,000}{[(€40 - €10)/€40]}$$

$$= \frac{€30,000}{75\%} = €40,000$$

Break-even on incremental investment

Break-even on incremental investment is a common form of break-even analysis. It examines the additional investment needed to pursue a marketing plan, and it calculates the additional sales required to cover that expenditure. Any costs or revenues that would have occurred regardless of the investment decision are excluded from this analysis.

Example John's Clothing Store employs three salespeople. It generates annual sales of $1 million and an average contribution margin of 30%. Rent is $50,000. Each sales person costs $50,000 per year in salary and benefits. How much would sales have to increase for John to break even on hiring an additional salesperson?

If the additional "investment" in a salesperson is $50,000, then break-even on the new hire will be reached when sales increase by $50,000/30%, or $166,666.67.

Data sources, complications and cautions

To calculate a break-even sales level, one must know the revenues per unit, the variable costs per unit and the fixed costs. To establish these figures, one must classify all costs as either fixed (those that do not change with volume) or variable (those that increase linearly with volume).

The time scale of the analysis can influence this classification. Indeed, one's managerial intent can be reflected in the classification. (Will the company fire employees and sub-let factory space if sales turn down?) As a general rule, all costs become variable in the long term. Firms generally view rent, for example, as a fixed cost. But in the long term, even rent becomes variable as a company may move into larger quarters when sales grow beyond a certain point.

Before agonising over these judgements, managers are urged to remember that the most useful application of the break-even exercise is to make a rough judgement about whether more detailed analyses are likely to be worth the effort. The break-even calculation enables managers to judge various options and proposals quickly. It is not, however, a substitute for more detailed analyses, including projections of target profits ("Profit-based sales targets", pages 85–88), risk, and the time value of money ("Customer lifetime value", pages 142–147 and "Evaluating multi-period investments", pages 313–318).

Related metrics and concepts

> Payback period: **The period of time required to recoup the funds expended in an investment. The payback period is the time required for an investment to reach break-even (see previous sections).**

Profit-based sales targets

> In launching a programme, managers often start with an idea of the profit they desire and ask what sales levels will be required to reach it. Target volume (N) is the unit sales quantity required to meet an earnings goal. Target revenue (£) is the corresponding figure for money sales. Both of these metrics can be viewed as extensions of break-even analysis.
>
> $$\text{Target volume (N)} = \frac{[\text{Fixed costs (£)} + \text{Target profit (£)}]}{\text{Contribution per unit (£)}}$$
>
> $$\text{Target revenue (£)} = \text{Target volume (N)} * \text{Selling price per unit (£)}$$
>
> or
>
> $$= \frac{[\text{Fixed cost (£)} + \text{Profit (£)}]}{\text{Contribution margin (\%)}}$$
>
> **Increasingly, marketers are expected to generate volumes that meet the target profits of their firm. This will often require them to revise sales targets as prices and costs change.**

Purpose: to ensure that marketing and sales objectives mesh with profit targets

In the previous section, we explored the concept of break-even, the point at which a company sells enough to cover its fixed costs. In target volume and target revenue calculations, managers take the next step. They determine the level of unit sales or revenues needed not only to cover a firm's costs but also to attain its profit targets.

Construction

> Target volume: **The volume of sales necessary to generate the profits specified in a company's plans.**

The formula for target volume will be familiar to those who have performed break-even analysis. The only change is to add the required profit target to the fixed costs. From another perspective, the break-even volume equation can be viewed as a special case of the general target volume calculation – one in which the profit target is zero, and a company seeks only to cover its fixed costs. In target volume calculations, the company broadens this objective to solve for a desired profit.

$$\text{Target volume (N)} = \frac{[\text{Fixed costs (£)} + \text{Profit (£)}]}{\text{Contribution per unit (£)}}$$

Example Mohan, an artist in the US, wants to know how many caricatures he must sell to realise a yearly profit objective of £15,000. Each caricature sells for £10 and costs £2.50 in materials to make. The fixed costs for Mohan's studio are £15,000 per year:

$$\text{Target volume} = \frac{(\text{Fixed costs} + \text{Profit})}{(\text{Sales price} - \text{Variable costs})}$$

$$= \frac{(£15,000 + £15,000)}{(£10 - £2.50)}$$

$$= 4,000 \text{ caricatures per year}$$

It is quite simple to convert unit target volume to target revenues. One need only multiply the volume figure by an item's price per unit. Continuing the example of Mohan's studio,

$$\text{Target revenue (\$)} = \text{Target volume (\#)} * \text{Selling price (\$)}$$

$$= 4,000 * £10 = £40,000$$

Alternatively, we can use a second formula:

$$\text{Target revenue} = \frac{[\text{Fixed costs (\$)} + \text{Profit (\$)}]}{\text{Contribution margin (\%)}}$$

$$= \frac{(£15,000 + £15,000)}{(£7.50/£10)}$$

$$= \frac{£30,000}{0.75} = £40,000$$

Data sources, complications and cautions

The information needed to perform a target volume calculation is essentially the same as that required for break-even analysis – fixed costs, selling price and variable costs. Of course, before determining target volume, one must also set a profit target.

The major assumption here is the same as in break-even analysis: costs are linear with respect to unit volume over the range explored in the calculation.

Related metrics and concepts

Target volumes *not* based on target profit

In this section, we have assumed that a firm starts with a *profit* target and seeks to determine the volume required to meet it. In certain instances, however, a firm might set a volume target for reasons other than short-term profit. For example, firms sometimes adopt top-line growth as a goal. Please do not confuse this use of target volume with the profit-based target volumes calculated in this section.

Returns and targets

Companies often set hurdle rates for return on sales and return on investment and require that projections achieve these before any plan can be approved. Given these targets, we can calculate the sales volume required for the necessary return. (See "Return on investment" on pages 309–310 for more details.)

Example Niesha runs business development at Gird, a company that has established a return on sales target of 15%. That is, Gird requires that all programmes generate profits equivalent to 15% of sales revenues. Niesha is evaluating a programme that will add £1,000,000 to fixed costs. Under this programme, each unit of product will be sold for £100 and will generate a contribution margin of 25%. To reach break-even on this programme, Gird must sell £1,000,000/£25 = 40,000 units of product. How much must Gird sell to reach its target return on sales (ROS) of 15%?

To determine the revenue level required to achieve a 15% ROS, Niesha can use either a spreadsheet model and trial and error, or the following formula:

$$\text{Target revenue} = \frac{\text{Fixed costs (£)}}{[\text{Contribution margin (\%)} - \text{Target ROS (\%)}]}$$

$$= \frac{£1,000,000}{(0.25 - 0.15)}$$

$$= \frac{£1,000,000}{0.1} = £10,000,000$$

Thus, Gird will achieve its 15% ROS target if it generates £10,000,000 in sales. At a selling price of £100 per unit, this is equivalent to unit sales of 100,000.

Product and portfolio management

Metrics covered in this chapter:

- Trial, repeat, penetration and volume projections

- Growth: percentage and CAGR

- Cannibalisation rate and fair share draw rate

- Brand equity metrics

- Conjoint utilities and consumer preference

- Segmentation and conjoint utilities

- Conjoint utilities and volume projection

Introduction

Effective marketing comes from customer knowledge and an understanding of how a product fits customers' needs. In this chapter, we'll describe metrics used in product strategy and planning. These metrics address the following questions: What volumes can marketers expect from a new product? How will sales of existing products be affected by the launch of a new offering? Is brand equity increasing or decreasing? What do customers really want, and what are they willing to sacrifice to obtain it?

We'll start with a section on trial and repeat rates, explaining how these metrics are determined and how they're used to generate sales forecasts for new products. Because forecasts involve growth projections, we'll then discuss the difference between year-on-year growth and compound annual growth rates (CAGR). Because growth of one product sometimes comes at the expense of an existing product line, it is important to understand cannibalisation metrics. These reflect the impact of new products on a portfolio of existing products.

Next, we'll cover selected metrics associated with brand equity – a central focus of marketing. Indeed, many of the metrics throughout this book can be useful in evaluating brand equity. Certain metrics, however, have been developed specifically to measure the "health" of brands. This chapter will discuss them.

Although branding strategy is a major aspect of a product offering, there are others, and managers must be prepared to make trade-offs among them, informed by a sense of the "worth" of various features. Conjoint analysis helps identify customers' valuation of specific product attributes. Increasingly, this technique is used to improve products and to help marketers evaluate and segment new or rapidly growing markets. In the final sections of this chapter, we'll discuss conjoint analysis from multiple perspectives.

Metric	Construction	Considerations	Purpose
Trial	First-time users as a percentage of the target population.	Distinguish "ever-tried" from "new" triers in current period.	Over time, sales should rely less on trial and more on repeat purchasers.
Repeat volume	Repeat buyers, multiplied by the number of products they buy in each purchase, multiplied by the number of times they purchase per period.	Depending on when trial was achieved, not all triers will have an equal opportunity to make repeat purchases.	Measure of the stability of a brand franchise.
Penetration	Users in the previous period, multiplied by repeat rate for the current period, plus new triers in the current period.	The length of the period will affect norms, that is, more customers buy in a year than in a month.	Measure of the population buying in the current period.
Volume projections	Combine trial volume and repeat volume.	Adjust trial and repeat rates for time frame. Not all triers will have time or opportunity to repeat.	Plan production and inventories for both trade sales and consumer off-take.

Metric	Construction	Considerations	Purpose
Year-on-year growth	Percentage change from one year to the next.	Distinguish unit and money growth rates.	Plan production and budgeting.
Compound annual growth rate (CAGR)	Ending value divided by starting value to the power of 1/N, in which N is the number of periods.	May not reflect individual year-on-year growth rates.	Useful for averaging growth rates over long periods.
Cannibalisation rate	Percentage of new product sales taken from existing product line.	Market expansion effects should also be considered.	Useful to account for the fact that new products often reduce the sales of existing products.
Fair share draw	Assumption that new entrants in a market capture sales from established competitors in proportion to established market shares.	May not be a reasonable assumption if there are significant differences among competing brands.	Useful to generate an estimate of sales and shares after entry of new competitor.
Brand equity metrics	Numerous measures, for example, conjoint utility attributed to brand.	Metrics tracking essence of brand may not track health and value.	Monitor health of a brand. Diagnose weaknesses, as needed.
Conjoint utilities	Regression coefficients for attribute levels derived from conjoint analysis.	May be function of number, level, and type of attributes in study.	Indicates the relative values that customers place on attributes of which product offerings are composed.

▶

Metric	Construction	Considerations	Purpose
Segment utilities	Clustering of individuals into market segments on the basis of sum-of-squares distance between regression coefficients drawn from conjoint analysis.	May be function of number, level and type of attributes in conjoint study. Assumes homogeneity within segments.	Uses customer valuations of product attributes to help define market segments.
Conjoint utilities and volume projection	Used within conjoint simulator to estimate volume.	Assumes awareness and distribution levels are known or can be estimated.	Forecast sales for alternative products, designs, prices and branding strategies.

Trial, repeat, penetration and volume projections

Test markets and volume projections enable marketers to forecast sales by sampling customer intentions through surveys and market studies. By estimating how many customers will try a new product, and how often they'll make repeat purchases, marketers can establish the basis for such projections.

$$\text{Trial rate (\%)} = \frac{\text{First-time triers in period } t \text{ (N)}}{\text{Total population (N)}}$$

$$\text{First-time triers in period } t \text{ (N)} = \text{Total population (N)} * \text{Trial rate (\%)}$$

$$\text{Penetration } t \text{ (N)} = [\text{Penetration in } t\text{-1 (N)} * \text{Repeat rate period } t \text{ (\%)}] + \text{First-time triers in period } t \text{ (N)}$$

$$\text{Projection of sales } t \text{ (N)} = \text{Penetration } t \text{ (N)} * \text{Average frequency of purchase (N)} * \text{Average units per purchase (N)}$$

Projections from customer surveys are especially useful in the early stages of product development and in setting the timing for product launch. Through such projections, customer response can be estimated without the expense of a full product launch.

Purpose: to understand volume projections

When projecting sales for relatively new products, marketers typically use a system of trial and repeat calculations to anticipate sales in future periods. This works on the principle that everyone buying the product will either be a new customer (a "trier") or a repeat customer. By adding new and repeat customers in any period, we can establish the penetration of a product in the marketplace.

It is challenging, however, to project sales to a large population on the basis of simulated test markets, or even full-fledged regional rollouts. Marketers have developed various solutions to increase the speed and reduce the cost of test marketing, such as stocking a store with products (or mock-ups of new products) or giving customers money to buy the products of their choice. These simulate real shopping conditions but require specific models to estimate full-market volume on the basis of test results. To illustrate the conceptual underpinnings of this process, we offer a general model for making volume projection on the basis of test market results.

Construction

The penetration of a product in a future period can be estimated on the basis of population size, trial rates and repeat rates.

> Trial rate (%): **The percentage of a defined population that purchases or uses a product for the first time in a given period.**

Example A cable TV company keeps careful records of the names and addresses of its customers. The firm's head of marketing notes that 150 households made first-time use of his company's services in March 2008. The company has access to 30,000 households. To calculate the trial rate for March, we can divide 150 by 30,000, yielding 0.5%.

> First-time triers in period t (N): **The number of customers who purchase or use a product or brand for the first time in a given period.**

$$\text{Penetration } t \text{ (N)} = [\text{Penetration in } t\text{-1 (N)} * \text{Repeat rate period } t \text{ (\%)}] + \text{First-time triers in period } t \text{ (N)}$$

Example A cable TV company started selling a monthly sports package in January. The company typically has an 80% repeat rate and anticipates that this will continue

▶

for the new offering. The company sold 10,000 sports packages in January. In February, it expects to add 3,000 customers for the package. On this basis, we can calculate expected penetration for the sports package in February.

$$\text{Penetration in February} = (\text{Penetration January} * \text{Repeat rate})$$
$$+ \text{First-time triers in February}$$

$$= (10{,}000 * 80\%) + 3{,}000 = 11{,}000$$

Later that year, in September, the company has 20,000 subscribers. Its repeat rate remains 80%. The company had 18,000 subscribers in August. Management wants to know how many new customers the firm added for its sports package in September:

$$\text{First-time triers} = \text{Penetration} - \text{Repeat customers}$$

$$= 20{,}000 - (18{,}000 * 80\%) = 5{,}600$$

From penetration, it is a short step to projections of sales.

$$\text{Projection of sales (N)} = \text{Penetration (N)} * \text{Frequency of purchase (N)}$$
$$* \text{Units per purchase (N)}$$

Simulated test market results and volume projections

Trial volume

Trial rates are often estimated on the basis of surveys of potential customers. Typically, these surveys ask respondents whether they will "definitely" or "probably" buy a product. As these are the strongest of several possible responses to questions of purchase intentions, they are sometimes referred to as the "top two boxes". The less favourable responses in a standard five-choice survey include "may or may not buy", "probably won't buy" and "definitely won't buy". (Refer to "Awareness, attitudes and usage (AAU)" on pages 32–36 for more on intention to purchase.)

Because not all respondents follow through on their declared purchase intentions, firms often make adjustments to the percentages in the top two boxes in developing sales projections. For example, some marketers estimate that 80% of respondents who say they'll "definitely buy" and 30% of those who say that they'll "probably buy" will in fact purchase a product when given the opportunity.[1] (The adjustment for customers following through is used in the following model.) Although some respondents in the bottom three boxes might buy a product, their number is assumed to be insignificant. By reducing the score for the top two boxes, marketers derive a more realistic estimate of the number of potential customers who will try a product, given the right circumstances. Those circumstances are often shaped by product awareness and availability.

Awareness

Sales projection models include an adjustment for lack of awareness of a product within the target market (see Figure 4.1). Lack of awareness reduces the trial rate because it excludes some potential customers who might try the product but don't know about it. By contrast, if awareness is 100%, then all potential customers know about the product, and no potential sales are lost due to lack of awareness.

Figure 4.1 Schematic of simulated test market volume projection

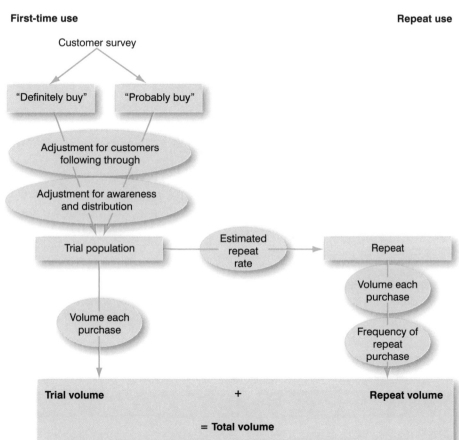

Distribution

Another adjustment to test market trial rates is usually applied: accounting for the estimated availability of the new product. Even survey respondents who say they'll "definitely" try a product are unlikely to do so if they can't find it easily. In making this adjustment, companies typically use an estimated distribution, a percentage of total stores that will stock the new product, such as ACV % distribution. (See "Numeric, ACV and PCV distribution, facings/share of shelf" on pages 176–183 for further detail.)

$$\text{Adjusted trial rate (\%)} = \text{Trial rate (\%)} * \text{Awareness (\%)} * \text{ACV (\%)}$$

After making these modifications, marketers can calculate the number of customers who are expected to try the product, simply by applying the adjusted trial rate to the target population.

$$\text{Trial population (N)} = \text{Target population (N)} * \text{Adjusted trial rate (\%)}$$

Estimated in this way, trial population (N) is identical to penetration (N) in the trial period.

To forecast trial volume, multiply trial population by the projected average number of units of a product that will be bought in each trial purchase. This is often assumed to be one unit because most people will experiment with a single unit of a new product before buying larger quantities.

$$\text{Trial volume (N)} = \text{Trial population (N)} * \text{Units per purchase (N)}$$

Combining all these calculations, the entire formula for trial volume is:

$$\text{Trial volume (N)} = \text{Target population (N)} * [(80\% * \text{Definitely buy (N)})$$
$$+ (30\% * \text{Probably buy (N)})] * \text{Awareness (\%)} * \text{ACV (\%)}$$
$$* \text{Units per purchase (N)}$$

Example The marketing team of an office supply manufacturer has a great idea for a new product – a safety stapler. To sell the idea internally, they want to project the volume of sales they can expect over the stapler's first year. Their customer survey yields the following results (see Table 4.1).

Table 4.1 Customer survey responses

	% of customers responding
Definitely will buy	20%
Probably will buy	50%
May/may not buy	15%
Probably won't buy	10%
Definitely won't buy	5%
Total	100%

On this basis, the company estimates a trial rate for the new stapler by applying the industry-standard expectation that 80% of "definites" and 30% of "probables" will in fact buy the product if given the opportunity.

$$\text{Trial rate} = 80\% \text{ of "definites"} + 30\% \text{ of "probables"}$$
$$= (80\% * 20\%) + (30\% * 50\%)$$
$$= 31\%$$

Thus, 31% of the population is expected to try the product if they are aware of it and if it is available in stores. The company has a strong advertising presence and a solid distribution network. Consequently, its marketers believe they can obtain an ACV of approximately 60% for the stapler and that they can generate awareness at a similar level. On this basis, they project an adjusted trial rate of 11.16% of the population:

$$\text{Adjusted trial rate} = \text{Trial rate} * \text{Awareness} * \text{ACV}$$
$$= 31\% * 60\% * 60\% = 11.16\%$$

The target population comprises 20 million people. The trial population can be calculated by multiplying this figure by the adjusted trial rate.

$$\text{Trial population} = \text{Target population} * \text{Adjusted trial rate}$$
$$= 20 \text{ million} * 11.16\% = 2.232 \text{ million}$$

Assuming that each person buys one unit when trying the product, the trial volume will total 2.232 million units.

We can also calculate the trial volume by using the full formula:

$$\text{Trial volume} = \text{Target population}$$
$$* [((80\% * \text{Definites}) + (30\% * \text{Probables})) * \text{Awareness} * \text{ACV}]$$
$$* \text{Units per purchase}$$
$$= 20m * [((80\% * 20\%) + (30\% * 50\%)) * 60\% * 60\%)] * 1$$
$$= 2.232 \text{ million}$$

Repeat volume

The second part of projected volume concerns the fraction of people who try a product and then repeat their purchase decision. The model for this dynamic uses a single estimated repeat rate to yield the number of customers who are expected to purchase again after their initial trial. In reality, initial repeat rates are often lower than subsequent repeat rates. For example, it is not uncommon for 50% of trial purchasers to make a first repeat purchase, but for 80% of those who purchase a second time to go on to purchase a third time.

$$\text{Repeat buyers (N)} = \text{Trial population (N)} * \text{Repeat rate (\%)}$$

To calculate the repeat volume, the repeat buyers' figure can then be multiplied by an expected volume per purchase among repeat customers and by the number of times these customers are expected to repeat their purchases within the period under consideration.

$$\text{Repeat volume (N)} = \text{Repeat buyers (N)} * \text{Repeat unit volume per customer (N)} * \text{Repeat occasions (N)}$$

This calculation yields the total volume that a new product is expected to generate among repeat customers over a specified introductory period. The full formula can be written as:

$$\text{Repeat volume (N)} = [\text{Repeat rate (\%)} * \text{Trial population (N)}] \\ * \text{Repeat volume per customer (N)} \\ * \text{Repeat occasions (N)}$$

Example Continuing the previous office supplies example, the safety stapler has a trial population of 2.232 million. Marketers expect the product to be of sufficient quality to generate a 10% repeat rate in its first year. This will yield 223,200 repeat buyers:

$$\text{Repeat buyers} = \text{Trial population} * \text{Repeat rate}$$
$$= 2.232 \text{ million} * 10\%$$
$$= 223,200$$

On average, the company expects each repeat buyer to purchase on four occasions during the first year. On average, each purchase is expected to comprise two units.

$$\text{Repeat volume} = \text{Repeat buyers} * \text{Repeat unit volume per customer} \\ * \text{Repeat occasions}$$
$$= 223,200 * 2 * 4$$
$$= 1,785,600 \text{ units}$$

This can be represented in the full formula:

$$\text{Repeat volume (N)} = [\text{Repeat rate (\%)} * \text{Trial population (N)}]$$
$$* \text{ Repeat volume per customer (N)}$$
$$* \text{ Repeat occasions (N)}$$
$$= (10\% * 2{,}232{,}000) * 2 * 4$$
$$= 1{,}785{,}600 \text{ units}$$

Total volume

Total volume is the sum of trial volume and repeat volume, as all volume must be sold to either new customers or returning customers.

$$\text{Total volume (N)} = \text{Trial volume} + \text{Repeat volume}$$

To capture total volume in its fully detailed form, we need only combine the previous formulas.

$$\text{Total volume (N)} = [\text{Target population} * ((0.8 * \text{Definitely buy} + 0.3 *$$
$$\text{Probably buy})$$
$$* \text{Awareness} * \text{ACV}) * \text{Units per trial purchase}]$$
$$+ [(\text{Repeat rate} * \text{Trial population})$$
$$* \text{Repeat volume per customer} * \text{Repeat occasions}]$$

Example Total volume in year one for the stapler is the sum of trial volume and repeat volume.

$$\text{Total volume} = \text{Trial volume} + \text{Repeat volume}$$
$$= 2{,}232{,}000 + 1{,}785{,}600$$
$$= 4{,}017{,}600 \text{ units}$$

A full calculation of this figure and a template for a spreadsheet calculation are presented in Table 4.2.

Table 4.2 Volume projection spreadsheet

Preliminary data	Source	
Definitely will buy	Customer survey	20%
Probably will buy	Customer survey	50%

Table 4.2 *Continued*

Preliminary data	Source	
Likely buyers		
Likely buyers from definites	= Definitely buy * 80%	16%
Likely buyers from probables	= Probably buy * 30%	15%
Trial rate (%)	Total of likely buyers	31%
Marketing adjustments		
Awareness	Estimated from marketing plan	60%
ACV	Estimated from marketing plan	60%
Adjusted trial rate (%)	= Trial rate * Awareness * ACV	11.2%
Target population (N) (thousands)	Marketing plan data	20,000
Trial population (N) (thousands)	= Target population * Adjusted trial rate	2,232
Unit volume purchased per trial (N)	Estimated from marketing plan	1
Trial volume (N) (thousands)	= Trial population * Volume per trier	2,232
Repeat rate (%)	Estimated from marketing plan	10%
Repeat buyers (N)	= Repeat rate * Trial population	223,200
Avg. volume per repeat purchase (N)	Estimated from marketing plan	2
Repeat purchase frequency* (N)	Estimated from marketing plan	4
Repeat volume (thousands) frequency	= Repeat buyers * Repeat volume per purchase * Repeat purchase	1,786
Total volume (thousands)		4,018

* The average frequency of repeat purchases per repeat purchaser should be adjusted to reflect the time available for first-time triers to repeat, the purchase cycle (frequency) for the category, and availability. For example, if trial rates are constant over the year, the number of repeat purchases would be about 50% of what it would have been if all had tried on day 1 of the period.

Data sources, complications and cautions

Sales projections based on test markets will always require the inclusion of key assumptions. In setting these assumptions, marketers face tempting opportunities to make the assumptions fit the desired outcome. Marketers must guard against that temptation and perform sensitivity analysis to establish a range of pre-dictions.

Relatively simple metrics such as trial and repeat rates can be difficult to capture in practice. Although strides have been made in gaining customer data – through customer loyalty cards, for example – it will often be difficult to determine whether customers are new or repeat buyers.

Regarding awareness and distribution, assumptions concerning the level of public awareness to be generated by launch advertising are fraught with uncer-tainty. Marketers are advised to ask: What sort of awareness does the product need? What complementary promotions can aid the launch?

Trial and repeat rates are both important. Some products generate strong results in the trial stage but fail to maintain ongoing sales. Consider the following example.

Example Let's compare the safety stapler with a new product, such as an enhanced envelope sealer. The envelope sealer generates less marketing buzz than the stapler but enjoys a greater repeat rate. To predict results for the envelope sealer, we have adapted the data from the safety stapler by reducing the top two box responses by half (reflecting its lower initial enthusiasm) and raising the repeat rate from 10% to 33% (showing stronger product response after use).

At the six-month mark, sales results for the safety stapler are superior to those for the envelope sealer. After one year, sales results for the two products are equal. On a three-year time scale, however, the envelope sealer – with its loyal base of cus-tomers – emerges as the clear winner in sales volume (see Figure 4.2).

The data for the graph is derived as shown in Table 4.3.

Figure 4.2 Time horizon influences perceived results

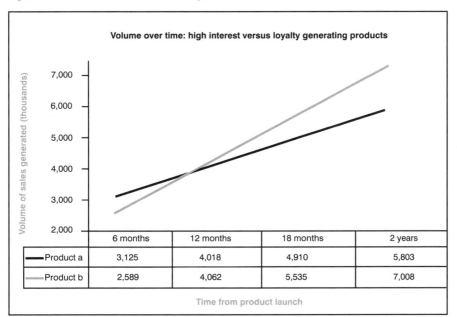

Volume over time: high interest versus loyalty generating products

	6 months	12 months	18 months	2 years
▬Product a	3,125	4,018	4,910	5,803
▬Product b	2,589	4,062	5,535	7,008

Time from product launch

Table 4.3 High initial interest or long-term loyalty: results over time

Preliminary data	Source	6 months Prod. A	6 months Prod. B	12 months Prod. A	12 months Prod. B	18 months Prod. A	18 months Prod. B	2 years Prod. A	2 years Prod. B
Definitely will buy	Customer survey	20%	10%	20%	10%	20%	10%	20%	10%
Probably will buy	Customer survey	50%	25%	50%	25%	50%	25%	50%	25%
Differences highlighted in yellow									
Likely buyers									
Likely buyers from definites	= Definitely buy * 80%	16%	8%	16%	8%	16%	8%	16%	8%
Likely buyers from probables	= Probably buy * 30%	15%	8%	15%	8%	15%	8%	15%	8%
Trial rate	Total of likely buyers	31%	16%	31%	16%	31%	16%	31%	16%
Marketing adjustments									
Awareness	Estimated from marketing plan	60%	60%	60%	60%	60%	60%	60%	60%
ACV	Estimated from marketing plan	60%	60%	60%	60%	60%	60%	60%	60%
Adjusted trial rate	= Trial rate * Awareness * ACV	11.2%	5.6%	11.2%	5.6%	11.2%	5.6%	11.2%	5.6%
Target population (thousands)	Marketing plan data	20,000	20,000	20,000	20,000	20,000	20,000	20,000	20,000

Trial population (thousands)	= Target population * Adjusted trial rate	2,232	1,116	2,232	1,116	2,232	1,116	2,232	1,116
Unit volume purchased at trial	Estimated from marketing plan	1	1	1	1	1	1	1	1
Trial volume (thousands)	= Trial population * Volume bought	2,232	1,116	2,232	1,116	2,232	1,116	2,232	1,116
Repeat rate	Estimated from marketing plan	10%	33%	10%	33%	10%	33%	10%	33%
Repeat buyers	= Repeat rate * Trial population	223.20	368.28	223.20	368.28	223.20	368.28	223.20	368.28
Repeat purchase unit volume	Estimated from marketing plan	2	2	2	2	2	2	2	2
Number of repeat purchases	Estimated from marketing plan	2	2	4	4	6	6	8	8
Repeat volume (thousands)	= Repeat buyers * Repeat volume * Number of repeat purchases	893	1,473	1,786	2,946	2,678	4,419	3,571	5,892
Total volume		3,125	2,589	4,018	4,062	4,910	5,535	5,803	7,008

Repeating and trying

Some models assume that customers, after they stop repeating purchases, are lost and do not return. However, customers may be acquired, lost, reacquired and lost again. In general, the trial–repeat model is best suited to projecting sales over the first few periods. Other means of predicting volume include share of requirements and penetration metrics (refer to "Penetration" on pages 23–26 and "Share of requirements" on pages 26–30). Those approaches may be preferable for products that lack reliable repeat rates.

	Market size	Pene-tration share	Share of require-ments	Heavy usage index	Market share	Units sold
New product	1,000,000	5%	80%	1.2	4.8%	48,000
Source	Estimated	Estimated	Estimated	Estimated	Penetration share * Share of require-ments * Heavy usage index	Share * Market size

Related metrics and concepts

Ever-tried

This is slightly different from trial in that it measures the percentage of the target population that has "ever" (in any previous period) purchased or consumed the product under study. Ever-tried is a cumulative measure and can never add up to more than 100%. Trial, by contrast, is an incremental measure. It indicates the percentage of the population that tries the product for the first time in a given period. Even here, however, there is potential for confusion. If a customer stops buying a product but tries it again six months later, some marketers will categorise that individual as a returning purchaser, others as a new customer. By the latter definition, if individuals can "try" a product more than once, then the sum of all "triers" could equal more than the total population. To avoid confusion, when reviewing a set of data, it's best to clarify the definitions behind it.

Variations on trial

Certain scenarios reduce the barriers to trial but entail a lower commitment by the customer than a standard purchase.

- **Forced trial:** No other similar product is available. For example, many people who prefer Pepsi-Cola have "tried" Coca-Cola in restaurants that only serve the latter, and vice versa.

- **Discounted trial:** Consumers buy a new product but at a substantially reduced price.

Forced and discounted trials are usually associated with lower repeat rates than trials made through volitional purchase.

Evoked set
The set of brands that consumers name in response to questions about which brands they consider (or might consider) when making a purchase in a specific category. Evoked sets for breakfast cereals, for example, are often quite large, while those for coffee may be smaller.

Number of new products
The number of products introduced for the first time in a specific time period.

Revenue from new products
Usually expressed as the percentage of sales generated by products introduced in the current period or, at times, in the most recent three to five periods.

Margin on new products
The money or percentage profit margin on new products. This can be measured separately but does not differ mathematically from margin calculations.

Company profit from new products
The percentage of company profits that is derived from new products. In working with this figure, it is important to understand how "new product" is defined.

Target market fit
Of customers purchasing a product, target market fit represents the percentage who belong in the demographic, psychographic or other descriptor set for that item. Target market fit is useful in evaluating marketing strategies. If a large percentage of customers for a product belongs to groups that have not previously been targeted, marketers may reconsider their targets – and their allocation of marketing spending.

Growth: percentage and CAGR

There are two common measures of growth. Year-on-year percentage growth uses the prior year as a base for expressing percentage change from one year to the next. Over longer periods of time, compound annual growth rate (CAGR) is a generally accepted metric for average growth rates.

$$\text{Year-on-year growth (\%)} = \frac{\text{Value } (\pounds,N,\%)\ t - \text{Value } (\pounds,N,\%)\ t - 1}{\text{Value } (\pounds,N,\%)\ t - 1}$$

> Compound annual growth rate, or = {[Ending value (£,N,%)/Starting value
> CAGR (%)   (£,N,%)] ^ [1/Number of years (N)]} − 1
>
> **Same stores growth = growth calculated only on the basis of stores that were fully established in both the prior and current periods.**

Purpose: to measure growth

Growth is the aim of virtually all businesses. Indeed, perceptions of the success or failure of many enterprises are based on assessments of their growth. Measures of year-on-year growth, however, are complicated by two factors:

1 Changes over time in the base from which growth is measured. Such changes might include increases in the number of stores, markets or salespeople generating sales. This issue is addressed by using "same store" measures (or corollary measures for markets, sales personnel and so on).

2 Compounding of growth over multiple periods. For example, if a company achieves 30% growth in one year, but its results remain unchanged over the two subsequent years, this would not be the same as 10% growth in each of three years. CAGR, the compound annual growth rate, is a metric that addresses this issue.

Construction

Percentage growth is the central plank of year-on-year analysis. It addresses the question: What has the company achieved this year, compared to last year? Dividing the results for the current period by the results for the prior period will yield a comparative figure. Subtracting one from the other will highlight the increase or decrease between periods. When evaluating comparatives, one might say that results in Year 2 were, for example, 110% of those in Year 1. To convert this figure to a growth rate, one need only subtract 100%.

The periods considered are often years, but any time frame can be chosen.

$$\text{Year-on-year growth (\%)} = \frac{\text{Value (£,N,\%) } t - \text{Value (£,N,\%) } t - 1}{\text{Value (£,N,\%) } t - 1}$$

Example Ed's is a small deli in New York, which has had great success in its second year of operation. Revenues in Year 2 are $570,000, compared with $380,000 in Year 1. Ed calculates his second-year sales results to be 150% of first-year revenues, indicating a growth rate of 50%.

$$\text{Year-on-year sales growth} = \frac{\$570,000 - \$380,000}{\$380,000} = 50\%$$

Same stores growth

This metric is at the heart of retail analysis. It enables marketers to analyse results from stores that have been in operation for the entire period under consideration. The logic is to eliminate the stores that have not been open for the full period to ensure comparability. Thus, same stores growth sheds light on the effectiveness with which equivalent resources were used in the period under study versus the prior period. In retail, modest same stores growth and high general growth rates would indicate a rapidly expanding organisation, in which growth is driven by investment. When both same stores growth and general growth are strong, a company can be viewed as effectively using its existing base of stores.

Example A small retail chain in Bavaria posts impressive percentage growth figures, moving from €58 million to €107 million in sales (84% growth) from one year to the next. Despite this dynamic growth, however, analysts cast doubt on the firm's business model, warning that its same stores growth measure suggests that its concept is failing (see Table 4.4).

Table 4.4 Revenue of a Bavarian chain store

Store	Opened	Revenue first year (m)	Revenue second year (m)
A	Year 1	€10	€9
B	Year 1	€19	€20
C	Year 1	€20	€15
D	Year 1	€9	€11
E	Year 2	n/a	€52
		€58	€107

Same stores growth excludes stores that were not open at the beginning of the first year under consideration. For simplicity, we assume that stores in this example were opened on the first day of Years 1 and 2, as appropriate. On this basis, same stores revenue in Year 2 would be €55 million – that is, the €107 million total for the year, less the €52 million generated by the newly opened Store E. This adjusted figure can be entered into the same stores growth formula:

$$\text{Same stores growth} = \frac{\text{(Stores A–D sales Year 2)} - \text{(Stores A–D sales Year 1)}}{\text{Stores A–D sales Year 1}}$$

$$= \frac{€55m - €58m}{€58} = -5\%$$

As demonstrated by its negative same stores growth figure, sales growth at this firm has been fuelled entirely by a major investment in a new store. This suggests serious doubts about its existing store concept. It also raises a question: Did the new store "cannibalise" existing store sales? (See the next section for cannibalisation metrics.)

Compounding growth, value at future period

By compounding, managers adjust growth figures to account for the iterative effect of improvement. For example, 10% growth in each of two successive years would not be the same as a total of 20% growth over the two-year period. The reason: growth in the second year is built upon the elevated base achieved in the first. Thus, if sales run £100,000 in Year 0 and rise by 10% in Year 1, then Year 1 sales come to £110,000. If sales rise by a further 10% in Year 2, however, then Year 2 sales do not total £120,000. Rather, they total £110,000 + (10% * £110,000) = £121,000.

The compounding effect can be easily modelled in spreadsheet packages, which enable you to work through the compounding calculations one year at a time. To calculate a value in Year 1, multiply the corresponding Year 0 value by one plus the growth rate. Then use the value in Year 1 as a new base and multiply it by one plus the growth rate to determine the corresponding value for Year 2. Repeat this process through the required number of years.

Example Over a three-year period, £100, compounded at a 10% growth rate, yields £133.10.

Year 0 to Year 1 £100 + 10% growth (that is, £10) = £110

Year 1 to Year 2 £110 + 10% growth (£11) = £121

Year 2 to Year 3 £121 + 10% growth (£12.10) = £133.10

There is a mathematical formula that generates this effect. It multiplies the value at the beginning – that is, in Year 0 – by one plus the growth rate to the power of the number of years over which that growth rate applies.

Value in future period (£,N,%) = Current value (£,N,%) $*$ [(1 + CAGR (%)) ^ Number of periods (N)]

Example Using the formula, we can calculate the impact of 10% annual growth over a period of three years. The value in Year 0 is £100. The number of years is 3. The growth rate is 10%.

Value in future period = Value in Year 0 $*$ (1 + Growth rate) ^ Number of years

$= £100 * (100\% + 10\%) \char`\^ 3$

$= £100 * 133.1\% = £133.10$

Compound annual growth rate (CAGR)
The CAGR is a constant year-on-year growth rate applied over a period of time. Given starting and ending values, and the length of the period involved, it can be calculated as follows:

CAGR (%) = {[Ending value (£,N)/Starting value (£,N)] ^ 1/ Number of periods (N)} − 1

Example Let's assume we have the results of the compounding growth observed in the previous example, but we don't know what the growth rate was. We know that the starting value was £100, the ending value was £133.10, and the number of years was 3. We can simply enter these numbers into the CAGR formula to derive the CAGR.

CAGR = [(Ending value/Starting value) ^ (1/Number of years)] − 1

$= [(£133.10/£100) \char`\^ 1/3] − 1$

$= [1.331 \text{ (the increase)} \char`\^ 1/3 \text{ (cube root)}] − 1 = 1.1 − 1 = 10\%$

Thus, we determine that the growth rate was 10%.

Data sources, complications and cautions

Percentage growth is a useful measure as part of a package of metrics. It can be deceiving, however, if not adjusted for the addition of such factors as stores, salespeople or products, or for expansion into new markets. "Same store" sales, and similar adjustments for other factors, tell us how effectively a company uses comparable resources. These very adjustments, however, are limited by their deliberate omission of factors that weren't in operation for the full period under study. Adjusted figures must be reviewed in tandem with measures of total growth.

Related metrics and concepts

Life cycle

Marketers view products as passing through four stages of development:

- **Introductory:** small markets not yet growing fast.
- **Growth:** larger markets with faster growth rates.
- **Mature:** largest markets but little or no growth.
- **Decline:** variable size markets with negative growth rates.

This is a rough classification. No generally accepted rules exist for making these classifications.

Cannibalisation rates and fair share draw

Cannibalisation is the reduction in sales (units or money) of a firm's existing products due to the introduction of a new product. The cannibalisation rate is generally calculated as the percentage of a new product's sales that represents a loss of sales (attributable to the introduction of the new entrant) of a specific existing product or products.

$$\text{Cannibalisation rate (\%)} = \frac{\text{Sales lost from existing products (N,£)}}{\text{Sales of new product (N,£)}}$$

Cannibalisation rates represent an important factor in the assessment of new product strategies.

Fair share draw constitutes an assumption or expectation that a new product will capture sales (in unit or money terms) from existing products in proportion to the market shares of those existing products.

Cannibalisation is a familiar business dynamic. A company with a successful product that has strong market share is faced by two conflicting ideas. The first is that it wants to maximise profits on its existing product line, concentrating on the current strengths that promise success in the short term. The second idea is that this company – or its competitors – may identify opportunities for new products that better fit the needs of certain segments. If the company introduces a new product in this field, however, it may "cannibalise" the sales of its existing products. That is, it may weaken the sales of its proven, already successful product line. If the company declines to introduce the new product, however, it will leave itself vulnerable to competitors who *will* launch such a product, and may thereby capture sales and market share from the company. Often, when new segments are emerging and there are advantages to being early to market, the key factor becomes timing. If a company launches its new product too early, it may lose too much income on its existing line; if it launches too late, it may miss the new opportunity altogether.

> **Cannibalisation: A market phenomenon in which sales of one product are achieved at the expense of some of a firm's other products.**

The cannibalisation rate is the percentage of sales of a new product that come from a specific set of existing products.

$$\text{Cannibalisation rate (\%)} = \frac{\text{Sales lost from existing products (N,£)}}{\text{Sales of new product (N,£)}}$$

Example A company has a single product that sold 10 units in the previous period. The company plans to introduce a new product that will sell 5 units with a cannibalisation rate of 40%. Thus 40% of the sales of the new product (40% * 5 units = 2 units) comes at the expense of the old product. Therefore, after cannibalisation, the company can expect to sell 8 units of the old product and 5 of the new product, or 13 units in total.

Any company considering the introduction of a new product should confront the potential for cannibalisation. A firm would do well to ensure that the amount of cannibalisation is estimated beforehand to provide an idea of how the product line's contribution as a whole will change. If performed properly, this analysis will tell a company whether overall profits can be expected to increase or decrease with the introduction of the new product line.

Example Lois sells umbrellas on a small beach where she is the only provider. Her financials for last month were as follows:

Umbrella sales price:	€20
Variable cost per umbrella:	€10
Umbrella contribution per unit:	€10
Total unit sales per month:	100
Total monthly contribution:	**€1,000**

Next month, Lois plans to introduce a bigger, lighter-weight umbrella called the "Big Block". Projected financials for the Big Block are as follows:

Big Block sales price:	€30
Variable cost per Big Block:	€15

▷ Big Block contribution per unit: €15
Total unit sales per month (Big Block): 50
Total monthly contribution (Big Block): €750

If there is no cannibalisation, Lois thus expects her total monthly contribution will be €1,000 + €750, or €1,750. Upon reflection, however, Lois thinks that the unit cannibalisation rate for Big Block will be 60%. Her projected financials after accounting for cannibalisation are therefore as follows:

Big Block unit sales: 50
Cannibalisation rate: 60%
Regular umbrella sales lost: 50 * 60% = 30
New regular umbrella sales: 100 − 30 = 70
New total contribution (regular): 70 Units * €10 Contribution per Unit = €700
Big Block total contribution: 50 Units * €15 Contribution per Unit = €750
Lois' total monthly contribution: €1,450

Under these projections, total umbrella sales will increase from 100 to 120, and total contribution will increase from €1,000 to €1,450. Lois will replace 30 regular sales with 30 Big Block sales and gain an extra €5 unit contribution on each. She will also sell 20 more umbrellas than she sold last month and gain €15 unit contribution on each.

In this scenario, Lois was in the enviable position of being able to cannibalise a lower-margin product with a higher-margin one. Sometimes, however, new products carry unit contributions lower than those of existing products. In these instances, cannibalisation reduces overall profits for the firm.

An alternative way to account for cannibalisation is to use a weighted contribution margin. In the previous example, the weighted contribution margin would be the unit margin Lois receives for Big Block after accounting for cannibalisation. Because each Big Block contributes €15 directly and cannibalises the €10 contribution generated by regular umbrellas at a 60% rate, Big Block's weighted contribution margin is €15 − (0.6 * €10), or €9 per unit. Because Lois expects to sell 50 Big Blocks, her total contribution is projected to increase by 50 * €9, or €450. This is consistent with our previous calculations.

If the introduction of Big Block requires some fixed marketing expenditure, then the €9 weighted margin can be used to find the break-even number of Big Block sales required to justify that expenditure. For example, if the launch of Big Block requires €360 in one-time marketing costs, then Lois needs to sell €360/€9, or 40 Big Blocks to break even on that expenditure.

If a new product has a margin lower than that of the existing product that it cannibalises, and if its cannibalisation rate is high enough, then its weighted contribution margin might be negative. In that case, company earnings will decrease with each unit of the new product sold.

Cannibalisation refers to a dynamic in which one product of a firm takes share from one or more other products of *the same firm*. When a product takes sales from a competitor's product, that is not cannibalisation ... though managers sometimes incorrectly state that their new products are "cannibalising" sales of a competitor's goods.

Though it is not cannibalisation, the impact of a new product on the sales of competing goods is an important consideration in a product launch. One simple assumption about how the introduction of a new product might affect the sales of existing products is called "fair share draw".

> **Fair share draw:** **The assumption that a new product will capture sales (in unit or money terms) from existing products in direct proportion to the market shares held by those existing products.**

Example Three rivals compete in the youth fashion market in a small town in the US. Their sales and market shares for last year appear in the following table.

Firm	Sales	Share
Threadbare	$500,000	50%
Too Cool for School	$300,000	30%
Tommy Hitchhiker	$200,000	20%
Total	$1,000,000	100%

A new entrant is expected to enter the market in the coming year and to generate $300,000 in sales. Two-thirds of those sales are expected to come at the expense of the three established competitors. Under an assumption of fair share draw, how much will each firm sell next year?

If the new firm takes two-thirds of its sales from existing competitors, then this "capture" of sales will total (2/3) * $300,000, or $200,000. Under fair share draw, the breakdown of that $200,000 will be proportional to the shares of the current competitors. Thus 50% of the $200,000 will come from Threadbare, 30% from Too Cool, and 20% from Tommy. The following table shows the projected sales and market shares next year of the four competitors under the fair share draw assumption:

Firm	Sales	Share
Threadbare	$400,000	36.36%
Too Cool for School	$240,000	21.82%
Tommy Hitchhiker	$160,000	14.55%
New entrant	$300,000	27.27%
Total	$1,100,000	100%

Notice that the new entrant expands the market by $100,000, an amount equal to the sales of the new entrant that *do not* come at the expense of existing competitors. Notice also that under fair share draw, the relative shares of the existing competitors remain unchanged. For example, Threadbare's share, relative to the total of the original three competitors, is 36.36/(36.36 + 21.82 + 14.55), or 50% – equal to its share before the entry of the new competitor.

Data sources, complications and cautions

As noted previously, in cannibalisation, one of a firm's products takes sales from one or more of *that* firm's other products. Sales taken from the products of competitors are not "cannibalised" sales, though some managers label them as such.

Cannibalisation rates depend on how the features, pricing, promotion and distribution of the new product compare to those of a firm's existing products. The greater the similarity of their respective marketing strategies, the higher the cannibalisation rate is likely to be.

Although cannibalisation is always an issue when a firm launches a new product that competes with its established line, this dynamic is particularly damaging to the firm's profitability when a low-margin entrant captures sales from the firm's higher-margin offerings. In such cases, the new product's weighted contribution margin can be negative. Even when cannibalisation rates are significant, however, and even if the net effect on the bottom line is negative, it may be wise for a firm to proceed with a new product if management believes that the original line is losing its competitive strength. The following example is illustrative.

Example A producer of powdered-milk formula in the US has an opportunity to introduce a new, improved formula. The new formula has certain attributes not found in the firm's existing products. Due to higher costs, however, it will carry a contribution margin of only $8, compared with the $10 margin of the established formula. Analysis suggests that the unit cannibalisation rate of the new formula will be 90% in its initial year. If the firm expects to sell 300 units of the new formula in its first year, should it proceed with the introduction?

Analysis shows that the new formula will generate $8 * 300, or $2,400 in direct contribution. Cannibalisation, however, will reduce contribution from the established line by $10 * 0.9 * 300, or $2,700. Thus, the company's overall contribution will decline by $300 with the introduction of the new formula. (Note also that the weighted unit margin for the new product is −$1.) This simple analysis suggests that the new formula should not be introduced.

The following table, however, contains the results of a more detailed four-year analysis. Reflected in this table are management's beliefs that without the new formula, sales of the regular formula will decline to 700 units in Year 4. In addition, unit sales of the new formula are expected to increase to 600 in Year 4, while cannibalisation rates decline to 60%.

	Year 1	Year 2	Year 3	Year 4	Total
Unit sales of standard formula *without* new product launch	1,000	900	800	700	3,400
		—		—	
Unit sales of new formula	300	400	500	600	1,800
Cannibalisation rate	90%	80%	70%	60%	—
Unit sales of standard formula *with* new product launch	730	580	450	340	2,100

Without the new formula, total four-year contribution is projected as $10 * 3,400, or $34,000. With the new formula, total contribution is projected as ($8 * 1,800) + ($10 * 2,100), or $35,400. Although forecast contribution is lower in Year 1 with the new formula than without it, total four-year contribution is projected to be higher with the new product due to increases in new-formula sales and decreases in the cannibalisation rate.

Brand equity metrics

> The value of a brand represents crucial information for a marketer. But it is quite difficult to measure. The metrics presented in this section will help marketers gain a deeper understanding of that most important intangible asset – the brand. Some of the models presented are proprietary; others are in the general domain. Commonly used models include the following:
> **Y&R brand asset valuator**
> **Interbrand's brand valuation model**

Purpose: to measure the value of a brand

There are a number of ways to assign a monetary value to one or more brands. If the owner of a brand portfolio has recently been acquired, then the goodwill component of its acquisition price may shed some light on the valuation of its brands.

Goodwill is the amount paid to acquire a company, in excess of the value of the tangible and measurable assets of the firm.

Marketers use various techniques in contemplating the value of a brand. Conjoint analysis, for example, can be used to estimate the worth of a brand from the customer's perspective (see next section). Brand equity metrics have also been proposed by several academic researchers. Some have been developed by commercial suppliers of market research data. Two commercial suppliers that have created widely used and influential measures of brand equity are Interbrand and the Young & Rubicam advertising agency (Y&R). Academic authorities on brand equity include David Aaker and Kevin Keller. Bill Moran has proposed interesting ways to capture three important aspects of brand equity – additional volume (market share), additional price premium, and loyalty (retention rates) – in a single index. Ailawadi et al. (2003) have developed and validated a measure of brand equality based on comparisons with private labels.

Construction

Y&R brand asset valuator

The BAV involves surveys of consumers regarding their beliefs and attitudes concerning brands.[2] Y&R maintains that four major dimensions dominate consumers' beliefs about brands. These include perceived differentiation in the market, relevance to consumer lifestyles, the esteem in which consumers hold the brand, and the perceived degree of knowledge of the brand that consumers possess. These four measures, Y&R claims, can help assess the strength and trends of brands. Stronger brands attain high values across all four measures. Growing brands show higher values for differentiation and relevance. Declining brands show relatively higher values for esteem and knowledge. Although these are proprietary scales, the concepts behind them have developed broad appeal and can be assessed through marketer judgements about a given brand relative to its competition.

Leon Ramsellar,[3] of Philips Consumer Electronics, reported using four key measures in evaluating brand equity and offered sample questions for assessing them:

- **Uniqueness:** Does this product offer something new to me?
- **Relevance:** Is this product relevant for me?
- **Attractiveness:** Do I want this product?
- **Credibility:** Do I believe in the product?

David Aaker's brand equity ten

This brand evaluation technique uses 10 (separate metrics for price and distribution coverage would raise the count to 11) unweighted tracking measures to diagnose brand strength: differentiation, satisfaction/loyalty, perceived quality, leadership/popularity, perceived value, brand personality, organisational associations, brand awareness, market share, market price and distribution coverage.[4]

This tool looks at year-on-year changes and relies on the combination of effective market share, relative price and durability (loyalty index).[5]

Brand equity methodology (Moran) (I) = Effective market share (%)
* Relative price (I)

* Durability (loyalty index) (I)

Effective market share is equal to the share of a market segment, weighted by that segment's percentage of brand sales. The higher the market share, the stronger the brand is assumed to be.

Relative price, also known as price premium (see pages 198–203), is the price of a product, divided by the average price in the market. Price indexes above 1 represent a price premium and a strong brand. If a brand receives a score of less than 1 along this dimension, it is selling at a discount and is deemed a weaker brand.

Ailawadi has published two very useful articles on using price and volume (sales) premiums to assess brand equity. In one, she cautions that for some marketers (such as discount department stores and low-price airlines), a price premium will not be a particularly useful indicator of brand equity.

Durability/loyalty can be calculated by considering how many of a brand's customers will repeat in the next year. A score of 1 indicates that all will repurchase, and the brand is assumed to enjoy strong loyalty within its customer base.

Example ILLI is a tonic drink that focuses on two geographic markets – eastern and western US metropolitan areas. In its western market, which represents 60% of ILLI's sales, the drink has a 30% share of the market. In the eastern market, ILLI has a 50% share of the market.

Effective market share is equal to the shares of the segments, weighted by the percentages of brand sales.

West = 30% * 60% = 0.18

East = 50% * 40% = 0.20

Effective market share = 0.38

Half of the people who purchase ILLI this year are expected to repeat next year, generating a loyalty index of 0.5. (Refer to pages 92–105 for a definition of repeat rates.)

The average price for tonic drinks in the market is $2.00, but ILLI enjoys a slight premium. It generally sells for $2.50. This yields a relative price of $2.50/$2.00, or $1.25.

With this information, ILLI's brand equity index can be calculated as follows:

Brand equity = Effective market share $*$ Relative price $*$ Durability/loyalty index

$$= 0.38 * 1.25 * 0.5$$

$$= 0.2375$$

On the basis of this brand equity index, a marketer could use the size of the market or the price of the brand, compared to the price of a private label good, to estimate the value of the brand.

Interbrand's brand valuation model

This proprietary measure is designed to separate tangible product value from intangible brand value. A figure for earnings associated with the brand is isolated by removing estimated earnings attributable to tangible assets from total earnings. Thus, this measure draws upon financial analyses or residual earnings forecasts, as well as market analysis of the role of brands in creating those earnings, in order to estimate the portion of profits attributable to the brands. This portion of profits is then combined with growth and discount rates (the latter also depend on the strength of the brand) to estimate a value for the brand. As most steps in this process are proprietary, this is, of necessity, only a general description.[6]

Data sources, complications and cautions

The methods described previously represent experts' best attempts to place a value on a very elusive entity. Almost all the metrics in this book are relevant to brand equity along one dimension or another.

Related metrics and concepts

Conjoint analysis

The value of a brand can be assessed through conjoint analysis (see next section). In performing such analysis, marketers simply need to treat brand as they would any other attribute of a product or service.

Conjoint utilities and consumer preference

Conjoint utilities measure consumer preference for an attribute level and then – by combining the valuations of multiple attributes – measure preference for an overall choice. Measures are generally made on an individual basis, although this analysis can also be performed on a segment level. In the frozen pizza market, for example, conjoint utilities can be used to determine how much a customer values superior taste (one attribute) versus paying extra for premium cheese (a second attribute).

Conjoint utilities can also play a role in analysing compensatory and non-compensatory decisions. Weaknesses in compensatory factors can be made up in other attributes. A weakness in a non-compensatory factor cannot be overcome by other strengths.

Conjoint analysis can be useful in determining what customers really want and – when price is included as an attribute – what they'll pay for it. In launching new products, marketers find such analyses useful for achieving a deeper understanding of the values that customers place on various product attributes. Throughout product management, conjoint utilities can help marketers focus their efforts on the attributes of greatest importance to customers.

Purpose: to understand what customers want

Conjoint analysis is a method used to estimate customers' preferences, based on how customers weight the attributes on which a choice is made. The premise of conjoint analysis is that a customer's preference between product options can be broken into a set of attributes that are weighted to form an overall evaluation. Rather than asking people directly what they want and why, in conjoint analysis, marketers ask people about their overall preferences for a set of choices described on their attributes and then decompose those into the component dimensions and weights underlying them. A model can be developed to compare sets of attributes to determine which represents the most appealing bundle of attributes for customers.

Conjoint analysis is a technique commonly used to assess the attributes of a product or service that are important to targeted customers and to assist in the following:

- product design
- advertising copy
- pricing
- segmentation
- forecasting.

Construction

> Conjoint analysis: **A method of estimating customers by assessing the overall preferences customers assign to alternative choices.**

An individual's preference can be expressed as the total of his or her baseline preferences for any choice, plus the partworths (relative values) for that choice expressed by the individual.

In linear form, this can be represented by the following formula:

Conjoint preference linear form (I) = [Partworth of attribute1 to individual (I) * Attribute level (1)] + [Partworth of attribute2 to individual (I) * Attribute level (2)] + [Partworth of attribute3 to individual (I) * Attribute level (3)] + etc.

Example Two attributes of a mobile phone, its price and its size, are ranked through conjoint analysis, yielding the results shown in Table 4.5.

This could be read as follows:

Table 4.5 Conjoint analysis: price and size of a mobile phone

Attribute	Rank	Partworth
Price	£50	0.9
Price	£100	0.1
Price	£200	−1
Size	Small	0.7
Size	Medium	−0.1
Size	Large	−0.6

A small phone for £50 has a partworth to customers of 1.6 (derived as 0.9 + 0.7). This is the highest result observed in this exercise. A small but expensive (£200) phone is rated as −0.3 (that is, −1 + 0.7). The desirability of this small phone is offset by its price. A large, expensive phone is least desirable to customers, generating a partworth of −1.6 (that is, (−1) + (−0.6)).

On this basis, we determine that the customer whose views are analysed here would prefer a medium-size phone at £100 (utility = 0) to a small phone at £200 (utility = −0.3). Such information would be instrumental to decisions concerning the trade-offs between product design and price.

This analysis also demonstrates that, within the ranges examined, price is more important than size from the perspective of this consumer. Price generates a range of effects from 0.9 to −1 (that is, a total spread of 1.9), while the effects generated by the most and least desirable sizes span a range only from 0.7 to −0.6 (total spread = 1.3).

Compensatory versus non-compensatory consumer decisions

A compensatory decision process is one in which a customer evaluates choices with the perspective that strengths along one or more dimensions can compensate for weaknesses along others.

In a non-compensatory decision process, by contrast, if certain attributes of a product are weak, no compensation is possible, even if the product possesses strengths along other dimensions. In the previous mobile phone example, for instance, some customers may feel that if a phone were greater than a certain size, no price would make it attractive.

In another example, most people choose a grocery store on the basis of proximity. Any store within a certain radius of home or work may be considered. Beyond that distance, however, all stores will be excluded from consideration, and there is nothing a store can do to overcome this. Even if it posts extraordinarily low prices, offers a stunningly wide assortment, creates great displays and stocks the freshest foods, for example, a store will not entice consumers to travel 400 miles to buy their groceries.

Although this example is extreme to the point of absurdity, it illustrates an important point: when consumers make a choice on a non-compensatory basis, marketers need to define the dimensions along which certain attributes *must* be delivered, simply to qualify for consideration of their overall offering.

One form of non-compensatory decision-making is elimination by aspect. In this approach, consumers look at an entire set of choices and then eliminate those that do not meet their expectations in the order of the importance of the attributes. In the selection of a grocery store, for example, this process might run as follows:

- Which stores are within 5 miles of my home?
- Which ones are open after 8 p.m.?
- Which carry the spicy mustard that I like?
- Which carry fresh flowers?

The process continues until only one choice is left.

In the ideal situation, in analysing customers' decision processes, marketers would have access to information on an individual level, revealing:

- whether the decision for each customer is compensatory or not
- the priority order of the attributes

- the "cut-off" levels for each attribute
- the relative importance weight of each attribute if the decision follows a compensatory process.

More frequently, however, marketers have access only to past behaviour, helping them make inferences regarding these items.

In the absence of detailed, individual information for customers throughout a market, conjoint analysis provides a means to gain insight into the decision-making processes of a sampling of customers. In conjoint analysis, we generally assume a compensatory process. That is, we assume utilities are additive. Under this assumption, if a choice is weak along one dimension (for example, if a store does not carry spicy mustard), it can compensate for this with strength along another (for example, it does carry fresh-cut flowers) at least in part. Conjoint analyses can approximate a non-compensatory model by assigning non-linear weighting to an attribute across certain levels of its value. For example, the weightings for distance to a grocery store might run as follows:

Within 1 mile:	0.9
1–5 miles away:	0.8
5–10 miles away:	−0.8
More than 10 miles away:	−0.9

In this example, stores outside a 5-mile radius cannot practically make up the loss of utility they incur as a result of distance. Distance becomes, in effect, a non-compensatory dimension.

By studying customers' decision-making processes, marketers gain insight into the attributes needed to meet consumer expectations. They learn, for example, whether certain attributes are compensatory or non-compensatory. A strong understanding of customers' valuation of different attributes also enables marketers to tailor products and allocate resources effectively.

Several potential complications arise in considering compensatory versus non-compensatory decisions. Customers often don't know whether an attribute is compensatory or not, and they may not be readily able to explain their decisions. Therefore, it is often necessary either to infer a customer's decision-making process or to determine that process through an evaluation of choices, rather than a description of the process.

It is possible, however, to uncover non-compensatory elements through conjoint analysis. Any attribute for which the valuation spread is so high that it cannot practically be made up by other features is, in effect, a non-compensatory attribute.

Example Among grocery stores, Juan prefers the Balzano market because it's close to his home, despite the fact that Balzano's prices are generally higher than those at the local Shoprite store. A third store, Vernon's, is located in Juan's apartment complex. But Juan avoids it because Vernon's doesn't carry his favourite soft drink.

From this information, we know that Juan's shopping choice is influenced by at least three factors: price, distance from his home, and whether a store carries his favourite soft drink. In Juan's decision process, price and distance seem to be compensating factors. He trades price for distance. Whether the soft drink is stocked seems to be a non-compensatory factor. If a store doesn't carry Juan's favourite soft drink, it will not win his business, regardless of how well it scores on price and location.

Data sources, complications and cautions

Prior to conducting a conjoint study, it is necessary to identify the attributes of importance to a customer. Focus groups are commonly used for this purpose. After attributes and levels are determined, a typical approach to conjoint analysis is to use a fractional factorial orthogonal design, which is a partial sample of all possible combinations of attributes. This is to reduce the total number of choice evaluations required by the respondent. With an orthogonal design, the attributes remain independent of one another, and the test doesn't weigh one attribute disproportionately to another.

There are multiple ways to gather data, but a straightforward approach would be to present respondents with choices and to ask them to rate those choices according to their preferences. These preferences then become the dependent variable in a regression, in which attribute levels serve as the independent variables, as in the previous equation. Conjoint utilities constitute the weights determined to best capture the preference ratings provided by the respondent.

Often, certain attributes work in tandem to influence customer choice. For example, a fast *and* sleek sports car may provide greater value to a customer than would be suggested by the sum of the fast and sleek attributes. Such relationships between attributes are not captured by a simple conjoint model, unless one accounts for interactions.

Ideally, conjoint analysis is performed on an individual level because attributes can be weighted differently across individuals. Marketers can also create a more balanced view by performing the analysis across a sample of individuals. It is appropriate to perform the analysis within consumer segments that have similar weights. Conjoint analysis can be viewed as a snapshot in time of a customer's desires. It will not necessarily translate indefinitely into the future.

It is vital to use the correct attributes in any conjoint study. People can only tell you their preferences within the parameters you set. If the correct attributes are not included in a study, while it may be possible to determine the relative importance of those attributes that *are* included, and it may technically be possible to form segments on the basis of the resulting data, the analytic results may not be valid for forming *useful* segments. For example, in a conjoint analysis of consumer preferences regarding colours and styles of cars, one may correctly group customers as to their feelings about these attributes. But if consumers really care most about engine size, then those segmentations will be of little value.

Segmentation using conjoint utilities

> Understanding customers' desires is a vital goal of marketing. Segmenting, or clustering similar customers into groups, can help managers recognise useful patterns and identify attractive subsets within a larger market. With that understanding, managers can select target markets, develop appropriate offerings for each, determine the most effective ways to reach the targeted segments and allocate resources accordingly. Conjoint analysis can be highly useful in this exercise.

Purpose: to identify segments based on conjoint utilities

As described in the previous section, conjoint analysis is used to determine customers' preferences on the basis of the attribute weightings that they reveal in their decision-making processes. These weights, or utilities, are generally evaluated on an individual level.

Segmentation entails the grouping of customers who demonstrate similar patterns of preference and weighting with regard to certain product attributes, distinct from the patterns exhibited by other groups. Using segmentation, a company can decide which group(s) to target and can determine an approach to appeal to the segment's members. After segments have been formed, a company can set strategy based on their attractiveness (size, growth, purchase rate, diversity) and on its own capability to serve these segments, relative to competitors.

Construction

To complete a segmentation based on conjoint utilities, one must first determine utility scores at an individual customer level. Next, one must cluster these customers into segments of like-minded individuals. This is generally done through a methodology known as cluster analysis.

> Cluster analysis: **A technique that calculates the distances between customers and forms groups by minimising the differences within each group and maximising the differences between groups.**

Cluster analysis operates by calculating a "distance" (a sum of squares) between individuals and, in a hierarchical fashion, starts pairing those individuals together. The process of pairing minimises the "distance" within a group and creates a manageable number of segments within a larger population.

Example The Samson-Finn Company has three customers. In order to help manage its marketing efforts, Samson-Finn wants to organise like-minded customers into segments. Toward that end, it performs a conjoint analysis in which it measures its customers' preferences among products that are either reliable or very reliable, either fast or very fast (see Table 4.6). It then considers the conjoint utilities of each of its customers to see which of them demonstrate similar wants. When clustering on conjoint data, the distances would be calculated on the partworths.

Table 4.6 Customer conjoint utilities

	Very reliable	Reliable	Very fast	Fast
Bob	0.4	0.3	0.6	0.2
Erin	0.9	0.1	0.2	0.7
Yogesh	0.3	0.3	0.5	0.2

The analysis looks at the difference between Bob's view and Erin's view on the importance of reliability on their choice. Bob's score is 0.4 and Erin's is 0.9. We can square the difference between these to derive the "distance" between Bob and Erin.

Using this methodology, the distance between each pair of Samson-Finn's customers can be calculated as follows:

Distances	Very reliable	Reliable	Very fast	Fast
Bob and Erin:	$= (0.4 - 0.9)^2$	$+ (0.3 - 0.1)^2$	$+ (0.6 - 0.2)^2$	$+ (0.2 - 0.7)^2$
	$= 0.25$	$+ 0.04$	$+ 0.16$	$+ 0.25$
	$= 0.7$			
Bob and Yogesh:	$= (0.4 - 0.3)^2$	$+ (0.3 - 0.3)^2$	$+ (0.6 - 0.5)^2$	$+ (0.2 - 0.2)^2$
	$= 0.01$	$+ 0.0$	$+ 0.01$	$+ 0.0$
	$= 0.02$			
Erin and Yogesh:	$= (0.9 - 0.3)^2$	$+ (0.1 - 0.3)^2$	$+ (0.2 - 0.5)^2$	$+ (0.7 + 0.2)^2$
	$= 0.36$	$+ 0.04$	$+ 0.09$	$+ 0.25$
	$= 0.74$			

On this basis, Bob and Yogesh appear to be very close to each other because their sum of squares is 0.02. As a result, they should be considered part of the same segment. Conversely, in light of the high sum-of-squares distance established by her preferences, Erin should not be considered a part of the same segment with either Bob or Yogesh.

Of course, most segmentation analyses are performed on large customer bases. This example merely illustrates the process involved in the cluster analysis calculations.

Data sources, complications and cautions

As noted previously, a customer's utilities may not be stable, and the segment to which a customer belongs can shift over time or across occasions. An individual might belong to one segment for personal air travel, in which price might be a major factor, and another for business travel, in which convenience might become more important. Such a customer's conjoint weights (utilities) would differ depending on the purchase occasion.

Determining the appropriate *number* of segments for an analysis can be somewhat arbitrary. There is no generally accepted statistical means for determining the "correct" number of segments. Ideally, marketers look for a segment structure that fulfils the following qualifications:

- Each segment constitutes a homogeneous group, within which there is relatively little variance between attribute utilities of different individuals.

- Groupings are heterogeneous across segments; that is, there is a wide variance of attribute utilities *between* segments.

Conjoint utilities and volume projection

> The conjoint utilities of products and services can be used to forecast the market share that each will achieve and the volume that each will sell. Marketers can project market share for a given product or service on the basis of the proportion of individuals who select it from a relevant choice set, as well as its overall utility.

Purpose: to use conjoint analysis to project the market share and the sales volume that will be achieved by a product or service

Conjoint analysis is used to measure the utilities for a product. The combination of these utilities, generally additive, represents a scoring of sorts for the expected popularity of that product. These scores can be used to rank products. However, further information is needed to estimate market share. One can anticipate that the top-ranked product in a selection set will have a greater probability of being chosen by an individual than products ranked lower for that individual. Adding the number of customers who rank the brand first should allow the calculation of customer share.

Data sources, complications and cautions

To complete a sales volume projection, it is necessary to have a full conjoint analysis. This analysis must include all the important features according to which consumers make their choice. Defining the "market" is clearly crucial to a meaningful result.

To define a market, it is important to identify all the choices in that market. Calculating the percentage of "first choice" selections for each alternative merely provides a "share of preferences". To extend this to market share, one must estimate (1) the volume of sales per customer, (2) the level of distribution or availability for each choice, and (3) the percentage of customers who will defer their purchase until they can find their first choice.

The greatest potential error in this process would be to exclude meaningful attributes from the conjoint analysis.

Network effects can also distort a conjoint analysis. In some instances, customers do not make purchase decisions purely on the basis of a product's attributes but are also affected by its level of acceptance in the marketplace. Such network effects, and the importance of harnessing or overcoming them, are especially evident during shifts in technology industries.

References and suggested further reading

Aaker, D.A. (1991). *Managing Brand Equity: Capitalizing on the Value of a Brand Name*, New York: The Free Press.

Aaker, D.A. (1996). *Building Strong Brands*, New York: The Free Press.

Aaker, D.A. and J.M. Carman. (1982). "Are You Overadvertising?" *Journal of Advertising Research*, 22(4), 57–70.

Aaker, D.A. and K.L. Keller. (1990). "Consumer Evaluations of Brand Extensions", *Journal of Marketing*, 54(1), 27–41.

Ailawadi, K. and K. Keller. (2004). "Understanding Retail Branding: Conceptual Insights and Research Priorities", *Journal of Retailing*, 80(4), 331–342.

Ailawadi, K., D. Lehman and S. Neslin. (2003). "Revenue Premium as an Outcome Measure of Brand Equity", *Journal of Marketing*, 67(4), 1–17.

Bruno, H.A., U. Parthasarathi and N. Singh, eds. (2005). "The Changing Face of Measurement Tools Across the Product Lifecycle", *Does Marketing Measure Up? Performance Metrics: Practices and Impact*, Marketing Science Institute, Conference Summary No. 05-301.

Harvard Business School Case: Nestlé Refrigerated Foods Contadina Pasta & Pizza (A) 9-595-035. Rev. 30 January 1997.

Customer profitability

5

Metrics covered in this chapter:

- Customers, recency and retention

- Customer profit

- Customer lifetime value

- Prospect value versus customer value

- Acquisition versus retention spending

Introduction

Chapter 2, "Share of hearts, minds and markets", presented metrics designed to measure how well the firm is doing with its customers as a whole. Previously discussed metrics were summaries of firm performance with respect to customers for entire markets or market segments. In this chapter, we cover metrics that measure the performance of individual customer relationships. We start with metrics designed to simply count how many customers the firm serves. As this chapter will illustrate, it is far easier to count the number of units sold than to count the number of people or businesses buying those units. The second section introduces the concept of customer profit. Just as some brands are more profitable than others, so too are some customer relationships. Whereas customer profit is a metric that summarises the past financial performance of a customer relationship, customer lifetime value looks forward in an attempt to value existing customer relationships. The third section discusses how to calculate and interpret customer lifetime value. One of the more important uses of customer lifetime value is to inform prospecting decisions. The fourth section explains how this can be accomplished and draws the careful distinction between prospect and customer value. The fifth section discusses acquisition and retention spending; two metrics firms track in order to monitor the performance of these two important kinds of marketing spending:

spending designed to acquire new customers and spending designed to retain and profit from existing customers.

Metric	Construction	Considerations	Purpose
Customers	The number of people (businesses) who bought from the firm during a specified time period.	Avoid double counting people who bought more than one product. Carefully define customer as individual/household/screen-name/division who bought/ordered/registered.	Measure how well the firm is attracting and retaining customers.
Recency	The length of time since a customer's last purchase.	In non-contractual situations, the firm will want to track the recency of its customers.	Track changes in number of active customers.
Retention rate	The ratio of customers retained to the number at risk.	Not to be confused with growth (decline) in customer counts. Retention refers only to existing customers in contractual situations.	Track changes in the ability of the firm to retain customers.
Customer profit	The difference between the revenues earned from and the costs associated with the customer relationship during a specified period.	Requires assigning revenues and costs to individual customers.	Allows the firm to identify which customers are profitable and which are not ... as a precursor to differential treatment designed to improve firm profitability.

Metric	Construction	Considerations	Purpose
Customer lifetime value	The present value of the future cash flows attributed to the customer relationship.	Requires a projection of future cash flows from a customer relationship. This will be easier to do in a contractual situation. Formulations of CLV differ with respect to the treatment of the initial margin and acquisition spending.	Customer relationship management decisions should be made with the objective of improving CLV. Acquisition budgeting should be based on CLV.
Prospect lifetime value	The response rate times the sum of the initial margin and the CLV of the acquired customer minus the cost of the prospecting effort.	There are a variety of equivalent ways to do the calculations necessary to see whether a prospecting effort is worthwhile.	To guide the firm's prospecting decisions. Prospecting is beneficial only if the expected prospect lifetime value is positive.
Average acquisition cost	The ratio of acquisition spending to the number of new customers acquired.	It is often difficult to isolate acquisition spending from total marketing spending.	To track the cost of acquiring new customers and to compare that cost to the value of the newly acquired customers.
Average retention cost	The ratio of retention spending to the number of customers retained.	It is often difficult to isolate retention spending from total marketing spending. The average retention cost number is not very useful to help make retention budgeting decisions.	To monitor retention spending on a per-customer basis.

Customers, recency and retention

These three metrics are used to count customers and track customer activity irrespective of the number of transactions (or monetary value of those transactions) made by each customer.

A customer is a person or business that buys from the firm.

- **Customer counts:** *These are the number of customers of a firm for a specified time period.*
- **Recency:** *This refers to the length of time since a customer's last purchase. A six-month customer is someone who purchased from the firm at least once within the last six months.*
- **Retention rate:** *This is the ratio of the number of retained customers to the number at risk.*

In contractual situations, it makes sense to talk about the number of customers currently under contract and the percentage retained when the contract period runs out.

In non-contractual situations (such as catalogue sales), it makes less sense to talk about the *current* number of customers, but instead to count the number of customers of a specified recency.

Purpose: to monitor firm performance in attracting and retaining customers

Only recently have most marketers worried about developing metrics that focus on individual customers. In order to begin to think about managing individual customer relationships, the firm must first be able to count its customers. Although consistency in counting customers is probably more important than formulating a precise definition, a definition is needed nonetheless. In particular, we think the definition of and the counting of customers will be different in contractual versus non-contractual situations.

Construction

Counting customers

In contractual situations, it should be fairly easy to count how many customers are currently under contract at any point in time. For instance, Vodafone Australia,[1] a global mobile phone company, was able to report 2.6 million direct customers at the end of the December quarter.

One complication in counting customers in contractual situations is the handling of contracts that cover two or more individuals. Does a family plan that includes five phones but one bill count as one or five? Does a business-to-business contract with one base fee and charges for each of 1,000 phones in use count as one or 1,000 customers? Does the answer to the previous question depend on whether the individual users pay Vodafone, pay their company or pay nothing? In situations such as these, the firm must select some standard definition of a customer (policy holder, member) and implement it consistently.

A second complication in counting customers in contractual situations is the treatment of customers with multiple contracts with a single firm. USAA, a global insurance and diversified financial services association, provides insurance and financial services to the US military community and their families. Each customer is considered a member, complete with a unique membership number. This allows USAA to know exactly how many members it has at any time – more than five million at the end of 2004 – most of whom avail themselves of a variety of member services.

For other financial services companies, however, counts are often listed separately for each line of business. The 2003 annual report for State Farm Insurance, for example, lists a total of 73.9 million policies and accounts with a pie chart showing the percentage breakdown among car, home-owners, life, annuities and so on. Clearly the 73.9 million is a count of policies and not customers. Presumably because some customers use State Farm for car, home and life insurance, they get double and even triple counted in the 73.9 million number. Because State Farm knows the names and addresses of all their policyholders, it seems feasible that they could count how many individual customers they serve. The fact that State Farm counts policies and not customers suggests an emphasis on selling policies rather than managing customer relationships.

Finally, we offer an example of a natural gas company that went out of its way to double count customers – defining a customer to be "a consumer of natural gas distributed in any one billing period at one location through one meter. An entity using gas at separate locations is considered a separate customer at each location." For this natural gas company, customers were synonymous with meters. This is probably a great way to view things if your job is to install and service meters. It is not such a great way to view things if your job is to market natural gas.

In non-contractual situations, the ability of the firm to count customers depends on whether individual customers are identifiable. If customers are not identifiable, firms can only count visits or transactions. Because Wal-Mart does not identify its shoppers, its customer counts are nothing more than the number of transactions that go through the cash registers in a day, week or year. These "traffic" counts are akin to turnstile numbers at sporting events and visits to a website. In one sense they count people, but when summed over several periods, they no longer measure separate individuals. So whereas home attendance at US baseball team Atlanta Braves games in 1993 was 3,884,720, the number of people attending one or more Braves games that year was some smaller number.[2]

In non-contractual situations with identifiable customers (direct mail, retailers with frequent shopper cards, warehouse clubs, purchases of hire cars and lodging that require registration), a complication is that customer purchase activity is sporadic. Whereas the *Independent* knows exactly how many *current* customers (subscribers) it has, the sporadic buying of catalogue retailer Littlewoods customers means that it makes no sense to talk about the number of *current* Littlewoods customers. Littlewoods will know the number of orders it receives daily, it will know the number of catalogues it mails monthly, but it cannot be expected to know the number of current customers it has because it is difficult to define a "current" customer.

Instead, firms in non-contractual situations count how many customers have bought within a certain period of time. This is the concept of recency – the length of time since the last purchase. Customers of recency one year or less are customers who bought within the last year. Firms in non-contractual situations with identifiable customers will count customers of various recencies.

> Recency: **The length of time since a customer's last purchase.**

For example, eBay reported 60.5 million active users in the first quarter of 2005. Active users were defined as the number of users of the eBay platform who bid, bought, or listed an item within the previous 12-month period. They go on to report that 45.1 million active users were reported in the same period a year ago.

Notice that eBay counts "active users" rather than "customers" and uses the concept of recency to track its number of active users across time. The number of active (12-month) users increased from 45.1 million to 60.5 million in one year. This tells the firm that the number of active customers increased due in part to customer acquisition. A measure of how well the firm maintained existing customer relationships is the percentage of the 45.1 million active customers one year ago who were active in the previous 12 months. That ratio measure is similar to retention in that it reflects the percentage of active customers who remained active in the subsequent period.

Retention

Applies to contractual situations in which customers are either retained or not. Customers either renew their magazine subscriptions or let them run out. Customers maintain a current account with a bank until they close it. Renters pay rent until they move out. These are examples of pure customer retention situations where customers are either retained or considered lost for good.

In these situations, firms pay close attention to retention rates.

> Retention rate: **The ratio of the number of customers retained to the number at risk.**

If 40,000 subscriptions to *Fortune* magazine are set to expire in July and the publisher convinces 26,000 of those customers to renew, we would say that the publisher retained 65% of its subscribers.

The complement of retention is attrition or churn. The attrition or churn rate for the 40,000 *Fortune* subscribers was 35%.

Notice that this definition of retention is a ratio of the number retained to the number at risk (of not being retained). The key feature of this definition is that a customer must be at risk of leaving in order to be counted as a customer successfully retained. This means that new *Fortune* subscribers obtained during July are not part of the equation, nor are the large number of customers whose subscriptions were set to run out in later months.

Finally, we point out that it sometimes makes better sense to measure retention in "customer time" rather than "calendar time". Rather than ask what the firm's retention rate was in 2004, it may be more informative to ask what percentage of customers surviving for three years were retained throughout Year 4.

Data sources, complications and cautions

The ratio of the total number of customers at the end of the period to the number of customers at the beginning of the period is not a retention rate. Retention during the period does affect this ratio, but customer acquisitions also affect the ratio.

The percentage of customers starting the period who remained customers throughout the period is a lot closer to being a retention rate. This percentage would be a true retention rate if all the customers starting the period were at risk of leaving during the period.

Advice on counting customers[3]

Defining the customer properly is critical

Marketers tend to count "customers" in ways that are easy and consequently get the wrong answers. They tend to gloss over the fundamental and critically important step of *defining the customer*. With the wrong definition, counting doesn't matter.

Banks look at "households" because they are "relationship" obsessed (*relationship* being defined as the number of products sold to customers with a common account address). Banks tend to emphasise the number of products sold. No matter that the household may contain a business owner with nearly all the accounts, a spouse who banks mostly elsewhere and children who do not bank at all. "Household" in this situation is meaningless. There are at least three "customers" here: business owner (a great customer), spouse (almost a non-customer) and children (definitely non-customers).

Retailers count transactions or "tickets" (cash register receipts), which may cover stuff sold to Mum, Dad and the kids, along with Aunt Mary and neighbour Sue. Or it may reflect a purchase by a spouse who is buying for his or her partner under specific instructions. In this circumstance, the spouse is the real customer, with the other taking on the role of dogsbody.

Defining the customer is nearly always hard because it requires a clear understanding of both business strategy and buyer behaviour.

▶

Not all "customers" are the same

Attracting and retaining "customers" cannot be measured for management action purposes without understanding the differences between customers. Last year, a major software firm we will call Zapp bought a single copy of a piece of software. Another company we will call Tancat bought 100 copies. Are these both "customers"? Of course not. Tancat is almost certainly a customer that needs to be retained and possibly expanded into other products. Zapp is probably just evaluating the product in order to stay on top of new software concepts and potentially copy it. One option is to follow up with Zapp with their one-copy purchase to see what is really going on. Zapp could become a great "customer" if we understand what motivated their purchase or if we use that purchase to gain a contact base.

Before you count anything, you have to segment your *potential and current* product or service users into groups that can be strategically addressed. Some current buyers like Zapp are actually potential buyers in terms of what you should do about them. You must count buyers and prospects who are *alike* in defined ways.

Where is the "customer"?

Large customers often buy independently from each user location. Is HSBC the customer, or is each branch office a customer? If Halifax were to buy centrally, how could you count it as one customer while HSBC counts as hundreds of customers?

Who is the "customer"?

Defining *who* is the customer is even trickier. Many "customers" are not those who place the order with your salespeople. The real customer is deep within the bowels of the buyer organisation, someone who may take a great deal of effort to even identify. The account name may be GM, but the real customer may be Burt Cipher, an engineer in some unknown facility. Or, the Ford buyer may have consolidated orders from several individuals scattered across the country. In this case, Ford is not the customer for anything but billing purposes. So, what do you count?

Even more common is the multi-headed customer. Buying decisions are made by several people. Different people may be central to a decision at different times or for different products. Big companies have sales teams dedicated to selling into such buying groups. Although they may be counted as a single customer, the dynamics of their buying decision is substantially more complicated than decisions made by a single individual.

Apparel retailers who sell pre-teen clothing have at least two customers: Mum and the pre-teen wearer. Do you count one or both as customers? Marketing might want to treat each as a customer for deciding how to design and place ads. The store might treat them both as a single customer or choose the pre-teen as their target.

The key thing to remember is that customer definition for counting depends fundamentally on the purpose of the count. You may have to count the same "customer" in different ways for different purposes. There is no universal customer definition.

Customer profit

Customer profit (CP) is the profit the firm makes from serving a customer or customer group over a specified period of time.

Calculating customer profitability is an important step in understanding which customer relationships are better than others. Often, the firm will find that some customer relationships are unprofitable. The firm may be better off (more profitable) without these customers. At the other end, the firm will identify its most profitable customers and be in a position to take steps to ensure the continuation of these most profitable relationships.

Purpose: to identify the profitability of individual customers

Companies commonly look at their performance in aggregate. A common phrase within a company is something like: "We had a good year, and the business units delivered £400,000 in profits." When customers are considered, it is often using an average such as "We made a profit of £2.50 per customer." Although these can be useful metrics, they sometimes disguise an important fact that not all customers are equal and, worse yet, some are unprofitable. Simply put, rather than measuring the "average customer", we can learn a lot by finding out what each customer contributes to our bottom line.[4]

Customer profitability: **The difference between the revenues earned from and the costs associated with the customer relationship during a specified period.**

The overall profitability of the company can be improved by treating dissimilar customers differently.

In essence, think of three different tiers of customer:

1. Top tier customers – REWARD: Your most valuable customers are the ones you most want to retain. They should receive more of your attention than any other group. If you lose these people, your profit suffers the most. Look to reward them in ways other than simply lowering your price. These

customers probably value what you do the most and may not be price-sensitive.

2   Second tier customers – GROW: The customers in the middle – with middle to low profits associated with them – might be targeted for growth. Here you have customers whom you may be able to develop into top tier customers. Look to the share of customer metrics described in the next section to help figure out which customers have the most growth potential.

3   Third tier customers – FIRE: The company loses money on servicing these people. If you cannot easily promote them to the higher tiers of profitability, you should consider charging them more for the services they currently consume. If you can recognise this group beforehand, it may be best not to acquire these customers in the first place.

A database that can analyse the profitability of customers at an individual level can be a competitive advantage. If you can figure out profitability by customer, you have a chance to defend your best customers and maybe even poach the most profitable consumers from your competitors.

Construction

In theory, this is a trouble-free calculation. Find out the cost to serve each customer and the revenues associated with each customer for a given period. Do the subtraction to get profit for the customer and sort the customers based on profit. Although painless in theory, large companies with a multitude of customers will find this a major challenge even with the most sophisticated of databases.

To do the analysis with large databases, it may be necessary to abandon the notion of calculating profit for each individual customer and work with meaningful groups of customers instead.

After you have the sorted list of customer profits (or customer-group profits), the custom is to plot cumulative percentage of total profits versus cumulative percentage of total customers. Given that the customers are sorted from highest to lowest profit, the resulting graph usually looks something like the head of a whale.

Profitability will increase sharply and tail off from the very beginning. (Remember, our customers have been sorted from most to least profitable.) Whenever there are some negative profit customers, the graph reaches a peak – above 100% – as profit per customer moves from positive to negative. As we continue through the negative-profit customers, cumulative profits decrease at an ever-increasing rate. The graph always ends at 100% of the customers accounting for 100% of the total profit.

Robert Kaplan (co-developer of Activity-Based Costing and the Balanced Scorecard) likes to refer to these curves as "whale curves".[5] In Kaplan's experience, the whale curve usually reveals that the most profitable 20% of customers can sometimes generate between 150% and 300% of total profits so that the resulting curve resembles a sperm whale rising above the water's surface. See Figure 5.2 for an example of a whale curve.

Example A catalogue retailer has grouped customers in 10 deciles based on profitability (see Table 5.1 and Figure 5.1). (A decile is a tenth of the population, so 0–10% is the most profitable 10% of customers.)

Table 5.1 Customer profitability ranked by profitability

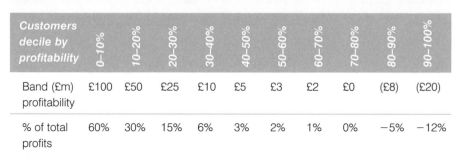

Customers decile by profitability	0–10%	10–20%	20–30%	30–40%	40–50%	50–60%	60–70%	70–80%	80–90%	90–100%
Band (£m) profitability	£100	£50	£25	£10	£5	£3	£2	£0	(£8)	(£20)
% of total profits	60%	30%	15%	6%	3%	2%	1%	0%	−5%	−12%

Here we have a clear illustration that if they were no longer to serve the least profitable 20% of customers, they would be £28 million better off.

Figure 5.1 Customer profitability by decile

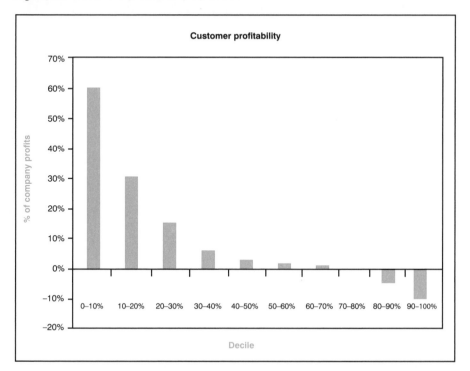

Table 5.2 Cumulative profitability peaks before all customers are served

Customers decile by profitability	0–10%	10–20%	20–30%	30–40%	40–50%	50–60%	60–70%	70–80%	80–90%	90–100%
Cumulative profits	£100	£150	£175	£185	£190	£193	£195	£195	£187	£167
Cumulative profits %	59.9	89.8	104.8	110.8	113.8	115.6	116.8	116.8	112.0	100.0

Table 5.2 presents this same customer information in cumulative form. Cumulative profits plotted across deciles begins to look like a whale with a steeply rising ridge reaching a peak of total profitability above 100% and tapering off thereafter (see Figure 5.2).

Figure 5.2 The whale curve

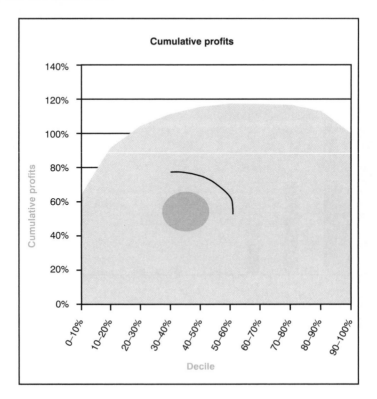

Data sources, complications and cautions

Measuring customer profitability requires detailed information. Assigning revenues to customers is often the easy part; assigning your costs to customers is much harder. The cost of goods sold obviously gets assigned to the customers based on the goods each customer purchased. Assigning the more indirect costs may require the use of some form of activity-based costing (ABC) system. Finally, there may be some categories of costs that will be impossible to assign to the customer. If so, it is probably best to keep these costs as company costs and be content with the customer profit numbers adding up to something less than the total company profit.

When considering the profits from customers, it must be remembered that most things change over time. Customers who were profitable last year may not be profitable this year. Because the whale curve reflects past performance, we must be careful when using it to make decisions that shape the future. For example, we may very well want to continue a relationship that was unprofitable in the past if we know things will change for the better in the future. For example, banks typically offer discount packages to students to gain their business. This may well show low or negative customer profits in the short term. The "plan" is that future profits will compensate for current losses. Customer lifetime value (addressed in the next section) is a forward-looking metric that attempts to account for the anticipated future profitability of each customer relationship.

When capturing customer information to decide which customers to serve, it is important to consider the legal environment in which the company operates. This can change considerably across countries, where there may be anti-discrimination laws and special situations in some industries. For instance, public utilities are sometimes obligated to serve all customers.

It is also worth remembering that intrusive capturing of customer-specific data can damage customer relationships. Some individuals will be put off by excess data gathering. For a food company, it may help to know which of your customers are on a diet. But the food company's management should think twice before adding this question to their next customer survey.

Sometimes there are sound financial reasons for continuing to serve unprofitable customers. For example, some companies rely on network effects. Take the case of the Royal Mail – part of its strength is the ability to deliver to the whole country. It may superficially seem profitable to stop deliveries to remote areas. But when that happens, the service becomes less valuable for all customers. In short, sometimes unprofitable customer relationships are necessary for the firm to maintain their profitable ones.

Similarly, companies with high fixed costs that have been assigned to customers during the construction of customer profit must ask whether those costs will go away if they terminate unprofitable customer relationships. If the costs do not go away, ending unprofitable relationships may only serve to make the surviving relationships look even less profitable (after the reallocation of costs) and result in the lowering of company profits. In short, make certain that the negative profit goes away if the relationship is terminated. Certainly the revenue and cost of goods sold will go away, but if some of the other costs do not, the firm could be better off maintaining a negative profit relationship as it contributes to covering fixed cost (refer to "Variable costs and fixed costs" on pages 70–76 and "Break-even analysis and contribution analysis" on pages 81–85).

Abandoning customers is a very sensitive practice, and a business should always consider the public relations consequences of such actions. Similarly, when you get rid of a customer, you cannot expect to attract them back very easily should they migrate into your profitable segment.

Finally, because the whale curve examines cumulative *percentage* of total profits, the numbers are very sensitive to the financial amount of total profit. When the total financial profit is a small number, it is fairly easy for the most profitable customers to represent a huge *percentage* of that small number. So when you hear that 20% of the firm's customers represent 350% of the firm's profit, one of the first things you should consider is the total monetary value of profits. If that total is small, 350% of it can also be a fairly small number of euros. To cement this idea, ask yourself what the whale curve would look like for a firm with €0 profit.

Customer lifetime value

Customer lifetime value (CLV) is the financial value of a customer relationship based on the present value of the projected future cash flows from the customer relationship.

When margins and retention rates are constant, the following formula can be used to calculate the lifetime value of a customer relationship:

$$\text{Customer lifetime value (£)} = \text{Margin (£)} * \frac{\text{Retention rate (\%)}}{1 + \text{Discount rate (\%)} - \text{Retention rate (\%)}}$$

Customer lifetime value is an important concept in that it encourages firms to shift their focus from quarterly profits to the long-term health of their customer relationships. Customer lifetime value is an important number because it represents an upper limit on spending to acquire new customers.

Purpose: to assess the value of each customer

As Don Peppers and Martha Rogers are fond of saying, "some customers are more equal than others".[6] We saw a vivid illustration of this in the last section, which examined the profitability of individual customer relationships. As we noted, customer profit (CP) is the difference between the revenues and the costs associated with the customer relationship during a specified period. The central difference between CP and customer lifetime value (CLV) is that CP measures the past and

CLV looks forward. As such, CLV can be more useful in shaping managers' decisions but is much more difficult to quantify. Quantifying CP is a matter of carefully reporting and summarising the results of past activity, whereas quantifying CLV involves forecasting future activity.

> Customer lifetime value (CLV): **The present value of the future cash flows attributed to the customer relationship.**

The concept of present value will be talked about in more detail in "Evaluating multiperiod investments" on pages 313–318. For now, you can think of present value as the discounted sum of future cash flows. We discount (multiply by a carefully selected number less than one) future cash flows before we add them together to account for the fact that there is a time value of money. The time value of money is another way of saying that everyone would prefer to get paid sooner rather than later and everyone would prefer to pay later rather than sooner. This is true for individuals (the sooner I get paid, the sooner I can pay off my credit card balance and avoid interest charges) as well as for firms. The exact discount factors used depend on the discount rate chosen (10% per year as an example) and the number of periods until we receive each cash flow (money received 10 years from now must be discounted more than money received five years in the future).

The concept of CLV is nothing more than the concept of present value applied to cash flows attributed to the customer relationship. Because the present value of any stream of future cash flows is designed to measure the single lump sum value today of the future stream of cash flows, CLV will represent the single lump sum value today of the customer relationship. Even more simply, CLV is the financial value of the customer relationship to the firm. It is an upper limit on what the firm would be willing to pay to acquire the customer relationship as well as an upper limit on the amount the firm would be willing to pay to avoid losing the customer relationship. If we view a customer relationship as an asset of the firm, CLV would present the financial value of that asset.

Cohort and incubate

One way to project the value of future customer cash flows is to make the heroic assumption that the customers acquired several periods ago are no better or worse (in terms of their CLV) than the ones we currently acquire. We then go back and collect data on a cohort of customers all acquired at about the same time and carefully reconstruct their cash flows over some finite number of periods. The next step is to discount the cash flows for each customer back to the time of acquisition to calculate that customer's sample CLV and then average all of the sample CLVs together to produce an estimate of the CLV of each newly acquired customer. We refer to this method as the "cohort and incubate" approach. Equivalently, one can calculate the present value of the *total* cash flows from the cohort and divide by the number of customers to get the average CLV for the cohort. If the value of customer relationships is stable across time, the average CLV of the cohort sample is an appropriate estimator of the CLV of newly acquired customers.

As an example of this "cohort and incubate" approach, Berger, Weinberg and Hanna (2003) followed all the customers acquired by a cruise-ship line in 1993. The 6,094 customers in the cohort of 1993 were tracked (incubated) for five years. The total net present value of the cash flows from these customers was $27,916,614. These flows included revenues from the cruises taken (the 6,094 customers took 8,660 cruises over the five-year horizon), variable cost of the cruises and promotional costs. The total five-year net present value of the cohort expressed on a per-customer basis came out to be $27,916,614/6,094 or $4,581 per customer. This is the average five-year CLV for the cohort.

> *"Prior to this analysis, [cruise-line] management would never spend more than $3,314 to acquire a passenger ... Now, aware of CLV (both the concept and the actual numerical results), an advertisement that [resulted in a cost per acquisition of $3 to $4 thousand] was welcomed—especially because the CLV numbers are conservative (again, as noted, the CLV does not include any residual business after five years.)"[7]*

The "cohort and incubate" approach works well when customer relationships are stationary – changing slowly over time. When the value of relationships changes slowly, we can use the value of incubated past relationships as predictive of the value of new relationships.

In situations where the value of customer relationships changes more rapidly, firms often use a simple model to forecast the value of those relationships. By a model, we mean some assumptions about how the customer relationship will unfold. If the model is simple enough, it may even be possible to find an equation for the present value of our model of future cash flows. This makes the calculation of CLV even easier because it now requires only the substitution of numbers for our situation into the equation for CLV.

Next, we will explain what is perhaps the simplest model for future customer cash flows and the equation for the present value of those cash flows. Although it's not the only model of future customer cash flows, this one gets used the most.

Construction

The model for customer cash flows treats the firm's customer relationships as something of a leaky bucket. Each period, a fraction (1 less the retention rate) of the firm's customers leave and are lost for good.

The CLV model has only three parameters: (1) constant margin (contribution after deducting variable costs including retention spending) per period, (2) constant retention probability per period, and (3) discount rate. Furthermore, the model assumes that in the event that the customer is not retained, they are lost for good. Finally, the model assumes that the first margin will be received (with probability equal to the retention rate) at the end of the first period.

The one other assumption of the model is that the firm uses an infinite horizon when it calculates the present value of future cash flows. Although no firm actually has an infinite horizon, the consequences of assuming one are discussed in the following.

Customer lifetime value

The CLV formula multiplies the per-period cash margin (hereafter we will just use the term "margin") by a factor that represents the present value of the expected length of the customer relationship:[8]

$$\text{Customer lifetime value (£)} = \text{Margin (£)} * \frac{\text{Retention rate (\%)}}{1 + \text{Discount rate (\%)} - \text{Retention rate (\%)}}$$

Under the assumptions of the model, CLV is a multiple of the margin. The multiplicative factor represents the present value of the expected length (number of periods) of the customer relationship. When retention equals 0, the customer will never be retained, and the multiplicative factor is zero. When retention equals 1, the customer is always retained, and the firm receives the margin in perpetuity. The present value of the margin in perpetuity turns out to be margin/discount rate. For retention values in between, the CLV formula tells us the appropriate multiplier.

Example An Internet service provider (ISP) charges $19.95 per month. Variable costs are about $1.50 per account per month. With marketing spending of $6 per year, their attrition is only 0.5% per month. At a monthly discount rate of 1%, what is the CLV of a customer?

$$\text{Contribution margin} = (\$19.95 - \$1.50 - \$6/12) = \$17.95$$

$$\text{Retention rate} = 0.995$$

$$\text{Discount rate} = 0.01$$

$$\text{Customer lifetime value (CLV)} = \text{Margin} * \frac{\text{Retention rate (\%)}}{1 + \text{Discount rate (\%)} - \text{Retention rate (\%)}}$$

$$\text{CLV} = \$17.95 * [0.995/(1 + 0.01 - 0.995)]$$

$$\text{CLV} = [\$17.95] * [66.33]$$

$$\text{CLV} = \$1,191$$

Data sources, complications and cautions

The retention rate (and by extension the attrition rate) is a driver of customer value. Very small changes can make a major difference to the lifetime value calculated. Accuracy in this parameter is vital to meaningful results.

The retention rate is assumed to be constant across the life of the customer relationship. For products and services that go through a trial, conversion and loyalty progression, retention rates will increase over the lifetime of the relationship.

In those situations, the model explained here might be too simple. If the firm wants to estimate a sequence of retention rates, a spreadsheet model might be more useful in calculating CLV.

The discount rate is also a sensitive driver of the lifetime value calculation – as with retention, seemingly small changes can make major differences to customer lifetime value. The discount rate should be chosen with care.

The contribution is assumed to be constant across time. If margin is expected to increase over the lifetime of the customer relationship, the simple model will not apply.

Take care not to use this CLV formula for relationships in which customer inactivity does not signal the end of the relationship. In catalogue sales, for example, a small percentage of the firm's customers purchase from any given catalogue. Don't confuse the percentage of customers active in a given period (relevant for the catalogue retailer) with the retention rates in this model. If customers often return to do business with the firm after a period of inactivity, this CLV formula does not apply.

Customer lifetime value (CLV) with initial margin

One final source of confusion concerns the timing assumptions inherent in the model. The first cash flow accounted for in the model is the margin received at the end of one period with probability equal to the retention rate. Other models also include an initial margin received at the beginning of the period. If a certain receipt of an initial margin is included, the new CLV will equal the old CLV plus the initial margin. Furthermore, if the initial margin is equal to all subsequent margins, there are at least two ways to write formulas for the CLV that include the initial margin:

$$\text{CLV with initial margin (£)} = \text{Margin (£)} + \text{Margin (£)} * \frac{\text{Retention rate (\%)}}{1 + \text{Discount rate (\%)} - \text{Retention rate (\%)}}$$

or

$$= \text{Margin (£)} * \frac{1 + \text{Discount rate (\%)}}{1 + \text{Discount rate (\%)} - \text{Retention rate (\%)}}$$

The second formula looks just like the original formula with 1 + Discount rate taking the place of the retention rate in the numerator of the multiplicative factor. Just remember that the new CLV formula and the original CLV formula apply to the same situations and differ only in the treatment of an initial margin. This new CLV formula includes it, whereas the original CLV formula does not.

The infinite horizon assumption

In some industries and companies it is typical to calculate four- or five-year customer values instead of using the infinite time horizon inherent in the previous formulas. Of course, over shorter periods customer retention rates are less likely to be affected by major shifts in technology or competitive strategies and are more likely to be captured by historical retention rates. For managers, the question is, "Does it make a difference whether I use the infinite time horizon or (for example) the five-year customer value?" The answer to this question is yes, sometimes, it can make a difference because the value over five years can be less than 70% of the value over an infinite horizon (see Table 5.3).

Table 5.3 calculates the percentages of (infinite horizon) CLV accruing in the first five years. If retention rates are higher than 80% and discount rates are lower than 20%, differences in the two approaches will be substantial. Depending on the strategic risks that companies perceive, the additional complexities of using a finite horizon can be informative.

Table 5.3 Finite-horizon CLV as a percentage of infinite-horizon CLV

Per cent of CLV accruing in first five years						
Discount rates	Retention rates					
	40%	50%	60%	70%	80%	90%
2%	99%	97%	93%	85%	70%	47%
4%	99%	97%	94%	86%	73%	51%
6%	99%	98%	94%	87%	76%	56%
8%	99%	98%	95%	89%	78%	60%
10%	99%	98%	95%	90%	80%	63%
12%	99%	98%	96%	90%	81%	66%
14%	99%	98%	96%	91%	83%	69%
16%	100%	99%	96%	92%	84%	72%
18%	100%	99%	97%	93%	86%	74%
20%	100%	99%	97%	93%	87%	76%

Prospect lifetime value versus customer value

> Prospect lifetime value is the expected value of a prospect. It is the value expected from the prospect minus the cost of prospecting. The value expected from the prospect is the expected fraction of prospects who will make a purchase times the sum of the average margin the firm makes on the initial purchase and the CLV of the newly acquired customer.
>
> Only if prospect lifetime value is positive should the firm proceed with the planned acquisition spending.

Purpose: to account for the lifetime value of a newly acquired customer (CLV) when making prospecting decisions

One of the major uses of CLV is to inform prospecting decisions. A prospect is someone whom the firm will spend money on in an attempt to acquire her or him as a customer. The acquisition spending must be compared not just to the contribution from the immediate sales it generates but also to the future cash flows expected from the newly acquired customer relationship (the CLV). Only with a full accounting of the value of the newly acquired customer relationship will the firm be able to make an informed, economic prospecting decision.

Construction

The expected prospect lifetime value (PLV) is the value expected from each prospect minus the cost of prospecting. The value expected from each prospect is the acquisition rate (the expected fraction of prospects who will make a purchase and become customers) times the sum of the initial margin the firm makes on the initial purchases and the CLV. The cost is the amount of acquisition spending per prospect. The formula for expected PLV is as follows:

$$\text{Prospect lifetime value (£)} = \text{Acquisition rate (\%)} * [\text{Initial margin (£)} + \text{CLV (£)}] - \text{Acquisition spending (£)}$$

If PLV is positive, the acquisition spending is a wise investment. If PLV is negative, the acquisition spending should not be made.

The PLV number will usually be very small. Although CLV is sometimes in the hundreds of pounds, PLV can come out to be only a few pennies. Just remember that PLV applies to prospects, not customers. A large number of small but positive-value prospects can add up to a considerable amount of value for a firm.

Example A service company in the US plans to spend $60,000 on an advertisement reaching 75,000 readers. If the service company expects the advertisement to convince 1.2% of the readers to take advantage of a special introductory offer (priced so low that the firm makes only $10 margin on this initial purchase) and the CLV of the acquired customers is $100, is the advertisement economically attractive?

Here acquisition spending is $0.80 per prospect, the expected acquisition rate is 0.012 and the initial margin is $10. The expected PLV of each of the 75,000 prospects is:

$$PLV = 0.012 * (\$10 + \$100) - \$0.80$$
$$= \$0.52$$

The expected PLV is $0.52. The total expected value of the prospecting effort will be 75,000 * $0.52 = $39,000. The proposed acquisition spending *is* economically attractive.

If we are uncertain about the 0.012 acquisition rate, we might ask what the acquisition rate from the prospecting campaign must be in order for it to be economically successful. We can get that number using Excel's goal seek function to find the acquisition rate that sets PLV to zero. Or we can use a little algebra and substitute $0 in for PLV and solve for the break-even acquisition rate:

$$\text{Break-even acquisition rate} = \frac{\text{Acquisition spending (\$)}}{\text{Initial margin (\$)} + \text{CLV (\$)}}$$

$$= \frac{\$0.80}{\$10 + \$100} = 0.007273$$

The acquisition rate must exceed 0.7273% in order for the campaign to be successful.

Data sources, complications and cautions

In addition to the CLV of the newly acquired customers, the firm needs to know the planned amount of acquisition spending (expressed on a per-prospect basis), the expected success rate (the fraction of prospects expected to become customers), and the average margin the firm will receive from the initial purchases of the newly acquired customers. The initial margin number is needed because CLV as defined in the previous section accounts for only the future cash flows from the relationship. The initial cash flow is not included in CLV and must be accounted for separately. Note also that the initial margin must account for any first-period retention spending.

Perhaps the biggest challenge in calculating PLV is estimating CLV. The other terms (acquisition spending, acquisition rate and initial margin) all refer to flows or outcomes in the near future, whereas CLV requires longer-term projections.

Another caution worth mentioning is that the decision to spend money on customer acquisition whenever PLV is positive rests on an assumption that the customers acquired would not have been acquired had the firm not spent the money. In other words, our approach gives the acquisition spending "full credit" for the subsequent customers acquired. If the firm has several simultaneous acquisition efforts, dropping one of them might lead to increased acquisition rates for the others. Situations such as these (where one solicitation cannibalises another) require a more complicated analysis.

The firm must be careful to search for the most economical way to acquire new customers. If there are alternative prospecting approaches, the firm must be careful not to simply go with the first one that gives a positive projected PLV. Given a limited number of prospects, the approach that gives the highest expected PLV should be used.

Finally, we want to warn you that there are other ways to do the calculations necessary to judge the economic viability of a given prospecting effort. Although these other approaches are equivalent to the one presented here, they differ with respect to what gets included in "CLV". Some will include the initial margin as part of "CLV". Others will include both the initial margin and the expected acquisition cost per acquired customer as part of "CLV". We illustrate these two approaches using the service company example.

Example A service company in the US plans to spend $60,000 on an advertisement reaching 75,000 readers. If the service company expects the advertisement to convince 1.2% of the readers to take advantage of a special introductory offer (priced so low that the firm makes only $10 margin on this initial purchase) and the CLV of the acquired customers is $100, is the advertisement economically attractive?

If we include the initial margin in "CLV" we get:

$$\text{"CLV" [with initial margin (\$)]} = \text{Initial margin (\$)} + \text{CLV (\$)}$$

$$= \$10 + \$100 = \$110$$

The expected PLV is now:

$$\text{PLV (\$)} = \text{Acquisition rate (\%)} * \text{"CLV" [with initial margin (\$)]} - \text{Acquisition cost (\$)}$$

$$= 0.012 * \$110 - \$0.85 = \$0.52$$

This is the same number as before, calculated using a slightly different "CLV" – one that includes the initial margin.

We illustrate one final way to do the calculations necessary to judge the economics of a prospecting campaign. This last way does things on a per-acquired-customer basis using a "CLV" that includes both initial margin and an allocated acquisition spending. The thinking goes as follows. The expected value of a new customer is $10 now plus $100 from future sales, or $110 in total. The expected cost to acquire a customer is the total cost of the campaign divided by the expected number of new customers. This average acquisition cost is calculated as $60,000/(0.012 * 75,000) = $66.67. The expected value of a new customer net of the expected acquisition cost per customer is $110 − $66.67 = $43.33. Because this new "net" CLV is positive, the campaign is economically attractive. Some will even label this $43.33 number as the "CLV" of a new customer.

Notice that $43.33 times the 900 expected new customers equals $39,000, the same total net value from the campaign calculated in the original example as the $0.52 PLV times the 75,000 prospects. The two ways to do the calculations are equivalent.

Acquisition versus retention cost

The firm's average acquisition cost is the ratio of acquisition spending to the number of customers acquired. The average retention cost is the ratio of retention spending directed toward a group of customers to the number of those customers successfully retained.

$$\text{Average acquisition cost } (\text{\pounds}) = \frac{\text{Acquisition spending } (\text{\pounds})}{\text{Number of customers acquired } (N)}$$

$$\text{Average retention cost } (\text{\pounds}) = \frac{\text{Retention spending } (\text{\pounds})}{\text{Number of customers retained } (N)}$$

These two metrics help the firm monitor the effectiveness of two important categories of marketing spending.

Purpose: to determine the firm's cost of acquisition and retention

Before the firm can optimise its mix of acquisition and retention spending, it must first assess the status quo. At the current spending levels, how much does it cost the firm (on average) to acquire new customers, and how much is it spending (on average) to retain its existing customers? Does it cost five times as much to acquire a new customer as it does to retain an existing one?

Construction

> Average acquisition cost: **This represents the average cost to acquire a customer and is the total acquisition spending divided by the number of new customers acquired.**

$$\text{Average acquisition cost (£)} = \frac{\text{Acquisition spending (£)}}{\text{Number of customers acquired (N)}}$$

> Average retention cost: **This represents the average "cost" to retain an existing customer and is the total retention spending divided by the number of customers retained.**

$$\text{Average retention cost (£)} = \frac{\text{Retention spending (£)}}{\text{Number of customers retained (N)}}$$

Example During the past year, a regional pest control service spent €1.4 million and acquired 64,800 new customers. Of the 154,890 customer relationships in existence at the start of the year, only 87,957 remained at the end of the year, despite about €500,000 spent during the year in attempts to retain the 154,890 customers. The calculation of average acquisition cost is relatively straightforward. A total of €1.4 million resulted in 64,800 new customers. The average acquisition cost is €1,400/64.8 = €21.60 per customer. The calculation of average retention cost is also straightforward. A total of €500,000 resulted in 87,957 retained customers. The average yearly retention cost is €500,000 / 87,957 = €5.68. Thus, for the pest control firm, it cost about *four* times as much to acquire a new customer as it did to retain an existing one.

Data sources, complications and cautions

For any specific period, the firm needs to know the total amount it spent on customer acquisition and the number of new customers that resulted from that spending. With respect to customer retention, the firm needs to measure the total amount spent during the period attempting to retain the customers in existence at the start of the period and the number of the existing customers successfully retained at the end of the period. Notice that retention spending directed at customers acquired within the period is not included in this figure. Similarly, the number retained refers only to those retained from the pool of customers in existence at the start of the period. Thus, the average retention cost calculated will be associated with the length of the period in question. If the period is a year, the average retention cost will be a cost per year per customer retained.

The calculation and interpretation of average acquisition cost is much easier than the calculation and interpretation of average retention cost. This is so because it is often possible to isolate acquisition spending and count the number of new customers that resulted from that spending. A simple division results in the average cost to acquire a customer. The reasonable assumption underlying this calculation is that the new customers would not have been acquired had it not been for the acquisition spending.

Things are not nearly so clear when it comes to average retention cost. One source of difficulty is that retention rates (and costs) depend on the period of time under consideration. Yearly retention is different from monthly retention. The cost to retain a customer for a month will be less than the cost to retain a customer for a year. Thus, the definition of average retention cost requires a specification of the time period associated with the retention.

A second source of difficulty stems from the fact that some customers will be retained even if the firm spends nothing on retention. For this reason it can be a little misleading to call the ratio of retention spending to the number of retained customers the average retention cost. One must not jump to the conclusion that retention goes away if the retention spending goes away. Nor should one assume that if the firm increases the retention budget by the average retention cost that it will retain one more customer. The average retention cost number is not very useful to help make retention budgeting decisions.

One final caution involves the firm's capability to separate spending into acquisition and retention classifications. Clearly there can be spending that works to improve both the acquisition and retention efforts of the firm. General brand advertisements, for example, serve to lower the cost of both acquisition and retention. Rather than attempt to allocate all spending as either acquisition or retention, we suggest that it is perfectly acceptable to maintain a separate category that is neither acquisition nor retention.

References and suggested further reading

Berger, P.D., B. Weinberg and R. Hanna. (2003). "Customer Lifetime Value Determination and Strategic Implications for a Cruise-Ship Line", *Database Marketing and Customer Strategy Management*, 11(1), 40–52.

Blattberg, R.C. and S.J. Hoch. (1990). "Database Models and Managerial Intuition: 50% Model + 50% Manager", *Management Science*, 36(8), 887–899.

Gupta, S. and D.R. Lehmann. (2003). "Customers as Assets", *Journal of Interactive Marketing*, 17(1), 9–24.

Kaplan, R.S. and V.G. Narayanan. (2001). "Measuring and Managing Customer Profitability", *Journal of Cost Management*, September/October, 5–15.

Little, J.D.C. (1970). "Models and Managers: The Concept of a Decision Calculus", *Management Science*, 16(8), B-466–B-485.

McGovern, G.J., D. Court, J.A. Quelch and B. Crawford. (2004). "Bringing Customers into the Boardroom", *Harvard Business Review*, 82(11), 70–80.

March, J.G., L.S. Sproull and M. Tamuz. (1989). "Learning from Samples of One or Fewer", *Organization Science*, 2(1), 1–12.

Peppers, D. and M. Rogers. (1997). *Enterprise One to One: Tools for Competing in the Interactive Age*, New York: Currency Doubleday.

Pfeifer, P.E., M.E. Haskins and R.M. Conroy. (2005). "Customer Lifetime Value, Customer Profitability, and the Treatment of Acquisition Spending", *Journal of Managerial Issues*, 17(1), 11–25.

Sales force and channel management

6

Metrics covered in this chapter:

- Sales force coverage

- Sales force goals

- Sales force results

- Sales force compensation

- Pipeline analysis

- Numeric distribution, ACV distribution and PCV distribution

- Facings and share of shelf

- Out-of-stock and service levels

- Inventory turns

- Mark-downs

- Gross margin return on inventory investment (GMROII)

- Direct product profitability (DPP)

Introduction

This chapter deals with push marketing. It describes how marketers measure the adequacy and effectiveness of the systems that provide customers with reasons and opportunities to buy their products.

The first sections discuss sales force metrics. Here, we list and define the most common measures for determining whether sales force effort and geographic coverage are adequate. We discuss pipeline analysis, which is useful in making sales forecasts and in allocating sales force effort to different stages of the selling process. Pipeline metrics are used to examine a sequence of selling activities, from lead generation, through follow-up, to conversion and sales. Although the most important of these represents the percentage of initial leads who ultimately buy, other measures of activity, productivity, efficiency and cost can be useful at each stage of the selling process.

In further sections of this chapter, we discuss measures of product distribution and availability. For manufacturers who approach their market through resellers, three key metrics provide an indication of "listings" – the percentage of potential outlets that stock their products. These include numeric distribution, which is unweighted; ACV, the industry standard; and PCV, a category-specific measure of product availability.

Marketing logistics tracking metrics are used to measure the operational effectiveness of the systems that service retailers and distributors. Inventory turns, out-of-stocks, and service levels are key factors in this area.

At the retail level, gross margin return on inventory investment (GMROII) and direct product profitability (DPP) offer SKU-specific metrics of product performance, combining movement rates, gross margins, costs of inventory and other factors.

Metric	Construction	Considerations	Purpose
Workload	Hours required to service clients and prospects.	Prospect numbers may be debatable. Time spent trying to convert prospects can vary by territory, salesperson and potential client.	To assess the number of salespeople required to service a territory, and to ensure balanced workloads.
Sales potential forecast	This comprises the number of prospects and their buying power.	Doesn't assess the likelihood of converting "potential" accounts. Definitions of buying power are more an art than a science.	To determine sales targets. Can also help identify territories worthy of an allocation of limited sales resources.

Metric	Construction	Considerations	Purpose
Sales total	Individual sales projections may be based on a salesperson's share of forecasted sales, on prior year sales and a share of increased district projections, or on a management-designed weighting system.	Setting individual targets on the basis of prior year sales can discourage optimal performance, as strong performance in one year leads to more aggressive targets in the next.	To set targets for individual salespeople and for territories.
Sales force effectiveness	Effectiveness metrics analyse sales in the context of various criteria, including calls, contacts, potential accounts, active accounts, buying power of territory, and expenses.	Depends on factors that also affect sales potential and workload.	To assess the performance of a salesperson or team.
Compensation	Total payments made to a salesperson, typically consisting of base salary, bonus and/or commission.	Perceived relationship between incentive reward and controllable activities may vary widely among industries and firms.	To motivate maximum sales effort. To enable salespeople and management to track progress toward goals.
Break-even number of employees	Sales revenue, multiplied by margin net of commission, divided by cost per staff member.	Margins may vary across products, time and salespeople. Sales are not independent of the number of salespeople.	To determine the appropriate personnel level for a projected sales volume.

▶

Metric	Construction	Considerations	Purpose
Sales funnel, sales pipeline	Portrayal of the number of clients and potential clients at various stages of the sales cycle.	Funnel dimensions depend on type of business and definition of potential clients.	To monitor sales effort and project future sales.
Numeric distribution	Percentage of outlets in a defined universe that stock a particular brand or product.	Outlets' size or sales levels are not reflected in this measure. Boundaries by which distribution universe is defined may be arbitrary.	To assess the degree to which a brand or product has penetrated its potential channels.
All commodity volume (ACV)	Numeric distribution, weighted by penetrated outlets' share of sales of all product categories.	Reflects sales of "all commodities", but may not reflect sales of the relevant product or category.	To assess the degree to which a brand or product has access to retail traffic.
Product category volume (PCV)	Numeric distribution, weighted by penetrated outlets' share of sales of the relevant product category.	Strong indicator of share potential, but may miss opportunities to expand category.	To assess the degree to which a brand or product has access to established outlets for its category.
Total distribution	Usually based on ACV or PCV. Sums the relevant measures for each SKU in a brand or product line.	Strong indicator of the distribution of a product *line*, as opposed to an individual SKU.	To assess the extent to which a product line is available.
Facings	Generally, an average of the total number of package views available in a typical stocking outlet.	Reflects visibility at retail. May reflect inventory as well, depending on whether "backroom" inventory is available.	To determine stock levels and visibility within stores.

Metric	Construction	Considerations	Purpose
Out-of-stock	Percentage of outlets that "list" or normally stock a product or brand, but have none available for sale.	Out-of-stocks can be measured in numeric, ACV or PCV terms.	To monitor the ability of logistics systems to match supply with demand.
Inventories	Total amount of product or brand available for sale in a channel.	May be held at different levels and valued in ways that may or may not reflect promotional allowances and discounts.	To calculate ability to meet demand and determine channel investments.
Mark-downs	Percentage discount from the regular selling price.	For many products, a certain percentage of mark-downs are expected. Too few mark-downs may reflect "under-ordering". If mark-downs are too high, the opposite may be true.	To determine whether channel sales are being made at planned margins.
Direct product profitability (DPP)	The adjusted gross margin of products, less direct product costs.	Cost allocation is often imprecise. Some products may be intended not to generate profit but to drive traffic.	To identify profitable SKUs and realistically calculate their earnings.
Gross margin return on inventory investment (GMROII)	Margin divided by the average monetary value of inventory held during a specific period of time.	Allowances and rebates must be considered in margin calculations. For "loss leaders" this measure may be consistently negative and still not present a problem. For most products, negative trends in GMROII are signs of future problems.	To quantify return on working capital invested in inventory.

Sales force coverage: territories

Sales force territories are the customer groups or geographic districts for which individual salespeople or sales teams hold responsibility. Territories can be defined on the basis of geography, sales potential, history, or a combination of factors. Companies strive to balance their territories because this can reduce costs and increase sales.

Workload (N) = [Current accounts (N) $*$ Average time to service an active account (N)] + [Prospects (N) $*$ Time spent trying to convert a prospect into an active account (N)]

Sales potential (£) = Number of possible accounts (N) $*$ Buying power (£)

Purpose: to create balanced sales territories

There are a number of ways to analyse territories.[1] Most commonly, territories are compared on the basis of their potential or size. This is an important exercise. If territories differ sharply or slip out of balance, sales personnel may be given too much or too little work. This can lead to under- or over-servicing of customers.

When sales personnel are stretched too thin, the result can be an *under-servicing* of customers. This can cost a firm business because over-taxed salespeople engage in sub-optimal levels of activity in a number of areas. They seek out too few leads, identify too few prospects and spend too little time with current customers. Those customers, in turn, may take their business to alternative providers.

Over-servicing, by contrast, may raise costs and prices and therefore indirectly reduce sales. Over-servicing in some territories may also lead to under-servicing in others.

Unbalanced territories also raise the problem of unfair distribution of sales potential among members of a sales force. This may result in distorted compensation and cause talented salespeople to leave a company, seeking superior balance and compensation.

Achieving an appropriate balance among territories is an important factor in maintaining satisfaction among customers, salespeople and the company as a whole.

Construction

In defining or redefining territories, companies strive to:

- balance workloads
- balance sales potential

- develop compact territories
- minimise disruptions during the redesigns.

These goals can have different effects on different stakeholders, as represented in Table 6.1.[2]

Table 6.1 Effects of balancing sales territories

		Balance the workload	Balance sales potential	Minimise disruption	Develop compact territories
Customers	Responsiveness	X			X
	Relationships			X	
Salespeople	Earnings opportunities		X		
	Manageable workload	X			X
	Reduced uncertainty			X	
	Control of overnights				X
Firm	Sales results	X	X	X	
	Effort control	X			
	Motivation	X	X	X	X
	Travel cost control				X

Before designing new territories, a sales force manager should evaluate the workloads of all members of the sales team. The workload for a territory can be calculated as follows:

Workload (N) = [Current accounts (N) * Average time to service an active account (N)] + [Prospects (N) * Time spent trying to convert a prospect into an active account (N)]

The sales potential in a territory can be determined as follows:

Sales potential (£) = Number of possible accounts (N) * Buying power (£)

Buying power is a monetary figure based on such factors as average income levels, number of businesses in a territory, average sales of those businesses and population demographics. Buying power indices are generally specific to individual industries.

Example Among the sales prospects in one of its territories, a photocopier manufacturer in the US has identified six small businesses, eight medium-sized firms and two large companies. Enterprises of these sizes have historically made annual photocopier purchases that average $500, $700, and $1,000, respectively. The sales potential for the territory is thus:

$$\text{Sales potential} = (6 * \$500) + (8 * \$700) + (2 * \$1,000) = \$10,600$$

In addition to workload and sales potential, a third key metric is needed to compare territories. This is size or, more specifically, travel time. In this context, travel time is more useful than size because it more accurately represents the factor that size implies – that is, the amount of time needed to reach customers and potential customers.

As a manager's goal is to balance workload and potential among sales personnel, it can be beneficial to calculate combined metrics – such as sales potential or travel time – in order to make comparisons between territories.

Data sources, complications and cautions

Sales potential can be represented in a number of ways. Of these, the most basic is population – the number of potential accounts in a territory. In the photocopier case cited earlier, this might be the number of offices in a territory.

Estimating the size of a territory might involve simply calculating the geographic area that it covers. It is likely, however, that average travel time will also be important. Depending on the quality of roads, density of traffic, or distance between businesses, one may find that territories of equal area entail very different travel time requirements. In evaluating such distinctions, sales force records of the time needed to travel from call to call can be useful. Specialised computer software programs are available for these purposes.

Redefining territories is a famously difficult process. To perform it well, in addition to the metrics cited earlier, disruption of customer relationships and feelings of ownership among sales personnel must also be considered.

Sales force objectives: setting goals

Sales goals are generally needed to motivate salespeople. These can have negative effects, however, if set too high or low. Means of establishing sales goals include the following:

Sales goal (£) = Salesperson's share of prior-year sales in district (%) * Forecasted sales for district (£)

Sales goal (£) = Salesperson's prior-year sales (£) + [Forecasted sales increase for district (£) * Territory's share of sales potential in district (%)]

Weighted share of sales allotment (%) = {Salesperson's share of prior-year sales in district (%) * Assigned weighting (%)} + {Territory's share of sales potential in district (%) * [1 − Assigned weighting (%)]}

Sales goal (£) = Weighted share of sales allotment (%) * Forecasted sales for district (£)

Many of these approaches involve a combination of historical results and a weighting of sales potential among the territories. This ensures that overall goals will be attained if all salespeople meet their individual goals.

Purpose: to motivate sales personnel and establish benchmarks for evaluating and rewarding their performance

In setting sales goals, managers strive to motivate their personnel to stretch themselves and generate the most sales possible. But they don't want to set the bar too high. The correct goal levels will motivate all salespeople and reward most of them.

When planning sales goals, certain guidelines are important. Under the SMART strategy recommended by Jack D. Wilner, author of *7 Secrets to Successful Sales Management*,[3] goals should be **S**pecific, **M**easurable, **A**ttainable, **R**ealistic and **T**ime-bound. Goals should be specific to a department, a territory and even a salesperson. They should be clear and applicable to each individual so that salespeople do not have to derive part of their goal. Measurable goals, expressed in concrete numbers such as "money sales" or "percentage increase" enable salespeople to set precise targets and track their progress. Vague goals, such as "more" or "increased" sales, are not effective because they make it difficult to measure progress. Attainable goals are in the realm of possibility. They can be visualised and understood by both the manager and the salesperson. Realistic goals are set high enough to motivate, but not so high that salespeople give up before they even start. Finally, time-bound goals must be met within a precise time frame. This applies pressure to reach them sooner rather than later and defines an endpoint when results will be checked.

Construction

There are numerous ways of allotting a company's forecast across its sales force. These methods are designed to set goals that are fair, achievable and in line with historic results. Goals are stated in terms of sales totals for individual salespeople. In the following formulas, which encapsulate these methods, a *district* is composed of the individual territories of multiple salespeople.

A sales goal or allocation based on prior-year sales can be calculated as follows:[4]

Sales goal (£) = Salesperson's share of prior-year sales in district (%) * Forecasted sales for district (£)

A sales goal based on prior-year sales *and* the sales potential of a territory can be calculated as follows:

Sales goal (£) = Salesperson's prior-year sales (£) + [Forecasted sales increase for district (£) * Territory's share of sales potential in district (%)]

Sales goals can also be set by a combined method, in which management assigns weightings to both the prior-year sales of each salesperson and the sales potential of each territory. These weightings are then used to calculate each salesperson's percentage share of the relevant sales forecast, and percentage shares are used to calculate sales goals in financial terms.

Weighted share of sales allotment (%) = {Salesperson's share of prior-year sales in district (%) * Assigned weighting (%)} + {Territory's share of sales potential in district (%)* [1 − Assigned weighting (%)]}

Sales goal (£) = Weighted share of sales allotment (%)* Forecasted sales for district (£)

Example A salesperson in the US achieved prior-year sales of $1,620, which represented 18% of the sales in her district. This salesperson was responsible for a territory that held 12% of the sales potential in the district. If the salesperson's employer mandates a district sales goal of $10,000 for the coming year – representing an overall increase of $1,000 over prior-year results – then the salesperson's individual sales goal can be calculated in several ways that involve different emphasis on historical sales versus sales potential. Here are four examples:

1 Sales goal based on prior-year sales = 18% * $10,000 = $1,800
2 Sales goals based on sales potential = 12% * $10,000 = $1,200
3 Sales goal based on prior-year sales + Sales potential * Increase = $1,620 + (12% * $1,000) = $1,740
4 Weighted share of sales allotment, in which prior-year sales and sales potential are weighted (for example) by a factor of 50% each = (18% * 50%) + (12% * 50%) = 15%. Then...

Sales goal based on weighted share of sales allotment = 15% * $10,000 = $1,500

Data sources, complications and cautions

Sales goals are generally established by using combinations of bottom-up and top-down procedures. Frequently, top management sets objectives at a corporate level, while the sales manager allocates shares of that overall goal among the various members of the sales force.

Top management generally uses multiple metrics to forecast sales, including prior-year sales of the product in question, total prior-year sales in the relevant market, prior-year sales by competitors, and the company's current market share. After the corporate sales forecast is derived, a sales force manager verifies that these targets are reasonable, pushing back where necessary. The manager then allots the projected sales among the sales force in a district, based at least in part on measures of individual performance from the prior year. Of greatest importance in this calculation are each salesperson's historic percentage of sales and the sales potential of his or her territory.

It is important to re-evaluate sales goals *during* the year to ensure that actual performance is running reasonably close to projections. If, at this checkpoint, it appears that more than 90% or less than 50% of the sales force is on track to achieve their goals, then it may be advisable to alter the goals. This will prevent salespeople from easing off too early because their goals are in sight, or giving up because their goals are unattainable. In setting goals, one possible rule of thumb would be to plan for a success rate of 75%. That would ensure that enough salespeople reach their goal *and* that the goal is sufficiently challenging.

If "rebudgeting" becomes necessary, it is important to ensure that this is properly recorded. Unless care is taken, revised sales goals can slip out of alignment with financial budgets and the expectations of senior management.

Sales force effectiveness: measuring effort, potential and results

By analysing sales force performance, managers can make changes to optimise sales going forward. Toward that end, there are many ways to gauge the performance of individual salespeople and of the sales force as a whole, in addition to total annual sales.

Sales force effectiveness ratios

$$= \frac{\text{Sales (£)}}{\text{Contacts with clients (calls) (N)}}$$

$$= \frac{\text{Sales (£)}}{\text{Potential accounts (N)}}$$

$$= \frac{\text{Sales (£)}}{\text{Active accounts (N)}}$$

$$= \frac{\text{Sales (£)}}{\text{Buying power (£)}}$$

$$= \frac{\text{Expenses (£)}}{\text{Sales (£)}} \quad \text{(also known as cost of sales)}$$

Each can also be calculated on a financial contribution basis.

Purpose: to measure the performance of a sales force and of individual salespeople

When analysing the performance of a salesperson, a number of metrics can be compared. These can reveal more about the salesperson than can be gauged by his or her total sales.

Construction

An authoritative source lists the following ratios as useful in assessing the relative effectiveness of sales personnel:[5]

$$\frac{\text{Sales (£)}}{\text{Contacts with clients (calls) (N)}}$$

$$\frac{\text{Sales (£)}}{\text{Potential accounts (N)}}$$

$$\frac{\text{Sales (£)}}{\text{Active accounts (N)}}$$

$$\frac{\text{Sales (£)}}{\text{Buying power (£)}}$$

These formulas can be useful for comparing salespeople from different territories and for examining trends over time. They can reveal distinctions that can be obscured by total sales results, particularly in districts where territories vary in size, in number of potential accounts or in buying power.

These ratios provide insight into the factors behind sales performance. If an individual's sales per call ratio is low, for example, that may indicate that the salesperson in question needs training in moving customers toward larger purchases. Or it may indicate a lack of closing skills. If the sales per potential account or sales per buying power metric is low, the salesperson may not be doing enough to seek out new accounts. These metrics reveal much about prospecting and lead generation because they're based on each salesperson's *entire* territory, including potential as well as current customers. The sales per active account metric provides a useful indicator of a salesperson's effectiveness in maximising the value of existing customers.

Although it is important to make the most of every call, a salesperson will not reach his or her goal in just one call. A certain amount of effort is required to complete sales. This can be represented graphically (see Figure 6.1).[6]

Although one can increase sales by expending more time and attention on a customer, at a certain point, a salesperson encounters diminishing returns in placing more calls to the same customers. Eventually, the incremental business generated by each call will be worth less than the cost of making the call.

Figure 6.1 Sales resulting from calls to customers

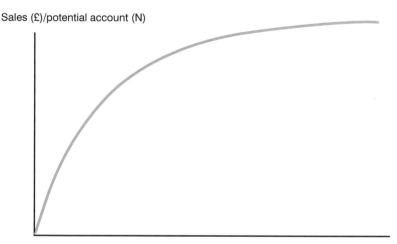

Sales (£)/potential account (N)

Calls (N)/potential account (N)

In addition to the formulas described earlier, one other important measure of effectiveness is the ratio of expenses to sales. This cost metric is commonly expressed as a percentage of sales and is calculated as follows:

$$\frac{\text{Expenses (£)}}{\text{Sales (£)}}$$

If this ratio is substantially higher for one salesperson than for others, it may indicate that the individual in question has poor control of his or her expenses. Examples of poor expense control could include making unnecessary trips to a client, overproducing product pamphlets or hosting too many dinners. Alternatively, expenses may represent a high percentage of sales if an individual possesses poor closing skills. If a salesperson's expenses are comparable to those of his peers, but his sales are lower, then he may be failing to deliver sales after spending significant money on a potential customer.

A more challenging set of sales force performance metrics involves customer service. Customer service is difficult to measure because there are no concrete numbers representing it, other than repeat rates or customer complaints. Each of those is telling, but how can a sales manager evaluate the service provided to customers who are not repeating, leaving or complaining? One possibility is to develop a survey, including an itemised scale to help customers quantify their opinions. After enough of these surveys are completed, managers will be able to calculate average scores for different service metrics. By comparing these with sales figures, managers can correlate sales with customer service and grade salespeople on their performance.

Example To translate customers' opinions into a metric, a company might pose survey questions such as the following:

Please circle the level of service your business received from our sales staff after shipment of the products you ordered:

1	2	3	4	5	6	7	8	9	10
Extremely poor				Satisfactory				Extremely good	

Data sources, complications and cautions

Calculating the effectiveness of a salesperson is not difficult, but it does require keeping track of a few important numbers. Fortunately, these are commonly recorded in the sales industry.

The most important statistics are the amount of each sale (in money) and the contribution generated by that sale. It may also be important to keep track of which items are sold if a salesperson has been instructed to emphasise a certain product line. Additional useful information would include measures of the number of calls made (including both face-to-face and phone meetings), total accounts active and total accounts in the territory. Of these, the latter two are needed to calculate the buying power of a territory.

The largest problem in performance review is a tendency to rely on only one or two metrics. This can be dangerous because an individual's performance on any one measure may be anomalous. A salesperson who generates £15,000 per call may be more valuable than one who generates £25,000 per call, for example, if he generates greater sales per potential account. A salesperson in a small territory may generate low total contribution but high monetary sales per buying power. If this is true, it may be advisable to increase the size of that person's territory. Another salesperson may show a dramatic increase in monetary sales per active account. If he achieves this simply by eliminating weaker accounts without generating incremental sales, it would not be grounds for reward. In reviewing sales personnel, managers are advised to evaluate as many performance metrics as possible.

Although the customer service survey described earlier is grounded upon a straightforward concept, managers can find it difficult to gather enough data – or sufficiently representative data – to make it useful. This could be because customers hesitate to fill out the surveys, or because they do so only when they encounter a problem. A small sample size or a prevalence of negative responses might distort the results. Even so, some effort to measure customer satisfaction is needed to ensure that salespeople don't emphasise the wrong issues – or neglect issues that have a substantial impact on customers' lifetime value.

Sales force compensation: salary/reward mix

"The incentive plan needs to align the salesperson's activities with the firm's objectives."[7] Toward that end, an effective plan may be based on the past (growth), the present (comparison with others) or the future (percentage of goal achieved). Key formulas in this area include the following:

$$\text{Compensation (£)} = \text{Salary (£)} + \text{Bonus 1 (£)} + \text{Bonus 2 (£)}$$

$$\text{Compensation (£)} = \text{Salary (£)} + [\text{Sales (£)} * \text{Commission (\%)}]$$

$$\text{Break-even number of employees (N)} = \frac{(\text{Sales (£)} * [\text{Margin (\%)} - \text{Commission (\%)}])}{[\text{Salary (£)} + \text{Expenses (£)} + \text{Bonus (£)}]}$$

Purpose: to determine the mix of salary, bonus and commission that will maximise sales generated by the sales force

When designing a compensation plan for a sales force, managers face four key considerations: level of pay, mix between salary and incentive, measures of performance, and performance–payout relationships. The level of pay, or compensation, is the amount that a company plans to pay a salesperson over the course of a year. This can be viewed as a range because its total will vary with bonuses or commissions.

The mix between salary and incentive represents a key allocation within total compensation. Salary is a guaranteed sum of money. Incentives can take multiple forms, including bonuses or commissions. In the case of a bonus, a salesperson will receive a lump sum for reaching certain sales targets. With a commission, the incentive is incremental and is earned on each sale. In order to generate incentives, it is important to measure accurately the role a salesperson plays in each sale. The higher the level of causality that can be attributed to a salesperson, the easier it is to use an incentive system.

Various metrics can be used to measure a salesperson's performance. With these, managers can evaluate a salesperson's performance in the context of past, present or future comparators, as follows:

- **The past:** Measure the salesperson's percentage growth in sales over prior-year results.
- **The present:** Rank salespeople on the basis of current results.
- **The future:** Measure the percentage of individual sales goals achieved by each salesperson.

Sales managers can also select the organisational level on which to focus an incentive plan. The disbursement of incentive rewards can be linked to results at the company, division or product-line level. In measuring performance and designing compensation plans along all these dimensions, managers seek to align salespeople's incentives with the goals of their firm.

Lastly, a time period should be defined for measuring the performance of each salesperson.

Construction

Managers enjoy considerable freedom in designing compensation systems. The key is to start with a forecast for sales and a range within which each salesperson's compensation should reside. After these elements are determined, there are many ways to motivate a salesperson.

In a multi-bonus system, the following formula can represent the compensation structure for a salesperson:

$$\text{Compensation (£)} = \text{Salary (£)} + \text{Bonus 1 (£)} + \text{Bonus 2 (£)}$$

In this system, bonus 1 might be attained at a level approximately halfway to the individual's sales goal for the year. The second bonus might be awarded when that goal is met.

In a commission system, the following formula would represent compensation for a salesperson:

$$\text{Compensation (£)} = \text{Salary (£)} + [\text{Sales (£)} * \text{Commission (\%)}]$$

Theoretically, in a 100% commission structure, salary might be set as low as £0. Many jurisdictions, however, place limits on such arrangements. Managers must ensure that their chosen compensation structures comply with employment law.

Managers can also combine bonus and commission structures by awarding bonuses on top of commissions at certain sales levels, or by increasing the commission rate at certain sales levels.

Example Tina earns a commission of 2% on sales up to €1,000,000, and a 3% commission on sales beyond that point. Her salary is €20,000 per year. If she makes €1,200,000 in sales, her compensation can be calculated as follows:

$$\text{Compensation} = €20,000 + (.02) * (€1,000,000) + (.03) * (€200,000)$$

$$= €46,000$$

After a sales compensation plan has been established, management may want to re-evaluate the size of its sales force. Based on forecasts for the coming year, a firm may have room to hire more salespeople, or it may need to reduce the size of the sales force. On the basis of a given value for projected sales, managers can determine the break-even number of employees for a firm as follows:

$$\text{Break-even number of employees (N)} = \frac{\text{Sales (£)} * [\text{Margin (\%)} - \text{Commission (\%)}]}{[\text{Salary (£)} + \text{Expenses (£)} + \text{Bonus (£)}]}$$

Data sources, complications and cautions

Measurements commonly used in incentive plans include total sales, total contribution, market share, customer retention and customer complaints. Because such a plan rewards a salesperson for reaching certain goals, these targets must be defined at the beginning of the year (or other time period). Continual tracking of these metrics will help both the salesperson and the company to plan for year-end compensation.

Timing is an important issue in incentive plans. A firm must collect data in a timely fashion so that both managers and salespeople know where they stand in relation to established goals. The time frame covered by a plan also represents an important consideration. If a company tries to generate incentives through weekly rewards, its compensation programme can become too expensive and time-consuming to maintain. By contrast, if the programme covers too long a period, it may slip out of alignment with company forecasts and goals. This could result in a sales force being paid too much or too little. To guard against these pitfalls, managers can develop a programme that mixes both short- and long-term incentives. They can link some rewards to a simple, short-term metric, such as calls per week, and others to a more complex, long-term target, such as market share achieved in a year.

A further complication that can arise in incentive programmes is the assignment of causality to individual salespeople. This can become a problem in a number of instances, including team collaborations in landing sales. In such a scenario, it can be difficult to determine which team members deserve which rewards. Consequently, managers may find it best to reward all members of the team with equal bonuses for meeting a goal.

A last concern: when an incentive programme is implemented, it may reward the "wrong" salespeople. To avoid this, before activating any newly proposed programme, sales managers are advised to apply that programme to the prior year's results as a test. A "good" plan will usually reward the salespeople whom the manager knows to be the best.

Sales force tracking: pipeline analysis

Pipeline analysis is used to track the progress of sales efforts in relation to all current and potential customers in order to forecast short-term sales and to evaluate sales force workload.

Purpose: to forecast upcoming sales and evaluate workload distribution

A convenient way to forecast sales in the short term and to keep an eye on sales force activity is to create a sales pipeline or sales funnel. Although this concept can be represented graphically, the data behind it are stored electronically in a database or spreadsheet.

The concept of the sales funnel originates in a well-known dynamic: if a sales force approaches a large number of potential customers, only a subset of these will actually make purchases. As salespeople proceed through multiple stages of customer interaction, a number of prospects are winnowed out. At the conclusion of each stage, fewer potential customers remain. By keeping track of the number of potential customers at each stage of the process, a sales force manager can balance the workload within a team and make accurate forecasts of sales.

This analysis is similar to the hierarchy of effects discussed in "Awareness, attitudes and usage (AAU)" on pages 32–36. Whereas the hierarchy of effects focuses on the impact of advertising or mass media, the sales funnel is used to track individual customers (often by name) and sales force efforts. (Note: In some industries, such as consumer packaged goods, the term "pipeline sales" can refer to sales into a distribution channel. Please do not confuse pipeline sales with a sales pipeline.)

Construction

In order to conceptualise a sales funnel or pipeline, it is helpful to draw a diagram showing the stages of the selling process (see Figure 6.2). At any point in the year, it is likely that all stages of the pipeline will include some number of customers. As Figure 6.2 illustrates, although there may be a large number of *potential* customers, those who actually make purchases represent only a percentage of these original leads.

Interest creation
This entails building awareness of a product through such activities as trade shows, direct mail and advertising. In the course of interest creation, salespeople can also generate leads. That is, they can identify targets to add to their pool of potential customers. Two main classifications of leads include cold leads and warm leads.

Figure 6.2 Sales force funnel

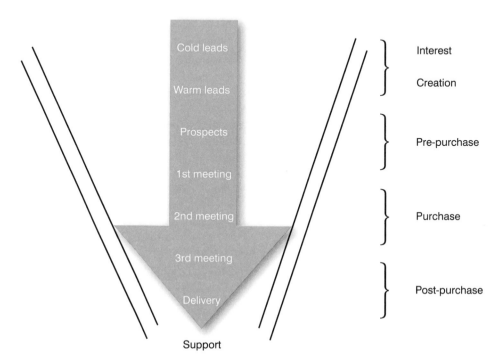

> Cold lead: **A lead that has not specifically expressed interest. These can be identified through mailing lists, phone books, business listings and so on.**
>
> Warm lead: **A lead that is expected to be responsive. These potential customers may have registered through a website or requested product information, for example.**

Pre-purchase

This stage involves identifying prospects from among cold and warm leads. Salespeople make this distinction through initial meetings with leads, in which they explain product features and benefits, and cooperate in problem solving with the customer. The desired result of such an early-stage meeting is not a sale but rather the identification of a prospect and the scheduling of another meeting.

> Prospect: **A potential customer who has been identified as a likely buyer, possessing the ability and willingness to buy.**[8]

Purchase

After prospects are identified and agree to additional calls, salespeople engage in second and third meetings with them. It is in these sessions that traditional "selling" takes place. Salespeople will engage in persuading, negotiating and/or bidding. If a purchase is agreed upon, a salesperson can close the deal through a written proposal, contract or order.

Post-purchase

After a customer has made a purchase, there is still considerable work to be done. This includes delivery of the product or service, installation (if necessary), collection of payments and possibly training. There is then an ongoing commitment to customer service.

After salespeople visualise the different stages represented in a sales funnel, they can track their customers and accounts more accurately. They can do this electronically by using a database or spreadsheet. If a sales pipeline file is maintained on a shared drive, any member of a sales force will be able to update the relevant data on a regular basis. This will also enable a sales manager to view the progress of the team at any point in time. Table 6.2 is an example of a spreadsheet form of a sales funnel.

A manager can use the information stored in such a funnel to prepare for sales in the near future. This is a form of *pipeline analysis*. When a firm faces inventory issues, or when sales goals are being missed, this represents vital information. By applying historical averages, a sales or marketing manager can improve sales forecasts by using the data in a sales funnel. This can be done manually or with specialised software. The underlying assumption behind a sales funnel is that failure at any stage eliminates a prospect from the funnel. The following example illustrates how this bottom-up forecasting could be applied.

Table 6.2 Spreadsheet sales funnel

Sales person	Interest creation		Pre-purchase		Purchase		Post-purchase	
	Cold leads	Warm leads	Prospects	$1^{st}/2^{nd}$ meeting	$2^{nd}/3^{rd}$ meeting		Delivery	Support
Sandy	56	30	19	5	8	7	25
Bob	79	51	33	16	4	14	35

Example Using the sales funnel from earlier, Sandy and Bob's manager wants to forecast the number of sales that will require fulfilment in the next five months. Toward that end, she applies certain historical averages:

- 2% of cold calls are converted to sales within five months.
- 14% of warm calls are converted to sales within four months.
- 25% of prospects are converted to sales within three months.
- 36% of customers who agree to a pre-purchase meeting are converted to sales within two months.
- 53% of customers who agree to a purchase meeting are converted to sales within one month.

On this basis:

$$\text{Upcoming sales} = [(56 + 79) * 2\%] + [(30 + 51) * 14\%] + [(19 + 33) * 25\%] \\ + [(5 + 16) * 36\%)] + [(8 + 4) * 53\%] = 41$$

Note: This example applies to only one product. Often, a firm will need multiple sales funnels for different products or product lines. Additionally, a sale may comprise a single item or thousands of items. In the latter case, it would be appropriate to use a metric for "average sale size/customer" in forecasting.

Data sources, complications and cautions

In order to populate a sales funnel correctly, salespeople must maintain records of all their current and potential customers, and the status of each within the purchase process. Each salesperson must also share this information, which can then be aggregated in a comprehensive database of sales force activities. By applying assumptions to these – including assumptions drawn from historical sales results – a firm can project future sales. For example, if 25% of warm leads are generally converted to sales within two months, and 200 warm leads currently appear in a sales funnel, management can estimate that 50 of these will be converted to sales within two months.

At times, the use of a sales funnel leads to the pitfall of over-prospecting. If the incremental contribution generated by a customer is less than the cost of acquiring that customer, then prospecting for that customer yields a negative result. Salespeople are advised to use customer lifetime value metrics as a guide in deciding the appropriate scale and direction of their prospecting. Increasing pre-purchase sales funnel metrics will not be worthwhile unless that increment leads to improved figures further down the pipeline as well.

Difficulties in the sales cycle can also arise when a salesperson judges that a potential customer may be a prospect because he or she has the willingness and ability to buy. To solidify this judgement, the salesperson must also confirm that the customer possesses the *authority* to buy. When prospecting, salespeople should take the time needed to verify that their contacts can make purchase decisions without approval from another source.

Numeric, ACV and PCV distribution, facings/share of shelf

Distribution metrics quantify the availability of products sold through resellers, usually as a percentage of all potential outlets. Often, outlets are weighted by their share of category sales or "all commodity" sales.

$$\text{Numeric distribution (\%)} = \frac{\text{Number of outlets carrying brand (N)}}{\text{Total number of outlets (N)}}$$

$$\text{All commodity volume (ACV) distribution (\%)} = \frac{\text{Total sales of outlets carrying brand (£)}}{\text{Total sales of all outlets (£)}}$$

$$\text{Product category volume (PCV) distribution[9] (\%)} = \frac{\text{Total category sales of outlets carrying brand (£)}}{\text{Total category sales of all outlets (£)}}$$

$$\text{Category performance ratio (\%)} = \frac{\text{PCV (\%)}}{\text{ACV (\%)}}$$

For marketers who sell through resellers, distribution metrics reveal a brand's percentage of market access. Balancing a firm's efforts in "push" (building and maintaining reseller and distributor support) and "pull" (generating customer demand) is an ongoing strategic concern for marketers.

Purpose: to measure a firm's ability to convey a product to its customers

In broad terms, marketing can be divided into two key challenges:

- The first – and most widely appreciated – is to ensure that consumers or end users want a firm's product. This is generally termed *pull* marketing.

- The second challenge is less broadly recognised, but often just as important. *Push* marketing ensures that customers are given opportunities to buy.

Marketers have developed numerous metrics by which to judge the effectiveness of the distribution system that helps create opportunities to buy. The most fundamental of these are measures of product availability.

Availability metrics are used to quantify the number of outlets reached by a product, the fraction of the relevant market served by those outlets, and the percentage of total sales volume in all categories held by the outlets that carry the product.

Construction

There are three popular measures of distribution coverage:

1 Numeric distribution.

2 All commodity volume (ACV).

3 Product category volume (PCV), also known as weighted distribution.

Numeric distribution

This measure is based on the number of outlets that carry a product (that is, outlets that list at least one of the product's stock-keeping units, or SKUs). It is defined as the percentage of stores that stock a given brand or SKU, within the universe of stores in the relevant market.

The main use of numeric distribution is to understand how many physical locations stock a product or brand. This has implications for delivery systems and for the cost of servicing these outlets.

To calculate numeric distribution, marketers divide the number of stores that stock at least one SKU of a product or brand by the number of outlets in the relevant market.

$$\text{Numeric distribution (\%)} = \frac{\text{Number of outlets carrying product (N)}}{\text{Total number of outlets in the market (N)}}$$

For further information about stock-keeping units (SKUs), refer to "Average price per unit and price per statistical unit" on pages 64–70.

Example Alice sells photo albums to gift shops. There are 60 such stores in her area. In order to generate adequate distribution coverage, Alice believes she must reach at least 60% of these. In initiating her relationship with each store, however, Alice must provide the store with €4,000 worth of inventory to build a presence. To attain her distribution goal, how much will Alice need to invest in inventory?

To reach her numeric distribution target of 60%, Alice must build a presence in 36 stores (that is, 0.60 * 60).

She will therefore have to spend at least €144,000 on inventory (36 stores * €4,000 per store).

All commodity volume

All commodity volume (ACV) is a weighted measure of product availability, or distribution, based on total store sales. ACV can be expressed as a monetary value or percentage.

> **All commodity volume (ACV):** The percentage of sales in all categories that are generated by the stores that stock a given brand (again, at least one SKU of that brand).

$$\text{All commodity volume (ACV distribution) (\%)} = \frac{\text{Total sales of stores carrying brand (£)}}{\text{Total sales of all stores (£)}}$$

$$\text{All commodity volume (ACV distribution) (£)} = \text{Total sales of stores carrying brand (£)}$$

Example The marketers at Madre's Tortillas in Arizona want to know the all commodity volume of their distribution network (Table 6.3).

Table 6.3 Madre's Tortillas' distribution

Outlet	All sales	Tortilla sales	Madre's Tortillas SKUs stocked	Padre's Tortillas SKUs stocked
Store 1	$100,000	$1,000	12 ct, 24 ct	12 ct, 24 ct
Store 2	$75,000	$500	12 ct	24 ct
Store 3	$50,000	$300	12 ct, 24 ct	None
Store 4	$40,000	$400	None	12 ct, 24 ct

Note: ct = count

Madre's Tortillas are carried by Stores 1–3, but not by Store 4. The ACV of its distribution network is therefore the total sales of Stores 1, 2 and 3, divided by the total sales of all stores. This represents a measure of the sales of all commodities in these stores, not just tortilla sales.

$$\text{Madre's Tortillas ACV (\%)} = \frac{\text{Sales stores } 1-3}{\text{All store sales}}$$

$$= \frac{(\$100k + \$75k + \$50k)}{(\$100k + \$75k + \$50k + \$40k)}$$

$$= \frac{\$225k}{\$265k} = 84.9\%$$

The principal benefit of the ACV metric, by comparison with numeric distribution, is that it provides a superior measure of customer traffic in the stores that stock a brand. In essence, ACV adjusts numeric distribution for the fact that not all retailers generate the same level of sales. For example, in a market composed of two small stores, one superstore and one kiosk, numeric distribution would weight each outlet equally, whereas ACV would place greater emphasis on the value of gaining distribution in the superstore. In calculating ACV when detailed sales data are not available, marketers sometimes use the square footage of stores as an approximation of their total sales volume.

The weakness of ACV is that it does not provide direct information about how well each store merchandises and competes in the relevant product category. A store can do a great deal of general business but sell very little of the product category under consideration.

Product category volume

Product category volume (PCV)[10] is a refinement of ACV. It examines the share of the relevant product category sold by the stores in which a given product has gained distribution. It helps marketers understand whether a given product is gaining distribution in outlets where customers look for its category, as opposed to simply high-traffic stores where that product may get lost in the aisles.

Continuing our example of the two small retailers, the kiosk and the superstore, although ACV may lead the marketer of a chocolate bar to seek distribution in the high-traffic superstore, PCV might reveal that the kiosk, surprisingly, generates the greatest volume in snack sales. In building distribution, the marketer would then be advised to target the kiosk as her highest priority.

> **Product category volume (PCV): The percentage share, or monetary value, of category sales made by stores that stock at least one SKU of the brand in question, in comparison with all stores in their universe.**

$$\text{Product category volume (PCV distribution) (\%)} = \frac{\text{Total category sales by stores carrying brand (£)}}{\text{Total category sales of all stores (£)}}$$

$$\text{Product category volume (PCV distribution) (£)} = \text{Total category sales of stores carrying brand (£)}$$

When detailed sales data are available, PCV can provide a strong indication of the market share within a category to which a given brand has access. If sales data are not available, marketers can calculate an approximate PCV by using square footage devoted to the relevant category as an indication of the importance of that category to a particular outlet or store type.

> **Total distribution: The sum of ACV or PCV distribution for all of a brand's stock-keeping units, calculated individually. By contrast with simple ACV or PCV, which are based on the all commodity or product category sales of all stores that carry at least one SKU of a brand, total distribution also reflects the number of SKUs of the brand that is carried by those stores.**
>
> **Category performance ratio: The relative performance of a retailer in a given product category, compared with its performance in all product categories.**

Example The marketers at Madre's Tortillas want to know how effectively their product is reaching the outlets where customers shop for tortillas. Using data from the previous example:

Stores 1, 2 and 3 stock Madre's Tortillas. Store 4 does not. The product category volume of Madre's Tortillas' distribution network can be calculated by dividing total tortilla sales in Stores 1–3 by tortilla sales throughout the market.

$$\text{PCV (\%)} = \frac{\text{(Tortilla sales of stores carrying Madre's)}}{\text{(Tortilla sales of all stores)}}$$

$$= \frac{(\$1,000 + \$500 + \$300)}{(\$1,000 + \$500 + \$300 + \$400)} = 81.8\%$$

By comparing PCV with ACV, the category performance ratio provides insight into whether a brand's distribution network is more or less effective in selling the category of which that brand is a part, compared with its average effectiveness in selling all categories in which members of that network compete.

$$\text{Category performance ratio (\%)} = \frac{\text{PCV (\%)}}{\text{ACV (\%)}}$$

If a distribution network's category performance ratio is greater than 1, then the outlets comprising that network perform comparatively better in selling the category in question than in selling other categories, relative to the market as a whole.

Example As noted earlier, the PCV of Madre's Tortillas' distribution network is 81.8%. Its ACV is 84.9%. Thus, its category performance ratio is 0.96.

Madre's has succeeded in gaining distribution in the largest stores in its market. Tortilla sales in those stores, however, run slightly below the average of all commodity sales in those stores, relative to the market as a whole. That is, outlets carrying Madre's show a slightly weaker focus on tortillas than the overall universe of stores in this market.

Data sources, complications and cautions

In many markets, there are data suppliers such as A.C. Nielsen, which specialise in collecting information about distribution. In other markets, firms must generate their own data. Sales force reports and shipment invoices provide a place to start.

For certain merchandise – especially low-volume, high-value items – it is relatively simple to count the limited number of outlets that carry a given product. For higher-volume, lower-cost goods, merely determining the number of outlets that stock an item can be a challenge and may require assumptions. Take, for instance, the number of outlets selling a specific soft drink. To arrive at an accurate number, one would have to include vending machines and street vendors as well as traditional grocery stores.

Total outlet sales are often approximated by quantifying selling space (measured in square feet or square metres) and applying this measure to industry averages for sales per area of selling space.

In the absence of specific category sales data, it is often useful to weight ACV to arrive at an approximation of PCV. Marketers may know, for example, that pharmacies, relative to their overall sales, sell proportionally more of given product than do superstores. In this event, they might increase the weighting of pharmacies relative to superstores in evaluating relevant distribution coverage.

Related metrics and concepts

Facing
A facing is a frontal view of a single package of a product on a fully stocked shelf.

Share of shelf
A metric that compares the facings of a given brand to the total facing positions available, in order to quantify the display prominence of that brand.

$$\text{Share of shelf (\%)} = \frac{\text{Facings for brand (N)}}{\text{Total facings (N)}}$$

Store versus brand measures
Marketers often refer to a grocery chain's ACV. This can be either a financial number (the chain's total sales of all categories in the relevant geographic market) or a percentage number (its share of financial sales among the universe of stores). A brand's ACV is simply the sum of the ACVs of the chains and stores that stock that brand. Thus, if a brand is stocked by two chains in a market, and these chains have 40% and 30% ACV respectively, then the ACV of that brand's distribution network is 30% + 40%, or 70%.

Marketers can also refer to a chain's market share in a specific category. This is equivalent to the chain's PCV (%). A brand's PCV, by contrast, represents the sum of the PCVs of the chains that stock that brand.

Inventory
This is the level of physical stock held. It will typically be measured at different points in a pipeline. A retailer may have inventory on order from suppliers, at warehouses, in transit to stores, in the stores' backrooms and on the store shelves.

Breadth of distribution
This figure can be measured by the number of SKUs held. Typically, a company will hold a wide range of SKUs – a high breadth of distribution – for the products that it is most interested in selling.

Features in store
The percentage of stores offering a promotion in a given time period. This can be weighted by product or by all commodity volume (ACV).

ACV on display
Distinctions can be made in all commodity volume metrics to take account of where products are on display. This will reduce the measured distribution of products if they are not in a position to be sold.

AVC on promotion
Marketers may want to measure the ACV of outlets where a given product is on promotion. This is a useful shorthand way of determining the product's reliance on promotion.

Supply chain metrics

Marketing logistics tracking includes the following metrics:

$$\text{Out-of-stocks (\%)} = \frac{\text{Outlets where brand or product is listed but unavailable (N)}}{\text{Total outlets where brand or product is listed (N)}}$$

$$\text{Service levels, percentage on-time delivery (\%)} = \frac{\text{Deliveries achieved in time frame promised (N)}}{\text{All deliveries initiated in the period (N)}}$$

$$\text{Inventory turns (I)} = \frac{\text{Product revenues (£)}}{\text{Average inventory (£)}}$$

Logistics tracking helps ensure that companies are meeting demand efficiently and effectively.

Purpose: to monitor the effectiveness of an organisation in managing the distribution and logistics process

Logistics are where the marketing rubber meets the road. A lot can be lost at the potential point-of-purchase if the right goods are not delivered to the appropriate outlets on time and in amounts that correspond to consumer demand. How hard can that be? Well, ensuring that supply meets demand becomes more difficult when:

- The company sells more than a few stock-keeping units (SKUs).
- Multiple levels of suppliers, warehouses and stores are involved in the distribution process.
- Product models change frequently.
- The channel offers customer-friendly return policies.

In this complex field, by monitoring core metrics and comparing these with historical norms and guidelines, marketers can determine how well their distribution channel is functioning as a supply chain for their customers.

By monitoring logistics, managers can investigate questions such as the following: Did we lose sales because the wrong items were shipped to a store that was running a promotion? Are we being forced to pay for the disposal of obsolete goods that stayed too long in warehouses or stores?

Construction

> Out-of-stocks: **This metric quantifies the number of retail outlets where an item is expected to be available for customers, but is not. It is typically expressed as a percentage of stores that list the relevant item.**

$$\text{Out-of-stocks (\%)} = \frac{\text{Outlets where brand or product is listed but unavailable (N)}}{\text{Total outlets where brand or product is listed (N)}}$$

Being "listed" by a chain means that a headquarters buyer has "authorised" distribution of a brand, SKU or product at the store level. For various reasons, being listed does not always ensure presence on the shelf. Local managers may not approve "distribution". Alternatively, a product may be distributed but sold out.

Out-of-stocks are often expressed as a percentage. Marketers must note whether an out-of-stock percentage is based on numeric distribution, ACV, PCV or the percentage of distributing stores for a given chain.

The in-stock percentage is the complement of the out-of-stock percentage. A 3% out-of-stock rate would be equivalent to a 97% in-stock rate.

> PCV net out-of-stocks: **The PCV of a given product's distribution network, adjusted for out-of-stock situations.**

Product category volume (PCV), net out-of-stocks

This out-of-stocks measure is calculated by multiplying PCV by a factor that adjusts it to recognise out-of-stock situations. The adjusting factor is simply one minus the out-of-stocks figure.

$$\text{Product category volume, net out-of-stocks (\%)} = \text{PCV (\%)} * [1 - \text{Out-of-stock (\%)}]$$

Service levels, percentage on-time delivery

There are various service measures in marketing logistics. One particularly common measure is on-time delivery. This metric captures the percentage of customer (or trade) orders that are delivered in accordance with the promised schedule.

$$\text{Service levels, percentage on-time delivery (\%)} = \frac{\text{Deliveries achieved in time frame promised (N)}}{\text{All deliveries initiated in the period (N)}}$$

Inventories, like out-of-stocks and service levels, should be tracked at the SKU level. For example, in monitoring inventory, an apparel retailer will need to know not only the brand and design of goods carried, but also their size. Simply knowing that there are 30 pairs of suede hiking boots in a store, for example, is not sufficient – particularly if all those boots are the same size and fail to fit most customers.

By tracking inventory, marketers can determine the percentage of goods at each stage of the logistical process – in the warehouse, in transit to stores or on the retail floor, for example. The significance of this information will depend on a firm's resource management strategy. Some firms seek to hold the bulk of their inventory at the warehouse level, for example, particularly if they have an effective transport system to ship goods quickly to stores.

Inventory turns

The number of times that inventory "turns over" in a year can be calculated on the basis of the revenues associated with a product and the level of inventory held. One need only divide the revenues associated with the product in question by the average level of inventory for that item. As this quotient rises, it indicates that inventory of the item is moving more quickly through the process. Inventory turns can be calculated for companies, brands or SKUs and at any level in the distribution chain, but they are frequently most relevant for individual trade customers. Important note: in calculating inventory turns, financial figures for both sales and inventory must be stated either on a cost or wholesale basis, or on a retail or resale basis, but the two bases must not be mixed.

$$\text{Inventory turns (I)} = \frac{\text{Annual product revenues (£)}}{\text{Average inventory (£)}}$$

Inventory days

This metric also sheds light on the speed with which inventory moves through the sales process. To calculate it, marketers divide the 365 days of the year by the number of inventory turns, yielding the average number of days of inventory carried by a firm. By way of example, if a firm's inventory of a product "turned" 36.5 times in a year, that firm would, on average, hold 10 days' worth of inventory of the product. High inventory turns – and, by corollary, low inventory days – tend to increase profitability through efficient use of a firm's investment in inventory. But they can also lead to higher out-of-stocks and lost sales.

$$\text{Inventory days (N)} = \frac{\text{Days in year (365)}}{\text{Inventory turns (I)}}$$

Inventory days represents the number of days' worth of sales that can be supplied by the inventory present at a given moment. Viewed from a slightly different perspective, this figure advises logistics managers of the time expected to elapse before they suffer a stock-out. To calculate this figure, managers divide product revenue for the year by the value of the inventory days, generating expected annual turns for that inventory level. This can be easily converted into days by using the previous equation.

Example An apparel retailer in California holds $600,000 worth of socks in inventory on 1 January, and $800,000 the following 31 December. Revenues generated by sock sales totalled $3.5 million during the year.

To estimate average sock inventory during the year, managers might take the average of the beginning and ending numbers: ($600,000 + $800,000)/2 = $700,000 average inventory. On this basis, managers might calculate inventory turns as follows:

$$\text{Inventory turns} = \frac{\text{Product revenues}}{\text{Average inventory}}$$

$$= \frac{\$3,500,000}{\$700,000} = 5$$

If inventory turns five times per year, this figure can be converted to inventory days in order to measure the average number of days' worth of stock held during the period.

$$\text{Inventory days} = \frac{\text{Days in year (365)}}{\text{Inventory turns}}$$

$$= \frac{365}{5} = 73 \text{ days' worth of inventory}$$

Data sources, complications and cautions

Although some companies and supply chains maintain sophisticated inventory tracking systems, others must estimate logistical metrics on the basis of less-than-perfect data. Increasingly, manufacturers may also have difficulty purchasing research because retailers that gather such information tend to restrict access or charge high fees for it. Often, the only readily available data may be drawn from incomplete store audits or reports filed by an overloaded sales force. Ideally, marketers would like to have reliable metrics for the following:

● Inventory units and monetary value of each SKU at each level of the distribution chain for each major customer.

● Out-of-stocks for each SKU, measured at both the supplier and the store level.

● Percentage of customer orders that were delivered on time and in the correct amount.

● Inventory counts in the tracking system that don't match the number in the physical inventory. (This would facilitate a measure of shrinkage or theft.)

When considering the monetary value of inventory, it is important to use comparable figures in all calculations. As an example of the inconsistency and confusion that can arise in this area, a company might value its stock on the retail shelf at the cost to the store, which might include an approximation of all direct costs. Or it might value that stock for some purposes at the retail price. Such figures can be difficult to reconcile with the cost of goods purchased at the warehouse and can also be different from accounting figures adjusted for obsolescence.

When evaluating inventory, managers must also establish a costing system for items that can't be tracked on an individual basis. Such systems include the following:

● **First in, first out (FIFO):** The first unit of inventory received is the first to be charged to expenses upon sale.

● **Last in, first out (LIFO):** The last unit of inventory received is the first to be charged to expenses upon sale.

The choice of FIFO or LIFO can have a significant financial impact in inflationary times. At such times, FIFO will hold down the cost of goods sold by reporting this figure at the earliest available prices. Simultaneously, it will value inventory at its highest possible level – that is, at the most recent prices. The financial impact of LIFO will be the reverse.

In some industries, inventory management is a core skill. Examples include the apparel industry, in which retailers must ensure that they are not left with prior seasons' fashions, and the technology industry, in which rapid developments make products hard to sell after only a few months.

In logistical management, firms must beware of creating reward structures that lead to sub-optimal outcomes. An inventory manager rewarded solely for minimising out-of-stocks, for example, would have a clear incentive to overbuy –

regardless of inventory holding costs. In this field, managers must ensure that incentive systems are sophisticated enough not to reward undesirable behaviour.

Firms must also be realistic about what will be achieved in inventory management. In most organisations, the only way to be completely in stock on every product all the time is to ramp up inventories. This will involve huge warehousing costs. It will tie up a great deal of the company's capital in buying stocks. And it will result in painful obsolescence charges to unload overpurchased items. Good logistics and inventory management entails finding the right trade-off between two conflicting objectives: minimising both inventory holding costs and sales lost due to out-of-stocks.

Related metrics and concepts

Rain checks, or make-goods on promotions

These measures evaluate the effect on a store of promotional items being unavailable. In a typical example, a store might track the incidents in which it offers customers a substitute item because it has run out of stock on a promoted item. Rain checks or make-goods might be expressed as a percentage of goods sold, or more specifically, as a percentage of revenues coded to the promotion but generated by sales of items not listed as part of the promotional event.

Misshipments

This measures the number of shipments that failed to arrive on time or in the proper quantities.

Deductions

This measures the value of deductions from customer invoices caused by incorrect or incomplete shipments, damaged goods, returns or other factors. It is often useful to distinguish between the reasons for deductions.

Obsolescence

This is a vital metric for many retailers, especially those involved in fashion and technology. It is typically expressed as the monetary value of items that are obsolete, or as the percentage of total stock value that comprises obsolete items. If obsolescence is high, then a firm holds a significant amount of inventory that is likely to sell only at a considerable discount.

Shrinkage

This is generally a euphemism for theft. It describes a phenomenon in which the value of actual inventory runs lower than recorded inventory, due to an unexplained reduction in the number of units held. This measure is typically calculated as a monetary figure or as a percentage of total stock value.

Pipeline sales

Sales that are required to supply retail and wholesale channels with sufficient inventory to make a product available for sale (refer to pages 172–176).

Consumer off-take

Purchases by consumers from retailers, as opposed to purchases by retailers or wholesalers from their suppliers. When consumer off-take runs higher than manufacturer sales rates, inventories will be drawn down.

Diverted merchandise or diverted goods

Products shipped to one customer that are subsequently resold to another customer. For example, if a retail pharmacy chain overbuys vitamins at a promotional price, it may ship some of its excess inventory to a pound shop.

SKU profitability: mark-downs, GMROII and DPP

Profitability metrics for retail products and categories are generally similar to other measures of profitability, such as unit and percentage margins. Certain refinements have been developed for retailers and distributors, however. Mark-downs, for example, are calculated as a ratio of discount to original price charged. Gross margin return on inventory investment (GMROII) is calculated as margin divided by the cost of inventory and is expressed as a "rate" or percentage. Direct product profitability (DPP) is a metric that adjusts gross margin for other costs, such as storage, handling and allowances paid by suppliers.

$$\text{Mark-down (\%)} = \frac{\text{Reduction in price of SKU (£)}}{\text{Initial price of SKU (£)}}$$

$$\text{Gross margin return on inventory investment (\%)} = \frac{\text{Gross margin on product sales in period (£)}}{\text{Average inventory value at cost (£)}}$$

$$\text{Direct product profitability (£)} = \text{Gross margin (£)} - \text{Direct product costs (£)}$$

By monitoring mark-downs, marketers can gain important insight into SKU profitability. GMROII can be a vital metric in determining whether sales rates justify inventory positions. DPP is a theoretically powerful measure of profit that has fallen out of favour, but it may be revived in other forms (for example, activity-based costing).

Purpose: to assess the effectiveness and profitability of individual product and category sales

Retailers and distributors have a great deal of choice regarding which products to stock and which to discontinue as they make room for a steady stream of new offerings. By measuring the profitability of individual stock-keeping units (SKUs), managers develop the insight needed to optimise such product selections. Profitability metrics are also useful in decisions regarding pricing, display and promotional campaigns.

Figures that affect or reflect retail profitability include mark-downs, gross margin return on inventory investment and direct product profitability.

Mark-downs are not always applied to slow-moving merchandise. Mark-downs in excess of budget, however, are almost always regarded as indicators of errors in product assortment, pricing or promotion. Mark-downs are often expressed as a percentage of regular price. As a stand-alone metric, a mark-down is difficult to interpret.

Gross margin return on inventory investment (GMROII) applies the concept of return on investment (ROI) to what is often the most crucial element of a retailer's working capital: its inventory.

Direct product profitability (DPP) shares many features with activity-based costing (ABC). Under ABC, a wide range of costs are weighted and allocated to specific products through cost drivers – the factors that cause the costs to be incurred. In measuring DPP, retailers factor such line items as storage, handling, manufacturer's allowances, warranties and financing plans into calculations of earnings on specific product sales.

Construction

Mark-down

This metric quantifies shop-floor reductions in the price of an SKU. It can be expressed on a per-unit basis or as a total for the SKU. It can also be calculated in monetary terms or as a percentage of the item's initial price.

$$\text{Mark-down (£)} = \text{Initial price of SKU (£)} - \text{Actual sales price (£)}$$

$$\text{Mark-down (\%)} = \frac{\text{Mark-down (£)}}{\text{Initial price of SKU (£)}}$$

Gross margin return on inventory investment (GMROII)

This metric quantifies the profitability of products in relation to the inventory investment required to make them available. It is calculated by dividing the gross margin on product sales by the cost of the relevant inventory.

$$\text{Gross margin return on inventory investment (\%)} = \frac{\text{Gross margin on product sales in period (£)}}{\text{Average inventory value at cost (£)}}$$

Direct product profitability (DPP)

Direct product profitability is grounded in a simple concept, but it can be difficult to measure in practice. The calculation of DPP consists of multiple stages. The first stage is to determine the gross margin of the goods in question. This gross margin figure is then modified to take account of other revenues associated with the product, such as promotional rebates from suppliers or payments from financing companies that gain business on its sale. The adjusted gross margin is then reduced by an allocation of direct product costs, described next.

Direct product costs
These are the costs of bringing a product to customers. They generally include warehouse, distribution and store costs.

$$\text{Direct product costs (£)} = \text{Warehouse direct costs (£)} + \text{Transportation direct costs (£)} + \text{Store direct costs (£)}$$

Direct product profitability (DPP)
Direct product profitability represents a product's adjusted gross margin, less its direct product costs.

As noted earlier, the concept of DPP is quite simple. Difficulties can arise, however, in calculating or estimating the relevant costs. Typically, an elaborate ABC system is needed to generate direct costs for individual SKUs. DPP has fallen somewhat out of favour as a result of these difficulties.

Other metrics have been developed, however, in an effort to obtain a more refined and accurate estimation of the "true" profitability of individual SKUs, factoring in the varying costs of receiving, storing and selling them. The variations between products in the levels of these costs can be quite significant. In the grocery industry, for example, the cost of warehousing and shelving frozen foods is far greater – per unit or per pound of sales – than the cost of warehousing and shelving canned goods.

$$\text{Direct product profitability (£)} = \text{Adjusted gross margin (£)} - \text{Direct product costs (£)}$$

Example The apparel retailer cited earlier wants to probe further into the profitability of its sock line. Toward that end, it assembles the following information. For this retailer, socks generate slotting allowances – in essence, fees paid by the manufacturer to the retailer in compensation for shelf space – in the amount of $50,000 per year. Warehouse costs for the retailer come to $10,000,000 per year. Socks consume 0.5% of warehouse space. Estimated store and distribution costs associated with socks total $80,000.

With this information, the retailer calculates an adjusted gross margin for its sock line.

$$\text{Adjusted gross margin} = \text{Gross margin} + \text{Additional margin}$$
$$= \$350,000 + \$50,000$$
$$= \$400,000$$

The retailer then calculates direct product costs for its sock line.

$$\text{Direct product costs} = \text{Store and distribution costs} + \text{Warehouse costs}$$
$$= \$80,000 + (0.5\% * \$10,000,000)$$
$$= \$80,000 + \$50,000$$
$$= \$130,000$$

On this basis, the retailer calculates the direct product profitability of its sock line.

$$\text{DPP} = \text{Adjusted gross margin} - \text{Direct product costs}$$
$$= \$400,000 - \$130,000$$
$$= \$270,000$$

Data sources, complications and cautions

For GMROII calculations, it is necessary to determine the value of inventory held, at cost. Ideally, this will be an average figure for the period to be considered. The average of inventory held at the beginning and end of the period is often used as a proxy, and is generally – but not always – an acceptable approximation. To perform the GMROII calculation, it is also necessary to calculate a gross margin figure.

One of the central considerations in evaluating direct product profitability is an organisation's ability to capture large amounts of accurate data for analysis. The DPP calculation requires an estimate of the warehousing, distribution, selling costs incurred in the store and other costs attributable to a product. To assemble these data, it may be necessary to gather all distribution costs and apportion them according to the cost drivers identified.

Inventory held, and thus the cost of holding it, can change considerably over time. Although one may usually approximate average inventory over a period by averaging the beginning and ending levels of this line item, this will not always be the case. Seasonal factors may perturb these figures. Also, a firm may hold substantially more – or less – inventory during the course of a year than at its beginning and end. This could have a major impact on any DPP calculation.

DPP also requires a measure of the ancillary revenues tied to product sales.

Direct product profitability has great conceptual strength. It tries to account for the wide range of costs that retailers incur in conveying a product to customers, and thus to yield a more realistic measure of the profitability of that product. The only significant weakness in this metric is its complexity. Few retailers have been able to implement it. Many firms continue to try to realise its underlying concept, however, through such programmes as activity-based costing.

Related metrics and concepts

> Shopping basket margin: **The profit margin on an entire retail transaction, which may include a number of products. This aggregate transaction is termed the "basket" of purchases that a consumer makes.**

One key factor in a firm's profitability is its capability to sell ancillary products in addition to its central offering. In some businesses, more profit can be generated through accessories than through the core product. Beverage and snack sales at cinemas are a prime example. With this in mind, marketers must understand each product's role within their firm's aggregate offering – be it a vehicle to generate customer traffic, or to increase the size of each customer's basket, or to maximise earnings on that item itself.

References and suggested further reading

Wilner, J.D. (1998). *7 Secrets to Successful Sales Management: The Sales Manager's Manual*, Boca Raton, Florida: St Lucie Press.

Zoltners, A.A., P. Sinha and G.A. Zoltners. (2001). *The Complete Guide to Accelerating Sales Force Performance*, New York: AMACOM.

Pricing strategy

7

Metrics covered in this chapter:

- Price premium

- Reservation price

- Per cent good value

- Price elasticity of demand

- Optimal prices, linear and constant demand

- "Own", "cross" and "residual" price elasticity

Introduction

"The cost of … lack of sophistication in pricing is growing day by day. Customers and Competitors operating globally in a generally more complex marketing environment are making mundane thinking about pricing a serious threat to the firm's financial well being."[1]

A full-fledged evaluation of pricing strategies and tactics is well beyond the scope of this book. However, there are certain key metrics and concepts that are fundamental to the analysis of pricing alternatives, and this chapter addresses them.

First we describe several of the more common methods of calculating price premiums – also called relative prices.

Next, we discuss the concepts that form the foundation of price – quantity schedules – also known as demand functions or demand curves. These include reservation prices and per cent good value.

In the third section, we explain the definition and calculation of price elasticity, a frequently used index of market response to changes in price. This relatively simple ratio of percentage changes in volumes and prices is complicated in practice by variations in measure and interpretation.

For managers, the purpose of understanding price elasticity is to improve pricing. With this in mind, we've devoted a separate section to determining optimal prices for the two main types of demand functions: linear and constant elasticity. The final portion of this chapter addresses the question of whether elasticity has been calculated in a manner that incorporates likely competitive reactions. It explains three types of elasticity – "own", "cross" and "residual" elasticity. Although these may seem at first glance to rest upon subtle or pedantic distinctions, they have major pragmatic implications. The familiar concept of the prisoner's dilemma helps explain their import.

Metric	Construction	Considerations	Purpose
Price premium	The percentage by which the price of a brand exceeds a benchmark price.	Benchmarks include average price paid, average price charged, average price displayed and price of a relevant competitor. Prices can be compared at any level in the channel and can be calculated on a gross basis or net of discounts and rebates.	Measures how a brand's price compares to that of its competition.
Reservation price	The maximum amount an individual is willing to pay for a product.	Reservation prices are difficult to observe.	One way to conceptualise a demand curve is as the aggregation of reservation prices of potential customers.
Per cent good value	The proportion of customers who consider a product to be a good value – that is, to have a selling price below their reservation price.	Easier to observe than individual reservation prices.	A second way to conceptualise a demand curve is as the relationship between per cent good value and price.

Metric	Construction	Considerations	Purpose
Price elasticity of demand	The responsiveness of demand to a small change in price, expressed as a ratio of percentages.	For linear demand, linear projections based on elasticity are accurate, but elasticity changes with price. For constant elasticity demand, linear projections are approximate, but elasticity is the same for all prices.	Measures the responsiveness of quantity to changes in price. If priced optimally, the margin is the negative inverse of elasticity.
Optimal price	For linear demand, optimal price is the average of variable cost and the maximum reservation price. For constant elasticity, optimal price is a known function of variable cost and elasticity. In general, optimal price is the price that maximises contribution after accounting for how quantity changes with price.	Optimal price formulas are appropriate only if the variable cost per unit is constant, and there are no larger strategic considerations.	Quickly determines the price that maximises contribution.
Residual elasticity	Residual elasticity is "own" elasticity plus the product of competitor reaction elasticity and cross elasticity.	Rests on an assumption that competitor reaction to a firm's price changes is predictable.	Measures the responsiveness of quantity to changes in price, after accounting for competitor reactions.

Price premium

Price premium, or relative price, is the percentage by which a product's selling price exceeds (or falls short of) a benchmark price.

$$\text{Price premium (\%)} = \frac{[\text{Brand A price (£)} - \text{Benchmark price (£)}]}{\text{Benchmark price (£)}}$$

Marketers need to monitor price premiums as early indicators of competitive pricing strategies. Changes in price premiums can also be signs of product shortages, excess inventories, or other changes in the relationships between supply and demand.

Purpose: to evaluate product pricing in the context of market competition

Although there are several useful benchmarks with which a manager can compare a brand's price, they all attempt to measure the "average price" in the marketplace. By comparing a brand's price with a market average, managers can gain valuable insight into its strength, especially if they view these findings in the context of volume and market share changes. Indeed, price premium – also known as relative price – is a commonly used metric among marketers and senior managers. Fully 63% of firms report the relative prices of their products to their boards, according to a recent survey conducted in the US, UK, Germany, Japan and France.[2]

Price premium: **The percentage by which the price charged for a specified brand exceeds (or falls short of) a benchmark price established for a similar product or basket of products. Price premium is also known as relative price.**

Construction

In calculating price premium, managers must first specify a benchmark price. Typically, the price of the brand in question will be included in this benchmark, and all prices in the benchmark will be for an equivalent volume of product (for example, price per litre). There are at least four commonly used benchmarks:

- The price of a specified competitor or competitors.
- Average price paid: the unit-sales weighted average price in the category.
- Average price displayed: the display-weighted average price in the category.
- Average price charged: the simple (unweighted) average price in the category.

Example Ali's company sells "gO2" mineral water in its EU home market at a 12% premium over the price of its main competitor. Ali would like to know whether the same price premium is being maintained in the Turkish market, where gO2 faces quite different competition. He notes that gO2 mineral water sells in Turkey for 2 (new) lira per litre, while its main competitor, Essence, sells for 1.9 lira per litre.

$$\text{Price premium} = \frac{(2.0 \text{ lira} - 1.9 \text{ lira})}{1.9 \text{ lira}}$$

$$= \frac{0.1 \text{ lira}}{1.9 \text{ lira}} = 5.3\% \text{ premium versus Essence}$$

When assessing a brand's price premium *vis-à-vis* multiple competitors, managers can use as their benchmark the average price of a selected group of those competitors.

Note also that changes in unit shares will affect the average price paid. If a low-price brand steals shares from a higher-priced rival, the average price paid will decline. This would cause a firm's price premium (calculated using the average price paid as a benchmark) to rise, even if its absolute price did not change. Similarly, if a brand is priced at a premium, that premium will decline as it gains share. The reason: a market share gain by a premium-priced brand will cause the overall average price paid in its market to rise. This, in turn, will reduce the price differential between that brand and the market average.

Example Ali wants to compare his brand's price to the average price paid for similar products in the market. He notes that gO2 sells for 2.0 lira per litre and has 20% of the unit sales in market. Its up-market competitor, Panache, sells for 2.1 lira and enjoys 10% unit market share. Essence sells for 1.9 lira and has 20% share. Finally, the budget brand, Besik, sells for 1.2 lira and commands 50% of the market.

Ali calculates the weighted average price paid as $(20\% * 2) + (10\% * 2.1) + (20\% * 1.9) + (50\% * 1.2) = 1.59$ lira.

$$\text{Price premium (\%)} = \frac{(2.00 - 1.59)}{1.59}$$

$$= \frac{0.41}{1.59}$$

$$= 25.8\%$$

To calculate the price premium using the average price paid benchmark, managers can also divide a brand's share of the market in value terms by its share in volume terms. If value and volume market shares are equal, there is no premium. If value share is greater than volume share, then there is a positive price premium.

$$\text{Price premium (\%)} = \frac{\text{Revenue market share (\%)}}{\text{Unit market share (\%)}}$$

Average price charged: **Calculation of the average price paid requires knowledge of the sales or shares of each competitor. A much simpler benchmark is the average price charged – the simple unweighted average price of the brands in the category. This benchmark requires knowledge only of prices. As a consequence, the price premium calculated using this benchmark is not affected by changes in unit shares. For this reason, this benchmark serves a slightly different purpose. It captures the way a brand's price compares to prices set by its competitors, without regard to customers' reactions to those prices. It also treats all competitors equally in the calculation of the benchmark price. Large and small competitors are weighted equally when calculating average price charged.**

Example Using the previous data, Ali also calculates the average price charged in the mineral water category as $(2 + 2.1 + 1.9 + 1.2)/4 = 1.8$ lira.

Using the average price charged as his benchmark, he calculates gO2's price premium as

$$\text{Price premium (\%)} = \frac{(2.00 - 1.8)}{1.8}$$

$$= \frac{0.2}{1.8}$$

$$= 11.1\% \text{ premium}$$

> **Average price displayed:** **One benchmark conceptually situated between average price paid and average price charged is the average price displayed. Marketing managers who seek a benchmark that captures differences in the scale and strength of brands' distribution might weight each brand's price in proportion to a numerical measure of distribution. Typical measures of distribution strength include numeric distribution, ACV (%) and PCV (%).**

Example Ali calculates the average price displayed using numeric distribution.

Ali's brand, gO2, is priced at 2 lira and is distributed in 500 of the 1,000 stores that carry bottled water. Panache is priced at 2.1 lira and stocked by 200 stores. Essence is priced at 1.9 lira and sold through 400 stores. Besik carries a price of 1.2 lira and has a presence in 900 stores.

Ali calculates relative weighting on the basis of numeric distribution. The total number of stores is 1,000. The weightings are therefore, for gO2, 500/1,000 = 50%; for Panache, 200/1,000 = 20%; for Essence, 400/1,000 = 40%; and for Besik, 900/1,000 = 90%. As the weightings thus total 200%, in calculating average price displayed, the sum of the weighted prices must be divided by that figure, as follows:

$$\text{Average price displayed} = \frac{[(2 * 50\%) + (2.1 * 20\%) + (1.9 * 40\%) + (1.2 * 90\%)]}{200\%}$$

$$= 1.63 \text{ lira}$$

$$\text{Price premium (\%)} = \frac{(2.00 - 1.63)}{1.63}$$

$$= \frac{0.37}{1.63}$$

$$= 22.7\% \text{ premium}$$

Data sources, complications and cautions

There are several practical aspects of calculating price premiums that deserve mention. Managers may find it easier to select a few leading competitors and focus their analysis and comparison on these. Often, it is difficult to obtain reliable data on smaller competitors.

Managers must exercise care when interpreting price premiums. Different benchmarks measure different types of premiums and must be interpreted accordingly.

Can a price premium be negative?

Yes. Although generally expressed in terms that imply only positive values, a price premium can be negative. If one brand doesn't command a positive premium, a competitor will. Consequently, except in the unlikely event that all prices are exactly equal, managers may want to speak in terms of *positive* premiums. When a given brand's price is at the low end of the market, managers may want to say that the competition holds a price premium of a certain value.

Should we use retail, manufacturer or distributor pricing?

Each is useful in understanding the market dynamics at its level. When products have different channel margins, their price premiums will differ, depending on the channel under consideration. When stating a price premium, managers are advised to specify the level to which it applies.

Prices at each level can be calculated on a gross basis, or net of discounts, rebates and coupons

Especially when dealing with distributors or retailers, there are likely to be substantial differences between manufacturer selling prices (retail purchase prices), depending on whether they are adjusted for discounts and allowances.

> Theoretical price premium: **This is the price difference that would make potential customers indifferent between two competing products. It represents a different use of the term "price premium" that is growing in popularity. The theoretical price premium can also be discovered through a conjoint analysis using brand as an attribute. The theoretical price premium is the point at which consumers would be indifferent between a branded and an unbranded item, or between two different brands. We have termed this a "theoretical" price premium because there is no guarantee that the price premiums observed in the market will take this value. (Refer to "Conjoint utilities and consumer preference" on pages 119–123 for an explanation of conjoint analysis.)**

Reservation price and per cent good value

> **The reservation price is the value a customer places on a product. It constitutes an individual's maximum willingness to pay. Per cent good value represents the proportion of customers who believe a product is a "good value" at a specific price.**
> **These are useful metrics in marketers' evaluation of pricing and customer value.**

Purpose: to evaluate maximum pricing latitude

Reservation prices provide a basis for estimating products' demand functions in situations where other data are not available. They also offer marketers insight into pricing latitude. When it is not possible or convenient to ask customers about their reservation prices, per cent good value can provide a substitute for that metric.

Construction

> Reservation price: **The price above which a customer will not buy a product. Also known as the maximum willingness to pay.**
>
> Per cent good value: **The proportion of customers who perceive a product to represent a good value, that is, to carry a selling price at or below their reservation price.**

By way of example, let's posit a market consisting of 11 individuals with reservation prices for a given product of £30, £40, £50, £60, £70, £80, £90, £100, £110, £120 and £130. The manufacturer of that product seeks to decide upon its price. Clearly, it might do better than to offer a single price. For now, however, let's assume tailored prices are impractical. The variable cost to produce the product is £60 per unit.

With these reservation prices, the manufacturer might expect to sell 11 units at £30 or less, 10 units at a price greater than £30 but less than or equal to £40, and so on. It would make no sales at a unit price greater than £130. (For convenience, we have assumed that people buy at their reservation price. This assumption is consistent with a reservation price being the *maximum* an individual is willing to pay.)

Table 7.1 shows this price–quantity relationship, together with the contribution to the firm at each possible price.

A table of quantities expected at each of several prices is often called a demand schedule (or curve). This example shows that one way to conceptualise a demand curve is as the accumulation of individual reservation prices. Although it will clearly be difficult in practice to measure individual reservation prices, the point here is simply to illustrate the use of reservation prices in pricing decisions. In this example, the optimal price – that is, the price that maximises total contribution – is £100. At £100, the manufacturer expects to sell 4 units. Its contribution margin is £40, yielding a total contribution of £160.

Table 7.1 Price–quantity relationship

Price	% good value	Quantity	Total contribution
£20	100.00%	11	−£440
£30	100.00%	11	−£330
£40	90.91%	10	−£200
£50	81.82%	9	−£90
£60	72.73%	8	£0
£70	63.64%	7	£70
£80	54.55%	6	£120
£90	45.45%	5	£150
£100	36.36%	4	£160
£110	27.27%	3	£150
£120	18.18%	2	£120
£130	9.09%	1	£70
£140	0.00%	0	£0
£150	0.00%	0	£0

Variable cost is £60 per unit.

This example also illustrates the concept of consumer surplus. At £100, the manufacturer sells three items at a price point below customers' reservation prices. The consumer with the reservation price of £110 enjoys a surplus of £10. The consumer with the reservation price of £120 receives a surplus of £20. Finally, the consumer with the highest reservation price, £130, receives a surplus of £30. From the manufacturer's perspective, the total consumer surplus – £60 – represents an opportunity for increased contribution if it can find a way to capture this unclaimed value.

Data sources, complications and cautions

Finding reservation prices is no easy matter. Two techniques that are frequently used to gain insight into this metric are as follows:

- **Second-price auctions:** In a second-price auction, the highest bidder wins but pays only the second-highest bid amount. Auction theory suggests that when bidding on items of known value in such auctions, individuals have an incentive to bid their reservation prices. Certain survey techniques have been designed to mimic this process. In one of these, customers are asked to name their prices for an item, with the understanding that these prices will then be subjected to a lottery. If the price drawn in the lottery is less than the price named, the respondent gains an opportunity to purchase the item in question at the drawn price.

- **Conjoint analysis:** In this analytical technique, marketers gain insight into customer perceptions regarding the value of any set of attributes through the trade-offs they are willing to make.

Such tests can, however, be difficult to construct and impractical in many circumstances. Consequently, as a fall-back technique, marketers can measure per cent good value. Rather than seeking to learn each customer's reservation price, they may find it easier to test a few candidate prices by asking customers whether they consider an item a "good value" at each of those prices.

Linear demand

The quantity–price schedule formed by an accumulation of reservation prices can take a variety of shapes. When the distribution of reservation prices is uniform – when reservation prices are equally spaced, as in our example – the demand schedule will be linear (see Figure 7.1). That is, each increment in price will reduce quantity by an equal amount. As the linear function is by far the most commonly used representation of demand, we provide a description of this function as it relates to the distribution of underlying reservation prices.

It takes only two points to determine a straight line. Likewise, it takes only two parameters to write an equation for that line. Generally, that equation is written as $Y = mX + b$, in which m is the slope of the line and b is its Y-intercept.

A line, however, can also be defined in terms of the two points where it crosses the axes. In the case of linear demand, these crossing points (intercepts) have useful managerial interpretations.

Figure 7.1 Maximum willing to buy and maximum reservation price

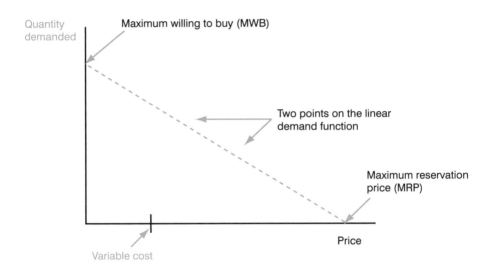

The quantity-axis intercept can be viewed as a representation of the maximum willing to buy (MWB). This is the total number of potential customers for a product. A firm can serve all these customers only at a price of zero. Assuming that each potential customer buys one unit, MWB is the quantity sold when the price is zero.

The price-axis intercept can be viewed as the maximum reservation price (MRP). The MRP is a number slightly greater than the highest reservation price among all those willing to buy. If a firm prices its product at or above MRP, no one will buy.

> Maximum reservation price: **The lowest price at which quantity demanded equals zero.**
>
> Maximum willing to buy (MWB): **The quantity that customers will "buy" when the price of a product is zero. This is an artificial concept used to anchor a linear demand function.**

In a linear demand curve defined by MWB and MRP, the equation for quantity (Q) as a function of price (P) can be written as follows:

$$Q = (MWB) * [1 - \frac{P}{MRP}]$$

Example Erin knows that the demand for her soft drink is a simple linear function of price. She can sell 10 units at a price of zero. When the price hits £5 per unit, demand falls to zero. How many units will Erin sell if the price is £3 (see Figure 7.2)?

Figure 7.2 Simple linear demand (price–quantity) function

For Erin's soft drink, the MRP (maximum reservation price) is £5 and the MWB (maximum willing to buy) is 10 units. At a price of £3, Erin will sell 10 * (1 − £3/£5), or 4 units.

When demand is linear, any two points on the price–quantity demand function can be used to determine MRP and MWB. If P_1 and Q_1 represent the first price-quantity point on the line, and P_2 and Q_2 represent the second, then the following two equations can be used to calculate MWB and MRP.

$$MWB = Q_1 - (\frac{Q_2 - Q_1}{P_2 - P_1}) * P_1$$

$$MRP = P_1 - (\frac{P_2 - P_1}{Q_2 - Q_1}) * Q_1$$

Example Early in this chapter, we met a firm that sells 5 units at a price of £90 and 3 units at a price of £110. If demand is linear, what are MWB and MRP?

$$MWB = 5 - (-2/£20) * £90$$
$$= 5 + 9$$
$$= 14$$
$$MRP = £90 - (£20/-2) * 5$$
$$= £90 + £50$$
$$= £140$$

The equation for quantity as a function of price is thus:

$$Q = 14 * \left(1 - \frac{P}{£140}\right)$$

The market in this example, as you may recall, comprises 11 potential buyers with reservation prices of £30, £40, ..., £120, £130. At a price of £130, the firm sells 1 unit.

Figure 7.3 Example of linear demand function

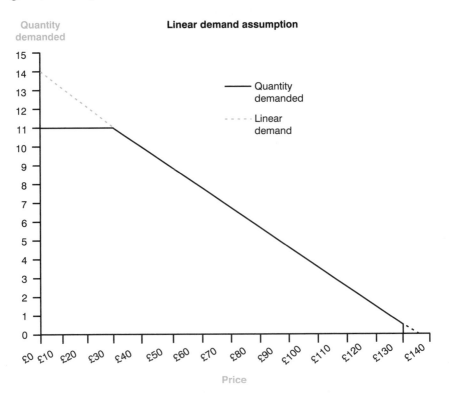

If we set price equal to £130 in the previous equation, our calculation does indeed result in a quantity of 1. For this to hold true, the MRP must be a number slightly higher than £130.

A linear demand function often yields a reasonable approximation of actual demand only over a limited range of prices. In our 11-person market, for example, demand is linear only for prices between £30 and £130. To write the equation of the linear function that describes demand between £30 and £130, however, we must use an MWB of 14 and an MRP of £140. When we use this linear equation, we must remember that it reflects actual demand only for prices between £30 and £130, as illustrated in Figure 7.3.

Price elasticity of demand

Price elasticity measures the responsiveness of quantity demanded to a small change in price.

$$\text{Price elasticity (I)} = \frac{\text{Change in quantity (\%)}}{\text{Change in price (\%)}}$$

Price elasticity can be a valuable tool, enabling marketers to set an optimal price.

Purpose: to understand market responsiveness to changes in price

Price elasticity is the most commonly employed measure of market responsiveness to changes in price. Many marketers, however, use this term without a clear understanding of what it entails. This section will help clarify some of the potentially dangerous details associated with estimates of price elasticity. This is challenging material but is well worth the effort. A strong command of price elasticity can help managers set optimal prices.

Price elasticity: **The responsiveness of demand to a small change in price, expressed as a ratio of percentages. If price elasticity is estimated at −1.5, for example, then we expect the percentage change in quantity to be approximately 1.5 times the percentage change in price. The fact that this number is negative indicates that when price rises, the quantity demanded is expected to decline, and vice versa.**

Construction

If we raise the price of a product, do we expect demand to hold steady or crash through the floor? In markets that are unresponsive to price changes, we say demand is inelastic. If minor price changes have a major impact on demand, we say demand is elastic. Most of us have no trouble understanding elasticity at a qualitative level. The challenges come when we quantify this important concept.

Challenge one: questions of sign

The first challenge in elasticity is to agree on its sign. Elasticity is the ratio of the percentage change in quantity demanded to the percentage change in price, for a small change in price. If an increase in price leads to a decrease in quantity, this ratio will be negative. Consequently, by this definition, elasticity will almost always be a negative number.

Many people, however, simply assume that quantity goes down as price goes up, and jump immediately to the question of "by how much". For such people, price elasticity answers that question and is a positive number. In their eyes, if elasticity is 2, then a small percentage increase in price will yield twice that percentage decrease in quantity.

In this book, under that scenario, we would say price elasticity is −2.

Challenge two: when demand is linear, elasticity changes with price

For a linear demand function, the slope is constant, but elasticity is not. The reason: elasticity is not the same as slope. Slope is the change in quantity for a small change in price. Elasticity, by contrast, is the *percentage* change in quantity for a small *percentage* change in price.

Example Consider three points on a linear demand curve: (£8, 100 units), (£9, 80 units) and (£10, 60 units) (see Figure 7.4). Each pound change in price yields a 20-unit change in quantity. The slope of this curve is a constant −20 units per pound.

As price rises from £8 to £9 (a 12.5% increase), quantity declines from 100 to 80 (a 20% decrease). The ratio of these percentages is 20%/12.5%, or −1.6. Similarly, as price rises from £8 to £10 (a 25% increase), quantity declines from 100 to 60 (a 40% decrease). Once again, the ratio (40%/25%) is −1.6. It appears that the ratio of percentage change in quantity to percentage change in price is −1.6, regardless of the size of the change made in the £8 price.

Consider, however, what happens when price rises from £9 to £10 (an 11.11% increase). Quantity declines from 80 to 60 (a 25% decrease). The ratio of these figures, 25%/11.11%, is now −2.25. A price decline from £9 to £8 also yields an elasticity ratio of −2.25. It appears that this ratio is −2.25 at a price of £9, regardless of the direction of any change in price.

▶

Figure 7.4 Linear demand function

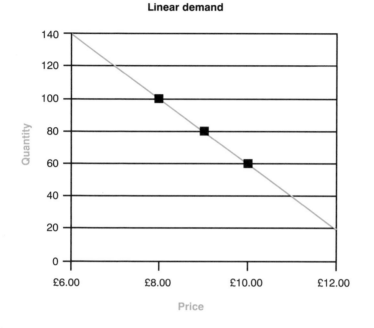

Linear demand

Exercise: Verify that the ratio of percentage change in quantity to percentage change in price at the price of £10 is −3.33 for every conceivable price change.

For a linear demand curve, elasticity changes with price. As price increases, elasticity gains in magnitude. Thus, for a linear demand curve, the absolute unit change in quantity for an absolute pound change in price (slope) is constant, while the percentage change in quantity for a percentage change in price (elasticity) is not. Demand becomes more elastic – that is, elasticity becomes more negative – as price increases.

For a linear demand curve, the elasticity of demand can be calculated in at least three ways:

$$\text{Elasticity } (P_1) = \cfrac{\cfrac{Q_2 - Q_1}{Q_1}}{\cfrac{P_2 - P_1}{P_1}}$$

$$= \frac{Q_2 - Q_1}{P_2 - P_1} * \left(\frac{P_1}{Q_1}\right)$$

$$= \text{Slope} * \left(\frac{P_1}{Q_1}\right)$$

To emphasise the idea that elasticity changes with price on a linear demand curve, we write *Elasticity (P)*, reflecting the fact that elasticity is a function of price. We also use the term "point elasticity" to cement the idea that a given elasticity applies only to a single point on the linear demand curve.

Equivalently, because the slope of a linear demand curve represents the change in quantity for a given change in price, price elasticity for a linear demand curve is equal to the slope, multiplied by the price, divided by the quantity. This is captured in the third equation here.

Example Revisiting the demand function from earlier, we see that the slope of the curve reflects a 20-unit decline in demand for each pound increase in price. That is, slope equals −20.

The slope formula for elasticity can be used to verify our earlier calculations. Calculate price/quantity at each point on the curve, and multiply this by the slope to yield the price elasticity at that point (see Table 7.2).

For example, at a price of £8, quantity sold is 100 units. Thus:

$$\text{Elasticity (£8)} = -20 * (8/100)$$

$$= -1.6$$

Table 7.2 Elasticities at a point calculated from the slope of a function

Price	Quantity demanded	Price/ quantity	Slope	Price elasticity at point
£8.00	100	0.08	(20.00)	(1.60)
£9.00	80	0.11	(20.00)	(2.25)
£10.00	60	0.17	(20.00)	(3.33)

In a linear demand function, point elasticities can be used to predict the percentage change in quantity to be expected for any percentage change in price.

Example Xavi manages the marketing of a toothpaste brand. He knows the brand follows a linear demand function. At the current price of $3.00 per unit, his firm currently sells 60,000 units with an elasticity of −2.5. A proposal is floated to raise the price to $3.18 per unit in order to standardise margins across brands. At $3.18, how many units would be sold?

The proposed change to $3.18 represents a 6% increase over the current $3 price. Because elasticity is −2.5, such an increase can be expected to generate a decrease in unit sales of 2.5 * 6, or 15%. A 15% reduction in current sales of 60,000 units would yield a new quantity of 0.85 * 60,000, or 51,000.

Constant elasticity: demand curve with a constantly changing slope

A second common form of function used to estimate demand entails constant elasticity.[3] This form is responsible for the term "demand curve" because it is, indeed, curved. In contrast with the linear demand function, the conditions in this scenario are reversed: elasticity is constant, while the slope changes at every point.

The assumption underlying a constant elasticity demand curve is that a small percentage change in price will cause the same percentage change in quantity, regardless of the value of the initial price. That is, the rate of change in quantity versus price, expressed as a ratio of percentages, is equal to a constant throughout the curve. That constant is the elasticity.

Figure 7.5 Constant elasticity

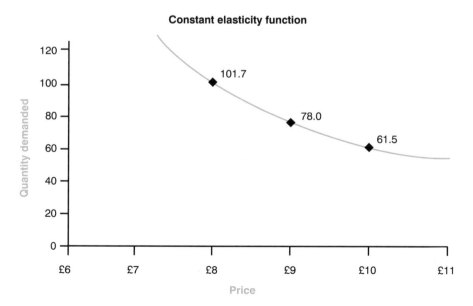

Constant elasticity function

In mathematical terms, in a constant elasticity demand function, slope multiplied by price divided by quantity is equal to a constant (the elasticity) for all points along the curve (see Figure 7.5). The constant elasticity function can also be expressed in an equation that is easily calculated in spreadsheets:

$$Q(P) = A * P^{ELAS}$$

In this equation, *ELAS* is the price elasticity of demand. It is usually a negative number. *A* is a scaling factor. It can be viewed as the quantity that would be sold at a price of £1 (assuming that £1 is a reasonable price for the product under consideration).

Example Plot a demand curve with a constant elasticity of −2.25 and a scaling factor of 10,943.1. For every point on this curve, a small percentage increase in price will yield a percentage decrease in quantity that is 2.25 times as great. This 2.25 ratio holds, however, only for the very smallest percentage changes in price. This is because the slope changes at every point. Using the 2.25 ratio to project the results of a finite percentage increase in price is always approximate.

The curve traced in this example should look like the constant elasticity curve in Figure 7.5. More exact figures for demand at prices £8, £9 and £10 would be 101.669, 78.000, and 61.538 units.

In its way, constant elasticity is analogous to the continuous compounding of interest. In a constant elasticity function, every small percentage increase in price generates the same percentage decrease in quantity. These percentage decreases compound at a constant rate, leading to an overall percentage decrease that does not precisely equal the continuous rate.

For this reason, given any two points on a constant elasticity demand curve, we can no longer calculate elasticity using finite differences as we could when demand was linear. Instead, we must use a more complicated formula grounded in natural logarithms:

$$ELAS = \frac{\ln(Q_2/Q_1)}{\ln(P_2/P_1)}$$

Example Taking any two points from the previous constant elasticity demand curve, we can verify that elasticity is −2.25.

At £8, for example, the quantity is 101.669. Call these P_1 and Q_1.

At £9 the quantity is 78.000. Call these P_2 and Q_2.

Inserting these into our formula, we determine that

$$ELAS = \frac{\ln(78.000/101.669)}{\ln(9/8)}$$

$$= \frac{-0.265}{0.118}$$

$$= -2.25$$

If we had set P_2 equal to £8, and P_1 equal to £9, we would have arrived at the same figure for elasticity. In fact, regardless of which two points we select on this constant elasticity curve, and regardless of the order in which we consider them, elasticity will always be −2.25.

In summary, elasticity is the standard measure of market responsiveness to changes in price. In general, it is the "percentage slope" of the demand function (curve) obtained by multiplying the slope of the curve for a given price by the ratio of price to quantity.

$$\text{Elasticity } (P) = \text{Slope} * \left(\frac{P}{Q}\right)$$

Elasticity can also be viewed as the percentage change in quantity for a small percentage change in price.

In a linear demand function, the slope is constant, but elasticity changes with price. In this scenario, marketers can use elasticity estimates to calculate the result of an anticipated price change in either direction, but they must use the elasticity that is appropriate for their initial price point. The reason: in a linear demand function, elasticity varies across price points, but projections based on these elasticities are accurate.

In a constant elasticity demand function, elasticity is the same at all price points, but projections based on these elasticities will be approximate. Assuming they are estimated with precision, using the constant elasticity demand function itself to make sales projections on the basis of price changes will be more accurate.

Data sources, complications and cautions

Price elasticity is generally estimated on the basis of available data. These data can be drawn from actual sales and price changes observed in the market, conjoint studies of customer intentions, consumer surveys about reservation prices or per cent good value, or test-market results. In deriving elasticity, price–quantity functions can be sketched on paper, estimated from regressions in the form of linear or constant elasticity equations, or estimated through more complex expressions that include other variables in the marketing mix, such as advertising or product quality.

To confirm the validity and usefulness of these procedures, marketers must thoroughly understand the implications of the resulting elasticity estimate for customer behaviour. Through this understanding, marketers can determine whether their estimate makes sense or requires further validation. That done, the next step is to use it to decide on pricing.

Optimal prices and linear and constant demand functions

The optimal price is the most profitable price for any product. In a linear demand function, the optimal price is halfway between the maximum reservation price and the variable cost of the product.

$$\text{Optimal price for a linear demand function (£)} = \frac{[\text{Maximum reservation price (£)} + \text{Variable cost (£)}]}{2}$$

Generally, the gross margin on a product at its optimal price will be the negative inverse of its price elasticity.

$$\text{Gross margin at optimal price (\%)} = \frac{-1}{\text{Elasticity (I)}}$$

Although it can be difficult to apply, this relationship offers a powerful insight: in a constant elasticity demand function, optimal margin follows directly from elasticity. This greatly simplifies the determination of the optimal price for a product of known variable cost.

Although "optimal price" can be defined in a number of ways, a good starting point is the price that will generate the greatest contribution by a product after deducting its variable cost – that is, the most profitable price for the product.

If managers set price too low, they forgo revenue from customers who would willingly have paid more. In addition, a low price can lead customers to value a product less than they otherwise might. That is, it causes them to lower their reservation prices.

By contrast, if managers set price too high, they risk losing contribution from people who could have been served profitably.

Construction

For linear demand, the optimal price is the midpoint between the maximum reservation price and the variable cost of the product.

In linear demand functions, the price that maximises total contribution for a product is always precisely halfway between the maximum reservation price (MRP) and the variable cost to produce that product. Mathematically, if P* represents the optimal price of a product, MRP is the X-intercept of its linear demand function, and VC is its variable cost per unit:

$$P* = (MRP + VC)/2$$

Example Jaime's business sells goods that cost €1 to produce. Demand is linear. If priced at €5, Jaime believes he won't sell anything. For every euro decrease in price, Jaime believes he will sell one additional unit.

Given that the variable cost is €1, the maximum reservation price is €5, and the demand function is linear, Jaime can anticipate that he'll achieve maximum contribution at a price midway between VC and MRP. That is, the optimal price is (€5 + €1)/2, or €3.00 (see Figure 7.6).[4]

In a linear demand function, managers don't need to know the quantity of a product demanded in order to determine its optimal price. For those who seek to examine Jaime's contribution figures, however, please find the details in Table 7.3.

Figure 7.6 Optimal price midway between variable cost and MRP

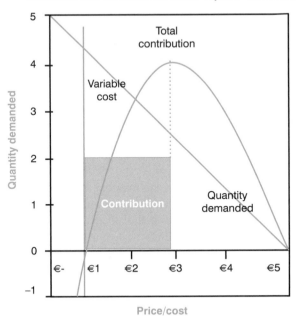

Maximum total contribution when "square" is formed

Table 7.3 Optimal price = $\frac{1}{2}$ (MRP + Variable cost)

Price	Quantity demanded	Variable cost per unit	Contribution per unit	Total contribution
€0	5	€1	(€1)	(€5)
€1	4	€1	€0	€0
€2	3	€1	€1	€3
€3	**2**	**€1**	**€2**	**€4**
€4	1	€1	€3	€3
€5	0	€1	€4	€0

The previous optimal price formula does not reveal the quantity sold at a given price or the resulting contribution. To determine optimal contribution, managers can use the following equation:

$$Contribution^* = (MWB/MRP) * (P^* - VC)^2$$

Example Jaime develops a new but similar product. Its demand follows a linear function in which the maximum willing to buy (MWB) is 200 and the maximum reservation price (MRP) is €10. Variable cost is €1 per unit. Jaime knows that his optimal price will be midway between MRP and variable cost. That is, it will be (€1 + €10)/2 = €5.50 per unit. Using the formula for optimal contribution, Jaime calculates total contribution at the optimal price:

Contribution at optimal price for a linear demand function (€)
= [MWB (N)/MRP (€)] * [Price (€) − Variable costs (€)] ^ 2
= (200/10) * (€5.50 − €1) ^ 2
= 20 * €4.5 ^ 2
= €405

Jaime builds a spreadsheet that supports this calculation (see Table 7.4).

Table 7.4 Contribution maximised at the optimal price

Price	Variable costs	Quantity demanded	Contribution per unit	Total contribution
€6	€1	80	€5.00	€400
€5.50	**€1**	**90**	**€4.50**	**€405**
€5	€1	100	€4.00	€400
€4	€1	120	€3.00	€360
€3	€1	140	€2.00	€280
€2	€1	160	€1.00	€160
€1	€1	180	€0.00	€0

This relationship holds across all linear demand functions, regardless of slope. For such functions, it is therefore possible to calculate the optimal price for a product on the basis of only two inputs: variable cost per unit and the maximum reservation price.

Example Brands A, B and C each have a variable cost of £2 per unit and follow linear demand functions as shown in Table 7.5.

Table 7.5 The optimal price formula applies to all linear demand functions

Price	Demand Brand A	Demand Brand B	Demand Brand C
£2	12	20	16
£3	10	18	15
£4	8	16	14
£5	6	14	13
£6	4	12	12
£7	2	10	11
£8	0	8	10
£9	0	6	9
£10	0	4	8
£11	0	2	7
£12	0	0	6

On the basis of these inputs, we can determine the maximum reservation price – the lowest price at which demand is zero. For Brand C, for example, we know that demand follows a linear function in which quantity declines by one unit for each pound increase in price. If 6 units are demanded at £12, then £18 will be the lowest price at which no one will buy a single unit. This is the maximum reservation price. We can make similar determinations for Brands A and B (see Table 7.6).

Table 7.6 In linear demand functions, the determination of optimal price requires only two inputs

	Brand A	Brand B	Brand C
Maximum reservation price	£8	£12	£18
Variable costs	£2	£2	£2
Optimal price	£5	£7	£10

To verify that the optimal prices so determined will generate the maximum attainable contribution, please see Table 7.7.

Table 7.7 The optimal prices for linear demand functions can be verified

Price	Variable	Contri-bution per unit	Demand Brand A	Contri-bution Brand A	Demand Brand B	Contri-bution Brand B	Demand Brand C	Contri-bution Brand C
P	VC	(C=P−VC)	Q (Given)	Q * C	Q (Given)	Q * C	Q (Given)	Q * C
£2	£2	£0	12	£0	20	£0	16	£0
£3	£2	£1	10	£10	18	£18	15	£15
£4	£2	£2	8	£16	16	£32	14	£28
£5	£2	£3	**6**	**£18**	14	£42	13	£39
£6	£2	£4	4	£16	12	£48	12	£48
£7	£2	£5	2	£10	**10**	**£50**	11	£55
£8	£2	£6	0	£0	8	£48	10	£60
£9	£2	£7	0	£0	6	£42	9	£63
£10	£2	£8	0	£0	4	£32	**8**	**£64**
£11	£2	£9	0	£0	2	£18	7	£63
£12	£2	£10	0	£0	0	£0	6	£60

Because slope doesn't influence optimal price, all demand functions with the same maximum reservation price and variable cost will yield the same optimal price.

Example A manufacturer of chair cushions operates in three different markets – urban, suburban and rural. These vary greatly in size. Demand is far higher in the city than in the suburbs or the country. Variable cost, however, is the same in all markets at $4 per unit. The maximum reservation price, at $20 per unit, is also the same in all markets. Regardless of market size, the optimal price is therefore $12 per unit in all three markets (see Figure 7.7 and Table 7.8).

The optimal price of $12 is verified by the calculations in Table 7.9.

Figure 7.7 Linear demand functions with the same MRP and variable cost

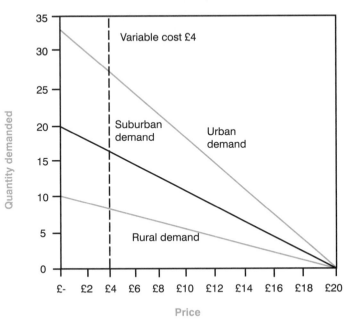

Different linear demand functions slopes with the same MRP and VC

Table 7.8 The slope doesn't influence optimal price

Maximum reservation price	£20
Variable cost	£4
Optimal price	£12

In this example, it might help to think of the urban, suburban and rural markets as groups of people with identical, uniform distributions of reservation prices. In each, the reservation prices are uniform between £0 and the maximum reservation price (MRP). The only difference between segments is the number of people in each. That number represents the maximum willing to buy (MWB). As might be expected, the *number* of people in a segment doesn't affect optimal price as much as the *distribution* of reservation prices in that segment. As all three segments here show the same distribution of reservation prices, they all carry the same optimal price.

Another useful exercise is to consider what would happen if the manufacturer in this example were able to increase everyone's reservation price by £1. This would raise the optimal price by half that amount, or £0.50. Likewise, the optimal price would rise by half the amount of any increase in variable cost.

Table 7.9 Linear demand functions with different slopes

Price	Contribution	Suburban demand	Rural demand	Urban demand	Suburban contribution	Rural contribution	Urban contribution
£0	(£4)	20	10	32	(£80)	(£40)	(£128)
£2	(£2)	18	9	29	(£36)	(£18)	(£58)
£4	£0	16	8	26	£0	£0	£0
£6	£2	14	7	22	£28	£14	£45
£8	£4	12	6	19	£48	£24	£77
£10	£6	10	5	16	£60	£30	£96
£12	**£8**	**8**	**4**	**13**	**£64**	**£32**	**£102**
£14	£10	6	3	10	£60	£30	£96
£16	£12	4	2	6	£48	£24	£77
£18	£14	2	1	3	£28	£14	£45
£20	£16	—	—	—	—	—	—

Optimal price in general

When demand is linear, we have an easy-to-use formula for optimal price. Regardless of the shape of the demand function, there is a simple relationship between gross margin and elasticity at the optimal price.

> Optimal price, relative to gross margin: **The optimal price is the price at which a product's gross margin is equal to the negative of the reciprocal of its elasticity of demand.[5]**

$$\text{Gross margin at optimal price (\%)} = \frac{-1}{\text{Elasticity at optimal price}}$$

A relationship such as this, which holds at the optimal price, is called an optimality condition. If elasticity is constant, then we can easily use this optimality condition to determine the optimal price. We simply find the negative of the reciprocal of the constant elasticity. The result will be the optimal gross margin. If variable costs are known and constant, then we need only determine the price that corresponds to the calculated optimal margin.

Example The manager of a stall selling replica sporting goods knows that the demand for football shirts has a constant price elasticity of −4. To price optimally, she sets her gross margin equal to the negative of the reciprocal of the elasticity of demand. (Some economists refer to the price–cost margin as the Lerner Index.)

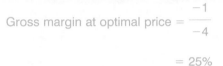

$$\text{Gross margin at optimal price} = \frac{-1}{-4}$$

$$= 25\%$$

If the variable cost of each shirt is £5, the optimal price will be £5/(1 − 0.25), or £6.67.

The optimal margins for several price elasticities are listed in Table 7.10.

Table 7.10 Optimal margins for sample elasticities

Price elasticity	Gross margin
−1.5	67%
−2	50%
−3	33%
−4	25%

Thus, if a firm's gross margin is 50%, its price will be optimal only if its elasticity at that price is −2. By contrast, if the firm's elasticity is −3 at its current price, then its pricing will be optimal only if it yields a gross margin of 33%.

This relationship between gross margin and price elasticity at the optimal price is one of the principal reasons that marketers take such a keen interest in the price elasticity of demand. Price elasticities can be difficult to measure, but margins generally are not. Marketers might now ask whether their current margins are consistent with estimates of price elasticity. In the next section, we will explore this issue in greater detail.

In the interim, if elasticity changes with price, marketers can use this optimality condition to solve for the optimal price. This condition applies to linear demand functions as well. Because the optimal price formula for linear demand is relatively simple, however, marketers rarely use the general optimality condition in this instance.

Data sources, complications and cautions

The shortcuts for determining optimal prices from linear and constant elasticity demand functions rest on an assumption that variable costs hold constant over the range of volumes considered. If this assumption is not valid, marketers will likely find that a spreadsheet model will offer the easiest way to determine optimal price.

We have explored these relationships in detail because they offer useful perspectives on the relationship between margins and the price elasticity of demand. In day-to-day management, margins constitute a starting point for many analyses, including those of price. One example of this dynamic would be cost-plus pricing.

Cost-plus pricing has received bad press in the marketing literature. It is portrayed not only as internally oriented, but also as naïve, in that it may sacrifice profits. From an alternative perspective, however, cost-plus pricing can be viewed as an attempt to maintain margins. If managers select the correct margin – one that relates to the price elasticity of demand – then pricing to maintain it may in fact be optimal if demand has constant elasticity. Thus, cost-plus pricing can be more customer-oriented than is widely perceived.

Related metrics and concepts

Price tailoring – a.k.a. price discrimination

Marketers have invented a variety of price discrimination tools, including coupons, rebates and discounts, for example. All are designed to exploit variations in price sensitivity among customers. Whenever customers have different sensitivities to price, or different costs to serve, the astute marketer can find an opportunity to claim incremental value through price tailoring.

Example The demand for a particular brand of sunglasses is composed of two segments: style-focused consumers who are less sensitive to price (more inelastic) and value-focused consumers who are more sensitive to price (more elastic) (see Figure 7.8). The style-focused group has a maximum reservation price of $30 and a maximum willing to buy of 10 units. The value-focused group has a maximum reservation price of $10 and a maximum willing to buy of 40 units.

Alternative A: one price for both segments

Suppose the sunglasses manufacturer plans to offer one price to both segments. Table 7.11 shows the contribution of several candidate prices. The optimal single price (to the nearest cent) is $6.77, generating a total contribution of $98.56.

Table 7.11 Two segments: one price for both segments

Single price	Value quantity demanded	Style quantity demanded	Total demand	Total contribution
$5	20	8.33	28.33	$85.00
$6	16	8.00	24.00	$96.00
$6.77	**12.92**	**7.74**	**20.66**	**$98.56**
$7	12	7.67	19.67	$98.33
$8	8	7.33	15.33	$92.00

 **Figure 7.8** Two segments form demand

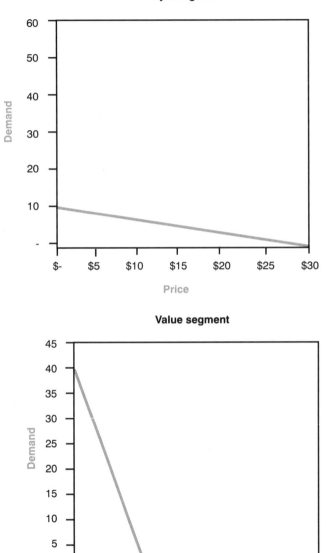

Alternative B: price per segment

If the manufacturer can find a way to charge each segment its own optimal price, it will increase total contribution. In Table 7.12, we show the optimal prices, quantities and contributions attainable if each segment pays a distinct optimal price.

Table 7.12 Two segments: price tailoring

	MRP	Variable costs	Optimal price	Quantity	Revenue	Contribution
Style	$30	$2	$16	4.67	$74.67	$65.33
Value	$10	$2	$6	16	$96.00	$64.00
Total				20.67	$170.67	**$129.33**

These optimal prices were calculated as the midpoints between maximum reservation price (MRP) and variable cost (VC). Optimal contributions were calculated with the formula:

$$\text{Contribution*} = (\text{MWB/MRP}) * (P* - VC)^2$$

In the style-focused segment, for example, this yields

$$\text{Contribution*} = (10/30) * (\$16 - \$2)^2$$
$$= (1/3) * (14^2) = \$65.33$$

Thus, through price tailoring, the sunglasses manufacturer can increase total contribution from $98.56 to $129.33 while holding quantity constant.

Where variable costs differ between segments, as in an airline's costs of service in business class versus economy class, the fundamental calculations are the same. To determine optimal prices, marketers need only change the variable cost per unit in each segment to correspond to actual costs.

Caution: regulation

In most industrial economies, governments have passed regulations concerning price discrimination. In Europe, several countries have their own regulations within the framework of EU rules. This creates some variation as to what practices are deemed to be anti-competitive. For example, some countries allow retail price maintenance whereas others do not. When operating in Europe it is important to understand the specific rules of the country and so we advise checking local legal advice before developing your pricing strategies that involve retail price maintenance and/or differential pricing.

"Own", "cross" and "residual" price elasticity

The concept of residual price elasticity introduces competitive dynamics into the pricing process. It incorporates competitor reactions and cross elasticity. This, in turn, helps explain why prices in daily life are rarely set at the optimal level suggested by a simpler view of elasticity. Marketers consciously or unconsciously factor competitive dynamics into their pricing decisions.

Residual price elasticity (I) = Own price elasticity (I) + [Competitor reaction elasticity (I) * Cross elasticity (I)]

The greater the competitive reaction anticipated, the more residual price elasticity will differ from a company's own price elasticity.

Purpose: to account for both customers' price elasticity and potential competitive reactions when planning price changes

Often, in daily life, price elasticity doesn't quite correspond to the relationships discussed in the previous section. Managers may find, for example, that their estimates of this key metric are not equal to the negative of the reciprocal of their margins. Does this mean they're setting prices that are not optimal? Perhaps.

It is more likely, however, that they're including competitive factors in their pricing decisions. Rather than using elasticity as estimated from current market conditions, marketers may estimate – or intuit – what elasticity *will be* after competitors respond to a proposed change in price. This introduces a new concept: residual price elasticity – customers' elasticity of demand in response to a change in price, *after* accounting for any increase or decrease in competitors' prices that may be triggered by the initial change.

Residual price elasticity is the combination of three factors:

1 **"Own" price elasticity:** the change in units sold due to the reaction of a firm's *customers* to its changes in price.

2 **"Competitor reaction" elasticity:** the reaction of *competitors* to a firm's price changes.

3 **"Cross" price elasticity:** the reaction of a firm's customers to price changes by its competitors.

These factors and their interactions are illustrated in Figure 7.9.

Own price elasticity: *How customers in the market react to our price changes.*

Competitive reaction elasticity: *How our competitors respond to our price changes.*

Cross elasticity: *How our customers respond to the price changes of our competitors.*

Figure 7.9 Residual price elasticity

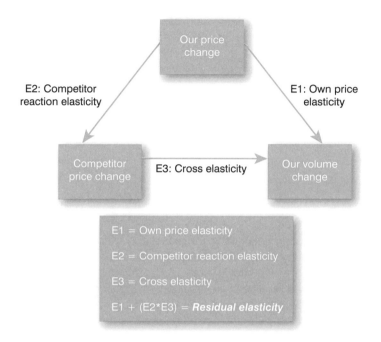

E1 = Own price elasticity

E2 = Competitor reaction elasticity

E3 = Cross elasticity

E1 + (E2*E3) = *Residual elasticity*

The distinction between own and residual price elasticity is not made clear in the literature. Some measures of price elasticity, for example, incorporate past competitive reactions and thus are more indicative of residual price elasticity. Others principally reflect own price elasticity and require further analysis to determine where sales and income will ultimately settle. The following sequence of actions and reactions is illustrative:

1 A firm changes price and observes the resulting change in sales. As an alternative, it may track another measure correlated with sales, such as share of choice or preference.

2 Competitors observe the firm's change in price and its increase in sales, and/or their own decrease in sales.

3 Competitors decide whether and by how much to change their own prices. The market impact of these changes will depend on (1) the direction and degree of the changes, and (2) the degree of cross elasticity, that is, the sensitivity of the initial firm's sales quantity to changes in competitors' prices. Thus, after tracking the response to its own price change, the initial firm may observe a further shift in sales as competitors' price changes take effect in the market.

Due to this dynamic, if a firm measures price elasticity only through customer response to its initial actions, it will miss an important potential factor: competitive reactions and their effects on sales. Only monopolists can make pricing decisions without regard to competitive response. Other firms may neglect or decline to consider competitive reactions, dismissing such analyses as speculation. But this generates a risk of shortsightedness and can lead to dangerous surprises. Still other firms may embrace game theory and seek a Nash Equilibrium to anticipate where prices will ultimately settle. (In this context, the Nash Equilibrium would be the point at which none of the competitors in a market has a profit-related incentive to change prices.)

Although a detailed exploration of competitive dynamics is beyond the scope of this book, we offer a simple framework for residual price elasticity next.

Construction

To calculate residual price elasticity, three inputs are needed:

1 **Own price elasticity:** The change in a firm's unit sales, resulting from its initial price change, assuming that competitors' prices remain unchanged.

2 **Competitor reaction elasticity:** The extent and direction of the price changes that are likely to be made by competitors in response to a firm's initial price change. If competitor reaction elasticity is 0.5, for example, then as a firm reduces its prices by a small percentage, competitors can be expected to reduce their own prices by half that percentage. If competitor reaction elasticity is −0.5, then as a firm reduces its prices by a small percentage, competitors will *increase* their prices by half that percentage. This is a less common scenario, but it is possible.

3 **Cross elasticity with regard to competitor price changes:** The percentage and direction of the change in the initial firm's sales that will result from a small percentage change in competitors' prices. If cross elasticity is 0.25, then a small percentage increase in competitors' prices will result in an increase of one-fourth that percentage in the initial firm's sales. Note that the sign of cross elasticity is generally the reverse of the sign of own price elasticity. When competitors' prices rise, a firm's sales will usually increase, and vice versa.

Residual price elasticity (I) = Own price elasticity (I) + [Competitor reaction elasticity (I) * Cross elasticity (I)]

The percentage change in a firm's sales can be approximated by multiplying its own price change by its residual price elasticity:

Change in sales from residual elasticity (%) = Own price change (%) * Residual price elasticity (I)

Forecasts of any change in sales to be generated by a price change thus should take into account the subsequent competitive price reactions that can be reasonably expected, as well as the second-order effects of those reactions on the sales of the firm making the initial change. The net effect of adjusting for such reactions might be to amplify, diminish or even reverse the direction of the change in sales that was expected from the initial price change.

Example A company decides to reduce price by 10% (price change = −10%). It has estimated its own price elasticity to be −2. Ignoring competitive response, the company would expect a 10% price reduction to yield an approximately 20% increase in sales (−2 * −10%). (Note: As observed in our earlier discussion of elasticity, projections based on point elasticity are accurate only for linear demand functions. Because this example does not specify the shape of the demand function, the projected 20% increase in sales is an approximation.)

The company estimates competitor reaction elasticity to be 1. That is, in response to the firm's action, competitors are expected to shift pricing in the same direction and by an equal percentage.

The company estimates cross elasticity to be 0.7. That is, a small percentage change in competitors' prices will result in a change in the firm's own sales of 0.7 per cent. On this basis,

$$\text{Residual elasticity} = \text{Own price elasticity} + (\text{Competitor reaction elasticity} * \text{Cross elasticity})$$
$$= -2(1 * .7)$$
$$= -2 + 0.7$$
$$= -1.3$$

$$\text{Sales increase} \approx \text{Change in price} * \text{Residual elasticity}$$
$$= -10\% * -1.3$$
$$= 13\% \text{ increase in sales}$$

Competitor reactions and cross elasticity are expected to reduce the firm's initially projected sales increase from 20% to 13%.

Data sources, complications and cautions

Accounting for potential competitive reactions is important, but there may be simpler and more reliable methods of managing price strategy in a contested market. Game theory and price leadership principles offer some guidance.

It is important for managers to distinguish between price elasticity measures that are inherently unable to account for competitive reactions and those that may already incorporate some competitive dynamics. For example, in "laboratory" investigations of price sensitivity – such as surveys, simulated test markets and conjoint analyses – consumers may be presented with hypothetical pricing scenarios. These can measure both own price elasticity and the cross elasticities that result from specific combinations of prices. But an effective test is difficult to achieve.

Econometric analysis of historical data, evaluating the sales and prices of firms in a market over longer periods of time (that is, annual or quarterly data), may be better able to incorporate competitive changes and cross elasticities. To the extent that a firm has changed price somewhat randomly in the past, and to the extent that competitors have reacted, the estimates of elasticity that are generated by such analyses will measure residual elasticity. Still, the challenges and complexities involved in measuring price elasticity from historical data are daunting.

By contrast, short-term test market experiments are unlikely to yield good estimates of residual price elasticity. Over short periods, competitors might not learn of price changes or have time to react. Consequently, elasticity estimates based on test markets are much closer to own price elasticity.

Less obvious, perhaps, are econometric analyses based on transactional data, such as scanner sales and short-term price promotions. In these studies, prices decline for a short time, rise again for a longer period, decline briefly, rise again, and so forth. Even if competitors conduct their own price promotions during the study period, estimates of price elasticity derived in this way are likely to be affected by two factors. First, competitors' reactions probably will not be factored into an elasticity estimate because they won't have had time to react to the initial firm's pricing moves. That is, their actions will have been largely motivated by their own plans. Second, to the extent that consumers stock up during price deals, any estimates of price elasticity will be higher than would be observed over the course of long-term price changes.

Prisoner's dilemma pricing

Prisoner's dilemma pricing describes a situation in which the pursuit of self-interest by all parties leads to sub-optimal outcomes for all. This phenomenon can lead to stability at prices above the expected optimal price. In many ways, these higher-than-optimal prices have the appearance of cartel pricing. But they can be achieved without explicit collusion, provided that all parties understand the dynamics, as well as their competitors' motivations and economics.

The prisoner's dilemma phenomenon derives its name from a story illustrating the concept. Two members of a criminal gang are arrested and imprisoned. Each prisoner is placed in solitary confinement, with no means of speaking to the other. Because the police don't have enough evidence to convict the pair on the principal charge, they plan to sentence both to a year in prison on a lesser charge. First, however, they try to get one or both to confess. Simultaneously, they offer each prisoner a Faustian bargain. If the prisoner testifies against his partner, he will go free, while the partner is sentenced to three years in prison on the main charge. But there's a catch . . . If *both* prisoners testify against each other, *both* will be sentenced to two years in jail. On this basis, each prisoner reasons that he'll do best by testifying against his partner, regardless of what the partner does.

For a summary of the choices and outcomes in this dilemma, please see Figure 7.10, which is drawn in the first person from the perspective of one of the prisoners. First-person outcomes are listed in bold. Partner outcomes are italicised.

Figure 7.10 Prisoner's dilemma pay-off grid

My partner refuses to testify	3 years I go free	1 year 1 year
My partner testifies	2 years 2 years	*My partner goes free* 3 years
	I testify	I refuse to testify

Continuing the first-person perspective, each prisoner reasons as follows: If my partner testifies, I'll be sentenced to two years in prison if I testify as well, or three years if I don't. On the other hand, if my partner refuses to testify, I'll go free if I testify, but serve one year in prison if I don't. In either case, I do better if I testify. But this raises a dilemma. If I follow this logic and testify – and my partner does the same – we end up in the lower-left cell of the table, serving two years in prison.

Figure 7.11 uses arrows to track these preferences – a dark arrow for the first-person narrator in this reasoning, and a light arrow for his partner.

The dilemma, of course, is that it seems perfectly logical to follow the arrows and testify. But when both prisoners do so, they both end up worse off than they would have if they'd both refused. That is, when both testify, both are sentenced to two years in prison. If both had refused, they both could have shortened that term to a single year.

Figure 7.11 Pay-off grid with arrows representing preferences for prisoners

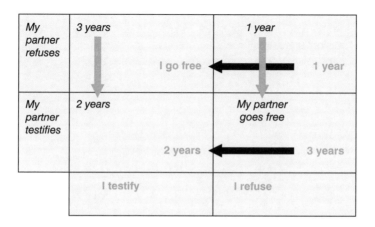

Admittedly, it takes a good deal of time to grasp the mechanics of the prisoner's dilemma, and far longer to appreciate its implications. But the story serves as a powerful metaphor, encapsulating a wide range of situations in which acting in one's own best interest leads to outcomes in which everyone is worse off.

In pricing, there are many situations in which a firm and its competitors face a prisoner's dilemma. Often, one firm perceives that it could increase profits by reducing prices, regardless of competitors' pricing policies. Simultaneously, its competitors perceive the same forces at work. That is, they too could earn more by cutting prices, regardless of the initial firm's actions. If *both* the initial firm and its competitors reduce prices, however – that is, if all parties follow their own unilateral best interests – they will, in many situations, all end up worse off. The industry challenge in these situations is to keep prices high despite the fact that each firm will benefit by lowering them.

Given a choice between high and low prices a firm faces a prisoner's dilemma pricing situation when the following conditions apply:

1 Its contribution is greater at the low price when selling against both high and low competitor prices.

2 Competitors' contribution is greater at their low price when selling against both the high and low prices of the initial firm.

3 For both the initial firm and its competitors, however, contribution is lower if all parties set their price low than it would have been if all parties had priced high.

Example As shown in Table 7.13, my firm faces one main competitor. Currently my price is £2.90, their price is £2.80, and I hold a 40% share of a market that totals 20 million units. If I reduce my price to £2.60, I expect my share will rise to 55% – unless, of course, they also cut their price. If they also reduce price by £0.30 – to £2.50 – then I expect our market shares to remain constant at 40/60. On the other hand, if my competitor cuts its price but I hold steady at £2.90, then I expect they'll increase their market share to 80%, leaving me with only 20%.

If we both have variable costs of £1.20 per unit, and market size remains constant at 20 million units, we face four possible scenarios with eight contribution figures – four for my firm and four for the competition:

Table 7.13 Scenario planning pay-off table

Pricing scenario	My price	My volume (m)	My sales (£m)	My variable costs (£m)	My contribution (£m)
My firm high. Competition high.	£2.90	8	£23.2	£9.6	£13.6
My firm high. Competition low.	£2.90	4	£11.6	£4.8	£6.8
My firm low. Competition low.	£2.60	8	£20.8	£9.6	£11.2
My firm low. Competition high.	£2.60	11	£28.6	£13.2	£15.4

Pricing scenario	Their price	Their volume (m)	Their sales (£m)	Their variable costs (£m)	Their contribution (£m)
My firm high. Competition high.	£2.80	12	£33.6	£14.4	£19.2
My firm high. Competition low.	£2.50	16	£40.0	£19.2	£20.8
My firm low. Competition low.	£2.50	12	£30.0	£14.4	£15.6
My firm low. Competition high.	**£2.80**	9	**£25.2**	**£10.8**	**£14.4**

Are we in a prisoner's dilemma situation?

Figure 7.12 shows the four contribution possibilities for both my firm and my competitor.

Figure 7.12 Pay-off grid with expected values (values are in the millions of pounds)

	My price = £2.60 Low	My price = £2.90 High
Their price = £2.80 High	£14.4 £15.4	£19.2 £13.6
Their price = £2.50 Low	£15.6 £11.2	£20.8 £6.8

Let's check to see whether the conditions for the prisoner's dilemma are met:

1 My contribution is higher at the low price for both high and low competitor prices (£15.4m > £13.6m, and £11.2m > £6.8m). No matter what my competitor does, I make more money at the low price.

2 My competitor's contribution is higher at the low price, regardless of my price (£15.6m > £14.4m, and £20.8m > £19.2m). They, too, are better off at the low price, regardless of my price.

3 For both my firm and my competitor, however, contribution is lower if we both price low than it would be if we both price high (£15.6m < £19.2m, and £11.2m < £13.6m).

The conditions for the prisoner's dilemma are met (see Figure 7.13).

Figure 7.13 Pay-off grid with expected values and preference arrows (values are in the millions of pounds)

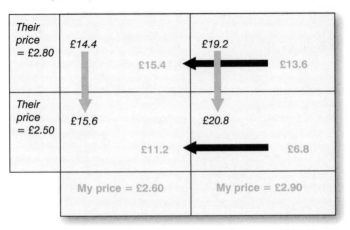

	My price = £2.60	My price = £2.90
Their price = £2.80	£14.4 £15.4	£19.2 £13.6
Their price = £2.50	£15.6 £11.2	£20.8 £6.8

The implication for my firm is clear: although it is tempting to lower my price, seeking increased share and a £15.4 million contribution, I must recognise that my competitor faces the same incentives. They, too, have an incentive to cut price, grab share and increase their contribution. But if they lower their price, I'll probably lower mine. If I lower my price, they'll probably lower theirs. If we both reduce our prices, I'll earn only £11.2m in contribution – a sharp decline from the £13.6m I make now.

Managerial note

To determine whether you face a prisoner's dilemma situation, project the financial contributions for both your firm and your competition at four combinations of high and low prices. Projections may require assumptions about your competitors' economics. These, in turn, will require care. If competitors' economics differ greatly from your projections, they may not face the decisions or motivations ascribed to them in your model. Additionally, there are a number of reasons that the logic of the prisoner's dilemma won't always hold, even if all assumptions are correct.

1 **Contribution may not be the sole criterion in decision-making:** In our example, we used contribution as the objective for both firms. Market share, however, may have importance to one or more firms, above and beyond its immediate, direct effect on contribution. Whatever a firm's objective may be, if it is quantifiable, we can place it in our table to better understand the competitive situation.

2 **Legal issues:** Certain activities designed to discourage competition and maintain high prices are illegal. Our purpose here is to help managers understand the economic trade-offs involved in competitive pricing. Managers should be aware of their legal environment and behave accordingly.

3 **Multiple competitors:** Pricing becomes more complicated when there are multiple competitors. The test for a multi-party prisoner's dilemma is the logical extension of the test described earlier. A major difference, however, arises in practice. As a general principle, the greater the number of independent competitors, the more difficult it will be to keep prices high.

4 **Single versus repeated play:** In our original story, two prisoners decide whether to testify in a single investigation. In game theory terms, they play the game a single time. Experiments have shown that in a single play of a prisoner's dilemma, the likely outcome is that both prisoners will testify. If the game is played repeatedly, however, it is more likely that both prisoners will refuse to testify. Because pricing decisions are made repeatedly, this evidence suggests that high prices are a more likely outcome. Most businesses eventually learn to live with their competition.

5 **More than two possible prices:** We have examined a situation in which each player considers two prices. In reality, there may be a wide range of prices under consideration. In such situations, we might extend our analysis

to more boxes. Once again, we might add arrows to track preferences. Using these more complex views, one sometimes finds areas within the table in which a prisoner's dilemma applies (usually at the higher prices), and others where it does not (usually at the lower prices). One might also find that the arrows lead to a particular cell in the middle of the table called the equilibrium. A prisoner's dilemma situation generally applies for prices higher than the set of equilibrium prices.

Applying the lessons of the prisoner's dilemma, we see that optimal price calculations based on own price elasticity may lead us to act in our own unilateral best interest. By contrast, when we factor residual price elasticity into our calculations, competitive response becomes a key element of our pricing strategy. As the prisoner's dilemma shows, over the long term, a firm is not always best served by acting in its apparent unilateral best interest.

References and suggested further reading

Dolan, R.J. and H. Simon. (1996). *Power Pricing: How Managing Price Transforms the Bottom Line*, New York: The Free Press, 4.

Roegner, E.V., M.V. Marn and C.C. Zawada. (2005). "Pricing", *Marketing Management*, 14(1), 23–28.

Promotion

8

Metrics covered in this chapter:

- Baseline sales, incremental sales and promotional lift

- Redemption rates for coupons/rebates

- Per cent sales on deal, per cent time on deal and average deal depth

- Pass-through and price waterfall

Introduction

Price promotions can be divided into two broad categories:

- temporary price reductions
- permanent features of pricing systems.[1]

With both of these, firms seek to change the behaviour of consumers and trade customers in ways that increase sales and profits over time, though a promotion's short-term effect on profits will often be negative. There are multiple routes to sales and profit growth and many potential reasons for offering price promotions. Such programmes might be aimed at affecting the behaviour of end users (consumers), trade customers (distributors or retailers), competitors or even a firm's own salespeople. Although the goal of a promotion is often to increase sales, these programmes can also affect costs. Examples of specific, short-term promotional objectives include the following:

- To acquire new customers, perhaps by generating trial.
- To appeal to new or different segments that are more price-sensitive than a firm's traditional customers.

- To increase the purchase rates of existing customers; to increase loyalty.
- To gain new trade accounts (that is, distribution).
- To introduce new SKUs to the trade.
- To increase shelf space.
- To blunt competitive efforts by encouraging the firm's customers to "load up" on inventory.
- To smooth production in seasonal categories by inducing customers to order earlier (or later) than they ordinarily would.

The metrics for many of these interim objectives, including trial rate and percentage of new product sales, are covered elsewhere. In this chapter, we focus on metrics for monitoring the acceptance of price promotions and their effects on sales and profits.

The most powerful framework for evaluating temporary price promotions is to partition sales into two categories: baseline and incremental. Baseline sales are those that a firm would have expected to achieve if no promotion had been run. Incremental sales represent the "lift" in sales resulting from a price promotion. By separating baseline sales from incremental lift, managers can evaluate whether the sales increase generated by a temporary price reduction compensates for the concomitant decrease in prices and margins. Similar techniques are used in determining the profitability of coupons and rebates.

Although the short-term effect of a price promotion is almost invariably measured by its increase in sales, over longer periods management becomes concerned about the percentage of sales on deal and the percentage of time during which a product is on deal. In some industries, list price has become such a fiction that it is used only as a benchmark for discussing discounts.

Average deal depth and the price waterfall help capture the depth of price cuts and explain how one arrives at a product's net price (pocket price) after accounting for all discounts. There are often major differences between the discounts offered to trade customers and the extent to which those discounts are accepted. There may also be a difference between the discounts received by the trade and those that the trade shares with its customers. The pass-through percentage and price waterfall are analytic structures designed to capture those dynamics and thus to measure the impact of a firm's promotions.

Metric	Construction	Considerations	Purpose
Baseline sales	Intercept in regression of sales as function of marketing variables. Baseline sales = total sales, less incremental sales generated by a marketing programme or programmes.	Marketing activities also contribute to baseline.	To determine the extent to which current sales are independent of specific marketing efforts.
Incremental sales, or promotional lift	Total sales, less baseline sales. Regression coefficient to marketing variables cited above.	Need to consider competitive actions.	To determine short-term effects of marketing effort.
Redemption rates	Coupons redeemed divided by coupons distributed.	Will differ significantly by mode of coupon distribution.	Rough measure of coupon "lift" after adjusting for sales that would have been made without coupons.
Costs for coupons and rebates	Coupon face amount plus redemption charges, multiplied by the number of coupons redeemed.	Does not consider margins that would have been generated by those willing to buy product without coupon.	Allows for budgeting of coupon expense.
Percentage sales with coupon	Sales via coupon, divided by total sales.	Doesn't factor in magnitude of discount offered by specific coupons.	A measure of brand dependence on promotional efforts.
Per cent sales on deal	Sales with temporary discounts as a percentage of total sales.	Does not make distinction for depth of discounts offered.	A measure of brand dependence on promotional efforts.

Metric	Construction	Considerations	Purpose
Per cent time on deal	Percentage of time during which temporary promotions are offered.	Does not reflect whether trade or consumers take advantage of discounts offered.	A measure of brand dependence on promotional efforts.
Average deal depth	Sales via coupon, divided by total sales.	Should be adjusted to account for forward buying and pass-through.	A measure of brand dependence on promotional efforts.
Pass-through	Promotional discounts provided by the trade to consumers, divided by discounts provided to the trade by the manufacturer.	Can reflect power in the channel, or deliberate management or segmentation.	To measure the extent to which a manufacturer's promotions generate promotional activity further along the distribution channel.
Price waterfall	Actual average price per unit divided by list price per unit. Can also be calculated by working backward from list price, taking account of potential discounts, weighted by the frequency with which each is exercised.	Some discounts may be offered at an absolute level, not on a per-item basis.	To indicate the price actually paid for a product, and the sequence of channel factors affecting that price.

Baseline sales, incremental sales and promotional lift

Estimates of baseline sales establish a benchmark for evaluating the incremental sales generated by specific marketing activities. This baseline also helps isolate incremental sales from the effects of other influences, such as seasonality or competitive promotions. The following equations can be applied for defined periods of time and for the specific element of the marketing mix that is used to generate incremental sales.

$$\text{Total sales } (£, N) = \text{Baseline sales } (£, N) + \text{Incremental sales from marketing } (£, N)$$

$$\begin{aligned}\text{Incremental sales from marketing } (£, N) = {} & \text{Incremental sales from advertising } (£, N) \\ & + \text{Incremental sales from trade promotion } (£, N) \\ & + \text{Incremental sales from consumer promotion } (£, N) \\ & + \text{Incremental sales from other } (£, N)\end{aligned}$$

$$\text{Lift (from promotion) } (\%) = \frac{\text{Incremental sales } (£, N)}{\text{Baseline sales } (£, N)}$$

$$\text{Cost of incremental sales } (£) = \frac{\text{Marketing spending } (£)}{\text{Incremental sales } (£, N)}$$

The justification of marketing spending almost always involves estimating the incremental effects of the programme under evaluation. However, because some marketing costs are often assumed to be fixed (for example, marketing staff and sales force salaries), one rarely sees incremental sales attributed to these elements of the mix.

Purpose: to select a baseline of sales against which the incremental sales and profits generated by marketing activity can be assessed

A common problem in marketing is estimating the sales "lift" attributable to a specific campaign or set of marketing activities. Evaluating lift entails making a comparison with baseline sales, the level of sales that would have been achieved without the programme under evaluation. Ideally, experiments or "control" groups would be used to establish baselines. If it were quick, easy and inexpensive to conduct such experiments, this approach would dominate. In lieu of such control groups, marketers often use historical sales adjusted for expected growth, taking care to control for seasonal influences. Regression models that attempt to control for the influence of these other changes are often used to improve estimates of baseline sales. Ideally, both controllable and uncontrollable factors, such as competitive spending, should be included in baseline sales regression models. When regression is used, the intercept is often considered to be the baseline.

Construction

In theory, determining incremental sales is as simple as subtracting baseline sales from total sales. Challenges arise, however, in determining baseline sales.

> Baseline sales: **Expected sales results, excluding the marketing programmes under evaluation.**

In reviewing historical data, total sales are known. The analyst's task then is to separate these into baseline sales and incremental sales. This is typically done with regression analysis. The process can also involve test market results and other market research data.

Total sales (£,N) = Baseline sales (£,N) + Incremental sales (£,N)

Analysts also commonly separate incremental sales into portions attributable to the various marketing activities used to generate them.

Incremental sales (£,N) = Incremental sales from advertising (£,N) +
Incremental sales from trade promotion (£,N) +
Incremental sales from consumer promotion (£,N)
+ Incremental sales from other (£,N)

Baseline sales are generally estimated through analyses of historical data. Firms often develop sophisticated models for this purpose, including variables to adjust for market growth, competitive activity and seasonality, for example. That done, a firm can use its model to make forward-looking projections of baseline sales and use these to estimate incremental sales.

Incremental sales can be calculated as total sales, less baseline sales, for any period of time (for example, a year, a quarter or the term of a promotion). The lift achieved by a marketing programme measures incremental sales as a percentage of baseline sales. The cost of incremental sales can be expressed as a cost per incremental sales pound or a cost per incremental sales unit (for example, cost per incremental case).

$$\text{Incremental sales } (\text{£,N}) = \text{Total sales } (\text{£,N}) - \text{Baseline sales } (\text{£,N})$$

$$\text{Lift } (\%) = \frac{\text{Incremental sales } (\text{£,N})}{\text{Baseline sales } (\text{£,N})}$$

$$\text{Cost of incremental sales } (\text{£}) = \frac{\text{Marketing spending } (\text{£})}{\text{Incremental sales } (\text{£,N})}$$

Example A retailer in the US expects to sell $24,000 worth of light bulbs in a typical month without advertising. In May, while running a newspaper ad campaign that cost $1,500, the store sells $30,000 worth of light bulbs. It engages in no other promotions or non-recurring events during the month. Its owner calculates incremental sales generated by the ad campaign as follows:

$$\text{Incremental sales } (\$) = \text{Total sales } (\$) - \text{Baseline sales } (\$)$$

$$= \$30,000 - \$24,000 = \$6,000$$

The store owner estimates incremental sales to be $6,000. This represents a lift (%) of 25%, calculated as follows:

$$\text{Lift } (\%) = \frac{\text{Incremental sales } (\$)}{\text{Baseline sales } (\$)}$$

$$= \frac{\$6,000}{\$24,000} = 25\%$$

The cost per incremental sales is $0.25, calculated as follows:

$$\text{Cost of incremental sales } (\$) = \frac{\text{Marketing spending } (\$)}{\text{Incremental sales } (\$)}$$

$$= \frac{\$1,500}{\$6,000} = 0.25$$

Total sales can be analysed or projected as a function of baseline sales and lift. When estimating combined marketing mix effects, one must be sure to determine whether lift is estimated through a multiplicative or an additive equation. Additive equations combine marketing mix effects as follows:

Total sales (£,N) = Baseline sales + [Baseline sales (£,N) * Lift (%) from advertising]
+ [Baseline sales (£,N) * Lift (%) from trade promotion]
+ [Baseline sales (£,N) * Lift (%) from consumer promotion]
+ [Baseline sales (£,N) * Lift (%) from other]

This additive approach is consistent with the conception of total incremental sales as a sum of the incremental sales generated by various elements of the marketing mix. It is equivalent to a statement that:

Total sales (£,N) = Baseline sales + Incremental sales from advertising + Incremental sales from trade promotion + Incremental sales from consumer promotion + Incremental sales from other

Multiplicative equations, by contrast, combine marketing mix effects by using a multiplication procedure, as follows:

Total sales (£,N) = Baseline sales (£,N) * (1 + Lift (%) from advertising) * (1 + Lift (%) from trade promotion) * (1 + Lift (%) from consumer promotion) * (1 + Lift (%) from other)

When using multiplicative equations, it makes little sense to talk about the incremental sales from a single mix element. In practice, however, one may encounter statements that attempt to do exactly that.

Example Company A collects data from past promotions and estimates the lift it achieves through different elements of the marketing mix. One researcher believes that an additive model would best capture these effects. A second researcher believes that a multiplicative model might better reveal the ways in which multiple elements of the mix combine to increase sales. The product manager for the item under study receives the two estimates shown in Table 8.1.

Table 8.1 Expected returns to marketing spending

	Additive			Multiplicative		
Spending	Advertising lift	Trade promotion lift	Consumer promotion lift	Advertising lift	Trade promotion lift	Consumer promotion lift
£0	0%	0%	0%	1	1	1
£100k	5.5%	10%	16.5%	1.05	1.1	1.15
£200k	12%	24%	36%	1.1	1.2	1.3

Fortunately, both models estimate baseline sales to be £900,000. The product manager wants to evaluate the following spending plan: advertising (£100,000), trade promotion (£0), and consumer promotion (£200,000). He projects sales using each method as follows:

Additive:

$$\text{Projected sales (£)} = £900,000 + [£900,000 * 5.5\%] + [£900,000 * 0] \\ + [£900,000 * 36\%]$$

$$= £900,000 + £49,500 + £0 + £324,000$$

$$= £1,273,500$$

Multiplicative:

$$\text{Projected sales} = \text{Baseline} * \text{Advertising lift} * \text{Trade promotion lift} \\ * \text{Consumer promotion lift}$$

$$= £900,000 * 1.05 * 1 * 1.3$$

$$= £1,228,500$$

Note: Because these models are constructed differently, they will inevitably yield different results at most levels. The multiplicative method accounts for a specific form of interactions between marketing variables. The additive method, in its current form, does not account for interactions.

When historic sales have been separated into baseline and incremental components, it is relatively simple to determine whether a given promotion was profitable *during the period under study*. Looking forward, the profitability of a proposed marketing activity can be assessed by comparing projected levels of profitability with and without the programme:

$$\text{Profitability of a promotion (£)} = \text{Profits achieved with promotion (£)} \\ - \text{Estimated profits without promotion} \\ \text{(that is, baseline) (£)}^2$$

Example Fred, the head of marketing, and Jeanne, the head of finance, receive estimates that sales will total 30,000 units after erecting special displays. Because the proposed promotion involves a considerable investment (€100,000), the CEO asks for an estimate of the incremental profit associated with the displays. Because this programme involves no change in price, contribution per unit during the promotion is expected to be the same as at other times, €12.00 per unit. Thus, total contribution during the promotion is expected to be 30,000 ∗ €12, or €360,000. Subtracting the incremental fixed cost of specialised displays, profits for the period are projected to be €360,000 − €100,000, or €260,000.

Fred estimates that baseline sales total 15,000 units. On this basis, he calculates that contribution without the promotion would be €12 ∗ 15,000 = €180,000. Thus, he projects that the special displays can be expected to generate incremental profit of €360,000 − €180,000 − €100,000 = €80,000.

Jeanne argues that she would expect sales of 25,000 units without the promotion, generating baseline contribution of €12 ∗ 25,000 = €300,000. Consequently, if the promotion is implemented, she anticipates an incremental *decline* in profits from €300,000 to €260,000. In her view, the promotion's lift would not be sufficient to cover its incremental fixed costs. Under this promotion, Jeanne believes that the firm would be spending €100,000 to generate incremental contribution of only €60,000 (that is, 5,000 units ∗ €12 contribution per unit).

The baseline sales estimate is a crucial factor here.

Example A luggage manufacturer faces a difficult decision regarding whether to launch a new promotion. The firm's data show a major increase in product sales in November and December, but its managers are unsure whether this is a permanent trend of higher sales or merely a blip – a successful period that can't be expected to continue (see Figure 8.1).

Figure 8.1 Monthly sales patterns

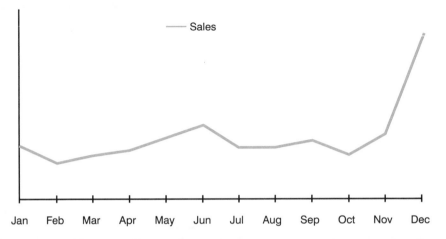

The firm's marketing director strongly supports the proposed promotion. He argues that the increased volume can't be expected to continue and that the firm's historic baseline (26,028 units) should be used as the level of sales that can be anticipated without the promotion. In addition, the marketing director argues that only the variable cost of each sale should be considered. "After all, the fixed costs will be with us whatever we do," he says. On this basis, the relevant cost per unit subject to analysis would be $25.76.

The CEO hires a consultant who has a very different opinion. In the consultant's view, the November–December sales increase was more than a blip. The market has grown, she says, and the strength of the firm's brand has grown with it. Consequently, a more appropriate estimate of baseline sales would be 48,960 units. The consultant also points out that in the long term, no costs are fixed. Therefore, for purposes of analysis, fixed costs should be allocated to the cost of the product because the product must ultimately generate a return after such expenses as factory rent are paid. On this basis, the full cost of each unit, $34.70, should be used as the cost of incremental sales (see Table 8.2).

Table 8.2 Baseline matters when considering profitability

	Consultant		Marketing director	
	Promotion	Baseline	Promotion	Baseline
Price	$41.60	$48.00	$41.60	$48.00
Cost	$34.70	$34.70	$25.76	$25.76
Margin	$6.90	$13.30	$15.84	$22.24
Sales	75,174	48,960	75,174	26.028
Profit	$518,701	$651,168	$1,190,756	$578,863
Profitability of promotion	($132,467)		$611,893	

The marketing director and the consultant make very different projections of the profitability of the promotion. Once again, the choice of the baseline matters. Also, we can see that establishing a shared understanding of costs and margins can be critical.

Data sources, complications and cautions

Finding a baseline estimate of what a company can be expected to sell, "all things being equal", is a complex and inexact process. Essentially, the baseline is the level of sales that can be expected without significant marketing activities. When certain marketing activities, such as price promotions, have been employed for several periods, it can be especially difficult to separate "incremental" and "baseline" sales.

In many companies, it is common to measure sales performance against historic data. In effect, this sets historic sales as the baseline level for analysis of the impact of marketing spending. For example, retailers can evaluate their performance on the basis of same store sales (to remove differences caused by the addition or removal of outlets). Further, they can compare each current period to the same period in the previous year, in order to avoid seasonality biases and to ensure that they measure periods of special activity (such as sales events) against times of similar activity.

It is also common practice to adjust the profitability of promotions for longer-term effects. These effects can include a decline in sales levels in periods immediately following a promotion, as well as higher or lower sales in related product categories that are associated with a promotion. Adjustments can be negative or positive. Additional long-term effects, such as obtaining trial by new consumers, gaining distribution with trade customers and increased consumption rates were discussed briefly in the chapter introduction.

Long-term effects of promotions

Over time, the effects of promotions may be to "ratchet" sales up or down (see Figures 8.2 and 8.3). Under one scenario, in response to one firm's promotions, competitors may also increase their promotional activity, and consumers and trade customers in the field may learn to wait for deals, increasing sales for no one (see the prisoner's dilemma on pages 232–234).

Figure 8.2 Downward spiral – promotional effectiveness

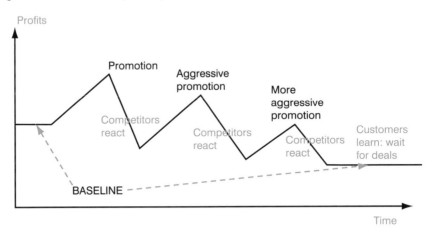

Under a different, more heartening scenario, promotions can generate trial for new products, build trade distribution and encourage loyalty, thus raising the long-term level of baseline sales.

Figure 8.3 Successful promotion with long-term benefits

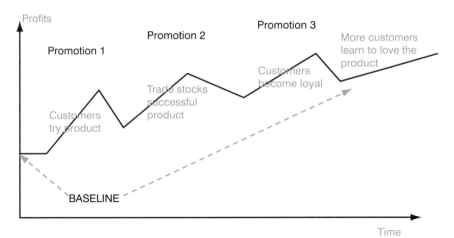

Redemption rates, costs for coupons and rebates, per cent sales with coupon

Redemption rate is the percentage of distributed coupons or rebates that are used (redeemed) by consumers.

$$\text{Coupon redemption rate (\%)} = \frac{\text{Coupons redeemed (N)}}{\text{Coupons distributed (N)}}$$

$$\text{Cost per redemption (£)} = \text{Coupon face amount (£)} + \text{Redemption charges (£)}$$

$$\text{Total coupon cost (£)} = [\text{Cost per redemption (£)} * \text{Coupons redeemed (N)}] + \text{Coupon printing and distribution cost (£)}$$

$$\text{Percentage sales with coupon (\%)} = \frac{\text{Sales with coupon (£)}}{\text{Sales (£)}}$$

The redemption rate is an important metric for marketers assessing the effectiveness of their coupon distribution strategy. It helps determine whether coupons are reaching the customers who are motivated to use them. Similar metrics apply to mail-in rebates (cashback sum).

Cost per redemption (£) measures variable costs per coupon redeemed. Coupon distribution costs are usually viewed as fixed costs.

Purpose: to track and evaluate coupon usage

Some people hate coupons. Some like them. And some say they hate coupons, but really like them. Businesses often say they hate coupons but continue to use them. Coupons and rebates are used to introduce new products, to generate trial of existing products by new customers and to "load" consumers' pantries, encouraging long-term consumption.

Almost all of the interim objectives discussed in the introduction to this chapter can apply to coupons and rebates. Coupons can be used to offer lower prices to more price-sensitive consumers. Coupons also serve as a form of advertising, making them dual-purpose marketing vehicles. Coupon clippers will see a brand name and pay closer attention to it – considering whether they desire the product – than would an average consumer exposed to an advertisement without a compelling offer. Finally, both rebates and coupons can serve as focus points for retailer promotions. To generate traffic, retailers can double or even triple coupon amounts – generally up to a declared limit. Retailers also often advertise prices "after rebates" in order to promote sales and perceptions of value.

Construction

$$\text{Coupon redemption rate (\%)} = \frac{\text{Coupons redeemed (N)}}{\text{Coupons distributed (N)}}$$

$$\text{Cost per redemption (£)} = \text{Coupon face amount (£)} + \text{Redemption charges (£)}$$

> **Total coupon cost: Reflects distribution,[3] printing and redemption costs to estimate the total cost of a coupon promotion.**

$$\text{Total coupon cost (£)} = [\text{Coupons redeemed (N)} * \text{Cost per redemption (£)}] + \text{Coupon printing and distribution cost (£)}$$

$$\text{Total cost per redemption (£)} = \frac{\text{Total coupon cost (£)}}{\text{Coupons redeemed (N)}}$$

$$\text{Percentage sales with coupon (\%)} = \frac{\text{Sales with coupon (£,N)}}{\text{Sales (£,N)}}$$

To determine the profitability of coupons and rebates, managers require approaches similar to those used in estimating baseline and incremental sales, as discussed in the previous section of this chapter. By themselves, redemption rates are not a good measure of success. Under certain circumstances, even low redemption rates can be profitable. Under other circumstances, by contrast, high redemption rates can be quite damaging.

Example Yvette is the Manager of Analysis for a small regional consumer pack-aged goods firm. Her product has a dominant share of the retail distribution in a narrow geographic area. Her firm decides to launch a coupon campaign, and Yvette is charged with reporting on the programme's success. Her assistant looks at the figures and realises that of the 100,000 coupons distributed in the local paper, 5,000 were used to buy product. The assistant is excited when he calculates that this represents a 5% redemption rate – a much higher figure than the company has ever previously seen.

Yvette, however, is more cautious in judging the promotion a success. She checks the sales of the relevant product and learns that these increased by only 100 units during the promotion period. Yvette concludes that the vast majority of coupon use was by customers who would have bought the product anyway. For most cus-tomers, the sole impact of the coupon was to reduce the price of the product below the level they would have willingly paid. Until she conducts a full profitability analysis, evaluating the profit generated by the 100 incremental sales and com-paring this to coupon costs and the value lost on most coupon sales, Yvette can't be sure that the programme made an overall loss. But she feels certain that she should curtail the celebrations.

Data sources, complications and cautions

To calculate coupon redemption rates, managers must know the number of coupons placed in circulation (distributed) as well as the number redeemed. Companies generally engage distribution services or media companies to place coupons in circulation. Redemption numbers are usually derived from the invoices presented by coupon clearing houses.

Related metrics and concepts

Mail-in rebates

The rebate, in effect, is a form of coupon that is popular with big-ticket items. Its usage dynamics are straightforward: customers pay the full price for a product, enabling retailers to meet a specific price point. The customer then exercises the rebate and receives back a specified amount of money (cashback sum).

By using rebates, marketers gain information about customers, which can be useful in remarketing and product control. Mail-in rebates also reduce the effective price of an item for customers who are sufficiently price-conscious to take advan-tage of them. Others pay full price. The "non-redemption rates" for rebates are sometimes called "breakage".

> Breakage: **The number of rebates not redeemed by customers. The breakage rate is the percentage of rebates not redeemed.**

Example A mobile phone company in the US sold 40,000 handsets in one month. On each purchase, the customer was offered a $30 rebate. Thirty thousand rebates were successfully claimed.

In volume terms, the rebate redemption rate can be calculated by dividing the number of rebates successfully claimed (30,000) by number offered (40,000):

$$\text{Redemption rate (in volume terms)} = \frac{30,000}{40,000} = 75\%$$

Managers often baulk at the cost of distributing coupons. Because promotions rely on adequate distribution, however, it is inadvisable to create arbitrary cutoffs for distribution costs. The total cost of incremental sales generated would represent a better metric to evaluate coupon efficiency – and thus to determine the point at which diminishing returns make further coupon distribution unattractive.

In evaluating a coupon or rebate programme, companies should also consider the overall level of benefit provided to consumers. Retailers commonly increase the value of coupons, offering customers a discount of double or even triple the coupons' face value. This enables retailers to identify price-sensitive customers and offer them additional savings. Of course, by multiplying the savings afforded consumers, the practice of doubling or tripling coupons undoubtedly raises some redemption rates.

Promotions and pass-through

Of the promotional value provided by a manufacturer to its retailers and distributors, the pass-through percentage represents the portion that ultimately reaches the consumer.

$$\text{Percentage sales on deal (\%)} = \frac{\text{Sales with any temporary discount (£,N)}}{\text{Total sales (£,N)}}$$

$$\text{Pass-through (\%)} = \frac{\text{Value of temporary promotional discounts provided to consumers by the trade (£)}}{\text{Value of temporary discounts provided to trade by manufacturer (£)}}$$

Manufacturers offer many discounts to their distributors and retailers (often called "the trade") with the objective of encouraging them to offer their own promotions, in turn, to their customers. If trade customers or consumers do not find promotions attractive, this will be indicated by a decline in percentage sales on deal. Likewise, low pass-through percentages can indicate that too many deals – or the wrong kinds of deals – are being offered.

Purpose: to measure whether trade promotions are generating consumer promotions

> **Pass-through:** The percentage of the value of manufacturer promotions paid to distributors and retailers that is reflected in discounts provided by the trade to their own customers.

"Middlemen" are a part of the channel structure in many industries. Companies may face one, two, three or even four levels of "resellers" before their product reaches the ultimate consumer. For example, a beer manufacturer may sell to an exporter, who sells to an importer, who sells to a local distributor, who sells to a retail store. If each channel adds its own margin, without regard for how others are pricing, the resulting price can be higher than a marketer would like. This sequential application of individual margins has been referred to as "double marginalisation".[4]

Construction

> **Percentage sales on deal:** Measures the percentage of company sales that are sold with a temporary trade discount of some form. Note: This usually would not include standard discounts such as those for early payment or cooperative advertising allowances (accruals).

$$\text{Percentage sales on deal (\%)} = \frac{\text{Sales with any temporary discount (N,£)}}{\text{Total sales (N,£)}}$$

Promotional discount represents the total value of promotional discounts given throughout the sales channel.

$$\text{Promotional discount (£)} = \text{Sales with any temporary discount (£)} * \text{Average depth of discount as per cent of list (\%)}$$

$$\text{Depth of discount as per cent of list} = \frac{\text{Unit discount (£)}}{\text{Unit list price (£)}}$$

Pass-through is calculated as the value of discounts given by the trade to their customers, divided by the value of temporary discounts provided by a manufacturer to the trade.

$$\text{Pass-through (\%)} = \frac{\text{Promotional discounts provided by the trade to consumers (£)}}{\text{Discounts provided to trade by manufacturer (£)}}$$

Manufacturers often compete with one another for the attention of retailers, distributors and other resellers. Toward that end, they build special displays for their products, change assortments to include new offerings, and seek to elicit increasing attention from resellers' sales personnel. Significantly, in their effort to increase channel "push", manufacturers also offer discounts and allowances to the trade. It is important to understand the rates and amounts of discounts provided to the trade, as well as the proportions of those discounts that are passed along to the resellers' customers. At times, when resellers' margins are thin, manufacturers' discounts are designed to enhance them. Market leaders often worry that trade margins are too thin to support push efforts. Other manufacturers may be concerned that retail margins are too high, and that too few of their discounts are being passed along. The metrics discussed in this chapter should be interpreted with these thoughts in mind.

Resellers may decide that optimising an entire product line is more important than maximising profits on any given product. If a reseller stocks multiple competing lines, it can be difficult to find an overall solution that suits both that reseller and its suppliers. Manufacturers strive to motivate resellers to market their goods aggressively and to grow their shared sales through such programmes as incentives for "exclusivity", or rebates based on increasing shares of category sales or on year-to-year growth in sales.

Resellers learn to adapt their buying and selling practices to take advantage of manufacturer pricing incentives. In this area, marketers must pay special attention to the law of unforeseen consequences. For example, resellers have been known to:

- Buy larger quantities of a product than they can sell – or want to sell – in order to qualify for volume discounts. The excess goods are then sold (diverted) to other retailers, stored for future sales, or even destroyed or returned to the manufacturer for "credit".

- Time their purchases at the ends of accounting periods in order to qualify for rebates and allowances. This results in "lumpy" sales patterns for manufacturers, making forecasting difficult, increasing problems with out-of-date products and returns and raising production costs.

In some instances, a particularly powerful channel "captain" can impose pricing discipline on an entire channel. In most cases, however, each "link" in the distribution chain can coordinate only its own pricing. A manufacturer, for example, may work out appropriate pricing incentives for wholesalers, and the wholesalers in turn may develop their own pricing incentives for retailers.

In many countries and industries, it is illegal for suppliers to dictate the selling prices of resellers. Manufacturers can't dictate wholesaler selling prices, and wholesalers can't dictate retail prices. Consequently, members of the channel seek indirect methods of influencing resellers' prices.

Price waterfall

The price waterfall is a way of describing the progression of prices from published list price to the final price paid by a customer. Each drop in price represents a drop in the "water level". For example:

100
List price
          Dealer discount
                    90
                    Cash discount
                         85
                         Annual rebate
                              82
                              Co-op advertising
                                   Net price £80

$$\text{Price waterfall (\%)} = \frac{\text{Net price per unit (£)}}{\text{List price per unit (£)}}$$

In this structure, the average price paid by customers will depend on the list price of a product, the sizes of discounts given and the proportion of customers taking advantage of those discounts.

By analysing the price waterfall, marketers can determine where product value is being lost. This can be especially important in businesses that allow the sales channel to reduce prices in order to secure customers. The price waterfall can help focus attention on deciding whether these discounts make sense for the business.

Purpose: to assess the actual price paid for a product, in comparison with the list price

In pricing, the bad news is that marketers can find it difficult to determine the right list price for a product. The good news is that few customers will actually pay that price anyway. Indeed, a product's net price – the price actually paid by customers – often falls between 53% and 94% of its base price.[5]

Net price: **The actual price paid for a product by customers after all discounts and allowances have been factored in. Also called the pocket price.**

List price: **The price of a good or service before discounts and allowances are considered.**

> **Invoice price:** The price specified on the invoice for a product. This price will typically be stated net of some discounts and allowances, such as dealer, competitive and order size discounts, but will not reflect other discounts and allowances, such as those for special terms and cooperative advertising. Typically, the invoice price will therefore be less than the list price but greater than the net price.
>
> **Price waterfall:** The reduction of the price actually paid by customers for a product as discounts and allowances are given at various stages of the sales process. Because few customers take advantage of all discounts, in analysing a product's price waterfall, marketers must consider not only the amount of each discount but also the percentage of sales to which it applies.

As customers vary in their use of discounts, net price can fall into a wide range relative to list price.

Construction

To assess a product's price waterfall, one must plot the price a customer will pay at each stage of the waterfall, specifying potential discounts and allowances in the sequence in which those are usually taken or applied. For example, broker commissions are generally applied *after* trade discounts.

> **Net price:** The actual average price paid for a product at a given stage in its distribution channel can be calculated as its list price, less discounts offered, with each discount multiplied by the probability that it will be applied. When all discounts are considered, this calculation yields the product's net price.

$$\text{Net price (£)} = \text{List price (£)} - [\text{Discount A (£)} * \text{Proportion of purchases on which discount A is taken (\%)}] - [\text{Discount B (£)} * \text{Proportion of purchases on which discount B is taken (\%)}] \text{ and so on} \ldots$$

$$\text{Price waterfall effect (\%)} = \frac{\text{Net price per unit (£)}}{\text{List price per unit (£)}}$$

Example Hakan manages his own firm. In selling his product, Hakan grants two discounts or allowances. The first of these is a 12% discount on orders of more than 100 units. This is given on 50% of the firm's business and appears on its invoicing system. Hakan also gives an allowance of 5% for cooperative advertising. This is not shown on the invoicing system. It is completed in separate procedures that involve customers submitting advertisements for approval. Upon investigation, Hakan finds that 80% of customers take advantage of this advertising allowance.

The invoice price of the firm's product can be calculated as the list price (50 dinar per unit), less the 12% order size discount, multiplied by the chance of that discount being given (50%).

Invoice price = List price − [Discount ∗ Proportion of purchases on which discount is taken]

= 50 dinar − [(50 ∗ 12%) ∗ 50%]

= 50 dinar − 3 dinar = 47 dinar

The net price further reduces the invoice price by the average amount of the cooperative advertising allowance granted, as follows:

Net price = List price − [Discount ∗ Proportion of purchases on which discount is taken] − [Advertising allowance ∗ Proportion of purchases on which advertising allowance is taken] = 50 dinar − [(50 ∗ 12%) ∗ 50%] − [(50 ∗ 5%) ∗ 80%] = 50 − 3 − 2 = 45 dinar

To find the effect of the price waterfall, divide the net price by the list price.

$$\text{Price waterfall (\%)} = \frac{45}{50} = 90\%$$

Data sources, complications and cautions

To analyse the impact of discounts, allowances and the overall price waterfall effect, marketers require full information about sales, in both revenue and unit volume terms, at an individual product level, including not only those discounts and allowances that are formally recorded in the billing system, but also those granted without appearing on invoices.

The major challenge in establishing the price waterfall is securing product-specific data at all of these various levels in the sales process. In all but the smallest businesses, this is likely to be quite difficult, particularly because many discounts are granted on an off-invoice basis, so they might not be recorded at a product level in a firm's financial system. Further complicating matters, not all discounts are based on list price. Cash discounts, for example, are usually based on net invoice price.

Where discounts are known in theory, but the financial system doesn't fully record their details, the problem is determining how to calculate the price waterfall. Toward that end, marketers need not only the amount of each discount, but also the percentage of unit sales for which customers take advantage of that discount.

The typical business offers a number of discounts from list prices. Most of these serve the function of encouraging particular customer behaviours. For example, trade discounts can encourage distributors and resellers to buy in full truckloads, pay invoices promptly and place orders during promotional periods or in a manner that smoothes production. Over time, these discounts tend to multiply as manufacturers find it easier to raise list price and add another discount than to eliminate discounts altogether.

Problems with discounts include the following:

- Because it's difficult to record discounts on a per-item basis, firms often record them in aggregate. On this basis, marketers may see the total discounts provided but have difficulty allocating these to specific products. Some discounts are offered on the total size of a purchase, exacerbating this problem. This increases the challenge of assessing product profitability.
- Once given, discounts tend to be sticky. It is hard to take them away from customers. Consequently, inertia often leaves special discounts in place, long after the competitive pressures that prompted them are removed.
- To the extent that discounts are not recorded on invoices, management often loses track of them in decision-making.

As the Professional Pricing Society advises, when considering the price of a product, "Look past the invoice price."[6]

Related metrics and concepts

Deductions:
Some "discounts" are actually deductions applied by a customer to an invoice, adjusting for goods damaged in shipment, incorrect deliveries, late deliveries or, in some cases, for products that did not sell as well as hoped. Deductions might not be recorded in a way that can be analysed, and they are often the subject of disputes.

Everyday low prices (EDLP)
EDLP refers to a strategy of offering the same pricing level from period to period. For retailers, there is a distinction between buying at EDLP and selling at EDLP. For example, some suppliers offer constant selling prices to retailers but negotiate periods during which a product will be offered on deal with display and other retail promotions. Rather than granting temporary price discounts to retailers, suppliers often finance these programmes through "market development funds".

HI-LO (high-low)
This pricing strategy constitutes the opposite of EDLP. In HI-LO pricing, retailers and manufacturers offer a series of "deals" or "specials" – times during which prices are temporarily decreased. One purpose of HI-LO pricing and other temporary discounts is to realise price discrimination in the economic – not the legal – sense of the term.

Price discrimination and tailoring

When firms face distinct and separable market segments with different willingness to pay (price elasticities), charging a single price means that the firm will "leave money on the table" – not capture the full consumer value.

There are three conditions for price tailoring to be profitable:

- Segments must have **different elasticities** (willingness to pay), and/or marketers must have different costs of serving the segments (say shipping expenses) and the incremental volume must be sufficiently large to compensate for the reduction in margin.
- Segments must be **separable** – that is, charging different prices does not just result in transfer between segments (for example, your father cannot buy your dinner and apply the senior citizen discount).
- The **incremental profit from price tailoring exceeds the costs** of implementing multiple prices for the same product or service.

Price tailoring is clearly a euphemism for price discrimination. However, the latter term is loaded with legal implications, and marketers understandably use it with caution.

When facing a total demand curve composed of identifiable segments with different demand slopes, a marketer can use optimal pricing for each segment recognised, as opposed to using the same price based upon aggregate demand. This is usually done by:

- **Time:** For example, cinemas charging a higher price during peak hours or products that are launched at a high price in the beginning, "skimming" profits from early adopters.
- **Geography:** Such as international market divisions – different prices for different regions for DVDs, for example.
- **Tolerable discrimination:** Identifying acceptable forms of segmentation, such as discriminating between students or senior citizens and the general public.

Price differences cause grey markets; goods are imported from low-price to high-price markets. Grey markets are common in some fashion goods and pharmaceuticals.

> ### Caution: regulations
>
> Most countries have regulations that apply to price discrimination. As a marketer, you should understand these regulations. In Europe, several countries have their own regulations within the framework of EU rules and this creates some variation as to what practices are deemed to be anti-competitive. When operating in Europe it is important to understand the specific rules of the country and so we advise checking local legal advice before developing your pricing strategies.

References and suggested further reading

Abraham, M.M. and L.M. Lodish. (1990). "Getting the Most Out of Advertising and Promotion", *Harvard Business Review*, 68(3), 50–58.

Ailawadi, K., P. Farris and E. Shames. (1999). "Trade Promotion: Essential to Selling Through Resellers", *Sloan Management Review*, 41(1), 83–92.

Christen, M., S. Gupta, J.C. Porter, R. Staelin and D.R. Wittink. (1997). "Using Market-level Data to Understand Promotion Effects in a Nonlinear Model", *Journal of Marketing Research*, 34(3), 322–334.

Roegner, E., M. Marn and C. Zawada. (2005). "Pricing", *Marketing Management*, 14(1), 23–28.

Advertising media and Web metrics

9

Metrics covered in this chapter:

- Advertising: impressions, gross rating points and opportunities-to-see

- Cost per thousand impressions (CPM) rates

- Reach/net reach and frequency

- Frequency response functions

- Effective reach and effective frequency

- Share of voice

- Impressions, pageviews and hits

- Clickthrough rates

- Cost per impression, cost per click and cost of acquisition

- Visits, visitors and abandonment

Introduction

Advertising is the cornerstone of many marketing strategies. The positioning and communications conveyed by advertising often set the tone and timing for many other sales and promotion efforts. Advertising is not only the defining element of the marketing mix, but it is also expensive and notoriously difficult to evaluate. This is because it is not easy to track the incremental sales associated with advertising decisions. For many marketers, media metrics are particularly confusing.

A command of the vocabulary involved in this field is needed to work with media planners, buyers and agencies. A strong understanding of media metrics can help marketers ensure that advertising budgets are spent efficiently and directed toward a specific aim.

In the first part of this chapter, we discuss media metrics that reveal how many people may be exposed to an advertising campaign, how often those people have an opportunity to see the ads, and the cost of each potential impression. Toward that end, we introduce the vocabulary of advertising metrics, including such terms as impressions, exposures, OTS, rating points, GRPs, net reach, effective frequency and CPMs.

In the second part of this chapter, we focus on metrics used in Web-based marketing efforts. The Internet increasingly provides valuable opportunities to augment traditional "broadcast" advertising with interactive media. In fact, many of the same advertising media terms, such as impressions, are used to describe and evaluate Web-based advertising. Other terms, such as clickthrough, are unique to the Web. Certain Web-specific metrics are needed because the Internet, like direct mail, serves not only as a communications medium, but also as a direct sales channel that can provide real-time feedback on the effectiveness of advertising in generating customer interest and sales.

Metric	Construction	Considerations	Purpose
Impressions	An impression is generated each time an advertisement is viewed. The number of impressions achieved is a function of an ad's reach (the number of people seeing it), multiplied by its frequency (number of times they see it).	As a metric, impressions do not account for quality of viewings. In this regard, a glimpse will have less effect than a detailed study. Impressions are also called exposures and opportunities-to-see (OTS).	To understand how many times an advertisement is viewed.
Gross rating points (GRPs)	Impressions divided by the number of people in the audience for an advertisement.	Impressions expressed in relation to population. GRPs are cumulative across media vehicles, making it possible to achieve GRPs of more than 100%. Target rating points (TRPs) are measured in relation to defined target populations.	To measure impressions in relation to the number of people in the audience for an advertising campaign.

Metric	Construction	Considerations	Purpose
Cost per thousand impressions (CPM)	Cost of advertising divided by impressions generated (in thousands).	CPM is a measure of cost per advertising impression, reckoning impressions in thousands. This makes it easier to work with the resulting financial figures than would be possible on the basis of cost per single impression.	To measure the cost-effectiveness of the generation of impressions.
Net reach	The number of people who receive an advertisement.	Equivalent to reach. Measures unique viewers of an advertisement. Often best mapped on a Venn diagram.	To measure the breadth of an advertisement's spread across a population.
Average frequency	The average number of times that an individual receives an advertisement, given that he or she is indeed exposed to the ad.	Frequency is measured only among people who have in fact seen the advertisement under study.	To measure how strongly an advertisement is concentrated on a given population.
Frequency response functions	Linear: All advertising impressions are equally impactful. Threshold: A certain number of impressions are needed before an advertising message will sink in.	Linear model is often unrealistic, especially for complex products. Threshold model is often used, as it is simple and intuitive.	Learning curve model may suggest spurious accuracy in an imprecise process. Should be tested for accuracy.
	Learning curve: An advertisement has little impact at first but gains force with repetition and then tails off as saturation is achieved.		To model the reaction of a population to exposure to an advertisement.

▶

Metric	Construction	Considerations	Purpose
Effective reach	Reach achieved among individuals who are exposed to an advertisement with a frequency greater than or equal to the effective frequency.	The effective frequency rate constitutes a crucial assumption in the calculation of this metric.	To measure the portion of an audience that is exposed to an advertisement enough times to be influenced.
Effective frequency	The number of times an individual must see an advertisement in order to register its message.	As a rule of thumb in planning, marketers often use an effective frequency of 3. To the extent that it promises to have a significant impact on campaign results, this assumption should be tested.	To determine optimal exposure levels for an advertisement or campaign, trading the risk of over-spending against the risk of failing to achieve the desired impact.
Share of voice	Quantifies the advertising "presence" of a brand, campaign or firm in relation to total advertising in a market.	Market definition is central to meaningful results. Impressions or ratings represent a conceptually strong basis for share of voice calculations. Often, however, such data are unavailable. Consequently, marketers use spending, an input, as a proxy for output.	To evaluate the relative strength of advertising programme within its market.
Pageviews	The number of times a Web page is served.	Represents the number of Web pages served. Hits, by contrast, represent pageviews multiplied by the number of files on a page, making it as much a metric of page design as of traffic.	To provide a top-level measure of the popularity of a website.

Metric	Construction	Considerations	Purpose
Clickthrough rate	Number of clickthroughs as a fraction of the number of impressions.	An interactive measure of Web advertising. Has great strengths, but clicks represent only a step toward conversion and are thus an intermediate advertising goal.	To measure the effectiveness of a Web advertisement by counting those customers who are sufficiently intrigued to click through it.
Cost per click	Advertising cost, divided by number of clicks generated.	Often used as a billing mechanism.	To measure or establish the cost-effectiveness of advertising.
Cost per order	Advertising cost, divided by number of orders generated.	More directly related to profit than cost per click, but less effective in measuring pure marketing. An advertisement may generate strong clickthrough but yield weak conversion due to a disappointing product.	To measure or establish the cost-effectiveness of advertising.
Cost per customer acquired	Advertising cost, divided by number of customers acquired.	Useful for purposes of comparison to customer lifetime value. Helps marketers determine whether customers are worth the cost of their acquisition.	To measure the cost-effectiveness of advertising.
Visits	The number of unique viewings of a website.	By measuring visits relative to pageviews, marketers can determine whether viewers are investigating multiple pages on a website.	To measure audience traffic on a website.

Metric	Construction	Considerations	Purpose
Visitors	The number of unique website viewers in a given period.	Useful in determining the type of traffic generated by a website – a few loyal adherents, or many occasional visitors. The period over which this metric is measured can be an important consideration.	To measure the reach of a website.
Abandonment rate	The rate of purchases started but not completed.	Can warn of weak design in an e-commerce site by measuring the number of potential customers who lose patience with a transaction process or are surprised and put off by "hidden" costs revealed toward its conclusion.	To measure one element of the close rate of Internet business.

Advertising: impressions, exposures, opportunities-to-see (OTS), gross rating points (GRPs) and target rating points (TRPs)

Advertising impressions, exposures and opportunities-to-see (OTS) all refer to the same metric: an estimate of the audience for a media "insertion" (one ad) or campaign.

Impressions = OTS = Exposures. In this chapter, we will use all these terms. It is important to distinguish between "reach" (number of unique individuals exposed to certain advertising) and "frequency" (the average number of times each such individual is exposed).

Rating point = Reach of a media vehicle as a percentage of a defined population (for example, a television show with a rating of 2 reaches 2% of the population).

> **Gross rating points (GRPs)** = Total ratings achieved by multiple media vehicles expressed in rating points (for example, advertisements on five television shows with an average rating of 30% would achieve 150 GRPs).
>
> Gross rating points are impressions expressed as a percentage of a defined population, and often total more than 100%. This metric refers to the defined population reached rather than an absolute number of people. Although GRPs are used with a broader audience, the term "target rating points" (TRPs) denotes a narrower definition of the target audience. For example, TRPs might consider a specific segment such as youths aged 15 to 19, whereas GRPs might be based on the total TV viewing population.

Purpose: to measure the audience for an advertisement

Impressions, exposures and opportunities-to-see (OTS) are the "atoms" of media planning. Every advertisement released into the world has a fixed number of planned exposures, depending on the number of individuals in its audience. For example, an advertisement that appears on a billboard on the Champs-Élysées in central Paris will have an estimated number of impressions, based on the flow of traffic from visitors and locals. An advertisement is said to "reach" a certain number of people on a number of occasions, or to provide a certain number of "impressions" or "opportunities-to-see". These impressions or opportunities-to-see are thus a function of the number of people reached and the number of times each such person has an opportunity to see the advertisement.

Methodologies for estimating opportunities-to-see vary by type of media. In magazines, for example, opportunities-to-see will not equal circulation because each copy of the magazine may be read by more than one person. In broadcast media, it is assumed that the quantified audience comprises those individuals available to hear or see an advertisement. In print and outdoor media, an opportunity-to-see might range from a brief glance to a careful consideration. To illustrate this range, imagine you're walking down a busy street. How many billboard advertisements catch your eye? You may not realise it, but you're contributing to the impressions of several advertisements, regardless of whether you ignore them or study them with great interest.

When a campaign involves several types of media, marketers may need to adjust their measures of opportunities-to-see in order to maintain consistency and allow for comparability among the different media.

Gross rating points (GRPs) are related to impressions and opportunities-to-see. They quantify impressions as a percentage of the population reached rather than in absolute numbers of people reached. Target rating points (TRPs) express the same concept but with regard to a more narrowly defined target audience.

Construction

> **Impressions, opportunities-to-see (OTS) and exposures: The number of times a specific advertisement is delivered to a potential customer. This is an estimate of the audience for a media "insertion" (one ad) or a campaign. Impressions = OTS = exposures.**

Impressions

The process of estimating reach and frequency begins with data that sum all of the impressions from different advertisements to arrive at total "gross" impressions.

$$\text{Impressions (N)} = \text{Reach (N)} * \text{Average frequency (N)}$$

The same formula can be rearranged as follows to convey the average number of times that an audience was given the opportunity to see an advertisement. Average frequency is defined as the average number of impressions per individual "reached" by an advertisement or campaign.

$$\text{Average frequency (N)} = \frac{\text{Impressions (N)}}{\text{Reach (N)}}$$

Similarly, the reach of an advertisement – that is, the number of people with an opportunity to see the ad – can be calculated as follows:

$$\text{Reach (N)} = \frac{\text{Impressions (N)}}{\text{Average frequency (N)}}$$

Although reach can thus be quantified as the number of individuals exposed to an advertisement or campaign, it can also be calculated as a percentage of the population. In this text, we will distinguish between the two conceptualisations of this metric as reach (N) and reach (%).

The reach of a specific media vehicle, which may deliver an advertisement, is often expressed in rating points. Rating points are calculated as individuals reached by that vehicle, divided by the total number of individuals in a defined population, and expressed in "points" that represent the resulting percentage. Thus, a television programme with a rating of 2 would reach 2% of the population.

The rating points of all the media vehicles that deliver an advertisement or campaign can be summed, yielding a measure of the aggregate reach of the campaign, known as gross rating points (GRPs).

> **Gross rating points (GRPs): The sum of all rating points delivered by the media vehicles carrying an advertisement or campaign.**

Example A campaign that delivers 150 GRPs might expose 30% of the population to an advertisement at an average frequency of 5 impressions per individual (150 = 30 * 5). If 15 separate "insertions" of the advertisement were used, a few individuals might be exposed as many as 15 times, and many more of the 30% reached would only have 1 or 2 opportunities-to-see (OTS).

$$\text{Gross rating points (GRPs) (\%)} = \text{Reach (\%)} * \text{Average frequency (N)}$$

$$\text{Gross Rating points (GRPs) (\%)} = \frac{\text{Impressions (N)}}{\text{Defined population (N)}}$$

Target rating points (TRPs): **The gross rating points delivered by a media vehicle to a specific target audience.**

Example A firm places 10 advertising insertions in a market with a population of 5 people. The resulting impressions are outlined in the following table, in which "1"

Insertion	Individual					Impressions	Rating points (impressions/population)
	A	B	C	D	E		
1	1	1	0	0	1	3	60
2	1	1	0	0	1	3	60
3	1	1	0	1	0	3	60
4	1	1	0	1	0	3	60
5	1	1	0	1	0	3	60
6	1	0	0	1	0	2	40
7	1	0	0	1	0	2	40
8	1	0	0	0	0	1	20
9	1	0	0	0	0	1	20
10	1	0	0	0	0	1	20
Totals	**10**	**5**	**0**	**5**	**2**	**22**	**440**

represents an opportunity-to-see, and "0" signifies that an individual did not have an opportunity to see a particular insertion.

In this campaign, the total impressions across the entire population = 22.

As insertion 1 generates impressions upon 3 of the 5 members of the population, it reaches 60% of that population, for 60 rating points. As insertion 6 generates impressions upon 2 of the 5 members of the population, it reaches 40% of the population, for 40 rating points. Gross rating points for the campaign can be calculated by adding the rating points of each insertion.

$$\text{Gross rating points (GRPs)} = \text{Rating points of insertion 1} + \text{Rating points of insertion 2} + \text{etc.}$$

$$= 440$$

Alternatively, gross rating points can be calculated by dividing total impressions by the size of the population and expressing the result in percentage terms.

$$\text{Gross rating points (GRPs)} = \frac{\text{Impressions}}{\text{Population}} * 100\% = \frac{22}{5} * 100\% = 440$$

Target rating points (TRPs), by contrast, quantify the gross rating points achieved by an advertisement or campaign among targeted individuals within a larger population. For the purposes of this example, let's assume that individuals A, B and C comprise the targeted group. Individual A has received 10 exposures to the campaign; individual B, 5 exposures; and individual C, 0 exposures. Thus, the campaign has reached 2 out of 3, or 66.67% of targeted individuals. Among those reached, its average frequency has been 15/2, or 7.5. On this basis, we can calculate target rating points by either of the following methods.

$$\text{Target rating points (TRPs)} = \text{Reach (\%)} * \text{Average frequency}$$

$$= 66.67\% * \frac{15}{2}$$

$$= 500$$

$$\text{Target rating points (TRPs)} = \frac{\text{Impressions (N)}}{\text{Targets (N)}} = \frac{15}{3} = 500$$

Data sources, complications and cautions

Data on the estimated audience size (reach) of a media vehicle are typically made available by media sellers. Standard methods also exist for combining data from different media to estimate "net reach" and frequency. An explanation of these procedures is beyond the scope of this book, but interested readers might want to consult a company dedicated to tracking rating points, such as Nielsen (www.nielsen.com), for further detail.

Two different media plans can yield comparable results in terms of costs and total exposures but differ in reach and frequency measures. In other words, one plan can expose a larger audience to an advertising message less often, while the other delivers more exposures to each member of a smaller audience. For an example, please see Table 9.1.

Table 9.1 Illustration of reach and frequency

	Reach	Average frequency*	Total exposures (impressions, OTS)
Plan A	250,000	4	1,000,000
Plan B	333,333	3	1,000,000

*Average frequency is the average number of exposures made to each individual who has received at least one exposure to a given advertisement or campaign. To compare impressions across media, or even within classes of media, one must make a broad assumption: that there is some equivalency between the different types of impressions generated by each media classification. Nonetheless, marketers must still compare the "quality" of impressions delivered by different media.

Consider the following examples. A billboard along a busy motorway and an underground railway advertisement can both yield the same number of impressions. Whereas the underground advertisement has a captive audience, however, members of the billboard audience are generally driving and concentrating on the road. As this example demonstrates, there may be differences in the quality of impressions. To account for these differences, media optimisers apply weightings to different media vehicles. When direct response data are available, they can be used to evaluate the relative effectiveness and efficiency of impression purchases in different media. Otherwise, this weighting might be a matter of judgement. A manager might believe, for example, that an impression generated by a TV commercial is twice as effective as one made by a magazine print advertisement.

Similarly, marketers often find it useful to define audience sub-groups and generate separate reach and frequency statistics for each. Marketers might weight sub-groups differently in the same way that they weight impressions delivered through different media.[1] This helps in evaluating whether an advertisement reaches its defined customer groups.

When calculating impressions, marketers often encounter an overlap of people who see an advertisement in more than one medium. Later in this text, we will discuss how to account for such overlap and estimate the percentage of people who are exposed to an advertisement multiple times.

Cost per thousand impressions (CPM) rates

Cost per thousand impressions (CPM) is the cost per thousand advertising impressions. This metric is calculated by dividing the cost of an advertising placement by the number of impressions (expressed in thousands) that it generates.

$$\text{Cost per thousand impressions (CPM)} = \frac{\text{Cost of advertising (£)}}{\text{Impressions generated (N in thousands)}}$$

CPM is useful in comparing the relative efficiency of different advertising opportunities or media and in evaluating the costs of overall campaigns.

Purpose: to compare the costs of advertising campaigns within and across different media

A typical advertising campaign might try to reach potential consumers in multiple locations and through various media. The cost per thousand impressions (CPM) metric enables marketers to make cost comparisons between these media, both at the planning stage and during reviews of past campaigns.

Marketers calculate CPM by dividing advertising campaign costs by the number of impressions (or opportunities-to-see) that are delivered by each part of the campaign. As the impression counts are generally sizeable, marketers customarily work with the CPM impressions. Dividing by 1,000 is an industry standard.

Cost per thousand impressions (CPM): **The cost of a media campaign, relative to its success in generating impressions or opportunities-to-see.**

Construction

To calculate CPM, marketers first state the results of a media campaign (gross impressions) in thousands. Second, they divide that result into the relevant media cost:

$$\text{Cost per thousand impressions (CPM) (£)} = \frac{\text{Advertising cost (£)}}{\text{Impressions generated (N in thousands)}}$$

Example An advertising campaign costs £4,000 and generates 120,000 impressions. On this basis, CPM can be calculated as follows:

$$\text{Cost per thousand impressions} = \frac{\text{Advertising cost}}{\text{Impressions generated (thousands)}}$$

$$= \frac{£4,000}{(120,000/1,000)}$$

$$= \frac{£4,000}{120} = £33.33$$

Data sources, complications and cautions

In an advertising campaign, the full cost of the media purchased can include agency fees and production of creative materials, in addition to the cost of media space or time. Marketers also must have an estimate of the number of impressions expected or delivered in the campaign at an appropriate level of detail. Internet marketers (see "Impressions, pageviews and hits" on pages 289–291) often can easily access these data.

CPM is only a starting point for analysis. Not all impressions are equally valuable. Consequently, it can make good business sense to pay more for impressions from some sources than from others.

In calculating CPM, marketers should also be concerned with their ability to capture the full cost of advertising activity. Cost items typically include the amount paid to a creative agency to develop advertising materials, amounts paid to an organisation that sells media, and internal salaries and expenses related to overseeing the advertisement.

Related metrics and concepts

Cost per point (CPP): **The cost of an advertising campaign, relative to the rating points delivered. In a manner similar to CPM, cost per point measures the cost per rating point for an advertising campaign by dividing the cost of the advertising by the rating points delivered.**

Reach, net reach and frequency

> Reach is the same as net reach; both of these metrics quantify the number or percentage of individuals in a defined population who receive at least one exposure to an advertisement. Frequency measures the average number of times that each such individual sees the advertisement.
>
> $$\text{Impressions (N)} = \text{Reach (N)} * \text{Frequency (N)}$$
>
> Net reach and frequency are important concepts in describing an advertising campaign. A campaign with a high net reach and low frequency runs the danger of being lost in a noisy advertising environment. A campaign with low net reach but high frequency can over-expose some audiences and miss others entirely. Reach and frequency metrics help managers adjust their advertising media plans to fit their marketing strategies.

Purpose: to separate total impressions into the number of people reached and the average frequency with which those individuals are exposed to advertising

To clarify the difference between reach and frequency, let's review what we learned in the first section. When impressions from multiple insertions are combined, the results are often called "gross impressions" or "total exposures". When total impressions are expressed as a percentage of the population, this measure is referred to as gross rating points (GRPs). For example, suppose a media vehicle reaches 12% of the population. That vehicle will have a single-insertion reach of 12 rating points. If a firm advertised in 10 such vehicles, it would achieve 120 GRPs.

Now, let's look at the composition of these 120 GRPs. Suppose we know that the 10 advertisements had a combined net reach of 40% and an average frequency of 3. Then their gross rating points might be calculated as 40 * 3 = 120 GRPs.

Example A commercial is shown once in each of three time slots. Nielsen keeps track of which households have an opportunity to see the advertisement. The commercial airs in a market with only five households: A, B, C, D and E. Time slots 1 and 2 both have a rating of 60 because 60% of the households view them. Time slot 3 has a rating of 20.

Time slot	Households with opportunity-to-see	Households with no opportunity-to-see	Rating points of time slot
1	A B E	C D	60
2	A B C	D E	60
3	A	B C D E	20
		GRP	140

$$GRP = \frac{\text{Impressions}}{\text{Population}} = \frac{7}{5} = 140 \; (\%)$$

The commercial is seen by households A, B, C and E, but not D. Thus, it generates impressions in four out of five households, for a reach (%) of 80%. In the four households reached, the commercial is seen a total of seven times. Thus, its average frequency can be calculated as 7/4, or 1.75. On this basis, we can calculate the campaign's gross rating points as follows:

$$GRP = \text{Reach (\%)} * \text{Average frequency} = \frac{4}{5} * \frac{7}{4} = 80\% * 1.75 = 140 \; (\%)$$

Unless otherwise specified, simple measures of overall audience size (such as GRPs or impressions) do not differentiate between campaigns that expose larger audiences fewer times and those that expose smaller audiences more often. In other words, these metrics do not distinguish between reach and frequency.

Reach, whether described as "net reach" or simply "reach", refers to the unduplicated audience of individuals who have been exposed at least once to the advertising in question. Reach can be expressed as either the number of individuals or the percentage of the population that has seen the advertisement.

> Reach: **The number of people or percentage of population exposed to an advertisement.**

Frequency is calculated by dividing gross impressions by reach. Frequency is equal to the average number of exposures received by individuals who have been exposed to at least one impression of the advertising in question. Frequency is calculated *only* among individuals who have been exposed to this advertising. On this basis: Total impressions = Reach * Average frequency.

> Average frequency: **The average number of impressions per reached individual.**

Media plans can differ in reach and frequency but still generate the same number of total impressions.

> Net reach: This term is used to emphasise the fact that the reach of multiple advertising placements is not calculated through the gross addition of all individuals reached by each of those placements. Occasionally, the word "net" is eliminated, and the metric is called simply reach.

Example Returning to our prior example of a 10-insertion media plan in a market with a population of five people, we can calculate the reach and frequency of the plan by analysing the following data. As previously noted, in the following table, "1" represents an opportunity-to-see, and "0" signifies that an individual did not have an opportunity to see a particular insertion.

| | Individual | | | | | | Rating points (impressions/ |
Insertion	A	B	C	D	E	Impressions	population)
1	1	1	0	0	1	3	60
2	1	1	0	0	1	3	60
3	1	1	0	1	0	3	60
4	1	1	0	1	0	3	60
5	1	1	0	1	0	3	60
6	1	0	0	1	0	2	40
7	1	0	0	1	0	2	40
8	1	0	0	0	0	1	20
9	1	0	0	0	0	1	20
10	1	0	0	0	0	1	20
Totals	**10**	**5**	**0**	**5**	**2**	**22**	**440**

Reach is equal to the number of people who saw at least one advertisement. Four of the five people in the population (A, B, D and E) saw at least one advertisement. Consequently, reach (N) = 4.

$$\text{Average frequency} = \frac{\text{Impressions}}{\text{Reach}} = \frac{22}{4} = 5.5$$

When multiple vehicles are involved in an advertising campaign, marketers need information about the overlap among these vehicles as well as sophisticated mathematical procedures in order to estimate reach and frequency. To illustrate this concept, the following two-vehicle example can be useful. Overlap can be represented by a graphic known as a Venn diagram (see Figure 9.1).

Figure 9.1  Venn diagram illustration of net reach

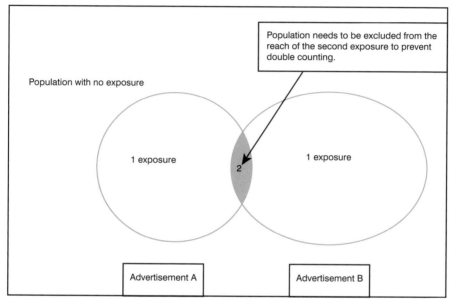

Example As an illustration of overlap effects, let's look at two examples. *Aircraft International* magazine offers 850,000 impressions for one advertisement. A second magazine, *Commercial Flying Monthly*, offers 1 million impressions for one advertisement.

Example 1: Marketers who place advertisements in both magazines should not expect to reach 1.85 million readers. Suppose that 10% of *Aircraft International* readers also read *Commercial Flying Monthly*. On this basis, net reach = (850,000 * .9) + 1,000,000 = 1,765,000 unique individuals. Of these, 85,000 (10% of *Aircraft International* readers) have received two exposures. The remaining 90% of *Aircraft International* readers have received only one exposure. The overlap between two different media types is referred to as external overlap.

Example 2: Marketers often use multiple insertions in the same media vehicle (such as the July and August issues of the same magazine) to achieve frequency. Even if the estimated audience size is the same for both months, not all of the same people will read the magazine each month. For purposes of this example, let's assume that marketers place insertions in two different issues of *Aircraft*

International, and that only 70% of readers of the July issue also read the August issue. On this basis, net reach is not merely 850,000 (the circulation of each issue of *Aircraft International*) because the groups viewing the two insertions are not precisely the same. Likewise, net reach is not 2 * 850,000, or 1.7 million, because the groups viewing the two insertions are also not completely disparate. Rather, net reach = 850,000 + (850,000 * 30%) = 1,105,000.

The reason: 30 per cent of readers of the August issue did not read the July issue and so did not have the opportunity to see the July insertion of the advertisement. These readers – and only these readers – represent incremental viewers of the advertisement in August, and so they must be added to net reach. The remaining 70% of August readers were exposed to the advertisement twice. Their total represents internal overlap or duplication.

Data sources, complications and cautions

Although we've emphasised the importance of reach and frequency, the impressions metric is typically the easiest of these numbers to establish. Impressions can be aggregated on the basis data originating from the media vehicles involved in a campaign. To determine net reach and frequency, marketers must know or estimate the overlap between audiences for different media, or for the same medium at different times. It is beyond the capability of most marketers to make accurate estimates of reach and frequency without access to proprietary databases and algorithms. Full-service advertising agencies and media buying companies typically offer these services.

Assessing overlap is a major challenge. Although overlap can be estimated by performing customer surveys, it is difficult to do this with precision. Estimates based on managers' judgement occasionally must suffice.

Frequency response functions

Frequency response functions help marketers to model the effectiveness of multiple exposures to advertising. We discuss three typical assumptions about how people respond to advertisements: linear response, learning curve response and threshold response.

In a linear response model, people are assumed to react equally to every exposure to an advertisement. The learning curve response model assumes that people are initially slow to respond to an advertisement and then respond more quickly for a time, until ultimately they reach a point at which their response to the message tails off. In a threshold response function, people are assumed to show little response until a critical frequency level is reached. At that point, their response immediately rises to maximum capacity.

Frequency response functions are not technically considered metrics. Understanding how people respond to the frequency of their exposure to advertising, however, is a vital part of media planning. Response models directly determine calculations of effective frequency and effective reach, metrics discussed in the next section.

Purpose: to establish assumptions about the effects of advertising frequency

Let's assume that a company has developed a message for an advertising campaign, and that its managers feel confident that appropriate media for the campaign have been selected. Now they must decide: how many times should the advertisement be placed? The company wants to buy enough advertising space to ensure that its message is effectively conveyed, but it also wants to ensure that it doesn't waste money on unnecessary impressions.

To make this decision, a marketer will have to make an assumption about the value of frequency. This is a major consideration: what is the assumed value of repetition in advertising? Frequency response functions help us to think through the value of frequency.

Frequency response function: **The expected relationship between advertising outcomes (usually in unit sales or financial revenues) and advertising frequency.**

There are a number of possible models for the frequency response functions used in media plans. A selection among these for a particular campaign will depend on the product advertised, the media used and the judgement of the marketer. Three of the most common models are described next.

Linear response: **The assumption behind a linear response function is that each advertising exposure is equally valuable, regardless of how many other exposures to the same advertising have preceded it.**

Learning curve response: **The learning or S curve model rests on the assumption that a consumer's response to advertising follows a progression. The first few times an advertisement is shown, it does not register with its intended audience. As repetition occurs, the message permeates its audience and becomes more effective as people absorb it. Ultimately, however, this effectiveness declines, and diminishing returns set in. At this stage, marketers believe that individuals who want the information already have it and can't be influenced further; others simply are not interested.**

> Threshold response: **The assumption behind this model is that advertising has no effect until its exposure reaches a certain level. At that point, its message becomes fully effective. Beyond that point, further advertising is unnecessary and would be wasted.**

These are three common ways to value advertising frequency. Any function that accurately describes the effect of a campaign can be used. Typically, however, only one function will apply to a given situation.

Construction

Frequency response functions are most useful if they can be used to quantify the effects of incremental frequency. To illustrate the construction of the three functions described in this section, we have tabulated several examples.

Tables 9.2 and 9.3 show the assumed incremental effects of each exposure to a certain advertising campaign. Suppose that the advertisement will achieve maximum effect (100%) at eight exposures. By analysing this effect in the context of various response functions, we can determine when and how quickly it takes hold.

Under a linear response model, each exposure below the saturation point generates one-eighth, or 12.5%, of the overall effect.

The learning curve model is more complex. In this function, the incremental effectiveness of each exposure increases until the fourth exposure and declines thereafter.

Under the threshold response model, there is no effect until the fourth exposure. At that point, however, 100% of the benefit of advertising is immediately realised. Beyond that point, there is no further value to be obtained through incremental advertising. Subsequent exposures are wasted.

The effects of these advertising exposures are tabulated cumulatively in Table 9.3. In this display, maximum attainable effectiveness is achieved when the response to advertising reaches 100%.

Table 9.2 Example of the effectiveness of advertising

Exposure frequency	Linear	Learning or S curve	Threshold value
1	0.125	0.05	0
2	0.125	0.1	0
3	0.125	0.2	0
4	0.125	0.25	1
5	0.125	0.2	0
6	0.125	0.1	0
7	0.125	0.05	0
8	0.125	0.05	0

Table 9.3 Assumptions: cumulative advertising effectiveness

Exposure frequency	Linear	Learning or S curve	Threshold value
1	12.5%	5%	0%
2	25.0%	15%	0%
3	37.5%	35%	0%
4	50.5%	60%	100%
5	62.5%	80%	100%
6	75.0%	90%	100%
7	87.5%	95%	100%
8	100.0%	100%	100%

We can plot cumulative effectiveness against frequency under each model (see Figure 9.2). The linear function is represented by a simple straight line. The threshold assumption rises steeply at four exposures to reach 100%. The cumulative effects of the learning curve model trace an S-shaped curve.

> **Frequency response function; linear:** Under this function, the cumulative effect of advertising (up to the saturation point) can be viewed as a product of the frequency of exposures and effectiveness per exposure.

Frequency response function; linear (I) = Frequency (N) * Effectiveness per exposure (I)

> **Frequency response function; learning curve:** The learning curve function can be charted as a non-linear curve. Its form depends on the circumstances of a particular campaign, including selection of advertising media, target audience, and frequency of exposures.
>
> **Frequency response function; threshold:** The threshold function can be expressed as a Boolean "if" statement, as follows:
>
> Frequency response function; threshold value (I) = if (frequency (N) ⩾ threshold (N), 1, 0)

Stated another way: in a threshold response function, if frequency is greater than or equal to the threshold level of effectiveness, then the advertising campaign is 100% effective. If frequency is less than the threshold, there is no effect.

Figure 9.2 Illustration of cumulative advertising effectiveness

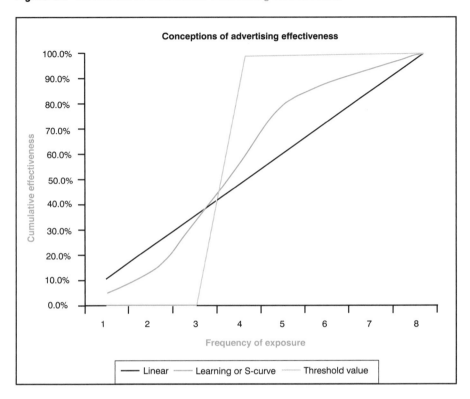

Data sources, complications and cautions

A frequency response function can be viewed as the structure of assumptions made by marketers in planning for the effects of an advertising campaign. In making these assumptions, a marketer's most useful information can be derived from an analysis of the effects of prior ad campaigns. Functions validated with past data, however, are most likely to be accurate if the relevant circumstances (such as media, creative, price and product) have not significantly changed.

In comparing the three models discussed in this section, the linear response function has the benefit of resting on a simple assumption. It can be unrealistic, however, because it is hard to imagine that every advertising exposure in a campaign will have the same effect.

The learning curve has intuitive appeal. It seems to capture the complexity of life better than a linear model. Under this model, however, challenges arise in defining and predicting an advertisement's effectiveness. Three questions emerge: At what point does the curve begin to ramp up? How steep is the function? When does it tail off? With considerable research, marketers can make these estimates. Without it, however, there will always be the concern that the learning curve function provides a spurious level of accuracy.

Any implementation of the threshold response function will hinge on a firm's estimate of where the threshold lies. This will have important ramifications. If the firm makes a conservative estimate, setting the tipping point at a high number of exposures, it may pay for ineffective and unnecessary advertising. If it sets the tipping point too low, however, it may not buy enough advertising media, and its campaign may fail to achieve the desired effect. In implementation, marketers may find that there is little practical difference between using the threshold model and the more complicated learning curve.

Related metrics and concepts

Wear-in: **The frequency required before a given advertisement or campaign achieves a minimum level of effectiveness.**

Wear-out: **The frequency at which a given advertisement or campaign begins to lose effectiveness or even yield a negative effect.**

Effective reach and effective frequency

The concept of effective frequency rests on the assumption that for an advertisement or campaign to achieve an appreciable effect, it must attain a certain number of exposures to an individual within a specified time period.

Effective reach is defined as the number of people or the percentage of the audience that receives an advertising message with a frequency equal to or greater than the effective frequency. That is, effective reach is the population receiving the "minimum" effective exposure to an advertisement or campaign.

Purpose: to assess the extent to which advertising audiences are being reached with sufficient frequency

Many marketers believe their messages require repetition to "sink in". Advertisers, like parents and politicians, therefore repeat themselves. But this repetition must be monitored for effectiveness. Toward that end, marketers apply the concepts of effective frequency and effective reach. The assumptions behind these concepts run as follows: the first few times people are exposed to an ad, it may have little effect. It is only when more exposures are achieved that the message begins to influence its audience.

With this in mind, in planning and executing a campaign, an advertiser must determine the number of times that a message must be repeated in order to be useful. This number is the effective frequency. In concept, this is identical to the threshold frequency in the threshold response function discussed in the previous section.

A campaign's effective frequency will depend on many factors, including market circumstances, media used, type of ad, and campaign. As a rule of thumb, however, an estimate of three exposures per purchase cycle is used surprisingly often.

Effective frequency: **The number of times a certain advertisement must be exposed to a particular individual in a given period to produce a desired response.**

Effective reach: **The number of people or the percentage of the audience that receives an advertising message with a frequency equal to or greater than the effective frequency.**

Construction

Effective reach can be expressed as the number of people who have seen a particular advertisement or the percentage of the population that has been exposed to that advertisement at a frequency greater than or equal to the effective frequency.

$$\text{Effective reach (N, \%)} = \text{Individuals reached with frequency equal to or greater than effective frequency}$$

Example An advertisement on the Internet was believed to need three viewings before its message would sink in. Population data showed the distribution in Table 9.4.

Table 9.4 Number of views of advertisement

Number of views	Population
0	140,000
1	102,000
2	64,000
3	23,000
4 or more	11,000
Total	**340,000**

Because the effective frequency is 3, only those who have seen the advertisement three or more times have been effectively reached. The effective reach is thus 23,000 + 11,000 = 34,000.

In percentage terms, the effective reach of this advertisement is 34,000/340,000 = 10% of the population.

The Internet has provided a significant boost to data gathering in this area. Although even Internet campaigns can't be totally accurate with regard to the number of advertisements served to each customer, data on this question in Web campaigns are far superior to those available in most other media.

Where data can't be tracked electronically, it's difficult to know how many times a customer has been in a position to see an advertisement. Under these circumstances, marketers make estimates on the basis of known audience habits and publicly available resources, such as TV ratings.

Although test markets and split-cable experiments can shed light on the effects of advertising frequency, marketers often lack comprehensive, reliable data on this question. In these cases, they must make – and defend – assumptions about the frequency needed for an effective campaign. Even where good historical data are available, media planning should not rely solely on past results because every campaign is different.

Marketers must also bear in mind that effective frequency attempts to quantify the *average* customer's response to advertising. In practice, some customers will need more information and exposure than others.

Share of voice

Share of voice quantifies the advertising "presence" that a specific product or brand enjoys. It is calculated by dividing the brand's advertising by total market advertising, and it is expressed as a percentage.

$$\text{Share of voice (\%)} = \frac{\text{Brand advertising (£, N)}}{\text{Total market advertising (£, N)}}$$

For purposes of share of voice, there are at least two ways to measure "advertising": in terms of financial spending; or in unit terms, through impressions or gross rating points (GRPs). By any of these measures, share of voice represents an estimate of a company's advertising, as compared to that of its competitors.

Purpose: to evaluate the comparative level of advertising committed to a specific product or brand

Advertisers want to know whether their messages are breaking through the "noise" in the commercial environment. Toward that end, share of voice offers one indication of a brand's advertising strength, relative to the overall market.

There are at least two ways to calculate share of voice. The classic approach is to divide a brand's advertising spend by the total advertising spend in the marketplace.

Alternatively, share of voice can be based on the brand's share of GRPs, impressions, effective reach or similar measures (see earlier sections in this chapter for more details on basic advertising metrics).

Construction

> Share of voice: **The percentage of advertising in a given market that a specific product or brand enjoys.**

$$\text{Share of voice (\%)} = \frac{\text{Brand advertising (£, N)}}{\text{Total market advertising (£, N)}}$$

Data sources, complications and cautions

When calculating share of voice, a marketer's central decision revolves around defining the boundaries of the market. One must ensure that these are meaningful to the intended customer. If a firm's objective is to influence savvy Web users, for example, it would not be appropriate to define advertising presence solely in terms of print media. Share of voice can be computed at a company level, but brand- and product-level calculations are also common.

In executing this calculation, a company should be able to measure its total advertising spend fairly easily. Determining the ad spending for the market as a whole can be fraught with difficulty, however. Complete accuracy will probably not be attainable. It is important, however, that marketers take account of the major players in their market. External sources such as annual reports and press clippings can shed light on competitors' ad spending. Services such as leading national advertisers (LNA) can also provide useful data. These services sell estimates of competitive purchases of media space and time. They generally do not report actual payments for media, however. Instead, costs are estimated on the basis of the time and space purchased and on published "rate cards" that list advertised prices. In using these estimates, marketers must bear in mind that rate cards rarely cite the discounts available in buying media. Without accounting for these discounts, published media spending estimates can be inflated. Marketers are advised to deflate them by the discount rates they themselves receive on advertising.

A final caution: some marketers might assume that the price of advertising is equal to the value of that advertising. This is not necessarily the case. With this in mind, it can be useful to augment a financial calculation of share of voice with one based on impressions.

Impressions, pageviews and hits

As noted in the first section, impressions represent the number of opportunities that have been presented to people to see an advertisement. The best available measures of this figure use technology in an effort to judge whether a given advertisement was actually seen. But this is never perfect. Many recorded impressions are not actually perceived by the intended viewer. Consequently, some marketers refer to this metric as opportunities-to-see.

In applying this concept to Internet advertising and publishing, pageviews represent the number of opportunities-to-see for a given Web page. Every Web page is composed of a variety of individual objects and files, which can contain text, images, audio and video. The total number of these files requested in a given period is the number of hits a website or Web server receives. Because pages composed of many small files generate numerous hits per pageview, one must take care not to be overly impressed by large hit counts.

Purpose: to assess website traffic and activity

To quantify the traffic a website generates, marketers monitor pageviews – the number of times a page on a website is accessed.

In the early days of e-commerce, managers paid attention to the number of hits a website received. Hits measure file requests. Because Web pages are composed of numerous text, graphic and multimedia files, the hits they receive are a function not only of pageviews, but also of the way those pages were composed by their Web designer.

As marketing on the Internet has become more sophisticated, better measures of Web activity and traffic have evolved. Currently, it is more common to use pageviews as the measure of traffic at a Web location. Pageviews aim to measure the number of times a page has been displayed to a user. It thus should be measured as close to the end user as possible. The best technology counts pixels returned to a server, confirming that a page was properly displayed. This pixel count technique[2] yields numbers closer to the end user than would a tabulation of requests to the server, or of pages sent from the server in response to a request. Good measurement can mitigate the problems of inflated counts due to servers not acting on requests, files failing to serve on a user's machine, or users terminating the serving of ads.

Hits: A count of the number of files served to visitors on the Web. Because Web pages often contain multiple files, hits is a function not only of pages visited, but also of the number of files on each page.

▶

> **Pageviews:** **The number of times a specific page has been displayed to users. This should be recorded as late in the page-delivery process as possible in order to get as close as possible to the user's opportunity-to-see. A page can be composed of multiple files.**

For marketing purposes, a further distinction needs to be made as to how many times an advertisement was viewed by unique visitors. For example, two individuals entering a Web page from two different countries might receive the page in their respective languages and might not receive the same ad. One example of an advertisement that changes with different visitors is an embedded link with a banner ad. Recognising this potential for variation, advertisers want to know the number of times that their specific advertisement was displayed to visitors, rather than a site's number of pageviews.

With this in mind, Internet advertisers often perform their analyses in terms of impressions – sometimes called ad impressions or ad views. These represent the number of times an advertisement is served to visitors, giving them opportunities to see it. (Many of the concepts in this section are in line with the terms covered in the advertising section – the first section of this chapter.)

For a single advertisement served to all visitors on a site, impressions are equal to the number of pageviews. If a page carries multiple advertisements, the total number of all ad impressions will exceed the number of pageviews.

Construction

Hits

The number of hits on a website is a function of the number of pageviews multiplied by the number of files comprising each page. Hit counts are likely to be more relevant to technicians responsible for planning server capacity than to marketers interested in measuring visitor activity.

$$\text{Hits (N)} = \text{Pageviews (N)} * \text{Files on the page (N)}$$

Pageviews

The number of pageviews can be easily calculated by dividing the number of hits by the number of files on the page.

$$\text{Pageviews (N)} = \frac{\text{Hits (N)}}{\text{Files on the page (N)}}$$

Example There are 250,000 hits on a website that serves five files each time a page is accessed. Pageviews = 250,000/5 = 50,000.

If the website served three files per page and generated 300,000 pageviews, then hits would total 3 * 300,000 = 900,000.

Data sources, complications and cautions

Pageviews, page impressions and ad impressions are measures of the responses of a Web server to page and ad requests from users' browsers, filtered to remove robotic activity and error codes prior to reporting. These measures are recorded at a point as close as possible to the user's opportunity to see the page or ad.[3]

A count of ad impressions can be derived from pageviews if the percentage of pageviews that contain the ad in question is known. For example, if 10% of pageviews receive the advertisement for a luxury car, then the impressions for that car ad will equal 10% of pageviews. Websites that serve the same advertisement to all Web users are much easier to monitor because only one count is required.

These metrics quantify opportunities-to-see without taking into account the number of ads actually seen or the quality of what is shown. In particular, these metrics do not account for the following:

- Whether the message appeared to a specific, relevant, defined audience.
- Whether the people to whom the pages appeared actually looked at them.
- Whether those who looked at the pages had any recall of their content, or of the advertising messages they contained, after the event.

Despite the use of the term "impression", these measures do not tell a business manager about the effect that an advertisement has on potential customers. Marketers can't be sure of the effect that pageviews have on visitors. Often, pageview results will consist of data that include duplicate showings to the same visitor. For this reason, the term "gross impressions" might be used to suggest a key assumption – that opportunities-to-see can be delivered to the same viewer on multiple occasions.

Clickthrough rates

Clickthrough rate is the percentage of impressions that lead a user to click on an ad. It describes the fraction of impressions that motivate users to click on a link, causing a redirect to another Web location.

$$\text{Clickthrough rate (\%)} = \frac{\text{Clickthroughs (N)}}{\text{Impressions (N)}}$$

Most Internet-based businesses use clickthrough metrics. Although these metrics are useful, they should not dominate all marketing analysis. Unless a user clicks on a "Buy Now" button, clickthroughs measure only one step along the path toward a final sale.

Purpose: to capture customers' initial response to websites

Most commercial websites are designed to elicit some sort of action, whether it be to buy a book, read a news article, watch a music video or search for a flight. People generally don't visit a website with the intention of viewing advertisements, just as people rarely watch TV with the purpose of consuming commercials. As marketers, we want to know the reaction of the Web visitor. Under current technology, it is nearly impossible to fully quantify the emotional reaction to the site and the effect of that site on the firm's brand. One piece of information that is easy to acquire, however, is the clickthrough rate. The clickthrough rate measures the proportion of visitors who initiated action with respect to an advertisement that redirected them to another page where they might purchase an item or learn more about a product or service. Here we have used "clicked their mouse" on the advertisement (or link) because this is the generally used term, although other interactions are possible.

Construction

> Clickthrough rate: **The clickthrough rate is the number of times a click is made on the advertisement divided by the total impressions (the times an advertisement was served).**

$$\text{Clickthrough rate (\%)} = \frac{\text{Clickthroughs (N)}}{\text{Impressions (N)}}$$

> Clickthroughs: **If you have the clickthrough rate and the number of impressions, you can calculate the absolute number of clickthroughs by multiplying the clickthrough rate by the impressions.**

$$\text{Clickthroughs (N)} = \text{Clickthrough rate (\%)} * \text{Impressions (N)}$$

Example There are 1,000 clicks (the more commonly used shorthand for clickthroughs) on a website that serves up 100,000 impressions. The clickthrough rate is 1%.

$$\text{Clickthrough rate} = \frac{1,000}{100,000} = 1\%$$

If the same website had a clickthrough rate of 0.5%, then there would have been 500 clickthroughs:

$$\text{Clickthrough rate} = 100,000 * 0.5\% = 500$$

If a different website had a 1% clickthrough rate and served up 200,000 impressions, there would have been 2,000 clicks:

$$\text{Number of clicks} = 1\% * 200{,}000 = 2{,}000$$

Data sources, complications and cautions

The number of impressions is a necessary input for the calculation. On simpler websites, this is likely to be the same as pageviews; every time the page is accessed, it shows the same details. On more sophisticated sites, different advertisements can be shown to different viewers. In these cases, impressions are likely to be some fraction of total pageviews. The server can easily record the number of times the link was clicked (see Figure 9.3).

First, remember that clickthrough rate is expressed as a percentage. Although high clickthrough rates might in themselves be desirable and help validate your ad's appeal, companies will also be interested in the total number of people who clicked through. Imagine a website with a clickthrough rate of 80%. It may seem like a highly successful website until management uncovers that only a total number of 20 people visited the site with 16 clicking through, compared with an objective of 500 visitors.

Also remember that a click is a very weak signal of interest. Individuals who click on an ad might move on to something else before the new page is loaded. This could be because the person clicked on the advertisement by accident or because the page took too long to load. This is a problem that is of greater significance with the increase in richer media advertisements. Marketers should understand their customers. Using large video files is likely to increase the number of people abandoning the process before the ad is served, especially if the customers have slower connections.

Figure 9.3 Clickthrough process

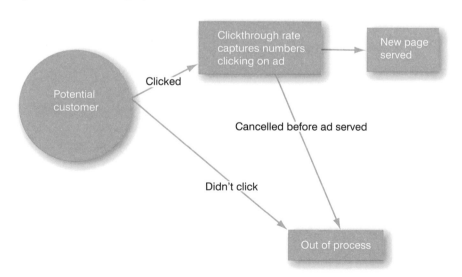

As with impressions, try to ensure that you understand the measures. If the measure is of clicks (the requests received from client machines to the server to send a file), then there may be a number of breakage points between the click-through rate and the impressions of the ad generated from a returned pixel count. Large discrepancies should be understood – is it technical (the size/design of the advertisement) or weak interest from clickers?

Clicks are the number of times the advertisement was interacted with, not the number of customers who clicked. An individual visitor can click on an ad several times – either in a single session or across multiple sessions. Only the most sophisticated websites control the number of times they show a specific advertisement to the same customer. This means that most websites can only count the number of times the ad was clicked, not the number of visitors who clicked on an ad. Finally, the clickthrough rate must be interpreted relative to an appropriate baseline. Clickthrough rates for banner ads are very low and continue to fall. In contrast, click-through rates for buttons that simply take visitors to the next page on a site should be much higher. An analysis of how clickthrough rates change as visitors navigate through various pages can help identify "dead end" pages that visitors rarely move beyond.

Cost per impression, cost per click and cost per order

These three metrics measure the average cost of impressions, clicks and customers. All three are calculated in the same way – as the ratio of cost to the number of resulting impressions, clicks or customers.

$$\text{Cost per impression (£)} = \frac{\text{Advertising cost (£)}}{\text{Number of impressions (N)}}$$

$$\text{Cost per click (£)} = \frac{\text{Advertising cost (£)}}{\text{Number of clicks (N)}}$$

$$\text{Cost per order (£)} = \frac{\text{Advertising cost (£)}}{\text{Orders (N)}}$$

These metrics are the starting point for assessing the effectiveness of a company's Internet advertising and can be used for comparison across advertising media and vehicles and as an indicator of the profitability of a firm's Internet marketing.

Purpose: to assess the cost-effectiveness of Internet marketing

In this section, we present three common ways of measuring the cost-effectiveness of Internet advertising. Each has benefits depending upon the perspective and end goal of the advertising activity.

> Cost per impression: **The cost to offer potential customers one opportunity to see an advertisement.**
>
> Cost per click: **The amount spent to get an advertisement clicked.**

Cost per click has a big advantage over cost per impression in that it tells us something about how effective the advertising was. Clicks are a way to measure attention and interest. Inexpensive ads that few people click on will have a low cost per impression and a high cost per click. If the main purpose of an ad is to generate a click, then cost per click is the preferred metric.

> Cost per order: **The cost to acquire an order.**

If the main purpose of the ad is to generate sales, then cost per order is the preferred metric.

Once a certain number of Web impressions are achieved, the quality and placement of the advertisement will affect clickthrough rates and the resulting cost per click (see Figure 9.4).

Figure 9.4 The order acquisition process

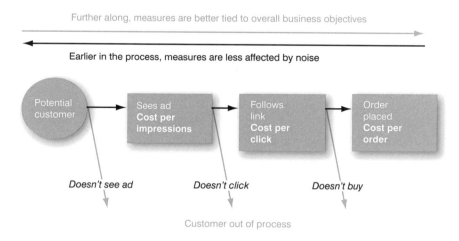

Construction

The formulas are essentially the same for the alternatives; just divide the cost by the appropriate number, for example, impressions, clicks or orders.

Cost per impression
This is derived from advertising cost and the number of impressions.

$$\text{Cost per impression (£)} = \frac{\text{Advertising cost (£)}}{\text{Number of impressions (N)}}$$

Remember that cost per impression is often expressed as cost per thousand impressions (CPM) in order to make the numbers easier to manage (for more on CPM, refer to pages 000–000).

Cost per click
This is calculated by dividing the advertising cost by the number of clicks generated by the advertisement.

$$\text{Cost per click (£)} = \frac{\text{Advertising cost (£)}}{\text{Clicks (N)}}$$

Cost per order
This is the cost to generate an order. The precise form of this cost depends on the industry and is complicated by product returns and multiple sales channels. The basic formula is:

$$\text{Cost per order (£)} = \frac{\text{Advertising cost (£)}}{\text{Orders placed (N)}}$$

Example An Internet retailer spent €24,000 on online advertising and generated 1.2 million impressions, which led to 20,000 clicks, with 1 in 10 clicks resulting in a purchase.

$$\text{Cost per impression} = \frac{€24,000}{1,200,000} = €0.02$$

$$\text{Cost per click} = \frac{€24,000}{20,000} = €1.20$$

If 1 in 10 of the clicks resulted in a purchase:

$$\text{Cost per order} = \frac{€24,000}{2,000} = €12.00$$

This last calculation is also called "cost per purchase".

Data sources, complications and cautions

The Internet has provided greater availability of advertising data. Consequently, Internet advertising metrics are likely to rely on data that are more readily obtainable than data from conventional channels. The Internet can provide more information about how customers move through the system and how individual customers behave at the purchase stage of the process.

For advertisers using a mix of online and "offline" media, it will be difficult to categorise the cause-and-effect relationships between advertising and sales from both online and offline sources. Banner ads might receive too much credit for an order if the customer has also been influenced by the firm's billboard advertisement. Conversely, banner ads might receive too little credit for offline sales.

The calculations and data we have discussed in this section are often used in contracts compensating advertisers. Companies may prefer to compensate media and ad agencies on the basis of new customers acquired instead of orders.

Search engines

Search engine payments help determine the placement of links on search engines. The most important search engine metric is the cost per click, and it is generally the basis for establishing the search engine placement fee. Search engines can provide plenty of data to analyse the effectiveness of a campaign. In order to reap the benefits of a great website, the firm needs to get people to visit it. In the previous section, we discussed how firms *measure* traffic. Search engines help firms *create* that traffic.

Although a strong brand helps drive traffic to a firm's site, including the firm's Web address in all of its offline advertising might not increase traffic count. In order to generate additional traffic, firms often turn to search engines. It was estimated that over $2.5 billion was spent on paid search marketing, which made up approximately 36% of total online spending of $7.3 billion in 2003.[4] Other online spending was composed of the following categories: 50% as impressions, 12% as banner ads and 2% as email advertising.

Paid search marketing is essentially paying for the placement of ads on search engines and content sites across the Internet. The ads are typically small portions of text (much like newspaper ads) made to look like the results of an unpaid or organic search. Payment is usually made only when someone clicks on the ad. It is sometimes possible to pay more per click in return for better placement on the search results page. One important subset of paid search is keyword search in which advertisers can bid to be displayed whenever someone searches for the keyword(s). In this case, companies bid on the basis of cost per click. Bidding a higher amount per click gets you placed higher. However, there is an added complexity, which is that if the ad fails to generate several clicks, its placement will be lowered in comparison to competing ads.

The measures for testing search engine effectiveness are largely the same as those used in assessing other Internet advertising.

Cost per click

The most important concept in search engine marketing is cost per click. Cost per click is widely quoted and used by search engine companies in charging for their services. Marketers use cost per click to build their budgets for search engine payments.

Search engines ask for a "maximum cost per click", which is a ceiling whereby the marketer imposes the maximum amount they are willing to pay for an individual click. A search engine will typically auction the placement of links and only charge for a click at a rate just above the next highest bid. This means the maximum cost per click that a company would be willing to pay can be considerably higher than the average cost per click they end up paying.

Marketers often talk about the concept of daily spend on search engines – just as it sounds, this is the total spent on paid search engine advertising during one day. In order to control spending, search engines allow marketers to specify maximum daily spends. When the maximum is reached, the advertisement receives no preferential treatment.

The formula is the multiple of average cost per click and the number of clicks:

Daily spend (£) = Average cost per click (£) * Number of clicks (N)

Example Andrei, the Internet marketing manager of an online music retailer in the US, decides to set a maximum price of $0.10 a click. At the end of the week he finds that the search engine provider has charged him a total of $350.00 for 1,000 clicks per day.

His average cost per click is thus the cost of the advertising divided by the number of clicks generated:

$$\text{Cost per click} = \frac{\text{Cost per week}}{\text{Clicks per week}}$$

$$= \frac{\$350}{7,000}$$

$$= \$0.05 \text{ a click}$$

Daily spend is also calculated as average cost per click times the number of clicks:

$$\text{Daily spend} = \$0.05 * 1,000$$

$$= \$50.00$$

Advice for search engine marketers

Search engines typically use auctions to establish a price for the search terms they sell. Search engines have the great advantage of having a relatively efficient market; all users have access to the information and can be in the same virtual location. They tend to adopt a variant on the second price auction. Buyers only pay the amount needed for their requested placement.

> **Cost per customer acquired: Similar to cost per order when the order came from a new customer. Refer to Chapter 5, "Customer Profitability", for a discussion on defining customer and acquisition costs.**

Visits, visitors and abandonment

Visits measures the number of sessions on the website. Visitors measures the number of people making those visits. When an individual goes to a website on Tuesday and then again on Wednesday, this should be recorded as two visits from one visitor. Visitors are sometimes referred to as "unique visitors". Visitors and unique visitors are the same metric.

Abandonment usually refers to shopping carts. The total number of shopping carts used in a specified period is the sum of the number abandoned and the number that resulted in complete purchases. The abandonment rate is the ratio of the number of abandoned shopping carts to the total.

Purpose: to understand website user behaviour

Websites can easily track the number of pages requested. As we saw earlier in "Impressions, pageviews and hits" on pages 289–291, the pageviews metric is useful but far from complete. In addition to counting the number of pageviews a website delivers, firms will also want to count the number of times someone visits the website and the number of people requesting those pages.

Visits: **The number of times individuals request a page on the firm's server for the first time. Also known as sessions.**

The first request counts as a visit. Subsequent requests from the same individual do not count as visits unless they occur after a specified time-out period (usually set at 30 minutes).

Visitors: **The number of individuals requesting pages from the firm's server during a given period. Also known as unique visitors.**

To get a better understanding of traffic on a website, companies attempt to track the number of visits. A visit can consist of a single pageview or multiple pageviews, and one individual can make multiple visits to a website. The exact specification of what constitutes a visit requires an accepted standard for a time-out period, which is the number of minutes of inactivity from the time of entering the page to the time of requesting a new page.

In addition to visits, firms also attempt to track the number of individual visitors to their website. Because a visitor can make multiple visits in a specified period, the number of visits will be greater than the number of visitors. A visitor is sometimes referred to as a unique visitor or unique user to clearly convey the idea that each visitor is only counted once.

The measurement of users or visitors requires a standard time period and can be distorted by automatic activity (such as "bots") that classify Web content. Estimation of visitors, visits and other traffic statistics are usually filtered to remove this activity by eliminating known IP addresses for "bots", by requiring registration or cookies, or by using panel data.

Pageviews and visits are related. By definition, a visit is a series of pageviews grouped together in a single session, so the number of pageviews will exceed the number of visits.

Consider the metrics as a series of concentric ovals as shown in Figure 9.5. In this view, the number of visitors must be less than or equal to the number of visits, which must be less than or equal to the number of pageviews, which must be equal to or less than the number of hits. (Refer to pages 289–291 for details of the relationship between hits and pageviews.)

Figure 9.5 Relationship of hits to pageviews to visits to visitors

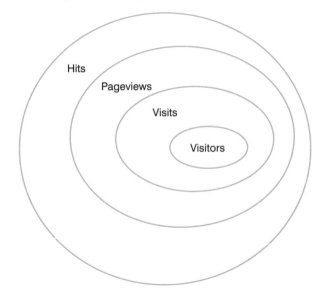

Figure 9.6 Example of online newspaper visitor

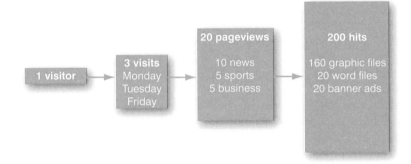

Another way to consider the relationship between visitors, visits, pageviews and hits is to consider the following example of one visitor entering a website of an online newspaper (see Figure 9.6). Suppose that the visitor enters the site on Monday, Tuesday and Friday. In her visit she looks at a total of 20 pageviews. Those pages are made up of a number of different graphic files, word files and banner ads.

The ratio of pageviews to visitors is sometimes referred to as the average pages per visit. Marketers track this average to monitor how the average visit length is changing over time.

It is possible to dig even deeper and track the paths visitors take within a visit. This path is called the clickstream.

> Clickstream: **The path of a user through the Internet.**

The clickstream refers to the sequence of clicked links while visiting multiple sites. Tracking at this level can help the firm identify the most and least appealing pages (see Figure 9.7).

Figure 9.7 A clickstream documented

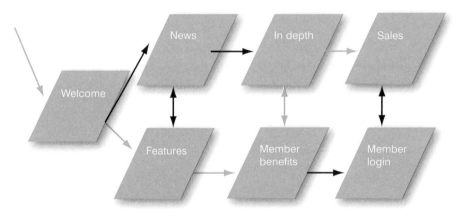

→ links   → clickstream, the actual path taken by a customer

The analysis of clickstream data often yields significant customer insights. What path is a customer most likely to take prior to purchase? Is there a way to make the most popular paths even easier to navigate? Should the unpopular paths be changed or even eliminated? Do purchases come at the end of lengthy or short sessions? At what pages do sessions end?

A portion of the clickstream that deserves considerable attention is the subset of clicks associated with the use of shopping carts. A shopping cart is a piece of software on the server that allows visitors to select items for eventual purchase. Although shoppers in bricks-and-mortar stores rarely abandon their carts, abandonment of virtual shopping carts is quite common. Savvy marketers count how many of the shopping carts used in a specified period result in a completed sale versus how many are abandoned. The ratio of the number of abandoned shopping carts to the total is the abandonment rate.

> Abandonment rate: **The percentage of shopping carts that are abandoned.**

To decide whether a visitor is a returning visitor or a new user, companies often employ cookies. A cookie is a file downloaded onto the computer of a person surfing the Web that contains identifying information. When the person returns, the Web server reads the cookie and recognises the visitor as someone who has been to the website previously. More advanced sites use cookies to offer customised content, and shopping carts make use of cookies to distinguish one shopping cart from another. For example, Amazon, eBay and easyJet all make extensive use of cookies to personalise the Web views to each customer.

> Cookie: **A small file that a website puts on the hard drive of visitors for the purpose of future identification.**

Construction

Visitors
Cookies can help servers track unique visitors, but these data are never 100% accurate (see the next section).

> Abandoned purchases: **The number of purchases that were not completed.**

Example An online comics retailer found that of the 25,000 customers who loaded items into their electronic baskets, only 20,000 actually purchased:

$$\text{Purchases not completed} = \text{Purchases initiated less purchases completed}$$

$$= 25{,}000 - 20{,}000 = 5{,}000$$

$$\text{Abandonment rate} = \frac{\text{Not completed}}{\text{Customer initiation}} = \frac{5{,}000}{25{,}000}$$

$$= 20\% \text{ abandonment rate}$$

Data sources, complications and cautions

Visits can be estimated from log file data. Visitors are much more difficult to measure. If visitors register and/or accept cookies, then at least the computer that was used for the visit can be identified.

Meaningful results are difficult to get for smaller or more narrowly focused websites.

It is possible to bring in professionals in competitive research and user behaviour. Nielsen, among other services, runs a panel in Europe and a number of major economies.[5]

References and suggested further reading

Farris, P. W., D. Reibstein and E. Shames. (1998). "Advertising Budgeting: A Report from the Field", New York: American Association of Advertising Agencies.

Forrester, J.W. (1959). "Advertising: A Problem in Industrial Dynamics", *Harvard Business Review*, 37(2), 100–110.

Interactive Advertising Bureau. (2004). Interactive Audience Measurement and Advertising Campaign Reporting and Audit Guidelines. United States Version 6.0b.

Lodish, L.M. (1997). "Point of View: J.P. Jones and M.H. Blair on Measuring Ad Effects – Another POV," *Journal of Advertising Research*, 37(5), 75–79.

NetGenesis Corp. (2000). *E-Metrics: Business Metrics for the New Economy*. NetGenesis and Target Marketing: Santa Barbara.

Tellis, G.J. and D.L. Weiss. (1995). "Does TV Advertising Really Affect Sales? The Role of Measures, Models, and Data Aggregation", *Journal of Advertising Research*, 24(3), 1–12.

Marketing and finance

10

Metrics covered in this chapter:

- Net profit and return on sales (ROS)

- Return on investment (ROI)

- Economic profit (EVA)

- Project metrics: payback, NPV, IRR

- Return on marketing investment

Introduction

As marketers progress in their careers, it becomes increasingly necessary to co-ordinate their plans with other functional areas. Sales forecasts, budgeting and estimating returns from proposed marketing initiatives are often the focus of discussions between marketing and finance. For marketers with little exposure to basic finance metrics, a good starting point is to gain a deeper understanding of "rate of return". "Return" is generally associated with profit, or at least positive cash flow. "Return" also implies that something has left – cash outflow. Almost all business activity requires some cash outflow. Even sales cost money that is only returned when bills are paid. In this chapter we provide a brief overview of some of the more commonly employed measures of profitability and profits. Understanding how the metrics are constructed and used by finance to rank various projects will make it easier to develop marketing plans that meet the appropriate criteria.

The first section covers net profits and return on sales (ROS). Next, we look at return on investment (ROI), the ratio of net profit to amount of investment. Another metric that accounts for the capital investment required to earn profits is economic profits (also known as economic value added – EVA), or residual income. Because EVA and ROI provide snapshots of the per-period profitability of firms, they are not appropriate for valuing projects spanning multiple periods. For multi-period projects, three of the most common metrics are payback, net present value (NPV) and internal rate of return (IRR).

The last section discuses the frequently mentioned but rarely defined measure, return on marketing investment (ROMI). Although this is a well-intentioned effort to measure marketing productivity, consensus definitions and measurement procedures for "marketing ROI" or ROMI have yet to emerge.

Metric	Construction	Considerations	Purpose
Net profit	Sales revenue less total costs.	Revenue and costs can be defined in a number of ways leading to confusion in profit calculations.	The basic profit equation.
Return on sales (ROS)	Net profit as a percentage of sales revenue.	Acceptable level of return varies between industries and business models. Many models can be described as high volume/low return or vice versa.	Gives the percentage of revenue that is being captured in profits.
Return on investment (ROI)	Net profits over the investment needed to generate the profits.	Often meaningless in the short term. Variations such as return on assets and return on investment capital analyse profits in respect of different inputs.	A metric that describes how well assets are being used.
Economic profit	Net operating profit after tax (NOPAT) less the cost of capital.	Requires a cost of capital to be provided/calculated.	Shows profit made in financial terms. Gives a clearer distinction between the sizes of returns than does a percentage calculation.

Metric	Construction	Considerations	Purpose
Payback	The length of time taken to return the initial investment.	Will favour projects with quick returns more than long-term success.	Simple return calculation.
Net present value (NPV)	The value of a stream of future cash flows after accounting for the time value of money.	The discount rate used is the vital consideration and should account for the risk of the investment too.	To summarise the value of cash flows over multiple periods.
Internal rate of return (IRR)	The discount rate at which the NPV of an investment is zero.	IRR does not describe the magnitude of return; £1 on £10 is the same as £1 million on £10 million.	An IRR will typically be compared to a firm's hurdle rate. If IRR is higher than hurdle rate, invest; if lower, pass.
Return on marketing investment (ROMI); revenue	Incremental revenue attributable to marketing over the marketing spending.	Marketers need to establish an accurate baseline to be able to meaningfully state what revenue is attributable to marketing.	Compares the sales generated in revenue terms with the marketing spending that helped generate the sales. The percentage term helps comparison across plans of varying magnitude.

Net profit and return on sales

Net profit measures the profitability of ventures after accounting for all costs. Return on sales (ROS) is net profit as a percentage of sales revenue.

$$\text{Net profit (£)} = \text{Sales revenue (£)} - \text{Total costs (£)}$$

$$\text{Return on sales (ROS) (\%)} = \frac{\text{Net profit (£)}}{\text{Sales revenue (£)}}$$

ROS is an indicator of profitability and is often used to compare the profitability of companies and industries of differing sizes. Significantly, ROS does not account for the capital (investment) used to generate the profit.

Purpose: to measure levels and rates of profitability

How does a company decide whether it is successful or not? Probably the most common way is to look at the net profits of the business. Given that companies are collections of projects and markets, individual areas can be judged on how successful they are at adding to the corporate net profit. Not all projects are of equal size, however, and one way to adjust for size is to divide the profit by sales revenue. The resulting ratio is return on sales (ROS), the percentage of sales revenue that gets "returned" to the company as net profits after all the related costs of the activity are deducted.

Construction

Net profit measures the fundamental profitability of the business. It is the revenues of the activity less the costs of the activity. The main complication is in more complex businesses when overhead needs to be allocated across divisions of the company (see Figure 10.1). Almost by definition, overheads are costs that cannot be directly tied to any specific product or division. The classic example would be the cost of headquarters staff.

Figure 10.1 Profits = revenues less costs

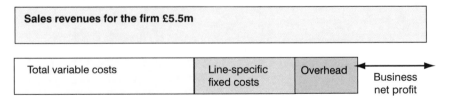

Simple view of business – revenues and costs

Data sources, complications and cautions

Although it is theoretically possible to calculate profits for any sub-unit, such as a product or region, often the calculations are rendered suspect by the need to allocate overhead costs. Because overhead costs often don't come in neat packages, their allocation among the divisions or product lines of the company can often be more art than science.

For return on sales, it is worth bearing in mind that a "healthy" figure depends on the industry and capital intensity (amount of assets per pound spent on sales). Return on sales is similar to margin (%), except that ROS accounts for overheads and other fixed costs that are often ignored when calculating margin (%) or contribution margin (%). (Refer to "Margins" on pages 47–53.)

Related metrics and concepts

Net operating profit after tax (NOPAT) deducts relevant income taxes but excludes some items that are deemed to be unrelated to the main ("operating") business.

Earning before interest taxes, depreciation and amortisation (EBITDA) is a measure of the "operating" profit of the business that excludes deductions related to decisions such as how to finance the business (debt or equity) and over what period to depreciate fixed assets. EBITDA is typically closer to actual cash flow than is NOPAT.

Return on investment

> Return on assets (ROA), return on net assets (RONA), return on capital (ROC) and return on invested capital (ROIC) are similar measures with variations on how "investment" is defined.
>
> Marketing not only influences net profits but also can affect investment levels too. New plants and equipment, inventories, and accounts receivable are three of the main categories of investments that can be affected by marketing decisions.

Purpose: to measure per-period rates of return on money invested in an economic entity

ROI and related metrics (ROA, ROC, RONA and ROIC) provide a snapshot of profitability adjusted for the size of the investment assets tied up in the enterprise. Marketing decisions have obvious potential connection to the numerator of ROI (profits), but these same decisions often influence assets usage and capital requirements (for example, receivables and inventories). The marketer should understand the position of their company and the returns expected. ROI is often compared to expected (or required) rates of return on money invested.

Construction

For a single period review just divide the return (net profit) by the resources that were committed (investment):

$$\text{Return on investment (\%)} = \frac{\text{Net profit (£)}}{\text{Investment (£)}}$$

Data sources, complications and cautions

Averaging the profits and investments over periods such as one year can disguise wide swings in profits and assets, especially inventories and receivables. This is especially true for seasonal businesses (such as some construction materials and toys). In such businesses it is important to understand these seasonal variations to relate quarterly and annual figures to each other.

Related metrics and concepts

Return on assets (ROA), return on net assets (RONA), return on capital employed (ROCE) and return on invested capital (ROIC) are commonly used variants of ROI. They are also calculated using net profit as the numerator, but they have different denominators. The relatively subtle distinctions between these metrics are beyond the scope of this book. Some differences are found in whether payables are subtracted from working capital and how borrowed funds and stockholder equity are treated.

Economic profit (EVA)

> Economic profit has many names, some of them trademarked as "brands". Economic value added (EVA) is Stern-Stewart's trademark. They deserve credit for popularising this measure of net operating profit after tax adjusted for the cost of capital.
>
> Economic profit (£) = Net operating profit after tax (NOPAT) (£) − Cost of capital (£)
>
> Cost of capital (£) = Capital employed (£) * WACC (%)
>
> Unlike percentage measures of return (for example, ROS or ROI), economic profit is a monetary metric. As such, it reflects not only the "rate" of profitability, but also the size of the business (sales and assets).

Purpose: to measure economic profits while accounting for required returns on capital invested

Economic profit, sometimes called residual income, or EVA, is different from "accounting" profit – in that economic profit also considers the cost of invested capital – the opportunity cost (see Figure 10.2). Like the discount rate for NPV calculations, this charge should also account for the risk associated with the investment. A popular (and proprietary) way of looking at economic profit is economic value added.[1]

Increasingly, marketers are being made aware of how some of their decisions influence the amount of capital invested or assets employed. First, sales growth almost always requires additional investment in fixed assets, receivables or inventories. Economic profit and EVA help determine whether these investments are justified by the profit earned. Second, the marketing improvements in supply chain

Figure 10.2  EVA is after-tax profit minus a charge for capital usage

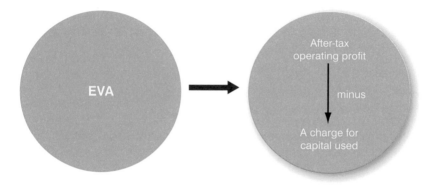

management and channel coordination often show up in reduced investments in inventories and receivables. In some cases, even if sales and profit fall, the investment reduction can be worthwhile. Economic profit is a metric that will help assess whether these trade-offs are being made correctly.

Construction

Economic profit/economic value added can be calculated in three stages. First, determine NOPAT (net operating profit after tax). Second, calculate the cost of capital by multiplying capital employed by the weighted average cost of capital.[2] The third stage is to subtract the cost of capital from NOPAT.

$$\text{Economic profit (£)} = \text{Net operating profit after tax (NOPAT) (£)} - \text{Cost of capital (£)}$$

$$\text{Cost of capital (£)} = \text{Capital employed (£)} * \text{WACC (\%)}$$

> Economic profit: **If your profits are less than the cost of capital, you have lost value for the firm. Where economic profit is positive, value has been generated.**

Example A company has profits – NOPAT – of £145,000.

They have a straightforward capital structure, half of which is supplied by shareholders. This equity expects a 12% return on the risk the shareholders are taking by investing in this company. The other half of the capital comes from a bank at a charge of 6%:

Weighted average cost of capital (WACC) therefore

$$= \text{Equity (12\% * 50\%)} + \text{Debt (6\% * 50\%)} = 9\%$$

The company employs total capital of £1 million. Multiplying the capital employed by the weighted average cost for the capital employed will give us an estimate of the profit (return) required to cover the opportunity cost of capital used in the business:

$$\text{Cost of capital} = \text{Capital employed} * \text{WACC}$$
$$= £1,000,000 * 9\%$$
$$= £90,000$$

Economic profit is the surplus of profits over the expected return to capital.

$$\text{Economic profit} = \text{NOPAT} - \text{Cost of capital}$$
$$= \text{£145,000} - \text{£90,000}$$
$$= \text{£55,000}$$

Data sources, complications and cautions

Economic profit can give a different ranking for companies than does return on investment. This is especially true for companies such as Wal-Mart and Microsoft that have experienced (achieved) high rates of growth in sales. Judging the results of the giant US retailer Wal-Mart by many conventional metrics will disguise its success. Although the rates of return are generally good, they hardly imply the rise to dominance that the company achieved. Economic profit reflects both Wal-Mart's rapid sales growth and their adequate return on the capital invested. This metric shows the magnitude of profits after the cost of capital has been subtracted. This combines the idea of a return on investment with a sense of volume of profits. Simply put, Wal-Mart achieved the trick of continuing to gain decent returns on a dramatically increasing pool of capital.

Evaluating multi-period investments

Multi-period investments are commonly evaluated with three metrics.

Payback (N) = The number of periods required to "pay back" or "return" the initial investment.

Net present value (NPV) (£) = The discounted value of future cash flows minus the initial investment.

Internal rate of return (IRR) (%) = The discount rate that results in an NPV of zero.

These three metrics are designed to deal with different aspects of the risk and returns of multi-period projects.

Purpose: to evaluate investments with financial consequences spanning multiple periods

Investment is a word business people like. It has all sorts of positive connotations of future success and wise stewardship. However, because not all investments can be pursued, those available must be ranked against each other. Also, some investments are not attractive even if we have enough cash to fund them. In a single period, the return on any investment is merely the net profits produced in the time considered divided by the capital invested. Evaluation of investments that produce returns over multiple periods requires a more complicated analysis – one that considers both the magnitude and timing of the returns.

> **Payback (N):** **The time (usually years) required to generate the (undiscounted) cash flow to recover the initial investment.**
>
> **Net present value (NPV) (£):** **The present (discounted) value of future cash inflows minus the present value of the investment and any associated future cash outflows.**
>
> **Internal rate of return (IRR) (%):** **The discount rate that results in a net present value of zero for a series of future cash flows after accounting for the initial investment.**

Construction

> **Payback:** **The years required for an investment to return the initial investment.**

Projects with a shorter payback period by this analysis are regarded more favourably because they allow the resources to be reused quickly. Also, generally speaking, the shorter the payback period, the less uncertainty is involved in receiving the returns. Of course the main flaw with payback period analysis is that it ignores all cash flows after the payback period. As a consequence, projects that are attractive but that do not produce immediate returns will be penalised with this metric.

Example Harry is considering buying a small chain of hairdressing salons in Vermont in the US. He estimates that the salons will produce a net income of $15,000 a year for at least five years. Harry's payback on this investment is $50,000/$15,000, or 3.33 years.

Net present value

Net present value (NPV) is the discounted value of the cash flows associated with the project.

The present value of £1 received in a given number of periods in the future is:

$$\text{Discounted value (£)} = \frac{\text{Cash flow (£)}}{[(1 + \text{Discount rate (\%)}) \char`\^ \text{Period (N)}]}$$

This is easiest to see when set out in spreadsheet form.

A 10% discount rate applied to £1 received now and in each of the next three years reduces in value over time as shown in Table 10.1.

Table 10.1 Discounting nominal values

	Year 0	Year 1	Year 2	Year 3
Discount formula	1	$1/(1+10\%)\char`\^1$	$1/(1+10\%)\char`\^2$	$1/(1+10\%)\char`\^3$
Discount factor	1	90.9%	82.6%	75.1%
Undiscounted cash flows	£1.00	£1.00	£1.00	£1.00
Present value	£1.00	£0.91	£0.83	£0.75

Spreadsheets make it easy to calculate the appropriate discount factors.

Example Harry wants to know the monetary value of his business opportunity. Although he is confident about the success of the venture, all future cash flows have a level of uncertainty. After receiving a friend's advice, he decides a 10% discount rate on future cash flows is about right.

He enters all the cash flow details into a spreadsheet (see Table 10.2).[3] Harry works out the discount factor using the formula and his discount rate of 10%:

$$\text{Discounted value} = \frac{\text{Face value}}{[1/[(1 + \text{Discount rate}) \char`\^ \text{Year}]}$$

$$\text{For year 1 cashflows} = \frac{\$15,000}{[(1 + 10\%) \char`\^ 1)]} = \frac{\$15,000}{(110\%) \char`\^ 1)}$$

$$= \frac{\$15,000}{90.9\%} = 13,636$$

Table 10.2 Discounted cashflow (10% discount rate)

	Year 0	Year 1	Year 2	Year 3	Year 4	Year 5	Total
Investment	($50,000)						($50,000)
Income		$15,000	$15,000	$15,000	$15,000	$15,000	$75,000
Undiscounted cashflow	($50,000)	$15,000	$15,000	$15,000	$15,000	$15,000	$25,000
Discount formula	$1/(1+DR)^0$	$1/(1+DR)^1$	$1/(1+DR)^2$	$1/(1+DR)^3$	$1/(1+DR)^4$	$1/(1+DR)^5$	
Discount factor	100.0%	90.9%	82.6%	75.1%	68.3%	62.1%	
Present value	($50,000)	$13,636	$12,397	$11,270	$10,245	$9,314	$6,862

The NPV of Harry's project is $6,862. Of course the NPV is lower than the sum of the undiscounted cash flows. NPV accounts for the fact that on a per-dollar basis, cash flows received in the future are less valuable than cash in the hand.

Internal rate of return

The internal rate of return is the percentage return made on the investment over a period of time. The internal rate of return is a feature supplied on most spreadsheets and thus is relatively easy to calculate.

> internal rate of return (IRR): **The discount rate for which the net present value of the investment is zero.**

The IRR is especially useful because it can be compared to a company's hurdle rate. The hurdle rate is the necessary percentage return to justify a project. Thus a company might decide only to undertake projects with a return greater than 12%. Projects that have an IRR greater than 12% get the green light; all others are thrown in the bin.

Example Returning to Harry, we can see that IRR is an easy calculation to perform using a software package. Enter the values given in the relevant periods on the spreadsheet (see Table 10.3).

Year 0 – now – is when Harry makes the initial investment; each of the next five years sees a $15,000 return. Applying the IRR function gives a return of 15.24%.

Table 10.3 Five-year cashflow

Cell reference	A	B	C	D	E	F	G
1		Year 0	Year 1	Year 2	Year 3	Year 4	Year 5
2	Cashflows	($50,000)	$15,000	$15,000	$15,000	$15,000	$15,000

In Microsoft Excel, the function is = IRR(B2:G2) which equals 15.24%.

The cell references in Table 10.3 should help in recreating this function. The function is telling Excel to perform an IRR on the range B2 (cashflow for year 0) to G2 (cashflow for year 5).

IRR and NPV are related

The internal rate of return is the percentage discount rate at which the net present value of the operation is zero.

Thus companies using a hurdle rate are really saying that they will only accept projects where the net present value is positive at the discount rate they specify as the hurdle rate. Another way to say this is that they will accept projects only if the IRR is greater than the hurdle rate.

Data sources, complications and cautions

Payback and IRR calculations require estimates of cash flows. The cash flows are the monies received and paid out that are associated with the project per period, including the initial investment. Topics that are beyond the scope of this book include the time frame over which forecasts of cash flows are made and how to handle "terminal values" (the value associated with the opportunity at the end of the last period).[4] Net present value calculations require the same inputs as payback and IRR, plus one other: the *discount rate*. Typically, the discount rate is decided at corporate level. This rate has a dual purpose to compensate for the following:

- The time value of money.
- The risk inherent in the activity.

A general principle to employ is that the riskier the project, the greater the discount rate to use. Considerations for setting the discount rates are also beyond the scope of this book. We will simply observe that, ideally, separate discount rates would be assessed for each individual project because risk varies by activity. A government contract might be a fairly certain project – not so for an investment by the same company in buying a fashion retailer. The same concern occurs when companies set a single hurdle rate for all projects assessed by IRR analysis.

> Cashflows and net profits: **In our examples cash flow equals profit, but in many cases they will be different.**

A note for users of spreadsheet programs

Microsoft Excel has an NPV calculator, which can be very useful in calculating NPV. The formula to use is NPV (rate, value 1, value 2, etc.) where the rate is the discount rate and the values are the cash flows by year, so year 1 = value 1, year 2 = value 2, and so on.

The calculation starts in period 1, and the cash flow for that period is discounted. If you are using the convention of having the investment in the period before period 0, you should not discount it but add it back outside the formula. Therefore Harry's returns discounted at 10% would be:

= NPV (rate, value 1, value 2, value 3, value 4, value 5)

= NPV (10%, 15000, 15000, 15000, 15000, 15000) or $56,861.80 less the initial investment of $50,000.

This gives the NPV of $6,861.80 as demonstrated fully in the example.

Return on marketing investment

> **Return on marketing investment (ROMI) is a relatively new metric. It is not like the other "return-on-investment" metrics because marketing is not the same kind of investment. Instead of moneys that are "tied up" in plants and inventories, marketing funds are typically "risked". Marketing spending is typically charged to expenses in the current period. There are many variations in the way this metric has been used, and although no authoritative sources for defining it exist, we believe the consensus of usage justifies the following:**

$$\text{Return on marketing investment (ROMI)} = \frac{[\text{Incremental revenue attributable to marketing} (£) * \text{Contribution} \% - \text{Marketing spending} (£)]}{\text{Marketing spending} (£)}$$

The idea of measuring the market's response in terms of sales and profits is not new, but terms such as marketing ROI and ROMI are used more frequently now than in past periods. Usually, marketing spending will be deemed as justified if the ROMI is positive.

Purpose: to measure the rate at which spending on marketing contributes to profits

Marketers are under more and more pressure to "show a return" on their activities. However, it is often unclear exactly what this means. Certainly, marketing spending is not an "investment" in the usual sense of the word. There is usually no tangible asset and often not even a predictable (quantifiable) result to show for the spending, but marketers still want to emphasise that their activities contribute to financial health. Some might argue that marketing should be considered an expense and the focus should be on whether it is a necessary expense. Marketers believe that many of their activities generate lasting results and therefore should be considered "investments" in the future of the business.[5]

Return on marketing investment (ROMI): The contribution attributable to marketing (net of marketing spending), divided by the marketing "invested" or risked.

Construction

A necessary step in calculating ROMI is the estimation of the incremental sales attributable to marketing. These incremental sales can be "total" sales attributable to marketing or "marginal". The following example, in Figure 10.3, should help clarify the difference:

Y_0 = Baseline sales (with £0 marketing spending),

Y_1 = Sales at marketing spending level X_1, and

Y_2 = Sales at marketing spending level X_2,

where the difference between X_1 and X_2 represents the cost of an incremental marketing budget item that is to be evaluated, such as an advertising campaign or a trade show.

1 **Revenue return to incremental marketing $= (Y_2 - Y_1)/(X_2 - X_1)$:** The additional revenue generated by an incremental marketing investment, such as a specific campaign or sponsorship, divided by the cost of that marketing investment.

2 **Revenue attributable to marketing $= Y_2 - Y_0$:** The increase in sales attributable to the entire marketing budget (equal to sales minus baselines sales).

3 **Revenue return to total marketing $= (Y_2 - Y_0)/(X_2)$:** The revenue attributable to marketing divided by the marketing budget.

4 **Return on marketing investment (ROMI) $= [(Y_2 - Y_0) \star$ Contribution% $- X_2]/X_2$:** The additional net contribution from all marketing activities divided by the cost of those activities.

5 **Return on incremental marketing investment (ROIMI) $= [(Y_2 - Y_1) \star$ Contribution % $- (X_2 - X_1)]/(X_2 - X_1)$:** The incremental net contribution due to the incremental marketing spending divided by the amount of incremental spending.

Figure 10.3 Evaluating the cost of an incremental marketing budget item

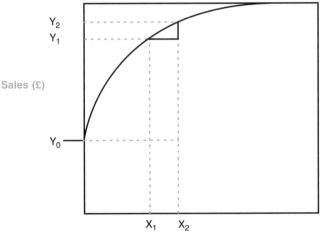

For some industries revenue return to incremental marketing might be a useful metric – those with low variable costs where the vast bulk of additional revenues go to contribution; it is thus a proxy for contribution. However, for most situations this metric is liable to be very misleading. There is no point in spending £20,000 on advertising to generate £100,000 of sales – a respectable 500% return to revenue – if high variable costs mean the marketing only generates a contribution of £5,000. Return on marketing investment (ROMI) accounts for the contribution from each sale. The key formula for judging the success of marketing investment is therefore:

$$\text{Return on marketing investment (ROMI) (\%)} = \frac{[\text{Revenue attributable to marketing} * \text{Contribution\% (\%)} - \text{Marketing cost (£)}]}{\text{Marketing cost (£)}}$$

Example A farm equipment company in Wisconsin in the US was considering a direct mail campaign to remind customers to have tractors serviced before spring planting. The campaign is expected to cost $1,000 and to increase revenues from $45,000 to $50,000. Baseline revenues for tractor servicing (with no marketing) were estimated at $25,000. The direct mail campaign was in addition to the regular advertising and other marketing activities costing $6,000. Contribution on tractor servicing revenues (after parts and labour) averages averages 60%.

Each of the metrics in this section can be calculated from the information in the example.

$$\text{Revenue return to incremental marketing} = \frac{(\$50,000 - \$45,000)}{(\$7,000 - \$6,000)}$$

$$= \frac{\$5,000}{\$1,000} = 500\%$$

Revenue attributable to marketing = $50,000 − $25,000 = $25,000 [note this figure applies if the additional direct mail campaign is used; otherwise it would be $20,000 ($45,000 − $25,000)]

Revenue returns to total marketing = $25,000/$7,000 = 357% [or, if the direct mail campaign is not used ($20,000/$6,000), 333%]

Return on marketing investment (ROMI) = ($25,000 * 60% − $7,000)/$7,000 = 114% [or, if the direct mail campaign is not used ($20,000 * .6 − $6,000)/$6,000 = 100%]

$$\text{Return on incremental marketing investment (ROIMI)} = \frac{(\$5,000 * 60\% - \$1,000)}{\$1,000} = 200\%$$

Data sources, complications and cautions

The first piece of information needed for marketing ROI is the cost of the marketing campaign, programme or budget. Although defining which costs belong in marketing can be problematic, a bigger challenge is estimating the incremental revenue, contribution and net profits attributable to marketing. This is similar to the distinction between baseline and lift discussed on pages 243–251.

A further complication of estimating ROMI concerns how to deal with important interactions between different marketing programmes and campaigns. The return on many marketing "investments" is likely to show up as an increase in the responses received for other types of marketing. For example, if direct mail solicitations show an increase in response because of television advertising, we could and should calculate that those incremental revenues had something to do with the TV campaign. As an interaction, however, the return on advertising would depend on what was being spent on other programmes. The function is not a simple linear return to the campaign costs.

For budgeting, one key element to recognise is that maximising the ROMI would probably reduce spending and profits. Marketers typically encounter diminishing returns, in which each incremental £1 will yield lower and lower incremental ROMI, and so low levels of spending will tend to have very high return rates. Maximising ROMI might lead to reduced marketing and eliminating campaigns or activities that are, on balance, profitable, even if the return rates are not as high. This issue is similar to the distinction between ROI (%) and EVA (£) discussed on pages 309–313. Additional marketing activities or campaigns that bring down average percentage returns but increase overall profits can be quite sensible. So, using ROMI or any percentage measure of profit to determine overall budgets is questionable. Of course, merely eliminating programmes with a negative ROMI is almost always a good idea.

The previous discussion intentionally does not deal with carryover effect, that is, marketing effects on sales and profits that extend into future periods. When marketing spending is expected to have effects beyond the current period, other techniques will be needed. These include payback, net present value and internal rate of return. Also, see "Customer lifetime value" (pages 142–147) for a more disaggregated approach to evaluating marketing spending designed to acquire long-lived customer relationships.

Related metrics

Media exposure return on marketing investment

In an attempt to evaluate the value of marketing activities such as sponsorships, marketers often commission research to gauge the number and quality of media exposures achieved. These exposures are then valued (often using "rate cards" to determine the cost of equivalent advertising space/time) and a "return" is calculated by dividing the estimated value by the costs.

$$\text{Media exposure return on marketing investment (MEROMI) (\%)} = \frac{\text{(Estimated value of media exposures achieved} - \text{Cost of marketing campaign, sponsorship or promotion)}}{\text{Cost of marketing campaign, sponsorship or promotion}}$$

This is most appropriate where there isn't a clear market rate for the results of the campaign and so marketers want to be able to illustrate the equivalent cost for the result for a type of campaign that has an established market rate.

Example A Japanese travel portal decides to sponsor a car at a Formula 1 event. They assume that the logo they put on the car will gain the equivalent of 500,000 impressions and will cost 10,000,000 yen. The cost per impression is thus 10 million yen/500,000 = or 20 yen per impression. This can be compared to the costs of other marketing campaigns.

References and suggested further reading

Hawkins, D.I., R.J. Best and C.M. Lillis. (1987). "The Nature and Measurement of Marketing Productivity in Consumer Durables Industries: A Firm Level Analysis", *Journal of the Academy of Marketing Science*, 1(4), 1–8.

The marketing metrics X-ray

The marketing metrics X-ray

Our purpose in this chapter is to give some examples of how marketing metrics can augment and complement traditional financial metrics when used to assess firm and brand performance. In particular, marketing metrics can serve as leading indicators of problems, opportunities and future financial performance. Just as X-rays are designed to provide deeper views of our bodies, marketing metrics can show problems (and opportunities) that would otherwise be missed.

Put your money where your metrics are

Table 11.1 shows common summary financial information for two hypothetical companies, Boom and Cruise. Income statement data from five years provide the basis for comparing the companies on several dimensions.

On which firm would you bet your grandparents' savings?

We have used this example with MBA students and executives many times – usually we ask them, "Assume that your grandparent wants to buy a partnership in one of these firms, using limited retirement savings. If these financial statements were the *only* data you had available or could obtain, which firm would you recommend?" These data are the metrics traditionally used to evaluate firm performance.

The table shows that gross margins and profits are the same for both firms. Although Boom's sales and marketing spending are growing faster, its return on sales (ROS) and return on investment (ROI) are declining. If this decline continues, Boom will be in trouble. In addition, Boom's marketing/sales ratio is increasing faster than Cruise's. Is this a sign of inefficient marketing?

Table 11.1 Financial statements

All £ in (thousands)	Boom				
	Year 1	Year 2	Year 3	Year 4	Year 5
Revenue	£833	£1,167	£1,700	£2,553	£3,919
Margin before marketing	£125	£175	£255	£383	£588
Marketing	£100	£150	£230	£358	£563
Profit	£25	£25	£25	£25	£25
Margin (%)	15%	15%	15%	15%	15%
Marketing/sales	12%	13%	14%	14%	14%
ROS	3.0%	2.1%	1.5%	1.0%	0.6%
Year-on-year revenue growth	—	40%	46%	50%	53%
CAGR revenue from year 1	—	40%	43%	45%	47%
Invested capital	£500	£520	£552	£603	£685
ROI	5.0%	4.8%	4.8%	4.1%	3.6%

All £ in (thousands)	Cruise				
	Year 1	Year 2	Year 3	Year 4	Year 5
Revenue	£1,320	£1,385	£1,463	£1,557	£1,670
Margin before marketing	£198	£208	£219	£234	£251
Marketing	£173	£183	£194	£209	£226
Profit	£25	£25	£25	£25	£25
Margin (%)	15%	15%	15%	15%	15%
Marketing/sales	13%	13%	13%	13%	14%
ROS	1.9%	1.8%	1.7%	1.6%	1.5%
Year-on-year revenue growth	—	5%	6%	6%	7%
CAGR revenue from year 1	—	5%	5%	6%	6%
Invested capital	£500	£501	£503	£505	£507
ROI	5.0%	5.0%	5.0%	5.0%	4.9%

On the basis of the information in Table 11.1, most people chose Cruise. Cruise is doing more with less. It's more efficient. Its trend in ROS looks much better, and Cruise has maintained a fairly consistent ROI of about 5%. About the only thing Boom has going for it is size and growth of the "top line" (sales revenue). Let's look deeper at the marketing metrics X-ray.

Using the marketing metrics X-ray

Table 11.2 presents the results of our marketing metrics X-ray of Boom and Cruise. It shows the number of customers each firm is serving and separates these into "old" (existing) and "new" customers.

This table allows us to see not only the rate at which the firm acquired new customers but also their retention (loyalty) rates. Now, Boom's spending on marketing looks a lot better because we now know that spending was used to generate new customers and keep old ones. In addition, Boom acquires new customers at a lower cost than Cruise. And although Cruise's customers spend more, Boom's stay around longer. Perhaps we should order another set of X-rays to examine customer profitability and lifetime value?

Table 11.3 uses the information in the previous table to calculate some additional customer metrics. Under an assumption of constant margins and retention rates, we can calculate the customer lifetime value (CLV) for the customers of each firm and compare this CLV with what the firms are spending to acquire the customers. The CLV represents the discounted margins a firm will earn from its customers over their life buying from the firm. Refer to pages 142–147 for details about the estimation of CLV and the process for using the number to value the customer base as an asset. The asset value is merely the customer lifetime value times the number of customers. For these examples, we have assumed that all marketing is used to acquire new customers, so the customer acquisition cost is obtained by dividing marketing spending by the new customers in year period.

Boom's aggressive marketing spending looks even better in this light. The difference between the CLV and acquisition cost is only £3.71 for Cruise but is £48.21 for Boom. From the viewpoint of the customer asset value at the end of year 5, Boom is worth almost five times as much as Cruise.

Table 11.4 gives us even more information on customers. Customer satisfaction is much higher for Boom, and Boom's customers are more willing to recommend the firm to others. As a consequence, we might expect Boom's acquisition costs to decline in the future. In fact, with such a stable and satisfied customer base, we could expect that brand equity (refer to pages 115–118) measures would be higher too.

Table 11.2 Marketing metrics

	Boom					Cruise				
	Year 1	Year 2	Year 3	Year 4	Year 5	Year 1	Year 2	Year 3	Year 4	Year 5
New customers (thousands)	1.33	2.00	3.07	4.77	7.50	1.86	1.97	2.09	2.24	2.43
Total customers (thousands)	3.33	4.67	6.80	10.21	15.67	3.86	4.05	4.28	4.55	4.88
Sales/customer	£250	£250	£250	£250	£250	£342	£342	£342	£342	£342
Marketing/new customer	£75	£75	£75	£75	£75	£93	£93	£93	£93	£93
Churn rate[1]	—	20%	20%	20%	20%	—	46%	46%	46%	46%

Table 11.3 Customer profitability

Customer value metric	Boom	Cruise
Customer CLV	£123.21	£96.71
Customer acquisition cost	£75.00	£93.00
Customer count (thousands)	15.67	4.88
Customer asset value (thousands)	£1,931	£472

Table 11.4 Customer attitudes and awareness

	Boom					Cruise				
	Year 1	Year 2	Year 3	Year 4	Year 5	Year 1	Year 2	Year 3	Year 4	Year 5
Awareness	30%	32%	31%	31%	33%	20%	22%	22%	23%	23%
Top of mind	17%	18%	20%	19%	20%	12%	12%	11%	11%	10%
Satisfaction	85%	86%	86%	87%	88%	50%	52%	52%	51%	53%
Willingness to recommend	65%	66%	68%	67%	69%	42%	43%	42%	40%	39%

Hiding problems in the marketing baggage?

The income statement for another example firm, Prestige Luggage, is depicted in Table 11.5. The company seems to be doing quite well. Unit and dollar sales are growing rapidly. Margins before marketing are stable and quite robust. Marketing spending and marketing to sales ratios are growing, but so is the bottom line. So what is not to like?

Table 11.5 Prestige Luggage income

	Statement			
	Year 1	Year 2	Year 3	Year 4
Sales revenue (thousands)	$14,360	$18,320	$23,500	$30,100
Unit sales (thousands)	85	115	159	213
Market share (unit)	14%	17%	21%	26%
Gross margin	53%	53%	52%	52%
Marketing	$1,600	$2,143	$2,769	$3,755
Profit	$4,011	$5,317	$7,051	$9,227
ROS	27.9%	29.0%	30.0%	30.7%
Marketing/sales	11.1%	11.7%	11.8%	12.5%

Using the marketing metrics X-ray

Let's take a deeper look at what's going on with Prestige Luggage by examining their retail customers. When we do, we'll get a better view of the marketing mechanics that underlie the seemingly pleasant financials in Table 11.5.

Table 11.6 (refer to pages 176–183 for distribution measures) shows that Prestige Luggage's sales growth comes from two sources: an expanding number of outlets stocking the brand and an increase (more than fourfold) in price promotions. Still, there are plenty of outlets that do not stock the brand. So there may be room to grow.

Table 11.7 reveals that although the overall sales are increasing, they are not keeping pace with the number of stores stocking the brand. (Sales per retail store are already declining.) Also, the promotional pricing by the manufacturer seems to be encouraging individual stores' inventories to grow. Soon, retailers may become irritated that the GMROII (gross margin return on inventory investment) has declined considerably. *Future sales may continue to slow further and put pressure on retail margins.* If retailer dissatisfaction causes some retailers to drop the brand from their assortment, manufacturer sales will decline precipitously.

Table 11.6 Prestige Luggage marketing and channel metrics

	Year 1	Year 2	Year 3	Year 4
Retail dollar sales (thousands)	$24,384	$27,577	$33,067	$44,254
Retail unit sales (thousands)	87	103	132	183
Number stocking outlets	300	450	650	900
Price premium	30.0%	22.3%	15.1%	8.9%
ACV distribution[2]	30%	40%	48%	60%
% sales on deal	10%	13%	20%	38%
Advertising spending (thousands)	$700	$693	$707	$721
Promotion spending (thousands)	$500	$750	$1,163	$2,034

Table 11.7 Luggage manufacturer retail profitability metrics

	Year 1	Year 2	Year 3	Year 4
Retail margin $	$9,754	$11,169	$13,557	$18,366
Retail margin %	40%	41%	41%	42%
Retail inventory (thousands)	15	27	54	84
Inventory per store	50	60	83	93
Sales/outlet (thousands)	$81	$61	$51	$49
Stores per point of AVC %	10	11	14	15
GMROII	385%	260%	170%	155%

In addition, the broadening of distribution and the increase of sales on deal suggest a possible change in how potential consumers view the previously exclusive image of the Prestige Luggage brand. The firm might want to order another set of X-rays to see if and how consumer attitudes about the brand have changed. Again, if these changes are by design, then maybe Prestige Luggage is okay. If not, then Prestige Luggage should be worried that its established strategy is falling apart. Add that to the possibility that some retailers are using deep discounts to unload inventory after they've dropped the brand, and suddenly Prestige Luggage faces a vicious cycle from which they may never recover.

Some things you can't make up, and this example is one. The actual company was "pumped up" through a series of price promotions, distribution was expanded and sales grew rapidly. Shortly after being bought by another company looking to add to their luxury goods portfolio of brands, the strategy unravelled. Many stores dropped the line, and it took years to rebuild the brand and sales.

These two examples illustrate the importance of digging behind the financial statements using tools such as the marketing X-ray. More numbers, in and of themselves, are only part of the answer. The ability to see patterns and meaning behind the numbers is even more important.

Smoking more but enjoying it less?

Table 11.8 displays marketing metrics reported by a major consumer-products company aimed at analysing the trends in competition by lower-priced discount brands. A declining market size, stagnant company market share and a growing share of firm sales accounted for by discount brands all made up a baleful picture of the future. The firm was replacing premium sales with discount brand sales. To top it off, the advertising and promotion budgets had almost doubled. In the words of Erv Shames, Darden Professor, it would be easy to conclude that the marketers had "run out of ideas" and were resorting to the bluntest of instruments: price.

Table 11.8 Market trends for discount brands and spending; Big Tobacco Company

Year	1987	1992
Market size (units)	4,000	3,850
Company unit share	25%	24%
Unit sales	1000	924
Premium brand units	925	774
Discount brand units	75	150
Advertising and promotion spend	$600	$1,225

The picture looks much brighter, however, after examining the metrics in Table 11.9. It turns out that in the same five years during which discount brands had become more prominent, sales revenue and operating income had both grown by over 50%. The reason is clear: prices had almost doubled, even though a large portion of

Table 11.9 Additional metrics

Year	1987	1992
Revenue (thousands)	$1,455	$2,237
Average unit price	$1.46	$2.42
Average premium price	$1.50	$2.60
Average discount price	$0.90	$1.50
Operating profit (thousands)	$355	$550

these price increases had been "discounted back" through promotions. Overall, the net impact was positive on the firm's bottom line.

Now you might be thinking that the messages in Table 11.9 are so obvious that no one would ever find the metrics in Table 11.8 to be as troubling as we made them out to be. In fact, our experience in teaching a case that contains all these metrics is that experienced marketers from all over the world tend to focus on the metrics in Table 11.8 and pay little or no attention to the additional metrics – even when given the same level of prominence.

The situation described by the two tables is a close approximation to the actual market conditions just before the now-famous "Marlboro Friday". Top management took action because they were concerned that the series of price increases that led to the attractive financials in 1992 would not be sustainable because the higher premium prices gave competitive discount brands more latitude to cut prices. On what later became known as "Marlboro Friday", 2 April 1993, Phillip Morris cut Marlboro prices by $0.40 a pack, reducing operating earnings by almost 40%. The stock price tumbled by 25%.

Note in this example the contrast from the preceding example. Prestige Luggage was increasing promotion expenditures to expand distribution. Prices were falling while promotion, or sales on deal, were increasing – an ominous sign. With Marlboro, they were constantly raising the price and then discounting back – a very different strategy.

Marketing dashboards

The presentation of metrics in the form of management "dashboards" has received a substantial amount of attention in the last several years. The basic notion seems to be that the manner of presenting complex data can influence management's ability to recognise key patterns and trends. Would a dashboard, a graphical depiction of the same information, make it easier for managers to pick up the ominous trends?

The metaphor of a car dashboard is appropriate because there are numerous metrics that could be used to measure a car's operation. The dashboard is to provide a *reduced set* of the *vital measures* in a form that is *easy for the operator to interpret and use*. Unfortunately, although all cars have the same key metrics, it is not as universal across all businesses. The set of appropriate and critical measures may differ across businesses.

Figure 11.1 presents a dashboard of five critical measures over time. It reveals strong sales growth while maintaining margins even though selling less expensive items. Disturbingly, however, the returns for the retailer (GMROII) have fallen precipitously while store inventories have grown. Sales per store have similarly dropped. The price premium that Prestige Luggage can command has fallen, and more of the company's sales are on deal. This should be a foreboding picture for the company and should raise concerns about the ability to maintain distribution.

Figure 11.1 Prestige Luggage: marketing management dashboard

Revenue and margins

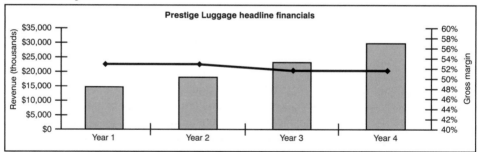

The financial metrics look healthy; revenue showing good growth while margins are almost unchanged.

Manufacturer prices to store prices

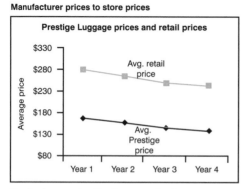

Prestige Luggage is selling less expensive items.

Store inventory and GMROII

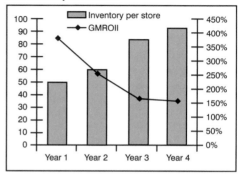

Prestige Luggage is making diminishing returns for retailer.

Distribution

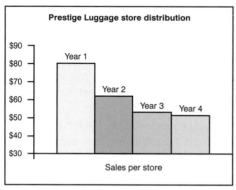

We are moving into smaller stores.

Pricing and promotions

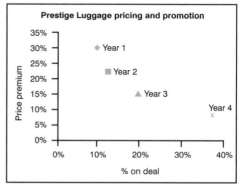

Prestige Luggage is becoming reliant on promotion.

Summary: marketing metrics + financial metrics = deeper insight

Dashboards, scorecards and what we have termed "X-rays" are collections of marketing and financial metrics that management believes are important indicators of business health. Dashboards are designed to provide depth of marketing understanding concerning the business. There are many specific metrics that may be considered important, or even critical, in any given marketing context. We do not believe it is generally possible to provide unambiguous advice on which metrics are most important or which management decisions are contingent on the values and trends in certain metrics. These recommendations would have to be of the "if, then" form, such as "If relative share is greater than 1.0 and market growth is higher than change in GDP, then invest more in advertising." Although such advice might be valuable under many circumstances, our aims were more modest – simply to provide a resource for marketers to achieve a deeper understanding of the diversity of metrics that exist.

Our examples, Boom versus Cruise, Prestige Luggage and Big Tobacco, showed how selected marketing metrics could give deeper insights into the financial future of companies. In situations such as these, it is important that a full array of marketing and financial metrics inform the decision. Examining a complete set of X-rays does not necessarily make the decisions any easier (the Big Tobacco example is debated by knowledgeable industry observers to this day!), but it does help ensure a more comprehensive diagnosis.

References and suggested further reading

Ambler, T., F. Kokkinaki and S. Puntoni (2004). "Assessing Marketing Performance: Reason for Metric Selection", *Journal of Marketing Management*, 20, 475–498.

McGovern, G., D. Court, J.A. Quelch and B. Crawford (2004). "Bringing Customers into the Boardroom", *Harvard Business Review*, 82(11), 70–80.

Meyer, C. (1994). "How the Right Measures Help Teams Excel", *Harvard Business Review*, 72(3), 95–103.

Conclusion

. . . metrics should be necessary (i.e., the company cannot do without them), precise, consistent, and sufficient (i.e., comprehensive) for review purposes.[1]

Understanding metrics will allow marketers to choose the right input data to give them meaningful information. They should be able to pick and choose from a variety of metrics depending upon the circumstances and create a dashboard of the most vital metrics to aid them in managing their business. After reading this work, we hope you agree that no one metric is going to give a full picture. It is only when you can use multiple viewpoints that you are likely to obtain anything approaching a full picture.

. . . results measures tell us where we stand in efforts to achieve goals, but not how we go there or what to do differently.[2]

Marketing metrics are needed to give a complete picture of a business's health. Financial metrics focus on money and periods of time, telling us how profits, cash and assets are changing. However, we also need to understand what is happening with our customers, products, prices, channels, competitors and brands.

The interpretation of marketing metrics requires knowledge and judgement. This book helps give you the knowledge so that you can know more about how metrics are constructed and what they measure. Knowing the limitations of individual metrics is important. In our experience, businesses are usually complex, requiring multiple metrics to capture different facets – to tell you what is going on.

Because of this complexity, marketing metrics often raise as many questions as they answer. Certainly, they rarely provide easy answers about what managers should do. Having a set of metrics based on a limited, faulty or outmoded view of the business can also blind you. Such a set of metrics can falsely reassure you that the business is fine when in fact trouble is developing. Like the ostrich with its head in the sand, it might be more comfortable to know less.

We don't expect that a command of marketing metrics will make your job easier. We do expect that such knowledge will help you do your job better.

Endnotes

Chapter 1

1. Bartlett, J. (1992). *Bartlett's Familiar Quotations*, 16th edition; Justin Kaplan, general editor.
2. Hauser, J. and G. Katz. "Metrics: You are What You Measure", *European Management Journal*, Vol. 16, No. 5, October 1998.
3. Kaplan, R.S. and D.P. Norton. (1996). *The Balanced Scorecard: Translating Strategy into Action*, Boston, MA: Harvard Business School Press.
4. Brady, D., with D. Kiley and Bureau Reports. (2004). "Making Marketing Measure Up", *Business Week*, 13 December, 112–113.
5. Strictly speaking, all the numbers can contain some error. Share may be estimated, for example, from retail sales to consumers. Sales might come from shipment to retailers.
6. Barwise, P. and J.U. Farley. (2003). "Which Marketing Metrics Are Used and Where?" Marketing Science Institute (03-111), working paper.
7. Ambler, T., F. Kokkinaki and S. Puntoni. (2004). "Assessing Marketing Performance: Reasons for Metrics Selection", *Journal of Marketing Management*, 20, 475–498.

Chapter 2

1. "Wal-Mart Shopper Update", *Retail Forward*, February 2005.
2. "Running Out of Gas", *Business Week*, 28 March 2005.
3. Check the Marketing Evaluations, Inc., website for more detail: http://www.qscores.com/. Accessed 12/08/08.
4. Claritas provides the Prizm analysis. For more details, visit the company website: http://www.claritas.com/target-marketing/market-research-services/marketing-data/marketing-segmentation/prizm.jsp. Accessed 12/08/08.

Chapter 3

1. "Running Out of Gas", *Business Week*, 28 March 2005.
2. This formula should be familiar if we consider that the supplier selling price is merely the cost to that layer of the chain. So this becomes Selling price = Cost/(1 − Margin %). This is the same as Sale £ = Cost £ + Margin £.
3. Those familiar with basic economics use the term "marginal cost" to refer to the cost of an additional unit of output. In this linear cost model, marginal cost is the same for all units and is equal to the variable cost per unit.
4. Both contribution per unit (£) and contribution margin (%) are closely related to unit margin (£) and margin (%). The difference is that contribution margins (whether unit or percentage based) result from a more careful separation of fixed and variable costs.

Chapter 4

1. Harvard Business School Case: Nestlé Refrigerated Foods Contadina Pasta & Pizza (A) 9-595-035. Rev. 30 January 1997.
2. Young & Rubicam can be found at: http://www.yr.com/yr/. Accessed 12/08/08.
3. Bruno, H., U. Parthasarathi and N. Singh, eds. (2005). "The Changing Face of Measurement Tools Across the Product Lifecycle", *Does Marketing Measure Up? Performance Metrics: Practices and Impact*, Marketing Science Institute, Conference Summary No. 05-301.
4. See Darden technical note and original research.
5. The information from Bill Moran comes from personal communications with the authors.
6. Interbrand can be contacted at: http://www.interbrand.com/. Accessed 12/08/08.

Chapter 5

1. "Vodafone Australia Gains Customers", *Sydney Morning Herald*, 26 January 2005.
2. "Atlanta Braves Home Attendance". Wikipedia, the free encyclopedia. http://en.wikipedia.org/wiki/Major_League_Baseball_attendance_records
3. Thanks to Gerry Allan, President, Anametrica, Inc. (developer of Web-based tools for managers) for his work on this section.
4. Pfeifer, P.E., M.E. Haskins and R.M. Conroy. (2005). "Customer Lifetime Value, Customer Profitability, and the Treatment of Acquisition Spending", *Journal of Managerial Issues*, 17(1), 11–25.
5. Kaplan, R.S. and V.G. Narayanan. (2001). "Measuring and Managing Customer Profitability", *Journal of Cost Management*, September/October, 5–15.
6. Peppers, D. and M. Rogers. (1997). *Enterprise One to One: Tools for Competing in the Interactive Age*, New York: Currency Doubleday.
7. Berger, P.D., B. Weinberg and R. Hanna. (2003). "Customer Lifetime Value Determination and Strategic Implications for a Cruise-Ship Line", *Database Marketing and Customer Strategy Management*, 11(1), 40–52.
8. Gupta, S. and D.R. Lehman. (2003). "Customers as Assets", *Journal of Interactive Marketing*, 17(1), 9–24.

Chapter 6

1. Material in pages 162–194 is based on a *Note on Sales Force Metrics*, written by Eric Larson, Darden MBA 2005.
2. Zoltners, A.A., P. Sinha and G.A. Zoltners. (2001). *The Complete Guide to Accelerating Sales Force Performance*, New York: AMACOM.
3. Wilner, J.D. (1998). *7 Secrets to Successful Sales Management: The Sales Manager's Manual*, Boca Raton, Florida: St Lucie Press.
4. For more on these total allocations, see Zoltners, A.A., P. Sinha and G.A. Zoltners. (2001). *The Complete Guide to Accelerating Sales Force Performance*, New York: AMACOM.
5. Zoltners, A.A., P. Sinha and G.A. Zoltners. (2001). *The Complete Guide to Accelerating Sales Force Performance*, New York: AMACOM.

6. Dolan, R.J. and B.P. Shapiro. "Milford Industries (A)", Harvard Business School, Case 584-012.
7. Zoltners, A.A., P. Sinha and G.A. Zoltners. (2001). *The Complete Guide to Accelerating Sales Force Performance*, New York: AMACOM.
8. Jones, E., C. Stevens and L. Chonko. (2005). *Selling ASAP: Art, Science, Agility, Performance*, Mason, Ohio: South Western, 176.
9. Product category volume is also known as weighted distribution.
10. The authors use the term "product category volume" (PCV) for this metric. However, this term is not as widely used in industry as "all commodity volume" (ACV).

Chapter 7

1. Dolan, R.J. and H. Simon. (1996). *Power Pricing: How Managing Price Transforms the Bottom Line*, New York: The Free Press, 4.
2. Barwise, P. and J.U. Farley. (2003). "Which Marketing Metrics Are Used and Where?" Marketing Science Institute (03-111) 2003, working paper.
3. Constant elasticity functions are also called log linear because they can be expressed as: log Q = log A + elasticity × log (p).
4. In graphing such relationships, economists often plot price on the vertical axis and quantity demanded on the horizontal axis. When reviewing a graph, managers are advised to always check the axis definitions.
5. If price elasticity is expressed in shorthand as a positive number, then we do not need the negative sign in the formula that follows.

Chapter 8

1. In this context, we use the term "permanent" with some flexibility, recognising that even long-term arrangements must be subject to change in response to market and industry dynamics.
2. Often, contribution can be used as a proxy for profits.
3. Distribution for coupons is used in the sense of postage and insertion costs, rather than retail and inventory logistics.
4. For a richer discussion, see Ailawadi, K., P. Farris and E. Shames. (1999). "Trade Promotion: Essential to Selling Through Resellers", *Sloan Management Review*, 41(1), 83–92.
5. Roegner, E., M. Marn and C. Zawada. (2005). "Pricing", *Marketing Management*, 14(1).
6. "How to Fix Your Pricing if it is Broken", by Ron Farmer, CEO, Revenue Technologies for the Professional Pricing Society: http://pricingsociety.com/members/articles/How-To-Fix-Your-Pricing-if-it-is-Broken.pdf. Accessed 12/08/08.

Chapter 9

1. Farris, P.W. (2003). "Getting the Biggest Bang for Your Marketing Buck", *Measuring and Allocating Marcom Budgets: Seven Expert Points of View*, Marketing Science Institute Monograph.
2. Known as client-side tagging, beacon and 1 × 1 clear pixel technology.

3. The Interactive Advertising Bureau gives the following definition of ad impression: "A measurement of responses from an ad delivery system to an ad request from the user's browser, which is filtered from robotic activity and is recorded at a point as late as possible in the process of delivery of the creative material to the user's browser – therefore closest to actual opportunity to see by the user." Interactive Audience Measurement and Advertising Campaign Reporting and Audit Guidelines. September 2004, United States Version 6.0b.
4. The spending data are taken from "Internet Weekly", Credit Suisse First Boston, 14 September 2004, 7–8.
5. http://www.nielsen-netratings.com/. Accessed 12/08/08.

Chapter 10

1. Economic value added is a trademark of Stern Stewart Consultants – http://www.sternstewart.com. Accessed 12/08/08.
2. The weighted average cost of capital, a.k.a. the WACC, is just the percentage return expected to capital sources. This finance concept is better left to specialist texts, but to give a simple example, if a third of a firm's capital comes from the bank at 6% and two-thirds from shareholders who expect a 9% return, then the WACC is the weighted average 8%. The WACC will be different for different companies, depending on their structure and risks.
3. Excel has a function to do this quickly, which we explain at the end of the section. However, it is important to understand what the calculation is doing.
4. A terminal value in a simple calculation might be assumed to be zero or some simple figure for the sale of the enterprise. More complex calculations consider estimating future cashflows; where this is done, ask about assumptions and importance. If the estimated terminal value is a significant area of the analysis, why have you curtailed the full analyses at this point?
5. Hawkins, D.I., R.J. Best and C.M. Lillis. (1987). "The Nature and Measurement of Marketing Productivity in Consumer Durables Industries: A Firm Level Analysis", *Journal of the Academy of Marketing Science*, 1(4), 1–8.

Chapter 11

1. Churn = per cent of customers lost each year.
2. ACV = all commodity volume, a measure of distribution coverage (refer to pages 176–183).

Conclusion

1. Ambler, T. (2000). *Marketing and the Bottom Line: The New Metrics of Corporate Wealth*, London: Prentice Hall.
2. Meyer, C. (1994). "How the Right Measures Help Teams Excel", *Harvard Business Review*, 72(3), 95.

Select bibliography

Aaker, D.A. (1991). *Managing Brand Equity: Capitalizing on the Value of a Brand Name*, New York: The Free Press.

Aaker, D.A. (1996). *Building Strong Brands*, New York: The Free Press.

Aaker, D.A. and J.M. Carman. (1982). "Are You Overadvertising?" *Journal of Advertising Research*, 22(4), 57–70.

Aaker, D.A. and K.L. Keller. (1990). "Consumer Evaluations of Brand Extensions", *Journal of Marketing*, 54(1), 27–41.

Abela, A., B.H. Clark and T. Ambler. "Marketing Performance Measurement, Performance, and Learning", working paper, 1 September 2004.

Abraham, M.M. and L.M. Lodish. (1990). "Getting the Most Out of Advertising and Promotion", *Harvard Business Review*, 68(3), 50–58.

Ailawadi, K., P. Farris and E. Shames. (1999). "Trade Promotion: Essential to Selling through Resellers", *Sloan Management Review*, 41(1), 83–92.

Ambler, T. and C. Styles. (1995). "Brand Equity: Toward Measures That Matter", working paper no. 95-902, London Business School, Centre for Marketing.

Barwise, P. and J.U. Farley. (2003). "Which Marketing Metrics Are Used and Where?" Marketing Science Institute (03-111), working paper.

Berger, P.D., B. Weinberg and R. Hanna. (2003). "Customer Lifetime Value Determination and Strategic Implications for a Cruise-Ship Line", *Database Marketing and Customer Strategy Management*, 11(1), 40–52.

Blattberg, R.C. and S.J. Hoch. (1990). "Database Models and Managerial Intuition: 50% Model + 50% Manager", *Management Science*, 36(8), 887–899.

Brady, D., with D. Kiley and Bureau Reports. (2004). "Making Marketing Measure Up", *Business Week*, 13 December 2004, 112–113.

Christen, M., S. Gupta, J.C. Porter, R. Staelin and D.R. Wittink. (1997). "Using Market-Level Data to Understand Promotion Effects in a Nonlinear Model", *Journal of Marketing Research*, 34(3), 322–334.

Clark, B.H., A.V. Abela and T. Ambler. (2004). "Return on Measurement: Relating Marketing Metrics Practices to Strategic Performance", working paper, 12 January.

Dekimpe, M.G. and D.M. Hanssens. (1995). "The Persistence of Marketing Effects on Sales", *Marketing Science*, 14, 1–21.

Dolan, R.J. and H. Simon. (1996). *Power Pricing: How Managing Price Transforms the Bottom Line*, New York: The Free Press, 4.

Farris, P.W., D. Reibstein and E. Shames. (1998). "Advertising Budgeting: A Report from the Field", New York: American Association of Advertising Agencies.

Forrester, J.W. (1959). "Advertising: A Problem in Industrial Dynamics", *Harvard Business Review*, 37(2), 100–110.

Forrester, J.W. (1959). "Modeling of Market and Company Interactions", Peter D. Bennett, ed. *Marketing and Economic Development,* American Marketing Association, Fall, 353–364.

Gregg, E., P.W. Farris and E. Shames. (revised, 2004). "Perspective on Brand Equity", Darden School Technical Notes, UVA-M-0668.

Greyser, S.A. (1980). "Marketing Issues", *Journal of Marketing*, 47, Winter, 89–93.

Gupta, S. and D.R. Lehman. (2003). "Customers as Assets", *Journal of Interactive Marketing*, 17(1), 9–24.

Harvard Business School Case: Nestlé Refrigerated Foods Contadina Pasta & Pizza (A) 9-595-035. Rev. 30 January 1997.

Hauser, J. and G. Katz. (1998). "Metrics: You Are What You Measure", *European Management Journal*, 16(5), 517–528.

Interactive Advertising Bureau. (2004). Interactive Audience Measurement and Advertising Campaign Reporting and Audit Guidelines. United States Version 6.0b.

Kaplan, R.S. and V.G. Narayanan. (2001). "Measuring and Managing Customer Profitability". *Journal of Cost Management*, September/October, 5–15.

Little, J.D.C. (1970). "Models and Managers: The Concept of a Decision Calculus", *Management Science*, 16(8), B-466–B-484.

Lodish, L.M. (1997). "Point of View: J.P. Jones and M.H. Blair on Measuring Ad Effects – Another POV", *Journal of Advertising Research*, 37(5), 75–79.

McGovern, G.J., D. Court, J.A. Quelch and B. Crawford. (2004). "Bringing Customers into the Boardroom", *Harvard Business Review*, 82(11), 70–80.

Meyer, C. (1994). "How the Right Measures Help Teams Excel", *Harvard Business Review*, 72(3), 95–103.

March, J.G., L.S. Sproull and M. Tamuz. (1989). "Learning from Samples of One or Fewer", *Organizational Science*, 2(1), 1–12.

Murphy, A.H. and B.G. Brown. (1984). "A Comparative Evaluation of Objective and Subjective Weather Forecasts in the United States", *Journal of Forecasting*, 3, 369–393.

NetGenesis Corp. (2000). *E-Metrics: Business Metrics for the New Economy*. NetGenesis and Target Marketing: Santa Barbara.

Peppers, D. and M. Rogers. (1997). *Enterprise One to One: Tools for Competing in the Interactive Age*, New York: Currency Doubleday.

Pfeifer, P.E., M.E. Haskins and R.M. Conroy. (2005). "Customer Lifetime Value, Customer Profitability, and the Treatment of Acquisition Spending", *Journal of Managerial Issues*, 17(1), 11–25.

Poundstone, W. (1993). *Prisoner's Dilemma*, New York: Doubleday, 118.

Reichheld, F.F. and E.W. Sasser, Jr. (1990). "Zero Defections: Quality Comes to Services", *Harvard Business Review*, September–October, 105–111.

Roegner, E., M. Marn and C. Zawada. (2005). "Pricing", *Marketing Management*, 14(1), 23–28.

Sheth, J.N. and R.S. Sisodia. (2002). "Marketing Productivity Issues and Analysis", *Journal of Business Research*, 55, 349–362.

Tellis, G.J. and D.L. Weiss. (1995). "Does TV Advertising Really Affect Sales? The Role of Measures, Models, and Data Aggregation", *Journal of Advertising Research*, 24(3), 1–12.

Wilner, J.D. (1998). *7 Secrets to Successful Sales Management: The Sales Manager's Manual*, Boca Raton, Florida: St Lucie Press.

Zoltners, A.A., P. Sinha and G.A. Zoltners. (2001). *The Complete Guide to Accelerating Sales Force Performance*, New York: AMACOM.

Index

£ (monetary terms) 6
% (percentage) 6

A.C. Nielsen 181
Aaker, David 116
  brand equity ten 116
AAU (Awareness, Attitudes and Usage) 32
  attitude 34
  awareness and knowledge 33
  calculating 33
  cautions 35–6
  data sources 35
  purpose 32
  usage 34–5
abandoned purchases 302
abandonment 299
abandonment rate 302
acceptors 26
accountability 2
acquisition versus retention 151–3
ACV (all commodity volume) 158, 176
  calculating 178–9
ad awareness 34
adjusting for periodic changes 35
advertising
  as a percentage of sales 80
  price versus cost 288
  See also impressions
advertising effectiveness 282, 284
advertising exposures 282
all commodity volume *see* ACV
allowances, slotting 80
apparel retailers, customers 136–7
assumptions
  infinite horizon assumption, customer lifetime
    value 147
  test markets 100–1
attitude, AAU 34
attitudes/liking/image 34
attrition 135
availability of data 3
AVC on display 183
AVC on promotion 183
average acquisition cost 152
average deal depth 240
average frequency 270, 273, 277
average margin 60–2
average price 64–5
average price charged 200–1
average price displayed 201
average price paid 199–200
average price per unit 65–6

calculating 66–9
  complications 69
  purpose 65–6
average retention cost 151–2
awareness 33
  customer awareness 329
  trial rate 95
Awareness, Attitudes and Usage *see* AAU

balancing sales force territories 160–2
banks, counting customers 135
baseline sales 241, 243
  calculating 244–9
  complications 249–50
  profitability 249
  purpose 244
BAV (brand asset valuator) 116
BCG (Boston Consulting Group) matrix 17–18
BDI (brand development index) 21
  calculating 21–2
  purpose 21
  segments 23
Big Tobacco Company 332–3
bonuses *see* sales force compensation
Boom
  customer awareness 329
  customer profit 328
  financial statements 325–6
  marketing metrics 328
Boston Consulting Group (BGC) matrix 17–18
brand asset valuator (BAV) 116
brand development index *see* BDI
brand equity methodology (Moran) 117
brand equity metrics 91, 115–18
  brand equity methodology (Moran) 117
  brand equity ten (David Aaker) 116
  brand valuation model 118
  purpose 115–16
  Y&R brand asset valuator 116
brand equity ten 116
brand penetration 23–4
brand valuation model 118
brand/product knowledge 34
brands, number of brands purchased 29
breadth of distribution 182
break-even analysis 81–5
  break-even on incremental investment 84
  classifying costs 84–5
  purpose 81
break-even number of employees 169, 171
break-even on incremental investment 84
break-even point 81–3

break-even sales level 46
breakage 253
Brita water filters 65
budgeting risk, assessing 76–7
budgets 2
buying power 161

CAGR (compound annual growth rates) 89, 91
  calculating 109
cannibalisation 110–13, 114
  weighted contribution margin 112
cannibalisation rates 91, 110–11
  complications 114–15
cash flows, internal rate of return 318
category development index see CDI
category performance ration 176, 180
cautions, AAU 35–6
CDI (category development index) 21, 22
  calculating 22
  purpose 21
  segments 23
chaining margins 53
channel margins 53
  complications 59
  hybrid channel margins 60
channel metrics, Prestige Luggage 331
choosing metrics 2–3
churn 134
classification of variable costs 75
clickstream 301–2
clickthrough rates 291–4
  calculating 292–3
  purpose 292
cluster analysis 124
CLV see customer lifetime value
cohort and incubate, customer lifetime value
    143–4
cold leads 174
commission see sales force compensation
commissioned sales costs 78
company profit from new products 105
comparing sales force territories 162
compensation 169, 171
  See also sales force compensation
compensatory decisions versus non-
    compensatory consumer decisions 121–3
competitor price elasticity 220, 230
competitor reaction elasticity 221, 228
complications
  average price per unit 69
  channel margins 59
compound annual growth rates see CAGR
compounding growth 106, 108–9
concentration ratio 19
conjoint analysis 118–19, 205
  calculating 120–1
  purpose 119
conjoint utilities 92, 119, 123
  complications 123

segmentation 124
  complications 126
  construction 124–5
  purpose 124
  volume projection and 126
constant elasticity 213–15
constructing frequency response functions 282–3
consumer off-take 189
consumer preference 119
  compensatory versus non-compensatory
      decisions 121–3
consumer ratings 34
contractual situations 132
  counting customers 133
contribution analysis 81
contribution margins 46, 48, 83
contribution per unit 46, 81–2
converting markups to margins 58–9
cookies 302
cost, total cost per unit 73
cost effectiveness, Internet marketing 294–5
cost of incremental sales 243
cost per click 295, 297–8
  calculating 296
cost per customer acquired 298
cost per impression 294–5, 297
  calculating 296
cost per order 295–7
cost per point (CPP) 275
cost per thousand impressions see CPM
cost-plus pricing 220–1, 225
costs
  assigning to customers 141
  average acquisition cost 152
  average retention cost 151–2
  classifying for break-even analysis 84–5
  commissioned sales costs 78
  fixed costs 70, 79
    calculating 70–1, 73–4
    classification of 75
    purpose 70
  overhead costs 309
  total cost 71, 74
  total selling costs 78
  total variable selling costs 78
  variable costs 70
    calculating 70–1, 73–4
    classification of 75
    purpose 70
counting customers 132, 135–7
  contractual situations 133
  non-contractual situations 133–4
  recency 132, 134
  retention 134–5
coupons 251–2
  evaluating 254
  percentage sales with coupons 251
  profitability 252–3
  redemption rate 252

coupons (*continued*)
  calculating 253
CP *see* customer profit
CPM (cost per thousand impressions) 265, 274–5
CPP (cost per point) 275
cross elasticity 221, 228
cross price elasticity 221, 228, 230
Cruise
  customer awareness 329
  customer profit 328
  financial statements 325–6
  marketing metrics 328
customer awareness 329
customer counts 132
customer lifetime value 129, 141–2, 149
  calculating 144–5
  cohort and incubate 143–4
  discount rate 146
  finite-horizon 147
  infinite horizon assumption 147
  versus prospect lifetime value 149–51
  purpose 142–3
  retention rate 145
customer lifetime value with initial margin 146
customer profit (CP) 129, 137–8, 141
  Boom 328
  calculating 138–40
  Cruise 328
  purpose 137–8
  quantifying 143
  whale curve 142
customer responses, separating customer from
    non-customer responses 35
customer satisfaction 37
  measuring 38–9
  purpose 37
  sample selection 40
  surveys 39
customer selling price 54, 55–6
customer service 168
customer survey data, triangulating 35–6
customer time 135
customers 132, 135
  abandoning 142
  acceptors 26
  acquisition versus retention 151–3
  assessing value of 142–3
  assigning cost to 141
  brand penetration 23–4
  counting 132, 135–7
    contractual situations 133
    non-contractual situations 133–4
    recency 132, 134
    retention 134–5
  deciding who to serve 141
  defining 135
  ever-tried customers 26
  impressions *see* impressions
  market penetration 23–4

purpose 132
Second Tier customers 138
surveys *see* surveys
Third Tier customers 138
Top Tier customers 137–8
total number of active customers 26
unprofitable customers 141

dashboards 333, 335
data, availability of 3
data parameters, market share 15–16
data sources
  AAU 35
  heavy usage index 31
decline, life cycle 110
decomposing market share 25
deductions 188, 260
demand
  linear demand
    optimal price 217, 219–23
    price elasticity 209–13
    reservation prices 205, 207–8
  price tailoring 261
demand curves, constant elasticity 213–15
demand functions 195
direct product costs 191
direct product profitability *see* DPP
discount rate 317
  customer lifetime value 146
  net present value 317
discounted trial 105
discounts 259–60
distribution, trial rates 95
distribution chains 53–4
distribution channels, calculating selling prices at
    each level in the distribution channel 54–5
distribution metrics 176
  ACV 178–9
  data sources 181–2
  numeric distribution 177–8
  PCV 180–1
  purpose 177
districts 164
diverted goods 189
diverted merchandise 189
double jeopardy 28
DPP (direct product profitability) 156, 159, 189, 192–3
  calculating 191–2
Drucker, Peter 43
durability/loyalty 117

earning before interest taxes, depreciation, and
    amortization (EBITDA) 309
eBay, active users 134
EBITDA (earning before interest taxes,
    depreciation, and amortization) 309
economic profit 306, 311, 312
  calculating 312–13
  purpose 311

economic value added (EVA) 305, 311
EDLP (everyday low prices) 260
effective frequency 266, 285–7
effective market share 117
effective reach 285–6
    calculating 286
    Internet 287
    purpose 285–6
effectiveness *see* sales force effectiveness
elasticity
    cross 221, 228
    See also price elasticity
EVA (economic value added) 305, 311
evaluating
    coupon programs 254
    inventories 187–8
    multi-period investments 313–14
    sales goals 165
    temporary price promotions 240
    workload distribution 172
ever-tried 104
ever-tried customers 26
everyday low prices (EDLP) 260
evoked set 105
examples
    Big Tobacco Company 332–3
    Boom *see* Boom
    Cruise *see* Cruise
    Prestige Luggage *see* Prestige Luggage
expenses, sales force effectiveness 168
exposures 268–9

facings 182
fair share draw 91, 110, 112–14
features in store 183
FIFO (First In, First Out) 187
financial statements, Boom and Cruise 325–6
finite-horizon, customer lifetime value 147
first channel member's selling price 57
First In, First Out (FIFO) 187
first-time triers in period 93
fixed costs 70, 79
    calculating 70–1, 73–4
    classification of 75
    purpose 70
forced trial 104
forecasting
    marketing spending 76–7
    trial volume 96
    upcoming sales 172
Fortune 134
frequency 276
    average frequency 277
    effective frequency *see* effective frequency
frequency response functions 265, 280–1,
    284–5
    construction 282–3
    learning curve response model 280–1
    linear response model 280–1

    purpose 281–2
    threshold response model 282

geo-clustering 36
globalisation 3
GM (General Motors), retail sales 43
GMROII (gross margin return on inventory
    investment) 156, 159, 189–91
goals, sales goals
    calculating 164–5
    purpose 163–4
goodwill 115–16
gross margin 53, 216
gross margin return on inventory investment *see*
    GMROII
gross rating points *see* GRPs
growth 106
    CAGR 109
    compounding 106, 108–9
    life cycle 110
    percentage growth 106
        adjusting 110
    same stores growth 107–8
    value of future period 108–9
    year-on-year growth 105
GRPs (gross rating points) 264, 269–70
    calculating 270–2, 277

heavy usage index 25, 30
    calculating 30–1
    data sources 31
    purpose 30
Herfindahl Index 19–20
HI-LO (high-low) 260
hierarchy of effects 35
hits 289–90
hybrid channel margins 60

I (Index) 6
identifying profitability of individual customers
    137–8
impressions 268–9
    calculating 270–1
    clickthrough rates 291–4
    complications 273
    cost per click 295–8
    cost per impression 294–7
    cost per order 295–7
    CPM *see* CPM
    data sources 273
    frequency response functions *see* frequency
        response functions
    GRPs 269–70
        calculating 270–2, 277
    net reach *see* net reach
    pageviews 289–91
    purpose 269
    share of voice 287–8
incentive plans 171–2

incentive plans (*continued*)
 timing 172
income statement, Prestige Luggage 330
incremental sales 243–4
 cost of 243
Index (I) 6
indexes
 brand development index 21–3
 CDI (category development index) 21–3
 heavy usage index 25, 30–1
 Herfindahl Index 19–20
indicators, separating leading from lagging
  indicators 36
infinite horizon assumption, customer lifetime
  value 147
inflation, estimating 69
intention to purchase 34
intentions 34
Interbrand 116
 brand valuation model 118
interest creation 173
internal rate of return (IRR) 307, 314, 316
 calculating 316–17
 cash flows 318
Internet 264
 assessing cost effectiveness 294–5
 effective reach 287
 search engine marketers 298
 search engines 297–8
 See also web pages
introductory life cycle 110
inventories, evaluating 187–8
inventory 182
inventory days 185–6
inventory tracking 185
inventory turns 183, 185
investments, evaluating multi-period investments
  313–14
invoice price 258–9
IRR *see* internal rate of return

Kaplan, Robert 138
Keller, Kevin 116
Kelvin, Lord 2
key assumptions, test markets 100–1
knowledge, brand/product knowledge 34

Last in, First Out (LIFO) 187
leading national advertisers (LNA) 288
learning curve 265
learning curve response model, frequency
  response functions 280–1
life cycle 110
LIFO (Last In, First Out) 187
likeability 36
linear cost model 75
linear demand
 optimal price 217, 219–23
 price elasticity 209–13

reservation prices 204, 206–8
linear response model, frequency response
  functions 280–1
list price 257
LNA (leading national advertisers) 288
loyalty 102, 327
 double jeopardy 28
 number of brands purchased 29
 willingness to search 40–2

mail-in rebates 253–4
make-goods on promotions 188
margin on new products 105
margins 43, 47
 average margin 60–2
 chaining 53
 channel margins *see* channel margins
 contribution margins 46, 48, 83
 converting from markups 58
 costs, including or excluding 53
 customer lifetime value with initial margin 146
 gross margin 53, 216
 versus markup 51–3
 as percentage of costs 50–1
 percentage margins 47
  calculating 48–9, 60–1
 purpose 47
 reported margins 50
 reporting 52
 selling prices, defining 51
 unit margins 47–9
 weighted contribution margins, cannibalisation
  112
markdowns 189–90
market concentration 17, 19
market penetration 23–4
market share 10, 14
 bias in reported shares 16
 data parameters 15–16
 decomposing 25
 effective market share 117
 measuring over time 16
 purpose of 14
 quantifying 15
 relative market share 17–19
 revenue market share 15
 served market 15
 unit market share 14, 15
market share rank 20
marketing as a percentage of sales 80
marketing budgets, developing 79–80
marketing dashboards 333, 335
marketing metrics 335
 Prestige Luggage 331
marketing spending 76
 calculating 78–9
 fixed costs 79
 purpose 76–7
 slotting allowances 80

markup
  converting to margins 58
  versus margins 51–3
Marlboro Friday 333
mastering metrics 3–4
mature life cycle 110
maximum reservation price *see* MRP
maximum willing to buy *see* MWB
measuring
  customer satisfaction 37–40
  market share, over time 17
media exposure return on marketing investment
    322–3
media plans, net reach 278
metrics
  defined 1
  reasons for having 2
middlemen 255
misshipments 188
Moran, Bill 116
MRP (maximum reservation price) 206–7, 217,
    220, 221, 222
multi-period investments, evaluating 313
MWB (maximum willing to buy) 206–7, 222

net operating profit after tax (NOPAT) 309
net present value (NPV) 307, 313, 314, 317
  calculating 315–16
  discount rate 318
net price 257, 258–9
net profit 306, 308
  calculating 308–9
  overhead costs 309
net reach 272, 276, 278
  complications 280
  overlap 279–80
  purpose 276–9
noise 35
non-compensatory consumer decisions versus
    compensatory decisions 121–3
non-contractual situations 132
  counting customers 133–4
NOPAT (net operating profit after tax) 309
NPV *see* net present value
number of complaints 40
number of new products 105
numeric distribution 158, 176
  calculating 177–8

obsolescence 188
opportunities-to-see (OTS) 268
optimal price 216
  calculating 220–1, 223–4
  complications 220–1, 224–5
  purpose 217
    linear demand 217, 219–23
  relative to gross margin 220, 223
  slope 221
optimality condition 220, 223

OTS (opportunities-to-see) 268
out-of-stock 159, 183–4
  PCV net out-of-stocks 184
over-servicing 160
overhead costs 309
overlap, assessing 280
overlap effects 279–80
own price elasticity 228, 230

pageviews 290, 300
pass-through 242, 255
  calculating 255
  complications 255–6
payback 314
payback period 85
PCV (product category volume) 158, 176
  calculating 180–1
PCV net out-of-stocks 184
penetration 23, 92
  brand penetration 23–4
    calculating 24, 93–4
  cautions 25
  market penetration 23–4
penetration rate 24
penetration share 23–5
Peppers, Don 142
perceived quality/esteem 34
perceived value for money 34
percent good value 203
percentage (%) 6
percentage growth 106
  adjusting 109–10
percentage margins 47
  calculating 48–9, 60–1
percentage of unit sales 60
percentage sales on deal 254
  calculating 255
percentage sales with coupons 251–2
performance 2
  monitoring firm performance in attracting and
    retaining customers 132
performance reviews *see* sales force effectiveness
periodic changes, adjusting for 35
Philips Consumer Electronics 116
pipeline analysis 172
  construction 173–5
  purpose 172–3
  sales funnel 175–6
pipeline sales 188
PLV *see* prospect lifetime value
post-purchases 174–5
pre-purchase 174, 175
Prestige Luggage 331
  income statement 330
  marketing and channel metrics 331
  retail margins 330
  retail profit 331
price discrimination 220, 225, 227, 261
  regulation 227, 261

price elasticity 197, 209, 216
  calculating 210–13
  constant elasticity 213–15
  linear demand 210–13
  purpose 209
price increases, evaluating 69
price of a specified competitor 199
price per statistical unit 45, 65, 67
  calculating 67–8
price premiums 198
  calculating 198–202
  complications 202
  purpose 198
price promotions see promotions
price tailoring 220, 225, 227, 261
  demand 261
  regulation 227, 261
price waterfalls 240, 242, 257
  calculating 258–9
  complications 259–60
  purpose 257
prices
  average price 64–5
  average price charged 200–1
  average price displayed 201
  average price paid 199–200
  average price per unit 65–6
    calculating 66–9
    complications 69
    purpose 65–6
  competitor price elasticity 220, 230
  cost-plus pricing 220–1, 225
  cross elasticity 221, 228
  cross price elasticity 221, 228, 230
  customer selling price 54, 55
    calculating 55–6
  first channel member's selling price 57
  invoice price 258
  list price 257
  net price 257–8
  optimal price 216
    calculating 220–1, 223–4
    complications 220–1, 224–5
    linear demand 217, 219–23
    purpose 217
    relative to gross margins 220, 223
    slope 221
  own price elasticity 220, 230
  percent good value 203
  prisoner's dilemma pricing 232–4, 235–7
    deciding if you face this situation 237–8
  relative price 117
  reservation price 203
    calculating 203, 205
    finding 205
    linear demand 205, 207–8
    purpose 203
  residual price elasticity 221, 228
    calculating 230–1

  complications 231–2
  purpose 228–30
selling price 54
  defining 50
  calculating prices at each level in the
    distribution channel 54–5
supplier selling price 53–4
  calculating 55–6
  calculating average 63
  theoretical price premiums 203
prisoner's dilemma pricing 232–4, 235–7
  deciding if you face this situation 237–8
Prizm, geo-clustering 36
product category volume see PCV
Professional Pricing Society 260
profit-based sales targets 85–6
profitability
  baseline sales 249
  coupons 252
  price tailoring 261
  redemption rates 252
profitability metrics 189
  complications 192–3
  DPP 189
    calculating 191–2
  GMROII 189–90
  markdowns 190
  purpose 190
profitability or promotions 247
projected volume, repeat volume 97–8
promotional discount 255
promotions 239
  baseline sales see baseline sales
  complications 256
  coupons see coupons
  evaluating temporary price promotions 240
  long-term effects of 250–1
  profitability 247–8
  rebates 251
    mail-in rebates 253
  redemption rates see redemption rates
  short-term promotional objectives 239
prospect lifetime value (PLV) 148
  calculating 148–9
  complications 149–51
  versus customer lifetime value 149–51
  purpose 148
prospects 174
pull marketing 177
purchases 174
push marketing 177

quantifying
  customer profit 142
  market share 15

R (Rating) 6
rain checks 188
Ramsellar, Leon 116

rating point 268–9
reach 276–8
  See also net reach
rebates 251
  mail-in rebates 253–4
recency 132, 134
redemption rates 251
  calculating 253–4
  coupon redemption rate 252
  profitability 252
  purpose 252
regulations, price discrimination 227, 261
relationships 136
relative market share 17
  calculating 18–19
  purpose 17–18
relative perceived quality 34
relative prices see price premiums
repeat 104
repeat rate 29–30, 101
repeat volume 97–8
reported margins 50
reporting margins 52
repurchase rate 29
resellers 256
reservation prices 203
  calculating 203, 205
  finding 205
  linear demand 205, 207–8
  purpose 203
residual price elasticity 221, 228
  calculating 221, 230–1
  complications 221, 231–2
  purpose 221, 228–30
response bias 39
responses, customer survey responses 96
retail margins 330
retail profit 331
retailers, apparel retailers (customers) 136–7
retention 29, 134–5
  versus acquisition 151–3
retention rate 132, 134
  customer lifetime value 145
return 305
return on assets (ROA) 310
return on capital (ROC) 310
return on incremental marketing investment
  (ROIMI) 320–1
return on invested capital (ROIC) 310
return on investments (ROI) 306, 309–10, 325
return on marketing investment (ROMI) 306, 307,
  319–20
  budgeting 322
  calculating 319–21
  complications 322
  media exposure return on marketing investment
    322–3
  purpose 319
return on net assets (RONA) 310

return on sales (ROS) 306, 308–9, 325
returns and target 87
revenue attributable to marketing 320–1
revenue from new products 105
revenue market share, calculating 15
revenue return to incremental marketing 320–1
revenue return to total marketing 320–1
revenue share of requirements 26
reward structures, supply chain metrics 187
ROA (return on assets) 310
ROC (return on capital) 310
Rogers, Martha 142
ROI (return on investment) 306, 309–10, 322–3
ROIC (return on invested capital) 310
ROIMI (return on incremental marketing
    investment) 320–1
ROMI see return on marketing investment
RONA (return on net assets) 310
ROS (return on sales) 306, 308–9, 325

salaries see sales force compensation
sales force compensation 169
  calculating 170–1
  incentive plans 171–2
  purpose 170
sales force effectiveness 166
  calculating 166–8
  customer service 168
  expenses 168
  purpose 166
sales force funnel 173
sales force objectives 163, 165
  calculating 164–5
  purpose 163–4
sales force territories 160
  balancing 160–1
  comparing 161
  estimating size of 162
  purpose 160
  redefining 162
sales force tracking see pipeline analysis
sales funnel 158, 175–6
sales goal 164
  evaluating 165
sales pipeline 158
sales potential 156, 160–2
  goals 163, 165
    calculating 164–5
    purpose 163–4
same stores growth 107–8
sample selection, customer satisfaction 39–40
search engine marketers 298
search engines 297–8
seasonal variations, return on investment 310
second-price auctions 205
segment utilities 92
segmentation by geography 36
segments
  BDI 21–2

segments (*continued*)
  CDI 22
  conjoint utilities 124–6
selling price 55
  calculating at each level in the distribution channel 54
  defining 50
separating customer responses from non-customer response 35
served market 16
service levels 183–5
Shames, Erv 332
share of category 20
share of requirements 25, 26
  calculating 27–8
  double jeopardy 28
  purpose 27
share of shelf 182
share of voice 287, 288
share of wallet *see* share of requirements
shopping basket margin 193
shrinkage 188
signals 35
SKU (stock keeping unit) 65–6, 190
slope, optimal price 221
slotting allowances 80
sole usage 28
sole usage percentage 29
spreadsheets, calculating NPV 318
State Farm Insurance 133
statistical units 67, 69
stepped payments 79
stock keeping unit (SKU) 65–6, 190
store versus brand measures 182
supplier selling price 53–4
  calculating 55–6
  calculating average 63
supply chain metrics 183
  complications 187–8
  inventories, evaluating 187–8
  inventory days 185–6
  inventory tracking 185
  inventory turns 185
  out-of-stocks 184
  purpose 183–4
  reward structures 187–8
  service levels 185
surveys 94
  customer satisfaction 39
  customer survey responses 96

target market fix 105
target rating points *see* TRPs
target revenue 86–7
target volume 46, 86
target volumes not based on target profit 87
targets, profit-based sales targets 85–6
terminal values 317

territories, sales force territories *see* sales force territories
test markets
  assumptions 100–1
  awareness 95
  distribution 95
  simulated results and volume projections, trial volume 94
  See also trials
'the trade' 254
theoretical price premiums 203
three (four) firm concentration ratio 19
threshold 265
threshold response model, frequency response functions 282
time, measuring market share over 16
tolerable discrimination 261
top of mind 33
total cost 71, 72, 74
total cost per unit 73
  versus variable cost per unit 75
total coupon cost 252
total distribution 158, 181
total number of active customers 26
total outlet sales 182
total selling costs 78
total variable selling costs 78
total volume 99
trade satisfaction 40
trial rates 93–4
  distribution 95
trial volume 96–7
trial-repeat model 104
trials 92, 101, 104
  discounted trials 105
  forced trials 104
  purpose 93
  repeat volume 97–8
  total volume 99
TRPs (target rating points) 264, 271–2

under-servicing 160
unit margin 47
  calculating 48–9
unit market share 14
unit share of requirements 26–7
units 47
USAA 133
usage, AAU 35
user behaviour, web sites 299–302

value of future period 108–9
variable cost per unit versus total cost per unit 75
variable costs 70
  calculating 70–1, 73–4
  classification of 75
  purpose 70
Venn Diagram 279
visitors 299, 302–3

visits 267, 299–300, 303
volume projection 92–3
    conjoint utilities 126
volume projection spreadsheet 99–100

Wal-Mart 9
    economic profit 313
warm leads 174
wear-in 285
wear-out 285
web pages
    hits 289
    pageviews 289–91, 300
    visitors 299, 303
    visits 299, 303

See also Internet
web sites, user behaviour 299–302
website traffic, assessing 289–90
weighted contribution margin, cannibalisation
    112–13
weighted share of sales allotment 164
whale curve, customer profit 142
willingness to recommend 37
willingness to search 40–2
workload 160
    evaluating workload distribution 172

Y&R (Young and Rubicam) 116
year-on-year growth 91, 105